Praise for
Green Breakdown

"Steve Goreham's latest book, *Green Breakdown*, is masterful. He has few peers when it comes to connecting dots and explaining complex energy, environmental, economic, and climate issues in ways that high school students (and even judges, regulators, and legislators) can readily understand. Think wind, solar, and battery energy can replace the fossil fuels that power industrialized societies? Goreham explains why it's not possible, certainly not without disrupting and destroying the Earth we love with mines, processing plants, and industrial installations unprecedented in human history."

— Paul Driessen, Senior Energy Policy Analyst for
    Committee for a Constructive Tomorrow, Author

"*Green Breakdown* is a must read for anyone looking to uncover the truth about energy production, energy use, and policies related to climate change. Steve Goreham presents an in-depth yet easily understandable examination and explanation of all components of energy, environment, and climate policy. This is a book that just begs to be given to young adults seeking a beacon to guide their efforts to make the world a better place."

— James Taylor, J.D., President, The Heartland Institute

"I love reading Steve Goreham's articles and books about climate issues. He has a unique ability to describe clearly the complex economic and technological issues involved and to do so in a way that offers important insights into the likely consequences if current trends continue. He makes an invaluable addition to the public's demand for more realism in climate policy."

— Robert Lyman, Economist, Principal at ENTRANS Policy Research Group

"In this clearly written, well researched book, Steve Goreham debunks climate catastrophism and explains why the so-called Net Zero agenda—a forced march to an all-renewables plus battery-storage energy system—is costly, dangerous, and doomed to fail. Citizens who want to more effectively engage in the critical debate over America's energy future should read this book."

— Marlo Lewis, Jr., Ph.D., Senior Fellow, Competitive Enterprise Institute

"*Green Breakdown* guides us through the myriad issues associated with energy policies, as well as the issues in the hyper-politicized scientific debates around climate change. Writing a book about energy policies is a tough task precisely because there is so much ground to cover and because so much of what's important is inherently technical and has become hyper-politicized. Steve Goreham is up to that challenge."

— Mark P. Mills, Senior Fellow, Manhattan Institute,
   Faculty Fellow, McCormick School of Engineering, Northwestern University
   Co-Founder, Montrose Lane Ventures, Author

"Steve Goreham's book, *Green Breakdown*, shows that our fossil fuels have created the miracle of modern transportation and provide most of our reliable electricity which enabled our enormous increase of wealth over the last 100 years. The book shows that the false ideology of climate catastrophe has put reliable energy under attack. The benefits of CO_2 fertilization exceed all harmful effects of warming due to greenhouse gas emissions. *Green Breakdown* shows that Net Zero policies will be enormously harmful to civilization because wind and solar power are environmentally harmful and can't be made reliable by any cost effective method. Capturing CO_2 would be enormously expensive. The book is entertaining and easy to read, is jam packed with facts and great graphics, presents comical failed predictions and makes a mockery of many green energy proposals."

— Ken Gregory, B.AppSc., P.Eng., Director, Friends of Science

"*Green Breakdown*, Steve Goreham's latest, continues his tradition of using superior organization, glossy graphics, and key quotations to expose the corrupt underbelly of climate alarmism and the forced energy transformation. Recommended for general audiences."

— Robert Bradley, Jr., PhD, CEO and Founder,
   Institute for Energy Research, Author

"Policy makers, business and industry leaders, and everyday citizens must read this book as soon as it comes out. *Green Breakdown* is filled with wonderful editorial cartoons and sidebars about crazy energy schemes 'to help save the planet.' If you only read one book this year, this must be it!"

— Jay Lehr, Senior Policy Analyst for the International Climate Science Coalition,
   Scientist, Author

GREEN BREAKDOWN

The Coming Renewable Energy Failure

STEVE GOREHAM

New Lenox Books

GREEN BREAKDOWN
The Coming Renewable Energy Failure

ISBN: 978-0-9824996-6-5
Library of Congress Control Number: 2023904905

www.stevegoreham.com

New Lenox Books, Inc.
New Lenox, IL USA 60451
newlenoxbooks@comcast.net

Printed in China

Credits
Chapter 1 cartoon by Loren Fishman, fishmantoons.com
Chapters 2–11 cartoons by Dan Rosandich
Image of broken light bulb on front cover by brandonheyer
Image of frozen wind turbine in Sweden on back cover
by Alpine Helicopter

CONTENTS

FOREWORD

Steve Goreham's *Green Breakdown* is a *cri de coeur*. It's no spoiler to reveal the bottom line that appears at the very end of this book; "The real tragedy of renewable energy polices is the vast misallocation" of the "trillions spent to pursue green energy." Amen. There is no escaping the evidence that policies to pursue green energy, through subsidies, taxes, and mandates, have cost trillions of dollars and will require much, much more yet to achieve just a fraction of the vision imagined in the so-called "energy transition."

Yes, we're aware of the rationale for that spending: to conquer the climate crisis. But as the world faces mounting financial challenges, and with so many unmet needs in so many areas of life, and with so many billions of people in the world living far below what the wealthy West calls the poverty line, we are reminded just how important it is and how hard it is to expand the world's wealth. Policies that dramatically and systemically increase the cost of energy are antithetical to human flourishing because everything depends on energy.

So it may seem odd to consider that economists don't include in measuring so-called "core inflation" the role of the cost of energy and its availability, which invariably translates into cost. Economists do recognize the crushing burden caused by inflating the cost of fuel and food, wherein the latter is deeply dependent on energy. But the assumption is that those costs are always temporary and short-lived because, in the simplistic but oft-noted summation, the cure for high-cost energy is high costs. In other words, consumers will find ways to consume less, which reduces demand and essentially increases supply, and producers will ramp up supply at higher prices. The combination quickly lowers prices. That's true unless governments mandate the use of more expensive energy. Since hydrocarbons supply over 80 percent of the world's energy, mandating the minor share to replace the major share will have consequences.

You have to get past click-bait headlines, slogans, and facile advocacy claims in order to understand that there is a staggering cost that is inherent with—not a temporary bug that's amenable to simple fixes—the nature of green energy technologies. For that, we have Steve Goreham's important and lucid tutorial, wherein *Green Breakdown* guides us through the myriad issues associated with energy policies, as well as the issues in the hyper-politicized scientific debates around climate change. Writing a book about energy policies is a tough task precisely because there is so much ground to cover and because so much of what's important is inherently technical and has become hyper-politicized. Steve is up to that challenge.

And when it comes to climate change arguments, whatever one believes about all the headline claims, Goreham takes pains to use primary sources for the data and offers clear explanations of what the data tell us. In the introduction, he asks the reader to be "open-minded" given that he's aware his viewpoint is in "a minority." We note you won't find the word "hoax" or any similar invectives often found used in the climate debate, but rather he seeks to show that there is an important distinction framed by what he calls the "alarmists." The key point of *Green Breakdown* is found in the indisputable fact there are always trade-offs with everything, and those being made with energy policies have enormous consequence. Steve brings to this critical issue of our time a vital contribution to understanding those tradeoffs in terms of the economic, social, and environmental costs. It's time to open your mind.

Mark P. Mills
Senior Fellow, Manhattan Institute
Faculty Fellow, McCormick School of Engineering, Northwestern University
Co-Founder, Montrose Lane Ventures

ACKNOWLEDGEMENTS

Green Breakdown builds on the writings and observations of a number of prestigious energy experts, economists, and scientists who have spoken out against the world's quest for renewable energy. Against an overwhelming tidal wave of green propaganda, these experts have courageously challenged society's renewable-energy obsession with facts and data. *Green Breakdown* attempts to capture their concerns and goes on to predict a coming renewable energy failure.

Canadian scientist Vaclav Smil has authored a number of excellent books on energy. His book *Power Density: A Key to Understanding Energy Sources and Uses* points out that wind, solar, and biofuels use vastly more land than hydrocarbon or nuclear sources of electric power. His other writings point out that today's society is based on heavy industry powered by hydrocarbon energy, and that a transition to renewable sources will take decades, if it is possible at all. Journalist Robert Bryce, author of *A Question of Power: Electricity and the Wealth of Nations*, debunks the idea that the world's energy needs can be met solely with renewables. Philosopher Alex Epstein, author of *Fossil Future: Why Global Human Flourishing Requires More Oil, Coal, and Natural Gas—Not Less*, effectively argues that hydrocarbon fuels will continue to be the basis for human prosperity for generations to come. Donn Dears, Marlo Lewis, Francis Menton, Mark Mills, and Stephen Moore provided valuable perspectives on the limits of renewable energy and the essential value of hydrocarbon fuels. *Green Breakdown* draws heavily from the works of these experts.

The data for graphs was gathered from excellent public sources, including BP, the US Energy Information Administration, the US Environmental Protection Agency, EurObservER, Eurostat, the International Energy Agency, and others. Max Roser's excellent website *Our World in Data* was also a valuable resource.

The discussion on global warming relies on the work of a growing number of skeptical scientists who challenge the theory of human-caused climate change. John Christy, Judith Curry, Will Happer, Craig Idso, Dick Lindzen, Willie Soon, Roy Spencer, Anthony Watts, and others have courageously spoken out for sound science, risking political attacks and damage to their careers. They will be vindicated when the theory of human-caused warming is discarded on the trash heap of history. Writings from members of the The Heartland Institute and the Global Warming Policy Foundation provided input for this book.

Special thanks go to Ken Gregory, Howard Hayden, Ed Hoskins, and Robert Lyman for technical review and correction of the text. Thanks to Mark Mills for writing the Foreword. Thanks to my editor, Janet Weber, for her professionalism and patience with me. Thanks to Henrik Weber for inputs on the cover design for the book. The great cartoons at the start of each chapter came from professional cartoonists Loren Fishman and Dan Rosandich.

I dedicate this book to my wife, Sue, who takes care of me and who has endured my endless frustrations with energy trends for more than a decade. Thanks also to my family and friends for their inspiration.

INTRODUCTION

"Essentially the entire developed part of the world is currently embarked on a crash program to eliminate fossil fuels from the energy system of the economy."
—FRANCIS MENTON (2022)[1]

An engineer who attended one of my recent presentations told me his wife had returned her electric vehicle (EV) to Tesla, the manufacturer. Her EV would not charge during the cold Cleveland winter of January 2022. Also in January, more than 100 insurance companies sued Texas electrical grid operator ERCOT because of the grid failure that happened in February 2021 due to the cold weather. The failure resulted in hundreds of deaths and tens of billions of dollars in damages. Former Swiss Environmental Minister Simonetta Sommaruga, seeking ways to reduce energy use, recently advised people to "shower together."[2] These examples point to growing problems with the world's rush to transition to renewable energy.

Over the last three decades, society has become convinced that a global energy transition is needed. The United Nations, the International Energy Agency, environmental groups, political leaders, and climate scientists warn that coal, oil, and natural gas, also known as hydrocarbon energy sources, must be eliminated. Instead, renewable sources, including wind, solar, biofuels, and hydrogen fuels, must be adopted. Carbon dioxide (CO_2) was branded a pollutant, with hydrocarbons to be eliminated or CO_2 emissions captured.

Political leaders claim that, without an energy transition, humanity is heading for climate change catastrophe. Melting icecaps, rising oceans, flooding coastal cities, stronger hurricanes and storms, droughts and floods, species extinction, and other disasters await us. They say we have only a few years to change course before the coming climate apocalypse.

1

Get With
The Herd!

**Google Aims to Run on
Carbon-Free Energy by 2030**
— *Reuters*, September 14, 2020[3]

Today, the world invests over $500 billion a year on renewable energy systems and EVs.[4] Thousands of climate change laws across more than 100 nations include feed-in tariffs, subsidies and mandates, laws to reduce energy demand, and statutes to force a transportation transition. Gas stoves and the sale of gasoline and diesel cars are now banned in several nations and cities. Carbon trading markets force businesses to price the emissions of CO_2 from industrial processes.

"Net Zero" has become the new badge of honor for climate compliance. Companies rush to demonstrate their allegiance to green ideology, with plans to reduce emissions, switch to carbon-free electricity, and achieve Net Zero. Utility companies bow to public pressure at the expense of ratepayers, building intermittent wind and solar arrays, while closing reliable coal and nuclear plants. Car companies extol the benefits of EVs, pledging to become 100 percent electric by a future date.

Over the last 20 years, the world has spent almost $5 trillion to promote wind, solar, biofuels, and electric vehicles but with surprisingly little to show for it.[5] Coal, oil, and natural gas continue to provide about 80 percent of the world's total energy supply, the same energy share as in the 1990s. Fuel from petroleum continues to power more than 90 percent of land vehicles and more than 99 percent of aircraft and ships. Heavy industries, such as cement, chemicals, fertilizer, plastics, and steel, remain overwhelmingly powered by natural gas or coal. For every year to date, the growth in energy output from renewable sources has been less than the incremental growth in world energy consumption.

Renewable energy suffers from a number of serious weaknesses, which emerge as penetration increases. With nuclear power out of favor, wind and solar are the only possible sources to replace hydrocarbon-generated electricity. But wind and solar are intermittent generators, requiring dispatchable power sources, such as natural gas, as backup to assure power reliability. Their arrays require vast amounts of land and thousands of miles of new transmission lines, which face rising local opposition. Wind and solar deployments boost required system capacity, hike electricity prices, and increase the risk of system blackouts.

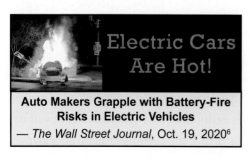

Electric Cars
Are Hot!

**Auto Makers Grapple with Battery-Fire
Risks in Electric Vehicles**
— *The Wall Street Journal*, Oct. 19, 2020[6]

Green advocates call for all vehicles to

transition to biofuels or electric drive. But bio-fuels are expensive and don't really reduce CO_2 emissions. EVs will penetrate car markets but face cost, charging, and consumer-preference barriers that will slow market acceptance.

Green Policies Require Coercion

New York City is Banning Natural Gas Hookups for New Buildings to Fight Climate Change
— *CNBC*, December 25, 2021[7]

Heavy industry poses the toughest problem for any green-energy transition. Leaders pro-pose carbon capture and storage (CCS) and hydrogen fuel to replace coal and natural gas fuels in industry. But CCS is expensive, and the huge volumes of carbon dioxide to be stored defeat any rational capture plans. Expensive hydrogen fuel requires enormous investment in hydrogen electrolyzers and an incredible amount of additional renewable energy capacity to power them.

Finally, a transition to renewables requires vast amounts of cobalt, copper, lithium, nickel, and other special materials, requiring a huge expansion in world mining, along with generating mountains of waste from used wind turbine blades, solar panels, and batteries. Mining requirements, metal shortages, and growing waste will raise the costs of electric vehicles and other renewables, stimulating opposition and slowing market penetration. The larger the renewable penetration, the larger mining and waste factors will become.

Green energy is headed for a breakdown. The 2022 world energy crisis may be just the first of several transnational energy shocks that demonstrate the futility of a renewable future. Europe's dependence on wind, solar, and imported natural gas, combined with Russia's invasion of Ukraine, resulted in a step-function drop in living standards and the severe destruction of industry on the continent. Energy shortages and astronomical costs may plague Europe for a decade. Green-minded states in the US and provinces in Australia may be next for power system failures and esca-lating costs as renewable energy is deployed.

Temporarily out of Gasoline OPEN for your other driving needs

Welcome to Net Zero

Energy Crisis: Will Hungarian Schools Be Heated with Wood?
"The Ministry is instructing educational institutions to immediately assess the feasibility of switching from gas to wood-burning as soon as possible by purchasing stoves."
— *Daily News Hungary*, July 29, 2022[8]

But an even larger specter looms over green energy. The fear of human-caused climate change, the reason for the demanded energy transition, is a foundation based on faulty science and misguided societal acceptance. Natural forces dominate Earth's climate, not industrial emissions. These forces may cause Earth to cool over the next two decades, extinguishing climate mania and removing the reason for endless mandates and spending to promote a renewable energy transition.

This book provides a minority point of view, but a view based on energy reality. We encourage readers to wade into it with an open mind. Chapter 1 discusses the Hydrocarbon Revolution, which brought energy abundance to developed nations, and also the situation in developing countries that still lack hydrocarbon energy. Chapter 2 covers the rise of renewable energy, which was driven by world oil crises, the need for cleaner air, and finally fears about human-caused climate change. Chapter 3 provides scientific evidence to show that the theory of man-made global warming is unfounded, that natural forces dominate Earth's temperatures, and that CO_2 is not a pollutant. Chapter 4 discusses the war on hydrocarbon energy. Chapter 5 discusses efforts to convert always-on electrical systems to intermittent wind and solar, with resultant rising electricity prices and system blackouts. Chapter 6 discusses programs to ban household use of natural gas and fears about small particle pollution. Chapter 7 covers the history and rise of EVs and their pros and cons compared to gasoline- and diesel-powered vehicles. Chapter 8 covers ships, planes, and trains, and alternative fuels. Chapter 9 discusses programs to try to decarbonize heavy industry using carbon capture and hydrogen. Chapter 10 covers the 2022 world energy crisis and discusses trends against further renewable growth. Chapter 11 predicts a renewable failure and proposes better pathways for the future.

Along the way we'll have some fun. This book is filled with sidebars about crazy energy schemes to help save the planet. From topping off gas tanks with beer-based vehicle fuel, to wearing carbon-dioxide-sucking T-shirts, to donning dresses that charge your smart phone, people think they are helping to solve the energy crisis. Green transportation is in, including dirigibles, wind-blown catamarans, charging stations powered by waste-fryer oil, and buses that run on human poo. All of the sidebars are actual articles and quotes from the media except "College Courses We Expect to See," which are spoofs.

But energy is serious business. Five-thousand-pound energy bills in the United Kingdom are no laughing matter. Unfortunately, citizens, businesses, and world leaders will learn a painful economic lesson. The drive to replace low-cost, always-on hydrocarbons with low-density, unreliable renewable sources is bound to come to a bitter end.

This book takes a look at the current worldwide push for green energy and the shortcomings of that energy. It predicts a coming green breakdown, the cracks of which are already apparent. Policy makers, business and industry leaders, and everyday citizens can learn from this realistic look at the future of energy.

ENERGY ABUNDANCE AND NEED

"Low-cost energy is the foundation of modern society."
—AUTHOR ROBERT BRYCE (2014)[1]

As energy expert Robert Bryce and others have observed, our modern society is based on low-cost, abundant, and reliable energy. Our organic vegetables are produced by farmers with tractors fueled by diesel. Assembly plants use modern energy to manufacture our flat-screen TVs and smart phones, built from plastics produced in refineries powered by natural gas. Our sport utility vehicles contain large amounts of steel from coal-powered mills, using smelted ores from energy-intensive mining operations. Our favorite music and movies come to our homes from internet data centers that use massive amounts of electrical power. Designer jeans, allergy pills, coffee beans, and many other goods arrive in our cities from the far corners of Earth on ships powered by heavy fuel oil and planes powered by aviation fuel.

Residents of developed nations take modern energy for granted. But those in developing nations are not so fortunate. About 900 million people, or 12 percent of the world's population, do not have access to electricity. Roughly three billion people, or 40 percent of the world's population, do not enjoy clean fuels for cooking, such as natural gas, propane, or electric stoves.[2] There is great need to extend modern fuels to the people of poor nations.

Unfortunately, leaders today insist that hydrocarbon fuels be eliminated and replaced by renewable energy, even though modern society runs on hydrocarbon energy, and poor nations desperately need to access those same sources of energy. Let's review the history that brought the wealthy world to abundant energy.

THE HYDROCARBON REVOLUTION

Over the last 300 years, mankind achieved an energy revolution that could be called the Hydrocarbon Revolution. The Hydrocarbon Revolution provided energy to drive the Industrial Revolution, pave the way for the miracles of modern transportation, power the new age of electricity, and set the stage for advances in agriculture and medicine. These successes generated huge growth in personal incomes, food production, education levels, life spans, and overall prosperity.

A hydrocarbon is an organic compound composed of the elements hydrogen and carbon. Crude oil and natural gas are our primary hydrocarbons. Coal is also considered a hydrocarbon, even though it contains small amounts of oxygen, sulfur, and other elements.

We live in a golden age of abundant, low-cost energy. Energy use has skyrocketed

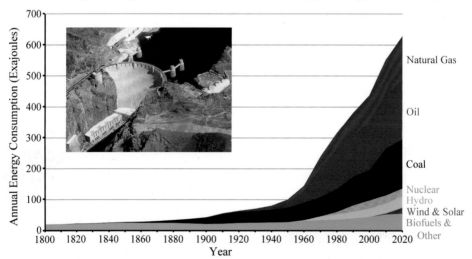

World Energy Consumption 1800–2020. Annual world energy consumption, measured in exajoules. Each exajoule is 1×10^{18} joules, equal to the energy from about 24 million metric tons of oil. Image of Hoover Dam in Nevada. (Smil, 2010; BP, 2020; IEA, 2020)[3]

over the last two centuries and continues to rise. Since 1800, global energy consumption increased by a factor of 30.[4] Human and animal muscle power and wood combustion dominated energy use in 1800, along with small amounts of coal and wind. Today, world energy consumption is dominated by hydrocarbons.

In 2021, world energy came from oil (29%), natural gas (23%), coal (25%), hydroelectric (6%), nuclear (4%), wind and solar (4%), and biomass and other fuels (9%).[5] Over 77 percent of energy consumption was supplied by hydrocarbons. Much of the biomass and other fuels were wood and charcoal, burned in developing nations for heating and cooking.

Back in the 1600s, before the age of modern energy, life was difficult in England. The majority of people were poor by today's standards, with many living in terrible poverty. Most people were illiterate. The vast majority of common English people lived on farms or in small communities. City dwellers usually resided in one-room apartments.[6]

Food for much of the population remained plain and monotonous. Many survived on bread, cheese, onions, and pottage, a kind of porridge. Most food was grown locally because it was difficult to transport and preserve.

Bubonic plague ravaged London in 1603, 1636, and 1665. Dysentery and diarrheal diseases were also common.[7] The average life expectancy at birth was only about 35 years. One in five babies died during their first year of life. Between one-third and one-half of children died before the age of 16. If English people survived their childhood years, they usually lived to an age of 50 to 60 or longer.[8]

Energy usage in England had remained mostly unchanged over the last 1,000 years. Wood and coal were burned for cooking and home heating. Horse-drawn vehicles provided transportation. Grain was sown by hand and harvested by hand-held sickle. Oil lamps and candles were used for light.

Life in England and across the world began to change with the Hydrocarbon Revolution. The Hydrocarbon Revolution consisted of three main elements: 1) the use of coal to power new machines, 2) the refining of oil into fuel for new vehicles, and 3) the harnessing of electricity, generated by burning hydrocarbon fuels. This revolution began at the end of the 1600s with the invention of the steam engine.

Thomas Savory, an English inventor and engineer, is credited with inventing the world's first steam-powered engine, which was patented

Don't Bet On It?

"Rail travel at high speed is not possible, because passengers, unable to breathe, would die of asphyxia."
— Dr. Dionysys Lander, University College of London, 1800[9]

in 1698. Savory's engine was a coal-fired pump used to "raise great quantities of water above eighty feet" and replace the efforts of "two horses working together," according to Savory's book *The Miner's Friend*.[10] The Savory pump used a vacuum to elevate the water and deliver two to four horsepower, but it was prone to boiler failure.

Around 1710, Thomas Newcomen, an English blacksmith, invented the first piston-based steam engine, an improvement on Savory's design. His engine reliably pumped water out of coal mines. Newcomen's engine worked 12 strokes a minute, raised 10 gallons of water per minute from a depth of 156 feet, delivered about 5.5 horsepower, and was powered by coal. When Newcomen died in 1729, more than 100 of his engines operated in Britain and across Europe.[11]

James Watt, a Scottish engineer and inventor, is regarded as the father of the modern steam engine. Watt improved Newcomen's design by adding a second chamber, named a condenser, where the steam could cool. This allowed the piston chamber to remain hot, improving the efficiency of the engine and saving 75 percent of the costs of coal fuel.

Watt partnered with industrialist Matthew Boulton of Birmingham, England, in 1773 to build the Boulton-Watt engines. Their first commercial engine began operation at the

---

Energy and Power Units Review

Energy is the amount of work that can be done by a force. Energy is measured in joules (J), megajoules (MJ, millions of joules), gigajoules (GJ, billions of joules), or British thermal units (Btu), which is a measure of heat energy. One Btu equals 1,054 joules. Total world energy usage can be measured in exajoules (EJ), which is 1×10^{18} joules (1 followed by 18 zeros).

Power is the amount of energy delivered per unit of time. Power is measured in watts (W) or horsepower (hp). One watt is the amount of power expended in delivering one joule of energy per second. One horsepower equals 746 watts.

Electrical power is measured in megawatts (MW, millions of watts) and gigawatts (GW, billions of watts). Electrical energy is measured as power delivered over time, in kilowatt-hours (kWh), megawatt-hours (MWh), or gigawatt-hours (GWh).[12]

Some examples:
- A healthy person can exert more than one horsepower for a few minutes.
- A weight lifter who lifts a 150 kilogram barbell over his head expends about 3,000 joules of energy.
- A laborer can exert about 100 watts of power over an eight-hour day and daily expends 800 watt-hours or 2.88 megajoules of energy.[13]
- A 12-gallon (45-litre) tank of gasoline contains about 1.6 GJ of energy.[14]
- A US residential customer uses about 11,000 kWh of electricity per year.[15]

Bentley Mining Company in March 1776. The engine "made 14 to 15 strokes per minute" and was able to empty a pit with 57 feet of water in less than an hour.[16]

Improved Boulton-Watt engines were broadly adopted by industry. By 1800, these engines were used in 84 British cotton mills, as well as in wool mills, flour mills, and saw-mills.[17] A 1796 model with a single-acting piston delivered 45 horsepower.[18]

The history of the Hydrocarbon Revolution and the Industrial Revolution is one of complimentary inventions in energy and

Boulton-Watt Rotative Beam Engine Built in 1788, the engine was used at Matthew Boulton's Soho Manufactory in Birmingham, England, where it drove 43 metal polishing machines for 70 years.[19]

mechanization. New steam engines lowered the costs of coal mining, which provided fuel for more steam engines. Lower-priced coal also drove iron smelting and the development of iron and steel tools of the Industrial Revolution. Improved tools then enabled engineers to develop better steam engines.

The invention of the coal-burning steam engine paved the way for the start of modern transportation. Robert Fulton built the steamship *Clermont* and started transportation service on the Hudson River between New York and Albany in 1807. In 1814, Fulton designed the world's first steam warship, the *Fulton*, for the United States government.[20] The Stockton & Darlington Railway, the world's first steam-powered railway, began service in England in 1825.[21]

The Baltimore & Ohio Railroad began the first rail service in the US in 1827.[22] During the first 40 years, the majority of America's locomotives burned wood fuel. Railroads began switching to coal after 1850.[23] By 1890, more than 163,000 miles of railroads were operating in the US, with most of the trains using coal.[24] But transportation required a better fuel.

MIRACLES IN TRANSPORTATION

On September 6, 1620, the *Mayflower* set sail from Plymouth, England, with 102 passengers and 28 crew aboard. The passengers were Puritans, separatists from the Church of England, now known in the US as the Pilgrims. They sought to build new lives in America.[25] The trip took 66 days, and one passenger died during the voyage. Today, a

Slow is the New Green

Climate Activist Greta Thunberg Completes Three-Week Catamaran Voyage across Atlantic

"…the crew had to grapple with tempestuous weather, including a lightning storm and 5-foot waves."
— *Salon*, December 6, 2019[26]

jet aircraft carries 300 passengers the same distance in under seven hours, and usually no one dies during the flight. Each day during 2019, more than 100,000 commercial aircraft carried more than 11 million passengers a combined total of over 14 billion passenger miles.[27]

Equally noteworthy, travel on the Oregon Trail during the 1800s was hazardous. From 1840 to 1860, 268,000 pioneers traveled the trail from St. Louis to the Willamette Valley in Oregon or to other endpoints in the American West. Settlers, miners, ranchers, businessmen and their families used wagons pulled by oxen to complete the 2,000-mile trip in six months. About five percent of the travelers who attempted the journey died on the trail. Cholera killed about half of those, with Native American attacks, freezing, wagon crashes, drownings, and shootings also causes of death.[28]

Today, a family of four can safely make the same journey in about 33 hours in the comfort of the air-conditioned family van. Each day, more than a billion automobiles around the world transport people.

In early 1800s' America, the day was over for most people when the sun went down. Light from candles and camphene, a flammable mixture of turpentine and alcohol, extended the day for some. The wealthy could afford whale oil to fuel their lamps. The US whaling fleet grew for over a century to a peak of more than 700 ships in the 1840s. But a single pint of whale oil cost more than a day's wages for many.[29]

Abraham Gesner, a Canadian chemist and geologist, invented kerosene in 1846. Kerosene was a fuel derived from coal, which burned cleaner than whale oil and could be used in the lamps of the day. By 1860, more than 30 companies were producing kerosene, which was also called "coal oil."[30] But commercial petroleum production began shortly after, an event that would dominate fuel for modern society.

On August 27, 1859, the world changed. A drill bit of the Seneca Oil Company reached a depth of 69 feet and struck oil near Titusville, Pennsylvania. Edwin Drake used a six-horsepower steam engine and a cable-tool drilling rig to drill through rock to access the oil. Drake is regarded as "the father of the petroleum industry" because of the drilling technology he devised to launch the industry. Drake's first customer, a Pittsburgh refinery, paid about $20 per barrel for the petroleum and refined "carbon oil" fuel for lamps, which sold at almost $40 per barrel.[31] The US produced about 2,000 barrels of oil during the year of 1859. By 1900, America was producing 2,000 barrels of oil every 17 minutes.[32]

While steam engines still provided power for industrial use, emerging small vehicles needed a compact engine using high-density fuel. The invention of the internal combustion engine (ICE) powered by fuels from petroleum revolutionized vehicular transportation. Steam engines typically use a combustion process to convert water to steam, which then forces a piston action. Internal combustion engines use a series of controlled explosions from a ready-to-explode fuel-air mixture in the cylinder of the engine. The explosions push a piston down along the axis of the cylinder, turning the drive shaft and the wheels of the vehicle.[34]

Modern ICEs use compression of the air-fuel mixture inside the cylinder to maximize engine efficiency. Gasoline engines use a spark-plug ignition system, while diesel engines rely on the heat and pressure of the engine itself to ignite the fuel-air mixture. The mixing of fuel and air down to an atomic level creates the explosive power of an internal combustion engine. One ton of gasoline, when burned in an automobile engine, releases more than 10 times the energy contained in a ton of the explosive TNT.[35]

The invention cycle of the internal combustion engine spanned more than a century. Leonardo da Vinci described a compression-less engine in 1509 but never actually built his concept. Robert Street patented and built the first compression-less internal combustion engine in England in 1794. Street's engine heated the bottom of the cylinder with fire and injected a small amount of tar or turpentine along with air into the cylinder, which became a vapor.[36] Follow-on inventors of the 1800s tried hydrogen, coal gas, and even gunpowder for fuel in mostly unsuccessful attempts to compete with steam engines. Dr. Nicholas Otto of Germany built the first commercially successful piston engine in 1862. It was a small stationary engine fueled by coal gas.[37]

Karl Benz of Germany is recognized as the inventor of the modern automobile. He followed a number of inventors of "steam carriages" during the early 1800s. Benz ran his first three-wheeled single-piston car on gasoline in 1885 and received a patent in 1886. His first commercial three-wheeler used a three-quarter-horsepower engine to reach a speed of

---

THE FOOL

Poor Prophecy

"In meeting the world's needs, however, the oil from the United States will continue to occupy a less and less dominant position, because within the next two to five years the oil fields of this country will reach their maximum production and from then on we will face an ever increasing decline."
— *Oil and Gas News*, October 23, 1919[33]

1885 Gasoline Car of Karl Benz[38]

10 miles per hour (16 kilometers per hour).[39]

The internal combustion engine and refined fuel from petroleum enabled the miracles of modern transportation. Fuel from oil was high in energy density and perfect for mobile applications. Petroleum fuels burned clean, leaving no ash residue after combustion. Today, about 90 percent of the world's cars, motorcycles, trucks, buses, trains, ships, and planes are powered by fuels from petroleum.

ELECTRICITY IS WHERE IT'S AT

Of the three elements of the Hydrocarbon Revolution, harnessing electricity delivered the greatest impact. Today's power plants generate electricity, our most flexible form of energy, from four sources: heat produced by burning natural gas, coal, or wood; heat produced by nuclear reactors or geothermal vents; mechanical energy of falling water or blowing wind; or voltage from sunlight captured by solar arrays. Electricity transformed and revolutionized our homes, industry, transportation, communications, health care, education, and science. In 2019, electricity provided 37 percent of US energy, with 28 percent of the energy used in transportation, and 35 percent consumed as heat for homes and industry.[40]

Electricity is personal energy. Your plug-in home wall outlet provides ready-to-use power for personal computers, big-screen TVs, coffee makers, refrigerators, and dozens of other applications. Batteries provide energy at your fingertips for headsets, smart phones, wall clocks, and portable devices of every shape and size. The alternator under the hood of your car powers your GPS navigation display, tail lights, and car battery.

Residents of developed nations take modern electrical wonders for granted, but electricity is either not available or scarce for about a third of the world's people. Electricity use drives prosperity in modern society. The nations that use the most electricity per person enjoy the highest levels of personal income.

The history of the development of electricity shows a remarkable mix of science, invention, and entrepreneurship. US inventor and statesman Benjamin Franklin demonstrated the electrical nature of lightning in June 1752. He flew a kite in a thunderstorm over Philadelphia and observed a spark from a key hung at the end of the kite string. Franklin would

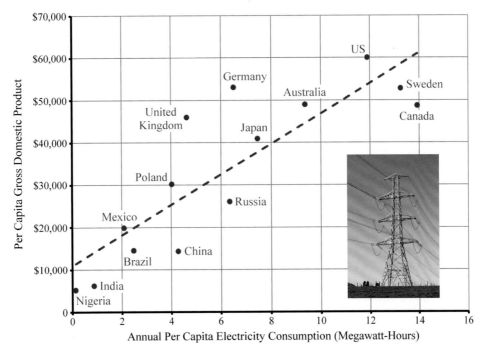

Electricity Use and Prosperity. Plot of per-person electricity use and per-person Gross Domestic Product for major nations in 2017. Prosperity is strongly correlated with the level of electricity use. Image of power lines in New Zealand. (World Bank, 2020; IEA, 2020)[41]

also invent the lightning rod to protect buildings and other structures from lightning.[42]

Italian physicist and chemist Alessandro Volta invented the first electrical battery in 1800. Volta stacked a column of discs of silver and zinc, separated with cards that were soaked with salt water, to produce electrical potential. Connecting the ends of the column caused electrical current to flow.[43]

Michael Faraday, an English chemist with only a basic education, became one of the greatest scientists in history and has been called "the father of electromagnetism." Faraday built on the work of Danish scientist Hans Christian Ørsted in 1821 to show that electricity has an effect on magnetism. Faraday brought a permanent magnet close to a wire carrying electricity and caused the wire to rotate around the pole of the magnet.[44] This meant that electricity in the presence of a magnet could do mechanical work, which is the basis of modern electrical motors.

Then in 1831, Faraday showed that a moving magnet inside a coil of wire produced an electrical current in the wire.[45] This meant that mechanical energy could be transformed into electrical energy, the opposite of his 1821 discovery. This property forms the basis for today's electricity generators. Modern generators use steam, falling water, or wind to turn turbines with an electromagnet to generate electrical power.

American inventor and entrepreneur Thomas Edison ushered in the age of commercial electricity in the late 1800s. Although best known as inventor of the incandescent light bulb, Edison actually invented and installed the first complete electrical power system in New York City in 1882. From 1878 to 1881, Edison established six different companies

What is Electricity?

Electricity is the separation of charge. Generators separate electrons from atoms, creating electrical potential. These separated electrons try to return to atoms that are short of electrons, providing electrical power. An electric grid routes separated electrons through wires, light bulbs, motors, and all of our other devices that are powered by electricity.

Electricity is a secondary energy source. Primary energy sources such as coal, natural gas, nuclear, water energy, wind energy, and solar energy produce electrical power. Electricity is also called an "energy carrier." It can be converted back into mechanical energy (such as with a motor) or into heat energy (such as with a stove).[46] Electricity can power almost any process, although it may not be cost effective to do so.

Batteries provide electrical potential based on chemical reactions that create a negative charge at the anode and a positive charge at the cathode. This potential can power flashlights, cell phones, and other devices. Battery chargers reverse the chemical reactions and restore electrical potential in a rechargeable battery.

Voltage is the potential of a battery or power system, measured in volts (V). Amperage is the current flow of electricity, measured in amps (A). Resistance is the opposition to current flow based on the properties of the conducting material, measured in ohms (Ω). Electricity flowing through conductors creates heat, a waste product.

Current flows atom to atom through a power grid at roughly one-half the speed of light in a vacuum.[47] Electric current is composed of individual charge carriers, which move though a conductor by pushing on charge carriers ahead, like marbles in a pipe. The current flow in a single circuit is the same at any point in the circuit.[48]

In direct current systems (DC), current flows continuously in the same direction. In alternating current systems (AC), current flow switches directions dozens of times per second, with a frequency measured in Hertz (Hz). Most power grids use AC to minimize long-distance resistance losses and allow use of transformers to easily change voltages.

Some examples:
- North American power systems use 120V alternating current at 60 Hz; European power systems use 230V alternating current at 50 Hz.
- A current as low as 100 milliamperes (0.1A) can be fatal to humans.[49]
- Electrical Voltages: Car battery (14V), stun gun (50,000V), long-distance power lines (230,000V)
- Electrical Resistances: Drinking water (about 2Ω per centimeter), dry human skin (about 50,000Ω), dry air (about 1,300,000,000,000Ω per centimeter)[50]

to design and manufacture electric lamps, power generators (called dynamos), copper conductors, lamp sockets, switches, electric motors, and other devices. These companies consolidated into the Edison General Electric Company in 1889, the forerunner of the General Electric Company of today.[51]

Energy Wisdom?

"It's pretty obvious that Western lifestyles which rely on gigantic amounts of electricity use up far more resources than a subsistence-based life. A little more poverty would be a good thing."
— Author Tom Hodgkinson,
The Guardian, November 10, 2009[52]

Edison's Pearl Street power plant began operation on September 4, 1882. The first phase of the world's first central power station provided direct current electricity to 400 lamps for 82 customers. Edison powered the Pearl Street facility with coal, which produced higher energy output per ton than wood. By 1884, the expanded Pearl Street facility served over 500 customers and over 10,000 lamps. By 1887, there were 121 Edison power stations across America.[53]

Thomas Edison is regarded as the greatest inventor in US history. In addition to his invention of the first commercially practical light bulb, he is credited with inventing the phonograph, the motion picture camera, an improved stock ticker, an electronic voting recorder, and many other devices. Edison established the first corporate research laboratory in Menlo Park, New Jersey, and received 1,093 patents during his lifetime.[54]

Despite Edison's successes, his power systems suffered from a major limitation. The direct current electricity he provided could only be delivered up to a mile from the generator without the need for larger, expensive copper wires to reduce transmission losses.

George Westinghouse, a prolific inventor like Edison but also with strong skills as a industrialist, established Westinghouse Electric Company in 1886 to manufacture DC electricity systems. Westinghouse hired the brilliant Serbian-American engineer Nikola Tesla, who convinced him to switch to AC, the superior long-distance power system. For the next six years, Edison, Westinghouse, and Tesla fought the "War of the Currents," which would establish the preferred power system for America and the world.[55]

By 1892, the battle was over. The AC system of Westinghouse provided long-distance power transmission, allowing a central generator to provide power over a wide area, a decisive low-cost advantage. Westinghouse won the contract to electrify the 1893 World's Columbian Exposition in Chicago, an event with 100,000 lights.[56] Edison's own General Electric Company merged with Thomson-Houston in 1892 and soon began work on AC systems, with Edison stepping aside.[57] The new energized world had begun.

AMERICA IN 1900 AND THE NEW ENERGIZED WORLD

By 1900, the energy innovations of the 1800s were just beginning to change life in America. But the societal transformation during the next century would be the greatest in history. The harnessing of hydrocarbon energy and electricity enabled huge advances in income, transportation, communication, life span, health, education, agriculture, and personal well-being, not only in the US but across the world.

US population numbered about 76 million in 1900.[58] It would grow to 330 million today. Back in those days, 60 percent of the population lived on farms or in small towns. Today, one in four lives in rural areas and three in four reside in cities or suburbs.[59] World population grew from 1.65 billion in 1900 to almost eight billion today.[60]

The average American family size was five persons in 1900. The full-time wage earner brought in a little over $800 per year,[61] or about $3,000 in today's dollars.[62] Today, the median income of a US family of four is about $86,000.[63]

Most regions of the world achieved remarkable growth in personal incomes during the twentieth century. Since 1950, income per person around the world more than quadrupled. Since 1900, per-person incomes in developed nations rose by a factor of nine.[64]

In 1900, the average US worker toiled 66 hours per week and earned about 25 cents per hour.[65] Jobs were primarily menial labor, and child labor and poor working conditions were common. The average family spent about 43 percent of their income on food, compared to about 15 percent today.[66] Eggs cost 21 cents per dozen. Fourteen cents bought a 10-pound bag of potatoes. Coffee cost as much at 35 cents per pound, and a small tin of tea leaves cost over 50 cents. A five-pound bag of sugar cost 31 cents, with chocolate costing a pricey 34 cents a pound.[67]

During the twentieth century, the power of hydrocarbon energy was increasingly applied to factory and industrial processes. A single barrel of oil contains more energy than the energy provided by 11 years of a human laboring 40 hours per week and 50 weeks per year.[68] Deployment of coal, oil, and natural gas in US industry enabled a work-week decline to 35 hours, boosting the time available for leisure activities.

Only six percent of Americans graduated from high school in 1900.[69] High-school-age youths worked in factories and fields. As energy automated industrial processes, child labor decreased, allowing the education level of society to rise. US years of education rose from seven to 12.8 during the twentieth century. Globally, years of education rose from two to almost eight during the same period.[70]

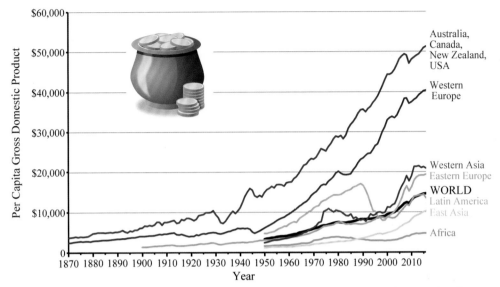

World Income Growth 1870–2016. Growth of per-person income (per capita Gross Domestic Product) for world regions in inflation-adjusted 2011 $US. (Maddison Project Database, 2018)[71]

Communications were limited in 1800. On January 8, 1815, General Andrew Jackson and a patchwork group of American fighters defeated a British army at the battle of New Orleans, ending the War of 1812. But the battle was fought 15 days after Great Britain and the United States signed the Treaty of Ghent, ending the conflict.[72] News of the treaty to end the war had not yet reached the armies near New Orleans prior to the battle.

By 1900, new methods of communication were shrinking the effective size of the world. During the 1830s, Samuel Morse and others used the battery technology invented by Alessandro Volta to produce a single-circuit telegraph. In 1844, Morse set up a telegraph for messaging between Washington, D.C., and Baltimore, Maryland. By 1861, Western Union laid the first transcontinental telegraph line, and, by 1866, the first telegraph line was laid across the Atlantic Ocean.[73]

Building on the development of the telegraph, Alexander Graham Bell and his partner, Thomas Watson, invented a receiver that could turn electricity into sound in 1875. Bell raced to the patent office to beat other competitive inventors and was granted a patent for the telephone in 1876. In 1877, the first telephone line began operation in Massachusetts. Telephone line construction exploded over the next few years. By 1880, almost 50,000 telephones were in use in America.[74] By 1900, about 10 percent of American homes had a telephone. A home with a phone made about 38 telephone calls per year, a figure that

Don't Bet On It?

"The telephone has too many shortcomings to be seriously considered as a means of communication."
— Western Union internal memo, 1876[75]

would grow to over 2,000 calls per year by the end of the twentieth century.[76]

Railroads, with engines powered by coal, crisscrossed America in 1900. A journey from St. Louis to San Francisco that once took six months by wagon could now be made in a few days. Trains belched clouds of smoke that annoyed passengers and residents of homes close to tracks.

The automobile revolution was just beginning. Only about 8,000 cars and about 10 miles of paved roads existed in 1900 America.[77] The maximum city speed limit was 12 miles per hour. Horse manure and urine from tens of thousands of horse-drawn carriages plagued major cities. Henry Ford established the Ford Motor Company in 1903 in Detroit and introduced the Model T in 1908.[78] By 1915, almost two million cars traveled US roads. Today, Americans drive more than 250 million vehicles.[79]

By 1900, about 10 percent of US homes had electricity for light bulbs and a telephone. In those days, an American worked six times as many hours to pay his electric bill than 100 years later.[80] Most US homes did not have indoor plumbing. Only 10 percent of homes had a bathtub. Most people washed their hair about once a month, using beaten egg mixed with water for shampoo.[81]

Clothes were washed by hand using a copper tub, mechanical agitators, a washboard, and hand-crank wringers. It took eight hours to wash a week's worth of laundry. Early versions of the automatic washing machine began to be sold in the US shortly after 1900. These electric machines used metal cups that agitated the clothes load and a wringer controlled by a switch.[82] One of the greatest time-saving inventions in history, electric and gas washers and dryers freed women from laundry drudgery.

Vast changes in cooking, heating, refrigeration, and air conditioning were underway for the 1900 American home. Wood and coal stoves of the 1800s began to be replaced by early electric and gas stoves. About half of homes had natural gas distribution lines by 1914. But almost half of US families still used their cook stove for heating before World War I, with wood or coal fuel in most cases.[83] Today, about 60 percent of US homes heat with natural gas, propane, kerosene, or fuel oil.[84]

The typical 1900 home used an ice box to cool food. A large block of ice inside a wood box lined with tin or zinc kept food cold. Ice was harvested from frozen lakes and stored in insulated warehouses during the winter, allowing daily deliveries of ice blocks to homes during the summer. Most families upgraded to electric refrigerators in the mid-1930s.[85]

We take our air conditioners for granted, but in 1900 open windows were the primary method used to cool the home. Commercial air conditioning was first demonstrated within the Missouri State Building at the St. Louis World's Fair in 1904. Americans flocked to air-conditioned movie theaters in the 1920s to watch the first Hollywood stars on the silver screen. Today, air conditioning is enjoyed in 90 percent of US homes.[86]

The life expectancy of a person born in the United States in 1900 was 49 years. Three of every 20 children born would die before their first birthday. More people died from tuberculosis than from cancer. Diphtheria, malaria, polio, smallpox, tuberculosis, typhoid, and whooping cough attacked American communities.

Thanks in large part to the new energy abundance and the use of electricity, life spans of people greatly increased during the twentieth century. Infectious diseases were largely eliminated in developed nations. Infant mortality dropped by a factor of 20 in the US and dropped by a factor of four globally.[87] US life expectancy rose from 49 years in 1900 to 79 years in 2015. World life expectancy rose from 32 years in 1900 to 72 years in 2015.[88]

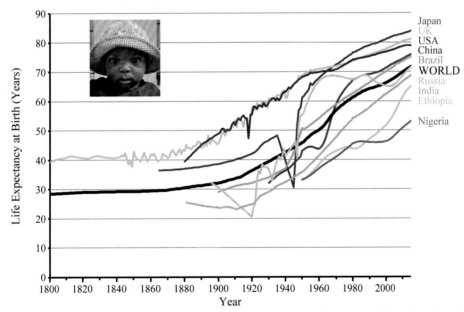

The Rise in Life Expectancy 1800–2015. Life expectancy for the world and selected nations is shown. Life expectancy is the average number of years a newborn would live if the pattern of mortality in the given year were to stay the same throughout his or her life. Image of an infant in Zimbabwe. (Our World in Data, 2020)[89]

Of course, the use of coal, oil, and natural gas, and the production of electricity didn't directly cause a reduction in infectious disease and infant mortality, or directly boost life spans. But the new energy abundance enabled revolutions in agriculture and medicine, which drove global advances in health and well-being.

The history of agriculture is a story about efforts to boost soil fertility. Animal and human manure provided the primary source of fertilizer for thousands of years. Ground-up bison bones in the US and bird guano from Peru were notable sources of fertilizer. But by 1900, the scarcity of nitrogen fertilizer endangered the growth of world population.

During the early 1900s, two Germans, Fritz Haber and Karl Bosch, invented a process to produce nitrogen-containing ammonia from air and methane under high temperature and very high pressure. This invention led to wide-scale production of synthetic nitrogen fertilizer by 1950. The Agricultural Revolution of the 1960s and 1970s that produced high-yielding varieties of wheat and rice depended upon synthetic nitrogen for success.

Today, the Haber-Bosch Process provides almost half of all fixed nitrogen atoms in human food and uses about two percent of world energy. The process requires methane feedstock and hydrocarbon fuel to provide the required high temperatures and pressures. It can't be done economically with renewable energy.[91]

Diesel fuel drives today's high-yield agriculture. The horse-drawn plow of ages past has been replaced by hydrocarbon-powered tractors, balers, combines, mowers, planters, and sprayers. World population more than doubled during the last 50 years, but world agricultural production more than tripled.[92] Farm automation contributed in large measure to the Agricultural Revolution of the twentieth century.

Health care, possibly more than any other industry, is dependent upon hydrocarbons and modern energy. Pacemakers, artificial heart valves, prosthetic legs, and contact lenses consist of plastics. Syringes, blood bags, surgical gloves, catheters, and intravenous tubes are made from nylon and flexible polyvinyl chloride. The durability, sterility, disposability, and low-cost nature of plastics made from oil and natural gas are essential for today's medicine.

Most pharmaceuticals come from petroleum-based chemicals. Anhydrides and carboxylic acids are used to make sedatives, tranquilizers, decongestants, antihistamines, and antibacterial soaps. Esters and alcohols are used to produce antibiotics. Petrochemical ingredients are essential for penicillin, cough syrup, radiological dyes, x-ray film, pill coatings, and many other medical materials.[93]

Electricity generated by hydrocarbon fuel powers respirators, dialysis equipment, CAT scanners, x-ray machines, operating rooms, laboratories, and air conditioning in today's hospitals. In addition, when hurricanes knock out the power, backup power usually comes from diesel, natural gas, or propane generators.

The US and most of the world have come a long way since 1900, thanks to the revolution in hydrocarbons and use of electricity. But billions still remain in energy poverty.

BILLIONS STILL IN ENERGY POVERTY

A long line stands outside the Papaye restaurant in Accra, the capital of Ghana, but the place looks closed. All of the lights are out in the Abeka neighborhood. Inside, management struggles to turn on the backup generator, producing a flash of light revealing two huge rooms packed with customers eating fried rice and chicken. After a few seconds, the diners are plunged back into darkness.[94]

The Ghanaians call it the *dumsor* (pronounced *doom-so*), which means "a period of time in which darkness is more prevalent than light." The Republic of Ghana is a West African nation of 31 million people situated just above the equator. Even though 85 percent of Ghanaians have access to electricity—one of the highest access rates in sub-Saharan Africa—the nation is plagued with power blackouts.[95]

Ghana's electricity production doubled in the last 10 years. The Akosombo Dam generates about 47 percent of the nation's power. Almost all of the remaining supply comes from gas (30%) and oil (23%). Ghana's government had a goal to reach 10 percent renewable electricity by 2020, but today the country gets less than one percent from solar and wind.[96]

Despite increasing production, demand grows faster than supply. When generated electricity can't meet demand, the Electric Company of Ghana allocates power to hospitals, police, military, and prisons and shuts down electricity to homes and businesses. Each week, one or two *dumsor* plague Ghana's residences and businesses with a typical outage lasting six hours.

The Emmanuel Printz printing press produces everything from newspapers to posters for local customers. But the company almost closed down because of the *dumsor*. The firm does not have a backup diesel generator like some competitors. To stay in business, employees returned to work day or night, whenever power was available.[97]

Ghana businesses pay $0.23 per kWh, one of the highest rates in the world, for their erratic supply of power. Exported products must compete with those from nations such as Vietnam, where electricity costs $0.07 per kWh with 99 percent reliability.[98]

As of 2019, 771 million, or 10 percent of the world's people, did not have access to residential electricity. Seventy-five percent, or 578 million, resided in sub-Saharan Africa. Most of the remaining people without power lived in Southeast and Central Asia, followed by those in the Middle East and Central America. Despite many still without access, the great news is that the portion of the world's people with access to electricity rose from 73 percent in 2000 to 90 percent today.[99] The United Nations Sustainable Development Goal 7 calls for access to electricity for all people by 2030.[100]

But access to electricity is only part of the story. Power blackouts persist not only in Ghana but in many countries. More than 900 million people live in the 47 nations classified by the UN as Least Developed Countries (LDCs).[101] Those LDC residents with electricity experience more than 10 blackouts per month. Pakistan is not classified as an LDC, but the 79 percent of residents in Pakistan that have electricity access experience an outage every day.[102] India also is not listed as an LDC and 99 percent of residents have access, but six of the most populous states of India face daily 11-hour blackouts.[103] In all, some three billion people have either no electricity or sporadic electricity.

The difference between electricity abundance and need is stark. More than three billion people in developing nations do not use as much electricity per person annually as the average air conditioner consumes in the United States.[105] More than 680 million people live in sub-Saharan Africa, where the average daily temperatures often exceed 30 degrees Celsius (86°F). But only about six percent of these people have air conditioning, and 40 percent don't even own an electric fan.[106] Hydrocarbon fuels are sorely needed to generate electrical power, boost national economies, and raise standards of living.

Students studying under streetlights in Mumbai, India.[104]

Electricity use is essential for modern societies, but another important factor is the use of hydrocarbon-fueled vehicles. Not only passenger cars for personal use, but buses for schools and transit systems, trucks for industry and transportation of freight, and tractors for agriculture are essential for economic growth.

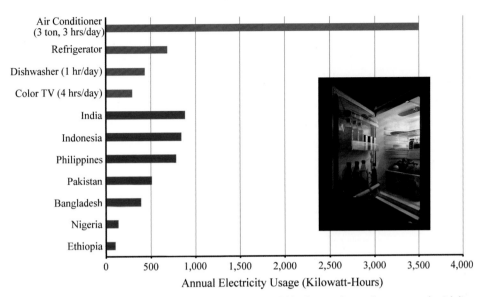

Electricity Use of US Appliances and in Selected Nations. Annual average electricity use of US appliances (blue bars) and per-person electricity use in selected developing nations. National electricity use is for year 2017. (World Bank, 2020; IEA 2020; US Dept. of Energy, 2020; Kompulsa, 2020)[107]

Developed nations enjoy a high level of motor vehicle ownership. There are 80 vehicles in use for every 100 persons in the US—almost one per person. Western Europe and Canada use more than one vehicle for every two residents. But vehicle ownership in the developing world remains very low. As of 2014, vehicle usage in India and Africa totaled fewer than four vehicles per 100 people.[108]

General Dwight D. Eisenhower led Allied armies to victory in Europe in 1945. While in Europe, Eisenhower was impressed with Germany's Autobahn system of highways. In 1956, as President of the US, Eisenhower initiated development of the Interstate Highway System (IHS), which is regarded as the world's largest public works project. The IHS now consists of more than 47,000 miles of roadway. Although the IHS comprises only 2.5 percent of US highways, the system carries 25 percent of all traffic and more than 50 percent of truck traffic. The system transports almost $14 trillion of goods each year.[109]

By contrast, roads in many parts of Africa and Southeast Asia are unpaved or non-existent. Businesses incur high costs because motor vehicles and paved roads are not available. Transportation limitations raise the price of delivery of materials and the cost of shipping finished goods. Improved roads and vehicle use are key to economic growth.

A third indicator of energy poverty is the lack of use of modern fuels for cooking and heating. Globally, about three billion people burn wood, charcoal, coal, or dung in inefficient open fires or simple cook stoves. Indoor air pollution from open fires causes respiratory infection in children and pulmonary disease, stroke, and lung cancer in adults, accounting for an estimated five percent of global mortality.[110] Emerging nations need modern fuels such as propane and natural gas to boost health and well-being. In 2016, Indian Prime Minister Narendra Modi launched a program to provide natural gas connections or propane gas cylinders to 200 million people, making India the second largest importer of liquid petroleum gas today.[111]

ENERGY UNDER ATTACK

Our modern world runs on low-cost, reliable, abundant energy. The production of coal, oil, and natural gas, the inventions of machine power and hydrocarbon-fueled transportation, and the harnessing of electricity transformed human society during the last 300 years more than anything else had in thousands of years of prior history. The modern energy revolution is spreading to billions in the developing world who are still in need.

Casualty in the War on Hydrocarbons

As Climate Change Tightens its Grip, Are Golf Courses a Luxury We can No Longer Afford?
— *The Salt Lake Tribune*, July 23, 2021[112]

But hydrocarbon energy is under attack. Because of fears about human-caused global warming, local, state, provincial, and national governments are implementing curbs on the use of hydrocarbon energy, while actively forcing adoption of renewable energy. Businesses succumb to pressure to join the demanded energy transition. And the United Nations and other organizations urge developing nations, many of whose residents live in poverty, to forego the use of coal, oil, and natural gas and endorse a risky jump to the use of renewables. In the next chapter, we'll look at the rise of renewable energy.

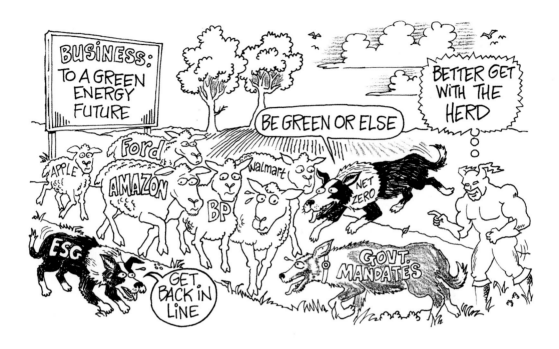

CHAPTER 2

THE RISE OF RENEWABLE ENERGY

"The future is green energy, sustainability, renewable energy."'
—ARNOLD SCHWARZENEGGER, ACTOR, POLITICAL LEADER (2012)[1]

Renewables have become the preferred source of energy for wealthy countries. State and provincial governments call for "zero carbon" electricity. Politicians condemn fracking and demand a halt to the use of petroleum and natural gas. Cities announce bans on traditional gasoline and diesel vehicles, and auto manufacturers respond with dozens of new electric car models. Big tech firms claim to power their businesses with wind and solar. Television car commercials love to show vehicles passing wind systems. Oil companies proclaim the wonders of biofuels from algae. "Sustainable Evanston" calls for Chicagoland to be "solarized."[2] Green energy is beautiful, baby.

Three major geopolitical factors stimulated the rise of renewable energy during the last decades of the twentieth century. These were the oil price shocks of the 1970s, the emergence of the modern environmental movement and a quest for clean air, and the

25

new-found fears about human-caused climate change. Each acted to pave the way for renewables, with climate change ascending as the core issue. But despite three decades of subsidies and mandates, renewable energy provides only a small part of global energy today. Let's take a look at the history and policies driving the growth of renewable energy.

OIL PRICES THAT SHOCKED THE WORLD

Back in 1970, coal, oil, and natural gas provided about 80 percent of global energy consumption, a share similar to today. Hydroelectric power accounted for about five percent of consumption. Almost all of the remainder came from burning biomass in developing nations.[3]

The United States reigned as the leading producer of crude oil, pumping 9.6 million barrels of crude oil per day, or 23 percent of the world's output. Oil cost about $3 per barrel.[4] The average US retail price of gasoline was $0.36 a gallon.[5]

Wind and solar were negligible in terms of world energy consumption. Windmills pumped water on farms. Solar systems heated water for household use or swimming pools but often cost more than natural gas alternatives. Renewable energy was still decades away from becoming a priority for society.

Changes in attitudes about energy began with the shock of the 1973 Arab oil embargo. Led by Saudi Arabia, the Organization of Petroleum Exporting Countries (OPEC) cut oil production and placed an embargo on shipments to nations that supported Israel in the Yom Kippur War of October 1973. Canada, Japan, the Netherlands, the United Kingdom, and the US were initial embargo targets.[6] Oil prices jumped to over $10 per barrel and reached $12 by 1976.[7] The price of US retail gasoline rose to $0.60 that same year.[8]

The embargo exposed a growing US dependency on foreign oil and natural gas. US crude oil production peaked in 1970 and began a 38-year decline.[10] During the late 1960s and early 1970s, the nation's electric power industry had shifted away from coal toward low-sulfur oil and natural gas fuel, increasing the demand for imported oil. Rising oil consumption now provided over 80 percent of New England's energy.[11] The share of US petroleum products imported increased from 21.5 percent in 1970 to 46.5 percent in 1977.[12]

Renewable Humor?

Drink Beer, Save the Planet! NZ Company Introduces World's First Beer-Based Fuel

"We drank beer and had an idea: taking the yeast and grain left over after we finish brewing DB Export, and turning it into a biofuel. We call it DB Export Brewtroleum."
— *RT News*, July 11, 2015[9]

The quadrupling of oil prices heavily impacted Europe and Japan, which imported more than 80 percent of their oil, most of it from the Middle East. Unemployment and inflation soared across Europe. The annual inflation rate in the UK rose to over 20 percent. The 1973 oil price shock ended 30 years of economic growth in Europe since the end of the Second World War and triggered a worldwide recession from 1973 to 1975.[14]

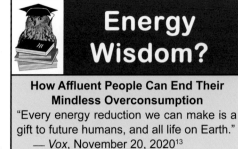

Energy Wisdom?

How Affluent People Can End Their Mindless Overconsumption
"Every energy reduction we can make is a gift to future humans, and all life on Earth."
— *Vox*, November 20, 2020[13]

In response to the crisis, US Presidents Richard Nixon and Gerald Ford introduced price controls on oil and gas, gasoline rationing, and a national 55-mph speed limit. The 1975 Energy Policy Conservation Act established the Strategic Petroleum Reserve to store crude oil in Gulf Coast salt domes. The act also set up the Corporate Average Fuel Economy (CAFE) standards for light-duty motor vehicles to try to reduce the growing demand for gasoline.[15]

The 1978 Iranian revolution triggered the second world oil shock in five years. Strikes in Iran's oil fields resulted in a decline of 4.8 million barrels per day, or about seven percent of global production. Oil prices rose from $13 per barrel in mid-1979 to $34 per barrel the next year.[16] To counter rising inflation, the US Federal Reserve tightened monetary policy, boosting home mortgage rates to double-digit levels. US unemployment soared to 10.8 percent during the resultant 1981–1982 recession.[17]

The oil shocks of the 1970s produced major changes in US and world energy policy. National governments ramped efforts to reduce oil and gas consumption, reduce oil imports, and boost domestic production where possible. America's electrical utilities reversed trends toward oil and natural gas fuel by building new plants to burn domestically available coal. The International Energy Agency was founded in 1974 to foster energy cooperation to counter OPEC. The Federal Energy Administration was formed the same year to respond to the embargo, becoming the US Department of Energy in 1977.[18]

In the wake of price shocks and declining US production, energy forecasters predicted global oil production would peak in coming decades. In 1956, M. King Hubbert, a geologist for Shell Oil, predicted that US oil production would peak about 1970, and that global output would peak in 2000, an expected event that would come to be called "peak oil."[19] During President Jimmy Carter's April 18, 1977 address to the nation, he stated,

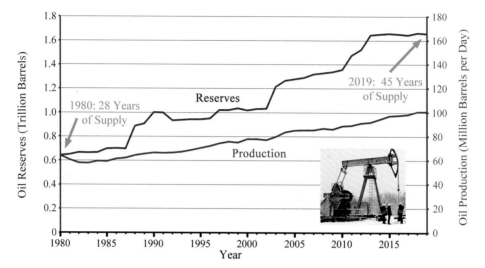

World Petroleum Production and Reserves 1980–2019. Over the last 39 years, world oil production increased from 64 million barrels per day to 101 million barrels per day. At the same time, global oil reserves increased from 28 years of supply to 45 years of supply at higher consumption rates. (US Energy Information Administration, 2020)[20]

Because we are now running out of gas and oil, we must prepare quickly for a third change, to strict conservation, and to the renewed use of coal, and to permanent renewable energy sources like solar power.[21]

But predictions of a near-term oil production peak were unfounded. The US Shale Revolution of the early 2000s opened up vast new sources of oil, allowing global production to continue climbing. Since 1980, both world oil reserves and natural gas reserves expanded faster than production and consumption. Nevertheless, oil price shocks, the resultant impact on national economies, and the fear of reaching peak oil have led governments to strive to reduce petroleum consumption and to look seriously at alternative energy sources.

ENVIRONMENTALISM AND CLEAN AIR

A second factor driving the rise of renewable energy was the quest for clean air and the emergence of the modern environmental movement. After World War II, 30 years of prosperity in Western nations increased population, urbanization, and industrialization, and many more people drove cars. These trends caused worsening levels of air pollution.

Pollution incidents plagued major cities. The expanding population and automobile fleet in Los Angeles generated recurring episodes of smog in the 1940s, which reduced visibility to three blocks, caused nausea and burned eyes.[22] Hydrogen fluoride and sulfur dioxide emissions from steel plants in Donora, Pennsylvania, killed 20 and sickened thousands in October 1948 in one of the worst air pollution incidents in US history.[23] The Great Smog of London killed between 4,000 and 12,000 residents over five days in December 1952.[24]

Prior to 1950, American air pollution control laws existed only at a city or county level. During the 1950s, eight states passed control laws. All 50 states enacted air pollution legislation by 1970. Congress passed the Clean Air Act of 1963 and established the Environmental Protection Agency as part of the Clean Air Act of 1970.[25]

As society struggled with air pollution, the modern environmental movement emerged during the 1950s–1970s. The early US conservation movement of the late 1800s and early 1900s, led by the Sierra Club and the National Audubon Society, had focused on fisheries and wildlife management and conservation of water, soils, and forests. The newly emerging environmental organizations of the 1950s raised concerns about air and water pollution, chemical pollution, and nuclear weapons testing. These organizations included The Nature Conservancy (founded in 1951), the World Wildlife Fund (1961), the Natural Resources Defense Council (1970), and Greenpeace (1971).[26] Environmental concerns would soon broaden into a wide array of issues, including population growth, genetically modified foods, and human-caused global warming.

Well-publicized events stimulated the rise of environmentalism. Hydrogen bomb testing at Bikini Atoll, oil spills off the coast of California, and the Cuyahoga River fire in Cleveland became rallying events for environmental protests. Rachel Carson's 1962 book *Silent Spring* criticized excessive use of pesticides, such as DDT, and became a worldwide bestseller. The first Earth Day was held April 22, 1970. Millions of Americans, including students from thousands of colleges, participated in rallies, marches, and educational events across the nation. Earth Day helped elevate concern for the environment to a leading national and global issue.[27]

Europe's environmental movement lagged behind developments in the US. Many Europeans regarded the widespread spraying of pesticides as a US problem. European agriculture did not have America's large farms and use of monoculture farming. But notable disasters shocked Europeans and launched environmental movements that eventually grew into

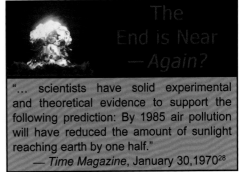

The End is Near — Again?

"... scientists have solid experimental and theoretical evidence to support the following prediction: By 1985 air pollution will have reduced the amount of sunlight reaching earth by one half."
— *Time Magazine*, January 30, 1970[28]

Europe's green parties. The supertanker *Torrey Canyon* struck a reef in 1967 and spilled oil that fouled hundreds of miles of coastline of southwestern Britain and northwestern France. A 1976 explosion at a chemical plant near Seveso, Italy, released a toxic cloud of dioxin, raising concerns about chemicals in the environment. The 1986 accident at the Chernobyl Nuclear Power Plant in Ukraine spread radiation across Europe, horrifying residents.[29]

Europe's first green parties started in the early 1970s. European Greens was founded in Brussels, Belgium, in 1984 to coordinate the activities of the various green groups. By the end of the 1980s, almost every country in Western Europe had a party known as the Greens. Green parties also developed in Argentina, Canada, Chile, and New Zealand. The Greens worked to build support for control of nuclear energy and reduce air and water pollution, along with writing proposals to dismantle NATO and demilitarize Europe.[30]

Many energy leaders predicted world-changing success for nuclear power, but growing opposition to nuclear weapons and atomic energy fueled the growth of the environmental movement. The first commercial nuclear power plant began operation at Calder Hall in England in October 1956. By 1970, many nuclear plants were under construction around the world. In 1971, Glenn Seaborg, chairman of the US Atomic Energy Commission, predicted that atomic energy would generate almost all of the world's electricity by 2000.[31] But also in 1971, a small group of activists in Vancouver, Canada, was formed to oppose underground nuclear weapons testing, which would become the international environmental organization Greenpeace.

Environmental groups would eventually sway public opinion against atomic energy. Reactor failures at Three Mile Island in Pennsylvania (1979), Chernobyl, Ukraine (1986), and Fukushima, Japan (2011), raised safety concerns. Rising costs from efforts to ensure reactor safety and problems with disposal of nuclear waste limited the construction of new nuclear plants. The nuclear share of world electricity peaked at 18 percent in 1996, dropping to about 10 percent by 2018.[33]

The 1970s oil crisis and concerns about air pollution, along with pressure from the environmental movement, stimulated efforts toward renewables. Between 1974 and 1981, the National Aeronautics and Space Administration (NASA) and the US Department of Energy funded research to develop wind

THE FOOL

Poor Prophecy

"It is estimated that nuclear power will provide more than one-quarter of this country's electrical production by 1985, and over half by the year 2000."
— President Richard Nixon, address to Congress, April 18, 1973[32]

turbine technology and photovoltaic solar cells.[34] The US government and California also established tax incentives to promote deployment of renewables.

Renewables *Need* A Handout

U.S. Wind Energy Production Tax Credit Extended through 2021

"The U.S. production tax credit (PTC), a per-kilowatt-hour (kWh) credit for electricity generated by eligible renewable sources, was first enacted in 1992 and has been extended and modified in the years since."
— Energy Information Administration, January 28, 2021[36]

The world's first wind array, consisting of twenty 30 kW turbines, was installed in 1980 on Crotched Mountain in New Hampshire. But wind took hold in California. By 1986, more than 10,000 turbines, mostly of 100 kW size, had been installed in California at Altamont Pass and Tehachapi Pass, providing more than 90 percent of US wind output.[35]

In 1982, a group of European agricultural equipment manufacturers visited California to assess the US market for wind turbines. By 1983, European manufacturers were exporting turbines to California, shipping almost half of the state's installed turbines during the 1980s. The first European wind installation began operation on the Greek island of Kythnos in 1982. With the help of government incentives, the first large-scale wind arrays began operation in Germany (1989) and Denmark (1990).[37]

Beginning in the 1980s and continuing until today, environmental groups expanded emphasis on wind, solar, and other renewables as the solution to reaching peak oil, air pollution, and rising fears of human-caused global warming. Denis Hayes, coordinator for the 1970 Earth Day, wrote in his 1977 book *Energy: The Solar Prospect*,

> About one-fifth of all energy used around the world now comes from solar resources: wind power, water power, biomass, and direct sunlight. By the year 2000, such renewable energy sources could provide 40 percent of the global energy budget; by 2025, humanity could obtain 75 percent of its energy from solar resources.[38]

Hayes's predictions were wrong, but his quote captured the desires of the environmental movement to adopt renewables and replace hydrocarbons.

In 2002, the Sierra Club started its Beyond Coal campaign. The campaign's objective was to retire existing coal-fired power plants and to prevent construction of new plants. Natural gas producer Chesapeake Energy contributed $26 million to the effort over four years, apparently hoping to suppress coal consumption and boost the market share of natural gas.[39] Then in 2012, the Sierra Club announced their Beyond Gas campaign and later broadened this to Beyond Gas & Oil.[40] Hydrocarbons still provide about 80 percent of the world's energy today, but environmental organizations now demand a ban on all use of coal, gas, and petroleum.

While environmentalists ramped up their war on hydrocarbons, developed nations successfully reduced levels of air pollution during the last four decades of the twentieth century. The use of unleaded gasoline, catalytic convertors, and particulate filters for vehicles dropped volatile organic compound emissions by 98 percent per mile from 1970 to 2019. These vehicle measures, along with the use of low-sulfur coal and the installation of scrubbers on exhaust towers of coal-fired plants, reduced US emissions of EPA criteria pollutants (carbon monoxide, lead, nitrogen dioxide, sulfur dioxide, ozone, and particulates) by 78 percent over the same period. US sulfur dioxide emissions peaked in 1970 and have since been steadily declining.[41] Europe's emissions of sulfur dioxide and nitrogen oxides peaked around 1980.[42] Air pollution levels continue to fall in all advanced nations.

Note that early deployments of wind and solar were largely irrelevant concerning air pollution and peak oil. Major developed nations installed conventional technologies to eliminate the majority of harmful air pollutant emissions by 2000, long before wind and

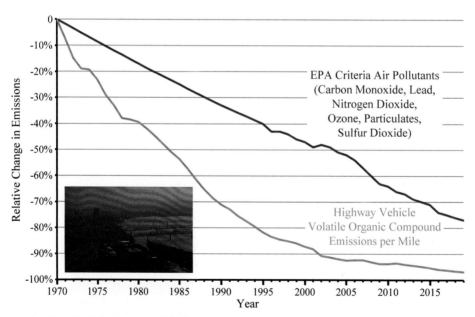

Reduction in Emissions of US Air Pollutants 1970–2019. The blue curve shows the aggregate decline in emissions of EPA criteria air pollutants (carbon monoxide, lead, nitrogen dioxide, ozone, particulates, and sulfur dioxide). The orange curve shows the decline in volatile organic compound emissions from vehicles per highway mile traveled. Image of pollution over Louisville, Kentucky, USA, in 1977. (EPA, 2020; FHA, 2020)[43]

solar output amounted to even one percent of world energy. The US Shale Revolution dispelled reaching peak oil as a near-term issue. But the vanishing air pollution problem and mistaken worries about peak oil were replaced by the fear of human-caused global warming to propel the world's growing rush to adopt renewable energy.

THE AGE OF CLIMATISM

The scene was the World Economic Forum in Davos, Switzerland. The date was January 25, 2019. Greta Thunberg, a 17-year-old climate activist from Sweden, scolded world leaders about their lack of action on human-caused climate change:

> Adults keep saying, "We owe it to the young people, to give them hope." But I don't want your hope. I don't want you to be hopeful. I want you to panic. I want you to feel the fear that I fear every day. And then I want you to act. I want you to act as if you would in a crisis. I want you to act as if the house was on fire, because it is.[44]

Ms. Thunberg's alarming presentation was followed by applause by the attending world diplomats. Indeed, more than 180 world heads of state say they believe that our modern society is causing dangerous climate change. This belief became the primary driver for global efforts to adopt renewable energy sources and to eliminate hydrocarbon energy.

As we will discuss, there is little empirical data to support the assertion that human industries, rather than natural factors, are caus-

Greta Thunberg at the
World Economic Forum, 2019.[45]

ing climate change, more correctly called global warming. Nor is there evidence that the one degree Celsius (°C) rise in temperatures since 1880 is harmful. Nevertheless, the world annually invests more than $500 billion in renewables, pursuing the futile expectation that this effort can control global temperatures. How did this massive cause get underway?

While the world struggled to cope with air pollution in the 1960s, the growing power of computer systems allowed the development of climate models of the Earth's atmosphere and oceans. A number of modelers noted that carbon dioxide was accumulating in the atmosphere and wanted to estimate the effects. Dr. Syukuro Manabe published a paper in 1967, concluding that a doubling of atmospheric carbon dioxide (CO_2) concentration would raise Earth's surface temperatures by about 2.3°C.[46]

The most renowned of the modelers was Dr. James Hansen at the NASA Goddard Institute for Space Studies in New York City. In 1981, Hansen and his team published a study that concluded that mankind's growing use of fossil fuel energy would cause an increase in Earth's average surface temperature of 2.5 to 4.5°C by 2100. Hansen projected dire effects, including regions of drought in North American and Central Asia and a possible sea level rise of five to six meters, flooding coastal cities around the world.[47]

In June 1988, global warming became headline news. Senator Tim Wirth convened the first-ever congressional hearing on the science of climate change. In testimony at the hearing, James Hansen drew three conclusions:

> Number one, the earth is warmer in 1988 than at any time in the history of instrumental measurements. Number two, the global warming is now large enough that we can ascribe with a high degree of confidence a cause and effect relationship to the greenhouse effect. And number three, our computer climate simulations indicate that the greenhouse effect is already large enough to begin to affect the probability of extreme events such as summer heat waves.[48]

That same year, the United Nations established the Intergovernmental Panel on Climate Change (IPCC). The IPCC website says that it is an international organization created to "provide policymakers with regular scientific assessments on climate change, its implications and potential future risks, as well as to put forward adaptation and mitigation options."[49]

More directly, the IPCC focuses on the perceived effects of human-caused climate change. In 1990, the IPCC issued its *First Assessment Report*, concluding that industrial emissions of greenhouse gases were significantly raising global temperatures. Just two years later at the 1992 Earth Summit in Rio de Janiero, 40 nations and the European Economic Community signed the Framework Convention on Climate Change, a treaty committing countries to reduce greenhouse emissions to mitigate the effects of climate change.[51]

Over the period of just four years, from 1988 to 1992, the world accepted Climatism, the belief that humans are causing dangerous global warming. Nations pledged efforts to halt the feared warming. Many scientists

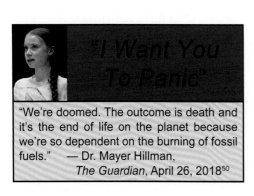

"We're doomed. The outcome is death and it's the end of life on the planet because we're so dependent on the burning of fossil fuels."   — Dr. Mayer Hillman, *The Guardian*, April 26, 2018[50]

disagreed with the findings of the IPCC and the conclusion of the Earth Summit and expressed disagreement by signing a petition.[52] But the IPCC and the UN, environmental groups, advocating nations such as the United Kingdom and Germany, scientists wielding projections from climate models, and sensationalism of climate fears by the media won the field. Climatism gained momentum and was reinforced with the signing of the Kyoto Protocol in 1997, where advanced countries agreed to mandatory reductions in emissions.[54]

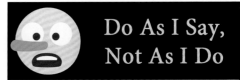

Do As I Say, Not As I Do

UN Environment Chief Resigns Amid "CO2 Hypocrisy"
"A draft internal UN audit … found Solheim had spent almost $500,000 on air travel and hotels in just 22 months, and was away 80% of the time."
— *The Guardian*, November 21, 2018[53]

Over the last 30 years, climate concern gave way to climate hysteria. The world now applauds scolding about global warming from a Swedish teenager hardly old enough to drive a car. Thousands of Extinction Rebellion protesters in London gather for weeks and carry signs that read "Business as Usual = DEATH."[55] Adoption of climate fear paved the way for the rise of renewable energy and an escalating war on hydrocarbon energy.

EARLY ADOPTERS AND SUBSIDIES

Driven by concerns first about energy security and air pollution, and finally about climate change, policy makers in selected states and nations took the lead in promoting the renewable revolution with lucrative subsidies and mandates. California, Denmark, and Germany were early adopters of renewables.

California Governor Jerry Brown established a 25 percent tax credit for wind and other renewables, triggering the California Wind Rush of the early 1980s. That credit, along with a 15 percent federal energy credit and a 10 percent federal investment tax credit, paid for about half of the installation cost of thousands of wind turbines.[56] California incentives also pioneered construction of the first large-scale solar systems. Between 1984 and 1991, nine solar generating systems were built in the Mojave Desert, using solar-trough reflecting mirrors to heat fluid flowing through pipes. These plants provided 95 percent of the world's solar-generated electricity at the time.[57]

The oil shocks of 1973 and 1979 highlighted Denmark's dependence on oil, which then provided over half of the nation's total energy. Denmark's leaders sought non-polluting energy sources to increase the electricity supply from renewables. Denmark's long coast

ENERGY CRISIS SOLVED?

PARK SPARK: Public Park Converts Dog Poo to Energy

"A new project in Cambridge, MA ... uses dog poop from the park to produce methane, which is then burned to light the park at night." — *Inhabit*, October 6, 2010[58]

pointed to wind energy as a possible solution.

In 1979, the Danish government introduced a subsidy that paid 30 percent of the installation price of a wind system. Joining this was a price-guarantee mandate at above market prices. Every wind operator was granted the right to deliver electricity to the grid and to receive a fixed guaranteed price per kilowatt-hour, paid for by electricity consumers.[59] This arrangement became known as a feed-in tariff (FIT). With these strong financial incentives, 2,665 onshore turbines had been installed by 1990.

Today, more than 6,000 wind turbines blanket Denmark's small countryside, one for every thousand Danish residents, the world's highest density of wind turbines. Wind generated about 45 percent of Denmark's electricity in 2019. Renewable energy rose from six percent of Denmark's total energy use in 1990 to 35 percent in 2019, with biomass becoming the leading renewable source, followed by wind.[60] At the same time, Danish electricity prices rose to the highest of any developed nation. Consumers paid 29 eurocents per kWh (32 US cents/kWh) in 2019, about triple the US residential electricity price.[61]

In 2010, the German government, led by Chancellor Angela Merkel, announced its energy concept policy, which soon became known as the *Energiewende*, meaning "energy transition." The policy called for increasing use of renewables as the "cornerstone of future energy supply," the phasing out of nuclear and hydrocarbon energy, and an emphasis on energy efficiency.[62] The 2010 Energiewende policy was more than 30 years in the making.

Germany's environmental movement grew throughout the 1970s and 1980s, first in opposition to atomic energy, but later in support of renewable energy. Germany's Green party won its first elected seats in 1980. The 1986 Chernobyl reactor incident turned German public opinion away from nuclear power and toward alternatives, with many in the Social Democrat SPD party changing their stance to oppose nuclear as well. No reactors were constructed in Germany after 1986.[63]

In 1991, Chancellor Helmut Kohl enacted a FIT in Germany, requiring utilities to accept electricity from renewable generators at a price of 90 percent of the retail electricity price. But renewables didn't take off until Kohl's conservatives were voted out in 1998, replaced by a coalition of Social Democrats and Greens. The new coalition passed the Renewable Energy Sources Act (EEG) in 2000, which established massive subsidies for wind and solar energy.

Beginning in 2000, electric utility companies were required to pay a tariff of between eight and nine eurocents per kWh to wind generators, roughly triple the wholesale electricity market price of three eurocents per kWh. Generators using biomass fuel received more than 10 eurocents per kWh. But solar energy received the largest subsidy. German residents that put solar panels on their roofs and fed electricity into the grid received a fixed tariff that averaged 45 to 50 eurocents per kWh, more than *10 times* the wholesale price. Solar feed-in tariffs were guaranteed for 20 years. FIT subsidies were paid by rate payers in the form of an EEG levy added to residential electric bills.[64]

Germany's generous EEG subsidy program produced an explosion in construction of renewable energy systems from 2000 to 2010. More than 20,000 wind turbines were installed[65] and more than one million homes and businesses generated electricity from solar voltaic rooftop installations by the end of 2010.[66] The rising EEG levy pushed German residential electricity bills upward in pace with those of Denmark.

A TRICKLE BECOMES A TORRENT

As California, Denmark, and Germany led the way in adoption of wind, solar, and biofuels, Climatism began to capture the hearts and minds of environmental leaders in universities, businesses, and governments. Climate change became the core issue for existence of environmental groups. Enlightened environmentalists set out to convince the public about the need for global change. Renewable energy was touted as the solution to global warming.

Former US Vice President Al Gore led the way with three books on climate, including his best-selling *An Inconvenient Truth*, which was made into an Academy Award-winning documentary movie in 2006. Gore and the Intergovernmental Panel on Climate Change shared the 2007 Noble Peace Prize for their efforts to "disseminate greater knowledge about man-made climate change."[67]

Television, articles, books, and websites warned the public about coming climate disasters. Rising oceans, stronger hurricanes and storms, droughts and floods, species extinction,

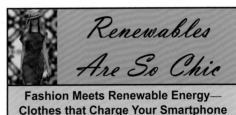

Renewables Are So Chic

Fashion Meets Renewable Energy— Clothes that Charge Your Smartphone

"The Wearable Solar collection currently consists of two designs, a coat and a dress made of wool and leather, which produce energy through their integrated solar cells. ... 'Everyone wants to look sexy and if you're creating a secondary benefit, such as producing your own energy, it's a win win.'" — *The Guardian*, August 4, 2014[68]

and ocean acidification were on the way. Universities and colleges taught students about the need for personal and societal change to save the planet, building the platform of Greta Thunberg and thousands of other green-eyed climate activists.

The UN, environmental groups, and the news media created a long list of climate and energy labels, soon to become household vocabulary. Each of us had a "carbon footprint." Hydrocarbon energy created "carbon pollution" and was "dirty" and "unsustainable," while renewable energy was "clean, green, and sustainable." Weather became "extreme" and characterized by "superstorms," "bomb cyclones," and "polar vortexes." Governments must tackle "anthropogenic greenhouse gas emissions" and lead us to a "low carbon," "zero carbon," and "carbon neutral" society if we are to "mitigate" climate change and avoid climate catastrophe. Those who publicly disagree with the theory of human-caused climate change are "anti-science" and "climate deniers."

Additional incentives and mandates joined feed-in tariffs in Europe and early tax credits in the US to boost renewable energy deployment. The US enacted a wind production tax credit (PTC) in 1992, providing wind generators with a tax credit of 1.5 cents per kWh. The PTC was extended five times, reaching 2.2 cents per kWh by 2012.[69] Twenty-nine states established Renewable Portfolio Standards laws, requiring state power utilities to purchase an increasing percentage of renewable electricity or be fined. Net metering programs were also adopted in a majority of US states. Net metering programs paid residences with roof-top solar systems the retail price of generated electricity, about three times the wholesale price received by other generators. European governments added renewable quotas to feed-in tariffs to force adoption of wind, solar, and biomass-generated electricity.

But climate campaigners and governments soon realized that electricity from renewables addressed only power plants, which accounted for about one-third of societal emissions. Residences and industry produced another third of emissions, and transportation the final third, both still dominated by hydrocarbon fuels.

Europe introduced its Emissions Trading System (ETS) in 2005 to "put a price on carbon" and to reduce industrial emissions. Today the ETS is the world's largest emissions cap-and-trade system. The ETS covers more than 11,000 European utility companies, industrial firms, and airlines.[71]

Cap-and-trade systems create artificial markets to place a tax on carbon dioxide-emitting industrial activity. Covered companies must purchase emissions allowances (the trade) and surrender those allowances to the government for each ton of CO_2 they emit. Government

Climate Change Magic?

Climate Change: Can Sending Fewer Emails Really Save the Planet?
— *BBC News*, November 19, 2020[72]

authorities set the total emissions limit (the cap) for each mandated industry. By 2020, carbon pricing systems operated in 47 countries, along with 13 states in the US and eight provinces in China.[73]

Biofuels were adopted as a solution to replace gasoline and diesel fuel in vehicles, first to reduce the demand for petroleum but later to reduce carbon dioxide emissions. The Energy Policy Act of 1978 launched the US ethanol industry, providing a 40-cents-per-gallon exemption on the gasoline excise tax to ethanol fuel producers. Between 1978 and 2011, US federal ethanol subsidies ranged between 40 and 60 cents per gallon.[74] Additional state incentives pushed the total ethanol subsidy to over $1 per gallon, stimulating a massive build-out of ethanol and biodiesel plants between 1995 and 2015. In 2019, the US blended 15.8 billion gallons of ethanol and 1.7 billion gallons of biodiesel with gasoline and diesel, providing about nine percent of US vehicle fuel.[75]

The European Biofuel Directive of 2003 called for biofuel to make up two percent of diesel fuel in 2005 and 5.75 percent by the end of 2010. The Renewable Energy Directive followed in 2009, mandating that at least 10 percent of road transport fuels be produced from renewable sources by 2020.[76] Millions of acres of land in Argentina, Brazil, and Indonesia were cleared to plant palm, rapeseed, and soybean crops to produce feedstock, which was then shipped thousands of miles to feed the growing biodiesel demand in Europe. Biofuels provided about eight percent of Europe's vehicle fuel in 2020.[77]

The high-energy density of Brazilian sugarcane, along with mandates, allowed Brazil to achieve the world's highest biofuel penetration. In 2020, Brazil directed that 27 percent of gasoline and 12 percent of diesel fuel be biofuel blends. In 2019, ethanol provided over 25 percent of the nation's gasoline, and biodiesel provided about 12 percent of its diesel fuel.[78]

But despite decades of aggressive biofuel programs in Brazil, Europe, and the US, biofuels only provided about three percent of the world's vehicle fuel in 2019,[79] requiring about three percent of the world's agricultural land to do so.[80] Scaling up biofuel production for a billion automobiles would require almost all of the world's farmland. All renewable proposals eventually run into the problem of scale, the vast size of global energy consumption.

SOME PERSPECTIVE—THE PROBLEM OF SCALE

Wind and solar energy, the two primary sources of the green energy revolution, have enjoyed strong growth over the last two decades. From 2000 to 2021, wind energy output grew at a compounded annual rate of 20.8 percent. Solar output grew at a rate of 38.8 percent per year over the same period.[81] As we have discussed, concerns about energy security, air pollution, and global warming drove this growth, backed by government subsidies and mandates. But today, wind and solar remain a tiny fraction of global energy supply.

Modern society uses vast amounts of energy. Each day the world consumes about 1.7 exajoules of energy, or 41 million metric tons of oil.[82] This is roughly equal to the energy carried by 200 oil tankers, each with a capacity of 200,000 metric tons, or the daily output of 43,000 Hoover Dams.[83]

Since 1965, global energy consumption more than tripled. The rate of world energy growth actually accelerated since the year 2000. From 2000 to 2021, world oil consumption increased 19 percent, natural gas consumption rose 69 percent, and coal consumption

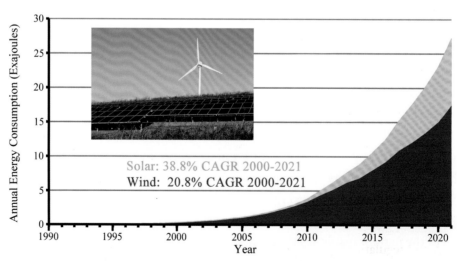

World Consumption of Wind and Solar Energy 1990—2021. Global consumption of wind and solar energy has grown at compounded annual growth rates above 20 percent over the last two decades. (BP, 2022)[84]

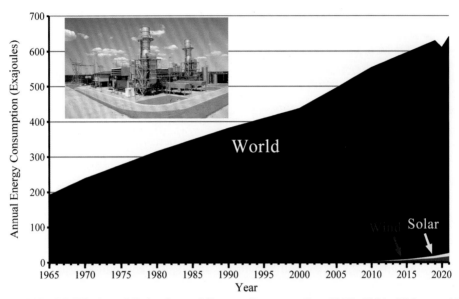

Total World, Wind, and Solar Annual Energy Consumption 1965–2021. Rising world consumption of energy and the share of wind and solar in exajoules. Image of gas-fired power plant in Orapa, Botswana. (Smil, 2010; BP, 2022; IEA, 2022)[85]

rose 62 percent.[86] World energy use fell in 2020 due to the COVID-19 pandemic but reached a new high in 2021 after pandemic fears subsided.

Despite the strong growth of wind and solar over the last two decades, the rising "energy mountain" continues to be dominated by hydrocarbons. Each year world demand grows by about 10 exajoules, equal to adding more than an additional United Kingdom's worth of energy consumption. To date, the annual growth of wind, solar, and other renewables has *never been able to generate enough new energy* to provide for that year-to-year growth, let alone replace our traditional energy sources.

RENEWABLE MANIA UNLEASHED

It seems that every politician rushes to endorse renewable energy. A 2020 study funded by the Grantham Foundation counted more than 1,800 national climate change laws in 133 nations.[87] Laws requiring renewable subsidies and mandates, statutes to reduce energy demand, and regulations promoting alternative fuels and electric vehicles have become the norm. Society responds to this huge mosaic of government directives with pledges to boost renewable energy and reduce hydrocarbon energy use.

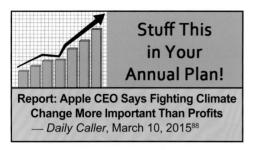

Stuff This in Your Annual Plan!

Report: Apple CEO Says Fighting Climate Change More Important Than Profits
— *Daily Caller*, March 10, 2015[88]

Electric power companies tout their green energy plans. Technology giants Apple, Facebook, and Google claim to be powered by 100 percent renewable electricity. Every automobile manufacturer announces their new line of plug-in electric vehicles, pursing what is now only eight percent of the global market. Even oil companies praise wind, solar, and bizarre solutions, such as fuel from algae. Renewables are now the preferred energy policy throughout most of the world.

Almost every nation, state, province, city, and organization must have zero-carbon goals. At the end of 2020, more than 2,600 entities had joined the Climate Ambition Alliance, pledging to achieve net-zero CO_2 emissions by 2050. Signers included 121 countries, 454 cities, 23 states and provinces, and 1,392 companies. According to the alliance, "All are united behind the same target because they recognize the benefits of the low-carbon transition."[89]

Environmental, Social, and Governance (ESG) recently gained traction with the world financial community. ESG claims to be an approach for evaluating how well a company works on behalf of social goals, beyond the usual role of maximizing returns to shareholders. Financial funds seek to invest in companies with high ESG ratings. In practice, ESG has become a vehicle to reject the use of hydrocarbon energy. Europe accounts for the highest concentration of high-ESG-rated investment assets globally. ESG is endorsed by the US Securities and Exchange Commission and most leading financial firms.[90]

Since many people are reluctant to sell their pickup truck or junk their gas stove, well-meaning governments must "help" them move down the green energy trail. Bans on gasoline and diesel vehicles and bans on gas appliances in new construction are new tools to herd them along.

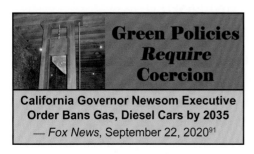

Green Policies Require Coercion

California Governor Newsom Executive Order Bans Gas, Diesel Cars by 2035
— *Fox News*, September 22, 2020[91]

The renewable trickle has become a green energy torrent, exceeding the bounds of any common sense. But will a low-carbon energy transition really provide the promised climate benefits? Let's examine the evidence for human-caused climate change in the next chapter.

CHAPTER 3

CLIMATE CHANGE FACT AND FICTION

"A myth is like an air mattress. There's nothing in it, but it is wonderfully comfortable." —MILTON FRIEDMAN, ECONOMIST (1977)[1]

Today's irresistible drive for renewable energy is founded on Climatism, the belief that carbon dioxide (CO_2) emissions cause dangerous global warming. Electric utilities deploy intermittent wind and solar energy, responding to government zero-carbon demands. Consumers believe they save the environment when they lease a plug-in electric car. Air travelers buy carbon offsets to compensate for emissions from their flight. Food companies claim to offer products that are "carbon free." Even oil companies announce that they are "beyond petroleum." According to Bloomberg, global investment in renewable energy and electric vehicles topped $500 billion in 2020.[2] But without climate change fear, renewable energy would remain a minor player in world energy markets.

The idea that human emissions of greenhouse gases cause dangerous climate change is only a theory that rests upon questionable scientific assumptions. The fact that most

43

people embrace Climatism does not validate the theory. Let's look first at the foundations of climate change theory and then at challenging empirical evidence.

THE FOUNDATIONS OF CLIMATE CHANGE THEORY

The theory of human-caused climate change rests on four concepts. These are: 1) rising global surface temperatures, 2) rising levels of atmospheric carbon dioxide, 3) the greenhouse effect, and 4) computer model projections. Proponents of the theory use these four foundational bases to warn that humans are causing dangerous global warming.

The first basis is rising global surface temperatures. Temperature metrics have been developed by the Climatic Research Unit (CRU) at the University of East Anglia in England, and also by the National Oceanic and Atmospheric Administration (NOAA) and the National Aeronautic and Space Administration (NASA) in the US, to track temperatures from the late 1800s until today. Thousands of individual thermometer measurements from all over the world, covering the last 140 years, were gathered and adjusted to produce global temperature averages.

According to the metric produced by the CRU at East Anglia, average global temperatures have increased about one degree Celsius since the late 1800s.[3] In response, the Intergovernmental Panel on Climate Change (IPCC) stated,

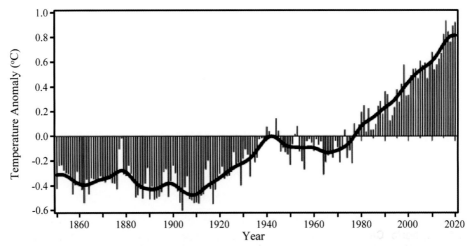

Global Surface Temperatures 1850–2020. Averaged global surface air temperatures from land and surface measuring stations. Temperature anomaly shows the difference from the 1961–1990 average. Data is from the HadCRUT5 analysis of the East Anglia University Climatic Research Unit and the UK Meteorological Office. (CRU, 2021)[4]

The increase in temperature in the 20th century is likely to have been the largest of any century during the past 1,000 years.[5]

The IPCC went on to conclude that it is "extremely likely" that most of the recent temperature rise was caused by human activity.[6] They reasoned that a one-degree rise in global temperatures was abnormal and that something abnormal must be causing it.

The second basis for the theory is rising atmospheric carbon dioxide levels. Dr. Charles Keeling conducted the first modern measurements of atmospheric carbon dioxide in 1958 at Mauna Loa Observatory on the island of Hawaii. At that time, Keeling measured a level of about 315 ppm in Earth's atmosphere.[7] Current measurements show that atmospheric CO_2 has risen to 415 ppm.[8] Other scientists estimate the pre-industrial background level"of carbon dioxide in the 1800s to be about 280 ppm. Scientists presume this rising level of atmospheric carbon dioxide to be an abnormal situation, supporting charges that CO_2 emissions from industry are pollution and must be controlled.

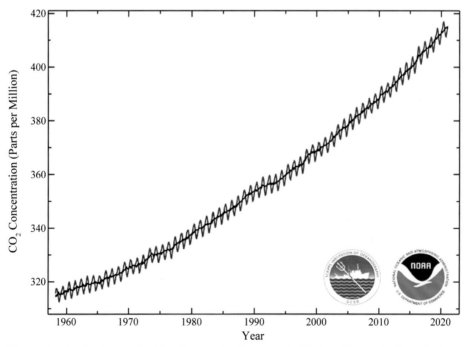

Atmospheric Carbon Dioxide Concentration 1958–2020. Atmospheric CO_2 has increased from about 315 ppm in 1958 to about 415 ppm in 2021. The red sawtooth curve shows the seasonal CO_2 variation, and the black line is the average. All atmospheric gas concentrations in this book are in parts per million by volume (ppmv). Data is from the Earth System Research Laboratory in Mauna Loa, Hawaii. (NOAA, 2021)[9]

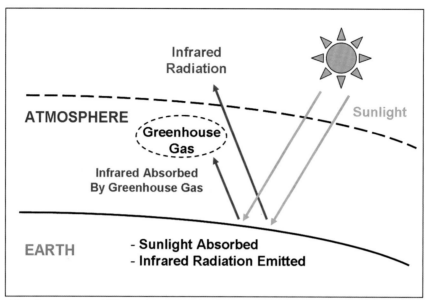

The Greenhouse Effect. Outgoing infrared radiation is absorbed by greenhouse gases in the atmosphere.

The greenhouse effect provides the third basis, and the theoretical foundation, for the theory of human-caused global warming. Sunlight, which is high-energy radiation, enters Earth's atmosphere. Sunlight that is not reflected or absorbed by clouds or the atmosphere is finally absorbed by Earth's surface. Like any warm body, the Earth emits radiation. Since Earth's temperature is lower than that of the Sun, Earth gives off lower-energy radiation called infrared radiation, which is not visible to our eyes. A tiny amount of emitted infrared passes directly out of our atmosphere to space, but almost all of the infrared is first absorbed by greenhouse gases in our atmosphere. This absorption of outgoing infrared radiation is called the greenhouse effect.

Greenhouse gases are those that absorb and emit infrared radiation. Water vapor and CO_2 are Earth's most important greenhouse gases, but methane, nitrous oxide, ozone, and other gases are also greenhouse gases. After absorbing outgoing infrared radiation, these gases reradiate a portion of the captured energy back to Earth, warming Earth's surface.

Natural climatic processes create the vast majority of Earth's greenhouse gases, so the greenhouse effect is a natural effect. But

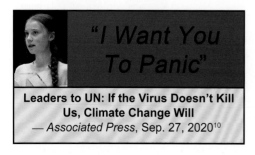

"I Want You To Panic"

Leaders to UN: If the Virus Doesn't Kill Us, Climate Change Will
— *Associated Press*, Sep. 27, 2020[10]

human emissions add to the effect. Climate change theory asserts that industrial emissions of CO_2 increase the level of atmospheric CO_2, enhancing Earth's greenhouse effect and forcing a rise in surface temperatures. According to climate alarmists, this is dangerous.

The fourth basis of the theory is computer model projections. For the last 50 years, General Circulation Models (GCMs) have been used to simulate Earth's evolving climate. The GCMs are tuned from past climate history and then run over and over to forecast the climate far into the future. They start from initial conditions and use the laws of physics and thermodynamics, many assumptions, and lots of computing power. Model outputs include temperature, air speed and direction, air pressure, and humidity at thou-

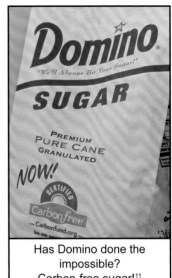

Has Domino done the impossible? Carbon-free sugar![11]

sands of points across the globe. GCMs of increasing complexity run on supercomputer systems that cost tens of millions of dollars each.

The IPCC uses outputs from more than 30 climate models to project a continuing rise in Earth's temperatures. Global surface temperatures have risen only about one degree Celsius over the last 140 years. But climate models project an additional rise of 0.5–3.5°C, or an average total rise of about 3°C or 5.4°F, by the year 2100.[12]

Based on these four concepts—rising global surface temperatures, rising atmospheric CO_2 concentration, the greenhouse effect, and model projections—proponents of the theory of human-caused warming warn of coming climate catastrophes. Rising oceans that will flood our coastal cities, stronger tropical storms, heat waves, droughts and floods, species extinction, and many other calamities are on the way. We are told that if we install wind and solar energy, eliminate gas for heating and cooking, drive electric cars, eat less meat, and have fewer children, these calamities can be avoided. But empirical evidence supports neither the foundations of Climatism nor the likelihood of coming climate disasters.

TEMPERATURE IN PERSPECTIVE

A temperature rise of one degree Celsius (1.8°F) in 140 years is not very much. A look at Chicago temperature records over the last 150 years shows that daily temperatures vary widely. Chicago's hottest temperature was 105°F, recorded on July 24, 1934. The city's

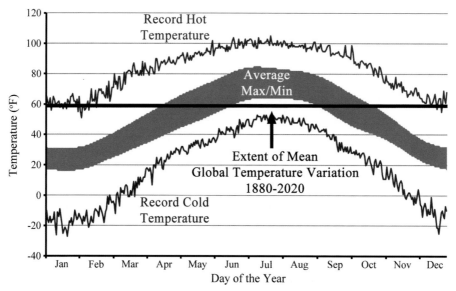

Chicago Temperatures and Global Temperature Change 1872–2020. Chicago record daily temperatures are shown in the red and blue graphs, using data from the last 148 years for each day of the year, from January 1 through December 31. The gray-shaded curve in the middle shows the average Chicago daily maximum and minimum temperature. Total global average temperature change for the last 140 years is captured *within* the thickness of the black line. (National Weather Service, 2021)[13]

coldest temperature was -27°F on January 20, 1985.[14] In a typical year, Chicago temperatures swing about 100 degrees Fahrenheit (about 56°C). Compare that variation to the 140-year 1.8-degree Fahrenheit rise in average global temperatures, which is captured *within* the thickness of the black line in the diagram above. Climate alarmists have only this tiny temperature rise and climate model projections to support their dire warnings.

But little empirical evidence exists to suggest that a one-degree rise in global temperatures since 1880 is abnormal. Modern thermometer records reach back only about 140 years. To estimate past temperatures, scientists use historical records and temperature proxies.

Written historical records tell us of a period of warm global temperatures about 1,000 years ago named the Medieval Warm Period (MWP). The MWP began about 900 AD and continued until about 1,300 AD. Viking explorers visited Newfoundland and established a colony in

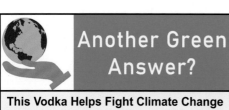

Another Green Answer?

This Vodka Helps Fight Climate Change
"Vodka is usually made from fermented grains, like rye. But Air Company's spirit is made out of captured carbon dioxide emissions." — *CNN*, July 20, 2021[15]

southwest Greenland during the MWP. Many of the great cathedrals of Europe were built during this period, including the cathedral in Cologne, Germany, which was started in 1248.

Climate crusaders characterize the Medieval Warm Period as a local event, but much evidence shows that the MWP was a global event. The evidence includes tree-ring proxies from Sweden, carbon and oxygen isotope analysis from cave stalagmites in South Africa, oxygen isotope proxies from plankton shells near Indonesia and in the Gulf of Mexico, charcoal and pollen records from the Altai Mountains in Central Asia, and historical records from China. These records also show that temperatures of the MWP were naturally warmer than today's temperatures.[16]

About 1300 AD, Earth's climate entered a period of cooler temperatures known as the Little Ice Age (LIA), which continued until about 1850. The LIA was not a true ice age but was a period of temperatures that were 1–2°C cooler than temperatures of the MWP or today. History describes the LIA as a difficult time for humanity. Growing seasons in Europe were shorter and were characterized by crop failures, famines, and increases in disease. In 1695, Iceland was completely surrounded by sea ice, which extended as far south as the Faroe Islands. The population of Iceland declined by half during the LIA.[17]

The Greenland Ice Core Project (GRIP) was a research project of the 1990s, organized by the European Science Foundation with eight participating nations. GRIP successfully

---

Temperature Proxies and Oxygen Isotopes

Scientists use proxy data to reconstruct past climate conditions. Temperature proxies are physical or chemical processes that change in concert with historical temperatures. Tree rings, ice cores, ocean sediments, fossil pollen, coral skeletons, and plankton shells are proxy sources that can capture and preserve a historical temperature record.[18]

Climatic conditions influence tree growth. In regions with a distinct growing season, trees generally produce one ring per year. Tree-ring width and cell density can provide a record of past temperatures.

The ratios of oxygen isotopes in ice cores, coral skeletons, and plankton shells can provide records of past temperatures. Each molecule of water contains two hydrogen atoms and one oxygen atom (H_2O). But water molecules also contain different isotopes of hydrogen and oxygen. Isotopes are elements with the same number of protons but differing numbers of neutrons. Water contains a mix of ^{16}O (oxygen atoms with 8 protons and 8 neutrons) and heavier ^{18}O (oxygen atoms with 8 protons and 10 neutrons).

Over tens of thousands of years, the Greenland Ice Cap grew by water evaporation from the oceans and deposition on Greenland's surface. When temperatures were warmer, more of the heavier water molecules with ^{18}O atoms evaporated from oceans and were deposited on top of the ice sheet. By measuring the ratio of ^{16}O to ^{18}O isotopes in deposited ice, scientists can create a record of past surface temperatures.[19]

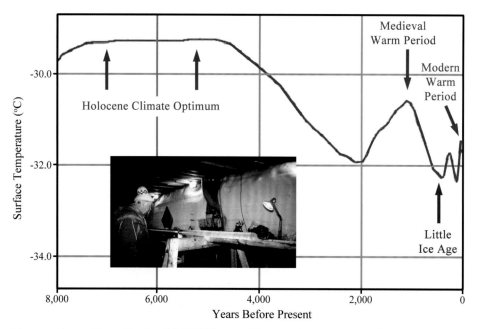

Temperatures Over the Last 8,000 Years. Temperature reconstructions show global temperatures were warmer than today for much of the last 8,000 years. The chart shows surface temperatures derived from oxygen isotope analysis of ice cores taken from the summit of the Greenland Ice Sheet. Present day on the chart is year 1995. Image of ice core researcher. (Dahl-Jensen et al., 1998)[20]

drilled and extracted a 3,029-meter ice core from the summit of the Greenland ice field. The ice deposited on the Greenland icecap provided a temperature record from the past 100,000 years.[21] The ice core clearly showed natural periods of warm temperatures, such as the Medieval Warm Period and the Holocene Climate Optimum, and our current Modern Warm Period, as well as the cool period of the Little Ice Age. Even more remarkable, the GRIP ice core record showed that temperatures near Greenland were naturally warmer than temperatures of today for much of the last 8,000 years.

Dr. Craig Idso provides an assembly of scientific evidence for The Medieval Warm Period on his excellent website, *CO2Science.org*. Idso provides summaries of 375 peer-reviewed papers describing climatic conditions during the MWP from all continents and corners of the globe, showing that the MWP was worldwide. More than 100 of these papers can be used to make qualitative temperature comparisons. These comparisons show that temperatures of the MWP were warmer than today's temperatures.[22]

Earth's temperatures during the Medieval Warm Period and the Little Ice Age were not caused by power plants or sport utility vehicles but instead by natural factors. If Earth was naturally warmer for much of the last 8,000 years than it is today, how can we conclude that the current warming is caused by human emissions, rather than natural factors?

EARTH'S COMPLEX CLIMATE

Earth's climate is amazingly complex. It is a chaotic, interdependent system shaped by powerful forces in the atmosphere, biosphere, and oceans. It's driven by gravitational forces of our solar system, radiation from the Sun, and cosmic rays from stars in deep space.

Sunlight drives all weather on Earth. It falls directly on the Equator and tropical regions, where much energy is absorbed. Sunlight falls indirectly on polar regions, where little energy is absorbed. Trade winds, storm fronts, hurricanes, jet streams, and other elements of Earth's weather, along with ocean currents, act to redistribute energy from the tropics to the poles.

Our oceans powerfully affect Earth's climate. The Gulf Stream current in the Atlantic Ocean carries huge volumes of heat to north latitudes to warm Europe and even western Russia. The El Niño cycle in the Pacific Ocean affects weather all over the world. Oceans have 250 times the mass of the atmosphere and hold more than 1,000 times the heat.

Aerosols, such as dust from volcanos, desert dust, and pollen from plants, rise into the atmosphere to shape the climate. In 1815, Mount Tambora in Indonesia exploded in the largest volcanic eruption in recorded history. The eruption expelled an estimated 36 cubic miles of ash, pumice, and rock into the atmosphere. These aerosols prevented significant amounts of sunlight from reaching Earth's surface, reducing average global temperatures by as much as 3°C (5.4°F) for the next year. Colder weather led to crop failures and starvation in some regions, and the year 1816 was named the "year without a summer."[23]

Earth's climate is *always* changing. Climatists earnestly proclaim that "climate change is real," a pronouncement indicating a grade-school level of understanding. Earth's climate changed continuously throughout all of history, dominated by long-, medium-, and short-term temperature cycles.

According to geologists, four ice ages have dominated Earth's history over the last 400,000 years, each about 85,000 years long. During these ice ages, much of the Northern Hemisphere was covered by thick ice, including

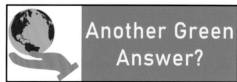

Another Green Answer?

Cows "Potty-Trained" in Experiment to Reduce Greenhouse Gas Emissions
"Calves taught to use toilet area with rewards and mild punishments, limiting ammonia release."
— *The Guardian*, September 13, 2021[24]

areas now occupied by Chicago, London, and New York. Each ice age was followed by a warm period of about 15,000 years. Transition periods from ice ages to warm periods and back provided temperature swings of 7–12°C (12–22°F). Today's temperatures are part of a warmer period that began 11,000 years ago.[26]

Most scientists believe planetary forces caused the long-term cycles of ice ages and intervening warm periods. These are named the Milankovitch Cycles for the Serbian astronomer Milutin Milankovitch, who developed theories to explain them. The Milankovitch Cycles, 20,000 to 100,000 years in length, are thought to be caused by changes in the angle and precession of Earth's axis, as well as the shape and tilt of Earth's orbit around the Sun.[27]

Medium-length cycles of about 1,500 years are well-documented in historical and proxy records since the last ice age. These include the Medieval Warm Period, the Little Ice Age, and our current Modern Warm Period. Medium-term temperature cycles show a change of about 1–2°C. These changes are probably caused by variations in the radiation and magnetic field of the Sun.[28]

Our planet also experiences short-term temperature cycles, which are associated with Earth's oceans. The El Niño Southern Oscillation (ENSO) is a very short, irregular cycle that occurs in the southern Pacific Ocean. The lesser-known part of ENSO is named La Niña. During La Niña, trade winds blow from east to west across the Pacific Ocean. Storms form above the warm pool of water in the western Pacific. Cold water from the deep ocean wells up near Peru.

Every few years, the ENSO shifts into the El Niño part of its cycle and a major temperature shift occurs in the Pacific Ocean. Trade winds change direction and blow from west to east, pushing a huge amount of heat thousands of miles to the east. Storms form in the central Pacific and move east to strike California, causing flooding and mud slides. Less cold water wells up near Peru, raising global temperatures. Weather conditions change in Africa, Australia, India, and all over the world. El Niño even reduces hurricane activity in the Atlantic Ocean.[29]

The Pacific Decadal Oscillation (PDO) is probably the most powerful of Earth's short-term cycles. The PDO is a cycle of sea surface temperatures in the northern Pacific Ocean that shows a temperature change of about one to two degrees Celsius over a period of about

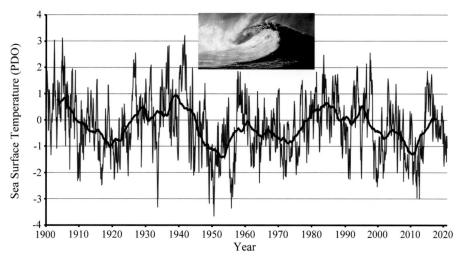

Pacific Decadal Oscillation 1900–2020. The PDO Index is a reconstruction of sea surface temperatures in the northern Pacific Ocean. The blue graph shows monthly PDO variation, and the dark line shows an 85-month (7-year) moving average. (NOAA, 2021)[30]

50 years. This cycle encompasses the very short-term changes of El Niño. The PDO was named by Dr. Stephen Hare in 1996 to explain the relationship between Alaskan salmon harvests and climate in the north Pacific. As shown in the graph above, the PDO generally cooled from 1940 to 1975, warmed from 1975 to 1995, and cooled from 1995 to 2010.[31]

The PDO and ENSO join the Atlantic Multidecadal Oscillation and short-term cycles in the Arctic, Antarctic, and Indian Oceans to shape global temperatures and global climate. Evidence shows that these cycles have been occurring for thousands of years, long before any significant level of man-made greenhouse gases existed.

Earth's climate cycled through warming and cooling, tropical periods, temperate periods, and ice ages throughout all of history. Climate is complex, shaped by forces from our solar system, the atmosphere, oceans, and land areas. But climate scientists are obsessed with the level of CO_2 in our atmosphere, though it's only a small part of the overall picture.

THE NATURAL GREENHOUSE EFFECT

Former New Jersey Governor Chris Christie stated, "… climate change is occurring and humans play a contributing role …"[32] This is a true statement but also a meaningless statement. Earth's climate is always changing, and my 12-pound dog plays a contributing role. The critical question is, what is the size of the human contribution to global warming compared to the role of natural factors?

When I present to groups about climate change, I typically ask the audience, "What is Earth's most abundant greenhouse gas?" Responders guess "carbon dioxide" or "methane," but the correct answer is water vapor. Anglo-Irish physicist John Tyndall is credited with the discovery of greenhouse gases. Tyndall remarked about water vapor in 1875,

> Aqueous vapor is a blanket, more necessary to the vegetable life of England than clothing is to man. Remove for a single summer-night the aqueous vapor from the air which overspreads this country, and you would assuredly destroy every plant capable of being destroyed by a freezing temperature.[33]

Most scientists agree that water vapor and clouds cause between 70 and 90 percent of Earth's greenhouse effect. Without the effect of water vapor and lesser greenhouse gases, Earth's average surface temperature would only be about -18°C (0°F), much colder than the warm average of 15°C (59°F) that we enjoy today.[34] Compared to water vapor, carbon dioxide is a trace gas. Only four of every 10,000 molecules in Earth's atmosphere are carbon dioxide. The amount of CO_2 that human industry could have added to the atmosphere in all of history is only a fraction of one of those 10,000 molecules.

To break down Earth's greenhouse effect, let's conservatively estimate that water vapor and clouds cause 75 percent of the effect. Then the last quarter of the effect is caused mostly by carbon dioxide, with a small amount due to ozone, methane and other gases. But how much of the last quarter is caused by natural emissions of CO_2 and how much by human emissions? The carbon dioxide dissolved in the oceans is 50 times larger than the CO_2 in the atmosphere. The oceans continuously release billions of tons of CO_2 into the air and absorb about the same amount. When plants grow, they absorb CO_2 and release it when they die. Land volcanos, and about 10 times as many undersea volcanos, release CO_2 and other gases continuously into the environment. Every day, nature emits over 20 times as much carbon dioxide into the atmosphere as all of human industry and absorbs about the same amount. Only about five percent of the CO_2 emitted each day is from industry.

After considering the dominance of water vapor and clouds, and the huge natural emissions of carbon dioxide, the human contribution to Earth's greenhouse effect is only about one or two parts in 100. This means that even if we eliminate all human emissions, the effect on global temperatures would likely be too small to measure.

Woke Or Joke?

Feeding Cattle Seaweed Reduces Their Greenhouse Gas Emissions 82 Percent
— *Physics.org*, March 17, 2021[35]
(So much for grass-fed beef!)

William van Wijngaarden and William Happer provide a more quantitative analysis of the contribution of various greenhouse gases to the greenhouse effect. These two physicists and atmospheric scientists analyzed the absorption of infrared radiation, also called outgoing longwave radiation (OLR), for water vapor, carbon dioxide, methane, ozone, and nitrous oxide at thousands of frequencies across the infrared spectrum.[36]

Their results show that for a transparent atmosphere without greenhouse gases, the radiated power of OLR averages about 394 watts for each square meter of Earth's surface. Adding water vapor, clouds, and minor greenhouse gases, but without carbon dioxide, OLR would be reduced to an average of 307 watts per square meter (W/m^2) as outgoing radiation is absorbed. Adding carbon dioxide reduces the outgoing radiation to about 277 W/m^2, or about 25 percent of the effect, which simulates today's greenhouse absorption. But doubling of atmospheric CO_2 from 400 ppm to 800 ppm by either natural or human causes reduces outgoing radiation from 277 to 274 W/m^2, a change of only about one percent. Doubling of atmospheric methane (CH_4) would increase the greenhouse absorption by only about 0.7 W/m^2, less than a 0.3 percent change, which is a negligible amount.

Wijngaarden and Happer point out that at current concentrations of atmospheric water vapor, carbon dioxide, and methane, the absorption of outgoing radiation is saturated. As

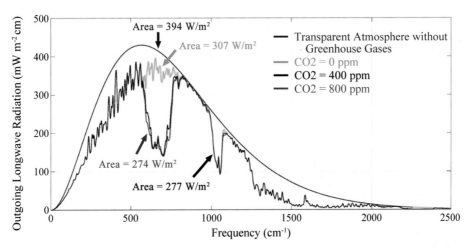

Outgoing Longwave Radiation. Simulations of Earth's outgoing longwave radiation (infrared) by frequency with levels of atmospheric carbon dioxide. The area under the blue curve shows a total outgoing radiated power of about 394 watts per square meter (W/m^2) without greenhouse gases (GHG) in the atmosphere. Outgoing power would be about 307 W/m^2 with water vapor and other GHG, but without CO_2. Outgoing power is about 277 W/m^2 at 400 ppm of CO_2 (black curve), which is about today's atmospheric level. Doubling CO_2 would reduce outgoing power to about 274 W/m^2 (red curve), a change of only one percent. (Wijngaarden and Happer, 2021)[37]

a result, adding additional H_2O, CO_2, or CH_4 to the atmosphere has only a tiny effect.

Earth's greenhouse absorption of outgoing infrared radiation is dominated by water vapor and clouds. Doubling atmospheric CO_2 would increase absorption by only about one percent. So how do the climate models arrive at their alarming projections?

CLIMATE-MODEL FAILURE

Every climate scientist knows that carbon dioxide, by itself, cannot cause dangerous global warming. Doubling of atmospheric CO_2 by either natural or human causes would only increase global temperatures by about one degree Celsius. To reach their alarming projections, climate models assume that as CO_2 is added to the atmosphere, the climate system will react to cause additional warming, a so-called positive feedback.

In his early climate model in the 1960s, Syukuro Manabe assumed that as the atmosphere warmed from carbon dioxide emissions, global relative humidity remained constant.[38] This meant that the atmosphere would hold increasing amounts of water vapor, adding additional greenhouse heating to that of CO_2. This positive feedback from water vapor is assumed to some degree in all climate models. The IPCC estimates that, for a doubling of atmospheric CO_2, positive feedback from water-vapor warming will cause about 60 percent of the projected temperature rise, doubling the warming expected from CO_2.[39]

But other studies provide evidence that the assumption based on positive feedback is incorrect. Richard Lindzen, an atmospheric scientist at the Massachusetts Institute of Technology, published evidence for negative feedback from clouds in 2001. Satellite data showed that high-level cirrus cloudiness over the tropical Pacific Ocean decreased as sea temperatures increased. This reduction in cloudiness increased outgoing infrared radiation, cooling Earth's surface and providing a negative feedback to rising temperatures. Lindzen called this an "iris effect" and showed that the effect would cancel the positive feedbacks in climate models.[41]

Good Thing We Can Control The Climate?

Why the 2020 Atlantic Hurricane Season Has Spun Out of Control

— *The Washington Post*, Sep. 24, 2020[40]

In 2009, Australian physicist Garth Partridge and others published a paper showing that weather balloon data from 1973 to 2007 showed a decline in the average humidity in the upper troposphere. The paper concluded,

Data would imply that long-term water vapor feedback is negative—that it would reduce rather than amplify the response of the climate system to external forcing such as that from increasing atmospheric CO_2.[42]

Actual measurements also show that temperature projections of the climate models are too high. In August 1990, the IPCC issued its *First Assessment Report*, which stated,

> Based on current model results, we predict ... under the IPCC Business-as-Usual emissions of greenhouse gases, a rate of increase of global mean temperature during the next century of about 0.3°C per decade (with an uncertainty range of 0.2°C to 0.5°C per decade).[43]

According to the IPCC, global surface temperatures should have risen by 0.9°C from 1990 to 2020. Their low estimate called for a minimum rise of 0.6°C. But satellite measurements show actual temperatures over the last 30 years to be consistently below the IPCC's low estimate. It's clear that the climate models have overstated the warming.

Despite the failed projections of the climate models and the evidence that global temperatures are dominated by natural factors, Climatists warn that climate calamities are already happening. In his January 2017 address at the Massachusetts Institute of Technology, then Secretary of State John Kerry warned:

> Glaciers are melting at an unprecedented rate. Sea levels are rising three times faster than they did in the twentieth century. The kind of intense storms that used to happen only twice or three times in a millennium are now becoming almost normal.[44]

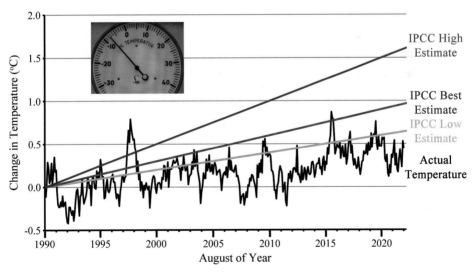

IPCC Projections and Actual Global Temperatures 1990–2022. High, best, and low estimates for global temperatures from the IPCC *First Assessment Report* in August 1990, derived from computer-model projections. The black curve shows actual low atmosphere temperatures measured by satellites. (IPCC, 1990, UAH, 2022)[45]

Like Mr. Kerry, other political speeches and media articles ring with endless warnings about glaciers, sea levels, storms, droughts, floods, heat waves, and forest fires, claiming that recent events are more extreme than in past ages, all because of human-caused climate change. Let's examine the evidence for these claims.

SEA LEVEL RISE

Melting icecaps and rising sea levels are regarded as the greatest threats from human-caused global warming. Warnings about the melting of the Greenland and Antarctic ice caps, and a resultant sea level rise of 5–6 meters, have been common over the last two decades. James Hansen of NASA predicted in 2006 that sea levels could rise 25 meters:

> A satellite study of the ice cap shows that it is melting far faster than scientists had feared. … The last time the world was three degrees warmer than today—which is what we expect later this century—sea levels were 25m higher. So that is what we can look forward to if we don't act soon.[46]

Sea level rise of even six meters by 2100, if it happened, would flood Copenhagen, Miami, Jakarta, Tokyo, Venice, and other coastal cities, bringing disaster to hundreds of millions.

Earth's seas have been rising naturally throughout modern history. NASA estimates that levels rose about 120 meters (390 feet) since the last ice age 20,000 years ago.[47] Tide gauges show that sea levels rose at a rate of about seven to eight inches per century over the last 150 years.[48]

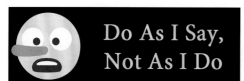

"Climate change, and especially rising seas, is a threat to our homeland security. … Along our coasts, thousands of miles of highways and roads, railways, energy facilities are all vulnerable. … A further increase in sea level of just one foot by the end of this century could cost our nation $200 billion."
— President Barack Obama, speech to US Coast Guard Academy, May 20, 2015[49]

Sea Level Rise? President Obama Just Bought a Beachside Property
— *WattsUpWithThat*, August 24, 2019[50]

After the start of the human-caused climate change era in 1988, scientists began measuring sea level rise using satellite radar altimeters. Satellites bounce radar waves off the surface of the oceans to measure the distance. Scientific organizations, such as the Sea Level Research Group at the University of Colorado, then use the satellite altimetry data to estimate sea level rise and acceleration.[51]

The IPCC agreed with moderate past sea level rise estimates from tide gauges but also claimed in its 2007 *Fourth Assessment Report* that the rate of sea level rise had increased:

Global average sea level rose at an average rate of 1.8 mm per year over 1961 to 2003. The rate was faster over 1993 to 2003: about 3.1 mm per year.[52]

The IPCC used tide-gauge data to state that sea level rise increased 1.8 mm per year (7.1 inches per century) until 2003, and satellite data to estimate a faster rate of rise of 3.1 mm per year (12 inches per century) after 1993.

In August 2015, a NOAA interagency task force began work to develop sea level rise and flood-hazard scenarios for the United States. The task force issued a 75-page report in January 2017, projecting a upper-bound global-mean sea level rise of 2.5 meters by 2100. The paper placed the recent historical rise at 0.2 meters (8 inches) per century but showed six different scenarios of rise from 0.3 meters (12 inches) to 2.5 meters (98.4 inches) by 2100.[53] It's clear from the report that scientists don't have much of a clue about future sea level rise. The report states that the twenty-first century rise could be anywhere from near-historical rise to extreme rise. The NOAA team used satellite altimetry data to project their widely varying scenarios.

But tide gauges disagree with satellite altimetry data regarding sea level rise. A 2019 paper by Dr. Craig Idso and others states, "The highest quality coastal tide gauges from around the world show no evidence of acceleration since the 1920s."[54] Tide gauges incur errors caused by land rise or subsidence and coastal processes, such as erosion and sedimentation. To get the best measure of sea level changes, high-quality gauge locations

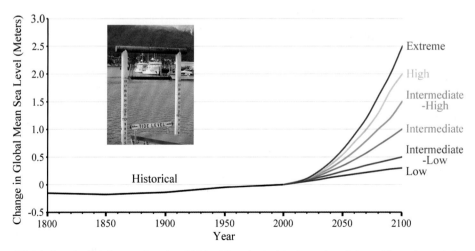

NOAA Sea Level Scenarios for 2021. Historical global sea level rise of less than eight inches (0.2 meter) per century from 1800 to 2000 and projections of mean global sea level rise for the twenty-first century. Six scenarios project a rise of 11.8 to 98.4 inches (0.3 to 2.5 meters) by 2100. Image of tide gauge at Juneau, Alaska. (NOAA, 2017)[55]

Sea Level Rise Uncertainty in Satellite Measurements[56]

Can satellites accurately measure sea level rise? The historical rate of 1.8 mm per year is about the thickness of a US quarter dollar. The claimed increase in sea level rise to 3.1 mm per year stacks a US dime on top of the quarter. Can scientists really measure a change in sea level rise over the course of a year, averaged across the world, that is the thickness of one dime?

Ocean-level variation is large and affected by many factors. If temperatures rise, water expands, adding to sea level rise. If icecaps melt, levels rise; but if icecaps grow due to increased snowfall, sea levels fall. If ocean saltiness changes, the water volume will also change. Shorelines rise and fall due to land rise and subsidence.

Tides are a major source of ocean variation, caused by the gravitational pull of the Moon and Sun, and the rotation of the Earth. These change more than 38 feet per day, the highest in the world, at the Bay of Fundy in Nova Scotia.[57] Tides rise and fall about one meter on average around the world, but this daily change is still 300 times the three-millimeter change that scientists claim to be able to measure over an entire year.

Storms and water are major factors affecting satellite measurements. Ocean-wave heights are irregular and measured in meters, dwarfing the annual rise in sea level. Winds also variably change the height of the sea. The easterly wind of a strong La Niña pushes seas around Singapore to a meter higher than in the eastern Pacific Ocean.

Satellites themselves have error bias. Satellite specifications claim a measurement accuracy of about one or two centimeters, almost 10 times larger than the annual change of three millimeters. The 1995 to 2019 satellite record contained data from four different satellites—the TOPEX, Jason-1, Jason-2, and Jason-3 satellites—each functioning for four to eight years before orbital decay. The same measurement taken by each satellite differed by as much as 75 millimeters and needed to be corrected.[58]

The satellite data set for sea level rise requires dozens of corrections by scientists to try to get to an accurate measurement. Scientists correct for satellite orbital drift, bias between altimeters, volcanic eruptions, ENSO cycles, data-spacing differences, seasonal variability, sea ice changes, atmospheric humidity, land- and ocean-basin changes, and other factors. Data-set adjustments are larger than the actual measurements.[59]

Dr. Carl Wunsch of the Massachusetts Institute of Technology commented on the satellite data in 2007, "It remains possible that the database is insufficient to compute mean sea level trends with the accuracy necessary to discuss the impact of global warming—as disappointing as this conclusion may be."[60]

must be used. A paper by Albert Parker and Clifford Ollier looked at six high-quality tide gauge data sets and concluded that "all consistently show a small sea level rate of rise and negligible acceleration."[61]

In summary, ocean levels have been rising for the last 20,000 years. No climate scientist knows when natural sea level rise stopped and man-made sea level rise began. Tide gauges show a rise of seven to eight inches per century, without acceleration. Satellite altimetry measurements of sea level suffer from inaccuracy due to large errors and adjustments.

ICECAP MELT

Earth's surface temperatures have gently warmed for the last 400 years as our climate moved from the cooler Little Ice Age to the Modern Warm Period. Icecaps experienced some shrinkage, and glaciers naturally receded as a result. Since the first satellite measurements in 1979, the area covered by sea ice in the Northern Hemisphere has declined by about 19 percent.[62] Global warming alarmists point to disappearing sea ice near the North Pole as the "canary in the coal mine,"[63] claiming that this reduction in ice must be caused by coal-fired power plants and your neighbor's SUV.

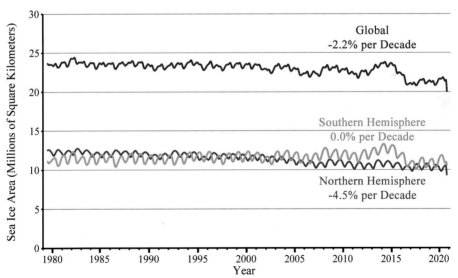

Global Sea Ice Area 1979–2021. Global, Northern Hemisphere, and Southern Hemisphere sea ice area over the last four decades in millions of square kilometers. Curves are 13-month running sums, so seasonal variations of up to 80 percent are not shown. Northern Hemisphere sea ice has been declining about 4.5 percent per decade. Southern Hemisphere sea ice is unchanged on net. Total global sea ice has declined about 2.2 percent per decade over the period. Data from satellites. (NOAA, 2021)[64]

But Arctic ice grows and shrinks with the natural warming and cooling cycles of Earth. In addition, Arctic ice is floating on the Arctic Ocean. If it melts entirely, whatever the cause, sea level rise would be minimal. Floating ice does not raise the level of water when it melts. Finally, Arctic ice is only a small part of the picture, just one to two percent of the world's ice.

The big dog in icecaps is Antarctic ice. The combination of Antarctic land ice and sea ice contains about 90 percent of Earth's ice. NASA satellite data shows that the sea ice area in the Southern Hemisphere, primarily Antarctic sea ice, has not changed over the last 40 years.[66]

Antarctic land ice is also stable. Observations from the University of Huntsville Alabama MSU satellite data set show that, while lower tropospheric temperatures for the Arctic region have risen about one degree Celsius over the last 40 years, temperatures for the Antarctic have not changed. The ice around the Amundsen-Scott South Pole Station has been thickening since 1956, forcing closure of the previous two stations. The current station employs hydraulic jack columns under buildings to periodically raise them over the accumulating ice.[67]

Although average Antarctic temperatures have not changed as a whole, thermometers show some warming on the Western Antarctic Ice Sheet. Some scientists fear that this

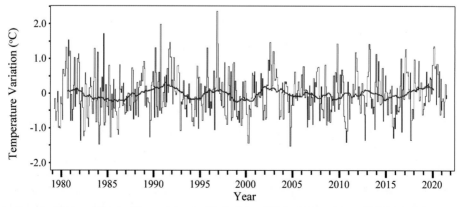

Antarctic Tropospheric Temperature Variation 1979–2021. Monthly Antarctic temperature data from MSU UAH satellites shows flat temperatures over the last 40 years. The thick line is a 37-month running average. (UAH, adapted from *Climate4You*, 2021)[68]

ice sheet could rapidly melt, raising sea levels by over three meters.[69] It's unlikely that global warming will cause this ice sheet to melt. But the sheet also sits above an undersea ridge with at least one active volcano, which should be of larger concern.[70]

The Greenland Icecap contains about 2.9 million kilometers of ice, or about eight percent of Earth's ice.[71] It has been shrinking for several decades during Earth's recent gentle warming. Since 2002, Gravity Recovery and Climate Experiment (GRACE) satellites have been measuring Greenland ice loss. The measurements show an average loss of 279 metric tons of ice per year. If this rate were to continue, Greenland would lose about 10 percent of its ice in 1,000 years, raising ocean levels by about 0.8 meters or 30 inches in 10 centuries.[72]

In summary, Antarctic ice is, on average, unchanging; Greenland ice is slowly melting and contributing about three inches of sea level rise per century; and Arctic sea ice is losing about 4.5 percent per decade without adding a measurable amount to sea levels. And since global warming is dominated by natural factors and not human emissions, a massive transition to renewable energy will not change these trends.

EXTREME WEATHER?

Hurricanes and storms have become the climate change effect most widely reported on by the media. Canadian zoologist Dr. David Suzuki has stated,

> As CO_2 levels rise, temperatures rise. The result: as the world gets warmer, the climate changes. And extreme weather events become more common.[73]

The US's *Fourth National Climate Assessment*, published in 2018, agrees. The document uses the word "extreme" more than 1,300 times in 1,526 pages of text to describe the weather. But the study relies on a history of the tiny one-degree Celsius rise in surface temperatures over the last 140 years and an eight-inch-per-century rise in sea levels, along with a heavy dose of climate-model projections. Few comparisons are made between current weather and storms and those of the past.[74] Historical data does not support the assertion of Dr. Suzuki or the assessment that extreme weather events today are more common.

Food to Save The Planet?

Swedish Scientist Advocates Eating Humans to Combat Climate Change
"After Söderlund's presentation, 8% of the audience raised their hands when asked if they would be willing to try human flesh."
— *Big Think*, September 8, 2019[75]

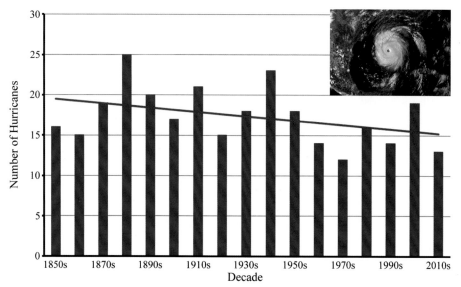

US Hurricane Landfalls by Decade 1850–2020. The chart shows a declining number of hurricanes making landfall in the United States per decade over the last 170 years. Hurricanes are storms with wind speeds that reach 64 knots or 74 mph. Image of Hurricane Katrina in the Gulf of Mexico, 2005. (NOAA, 2021)[76]

An example is the number of hurricanes striking the United States. NOAA was the lead agency for the *Fourth National Climate Assessment*, but it did not include its own data on US hurricane landfalls. Each year on average, about two hurricanes strike the US. NOAA data shows that the number of hurricanes making landfalls in the US has been flat to declining since 1850.[77]

A wind scatterometer is a microwave radar designed to measure wind speed and direction near the surface of the Earth.[78] Scatterometers mounted on NASA satellites measure the wind speed of every tropical storm for each day of the life of the storm. Meteorologist Dr. Ryan Maue uses NASA data to track the number and strength of tropical cyclones globally, including both tropical storms and stronger hurricanes.

The Climate Apocalypse

Zombie Storms are Rising from the Dead Thanks to Climate Change
— *Live Science*, September 25, 2020[79]

The data shows that during each 12-month period, roughly 90 tropical storms are active on Earth's surface. These are cyclones that reach tropical-storm strength, which is a maximum-lifetime wind speed of at least 34 knots. About half of these storms also attain hurricane-strength wind speeds of a maximum-lifetime

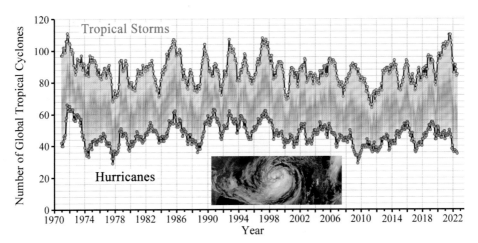

Global Tropical Cyclones 1971–2022. The number of tropical storms (top line) and stronger hurricanes (bottom line) observed worldwide by satellites over the last 51 years. Numbers are 12-month running sums. No trend of increasing tropical storm frequency or strength can be seen. Image of Tropical Storm Isaac, 2012. (Maue, 2022)[80]

speed of 64 knots. The number of tropical storms and hurricanes varies each year by about 20 percent from the average.[81]

But a review of tropical cyclones from 1971 to 2022, the period for which satellite data is available, shows no increasing trend in either the number of tropical storms or the number of hurricanes. The chart above is also a measure of trends in storm strength. If storms were getting stronger over time, more would attain hurricane-strength wind speeds, so the number of hurricanes would be increasing. But it isn't happening.

Most deaths from natural disasters result from droughts or floods. According to the Emergency Events Database (EM-DAT), from 1900 to 2015, droughts caused 51 percent of deaths, while floods caused 30 percent of deaths.[82] Of course, those who fear climate change claim that both droughts and floods are growing more extreme.

Tim Flannery, zoologist and former professor at Macquarie University in Sydney, has been called the "Al Gore of Australia." In 2005, Flannery said, "If the computer models are right then drought conditions will become permanent in Australia."[84]

Global Warming Makes Couples Cheat, Says Dating Website
— *Miami New Times*, May 28, 2014[83]

College Courses 😀
We Expect to See?[85]

Environmental Science 300
**Elementary
Hurricane Mitigation**

But in 2021, widespread flooding hit Queensland and New South Wales, the two eastern provinces of Australia. The once-in-a-century event drenched the area with 24 inches of rain in a week, about the amount received in six months in a typical year.[86] Of course, other climate advocates pointed to the flooding event as evidence of human-caused climate change.[87]

The *Fourth National Climate Assessment* states several times that a warming climate will lead to "intensifying droughts" and "more severe floods." But aside from anecdotal examples, the assessment provides no evidence that droughts and floods are becoming more extreme.[88]

NOAA tracks very dry and very wet conditions for the continental US using a metric called the Palmer Drought Index. A look at dry and wet conditions over the last century shows many years with very dry and very wet conditions. But no trend of increasing drought or flood is apparent.[89] This data was also somehow omitted from the 2018 assessment.

Other scientific studies show that droughts and floods during past centuries exceeded the conditions observed during the last 100 years. Dr. Henry Lamb of the University of

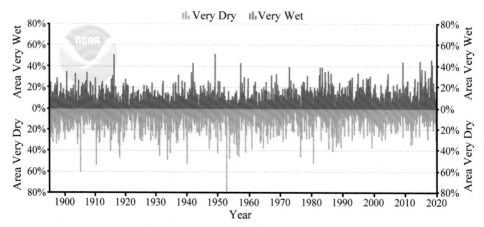

United States Very Wet/Very Dry Area 1895–2020. Percentage of area in the continental United States that was very wet or very dry over the last 125 years. No trend of increasing drought or flood can be seen. (NOAA, 2021)[90]

Wales analyzed sediments from the bottom of Lake Hayq in northern Ethiopia. Lamb and his team found many periods of drought and flood over the last 2,000 years that exceeded twentieth century conditions.[91] Ecologist Masaki Sano and others created a 535-year historical record of drought and flood for Southeast Asia from tree rings in Vietnam. Their work found major droughts during the 1300s, 1400s, and 1700s that exceeded modern events.[92]

WILDFIRES CAUSED BY GLOBAL WARMING?

A latest climate fad is to blame wildfires on global warming, particularly in California. The *Fourth National Climate Assessment* of 2018 featured a fire on its cover.[93] California Governor Gavin Newsom commented regarding his state's fires, "If anyone is wondering if climate change is real, come to California."[94] CNN's headline shouted, "How the climate crisis is fueling wildfires and changing life in the golden state."[95]

Damage from California forest fires is rising. Ten of the 20 largest California wildfires (in terms of acres burned) raged during the last decade.[96] But an honest assessment should conclude that rising temperatures had not caused the rise in fires, which were caused instead by poor forest management.

NASA uses imaging spectroradiometers on satellites to detect fires and to track the area burned by fires worldwide. About 10,000 fires burn around the world during an average

---

Are California Wildfires Caused by Global Warming?

A report by the Little Hoover Commission in 2018 pointed out that a century of forest fire suppression efforts in California produced "disastrous results." Fire suppression created crowded forests choked with tinder-dry brush and worsened conditions for insect damage and disease. According to the report, "frequent low-intensity fire" should be a "critical component for California's forest ecosystems."[97]

In part, due to strong opposition from environmental groups, the California forestry industry has been in decline for more than three decades. California harvested only 1.4 billion board-feet of timber in 2019,[98] down 35 percent from 2000 and down 65 percent from the late 1980s.[99] Declining forest harvests added fuel to recent destructive fires.

Insect damage is also a major factor. Forest overcrowding due to fire suppression created ideal conditions for bark beetle infestation of California's conifers. Millions of trees now die each year from overcrowding, drought, and the bark beetle. The US Forest Service estimated in 2018 that California had 147 million dead trees, with most dying since 2010.[100]

Because of poor forest management, California forests are packed with fuel and ripe for continued destructive combustion. Improved forest management is the solution to reducing wildfire damage, not a shift to electric cars.

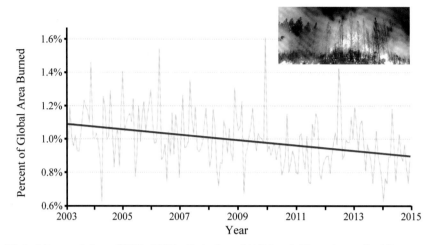

Global Burned Area 2003–2015. Data from NASA satellites shows that the area burned around the world each year has been declining for more than a decade. Image of fire in Stanislaus National Forest in California in 2013. (NASA, 2019)[101]

day in August. Interestingly, NASA data shows that the expanse of area burned by wildfires annually *declined* about 20 percent from 2003–2015.[102] If this is true, how can rising California fires be due to global warming?

CARBON POLLUTION?

One of the greatest misconceptions of our time is that carbon dioxide is pollution. Former EPA Administrator Gina McCarthy said,

> I view climate as a pollution problem. It is, in my words, carbon pollution. It's just like every other pollutant.[103]

Ms. McCarthy and many others mistakenly call carbon dioxide "carbon" and consider it a pollutant.

Labeling carbon dioxide "carbon" is as foolish as calling salt "chlorine." Carbon and carbon dioxide are completely different substances. The term "carbon" conveys an image of black pencil lead or soot, but CO_2 is an invisible gas. It appears that it's deliberately being misnamed to convey a negative image.

Furthermore, carbon dioxide is not a pollutant. Carbon dioxide is an odorless, harmless gas. It doesn't cause smoke or smog. The white cloud rising from the cooling tower of a power plant isn't carbon dioxide, it's condensing water vapor. You can't see carbon dioxide.

Pigeon Pea Growth and CO₂. Pigeon pea growth differences in plant size, stem thickness, and root-system size for recent (395 ppm) and elevated (550 ppm) atmospheric carbon dioxide concentrations. (Sreeharsha, 2014)[104]

We inhale only a trace of CO_2, but as we burn sugars in our bodies, we continuously produce carbon dioxide. Each time we exhale, we exhaust air with 100 times the carbon dioxide concentration that is in the atmosphere. The average person exhales about two pounds (0.9 kilograms) of CO_2 per day.[105]

As a matter of fact, CO_2 is green! Carbon dioxide is plant food. Hundreds of peer-reviewed studies show that CO_2 makes plants grow larger and faster. Plants grow larger fruits, larger vegetables, thicker stems, and bigger root systems, and they are more resistant to drought with higher levels of atmospheric carbon dioxide. Studies show that all 45 of the crops that provide 95 percent of the world's total food production grow significantly larger with increased levels of CO_2.[106] Carbon dioxide joins water and oxygen as one of the three essential substances for life on Earth. Yet many companies and most universities now foolishly measure their "carbon footprint" and strive to reduce CO_2 emissions.

Rather than negatively impacting global ecosystems, the recent rise in atmospheric carbon dioxide has been beneficial. Based on satellite observations, Dr. Randall Donohue of the Commonwealth Scientific and Industrial Research Organization of Australia (CSIRO) found that CO_2 fertilization from rising atmospheric carbon dioxide correlated with an 11 percent increase in foliage cover from 1982–2010 across arid areas of Australia,

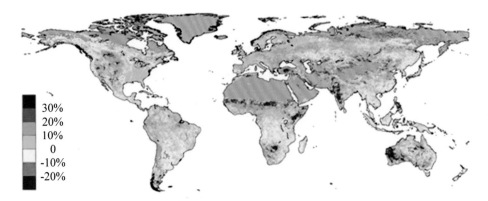

Change in Foliage Globally 1982–2010. Satellite observations indicate an 11 percent increase in foliage cover in areas studied from 1982 to 2010. (Donohue, CSIRO, 2013)[107]

North America, the Middle East, and Africa.[108] Further work by Vanessa Haverd and others of CSIRO estimated that photosynthesis had risen globally by 30 percent over the last century, in concert with the rise in atmospheric CO_2.[109] Carbon dioxide is probably the best compound that humanity could put into the environment.

THE FALSE DRIVER FOR RENEWABLE ENERGY

The global drive for renewable energy is based on the greatest superstition in modern history, the notion that human industry is causing dangerous climate change. Governments, industry, and academia mistakenly believe we can lower global temperatures by shifting our energy consumption from hydrocarbon energy to renewable energy.

But Earth's temperatures are dominated by natural, not human-caused, factors. Water vapor is Earth's dominant greenhouse gas. Human industry is responsible for only about one to two percent of Earth's greenhouse effect. Doubling of atmospheric CO_2 concentration from either natural causes or human emissions would reduce outgoing infrared radiation by only about one percent, an effect too small to measure.

A look at history shows that global temperatures were naturally warmer for much of the last 10,000 years than they are today. Storms, droughts, and floods are neither more frequent nor more intense today than in past centuries. Tide gauges show sea levels to be rising at seven to eight inches per century, about the same rate as during the last 150 years.

Fear of dangerous global warming drives not only the rise of renewable energy, but also unprecedented attacks on coal, oil, and natural gas industries. Let's take a look at the war on hydrocarbons in the next chapter.

CHAPTER 4

THE WAR ON HYDROCARBON ENERGY

"A century ago, petroleum—what we call oil—was just an obscure commodity;
today it is almost as vital to human existence as water."
—JAMES BUCHAN, SCOTTISH NOVELIST AND HISTORIAN (2006)[1]

Hydrocarbons have provided, and continue to provide, the low-cost energy that is the basis for modern society. As we discussed in the first chapter, the hydrocarbon revolution drove the rise in industrialization, transportation, and electrical power, and laid the foundation for the internet age. Hydrocarbon energy paved the way for the rise in global incomes, increase in life spans, improvements in education, and gains in almost every aspect of modern life. Oil powers our cars, aircraft, and trains. Natural gas heats our homes and cooks our food. Our medicines, cosmetics, playground equipment, toys, smart phones, and tires are made of materials from hydrocarbons.

Hydrocarbon energy is under attack. As renewable energy is touted, coal, natural gas, and oil are under assault as never before, particularly in wealthy nations. Every aspect

Protesting the Shell Oil Drilling Platform in Seattle Harbor, 2015

Kayakers wear gore-tex paddling jackets, personal flotation devices made of nylon and foam, and neoprene spray skirts, while holding carbon-fiber paddles and sitting in fiberglass or polyethylene boats. This clothing and equipment is all made from oil or natural gas.[2]

of the production and use of hydrocarbon energy is challenged. Protests at pipeline and airport-runway construction sites are common. Lawsuits brought by cities, states, and provinces against oil and gas companies are multiplying. Banks and nations restrict funding for coal, gas, and petroleum projects, even to bring electricity to poor nations. Bans on hydraulic fracturing, oil and gas exploration, and even the sale of gasoline cars and gas appliances are becoming common in developed nations. Let's take a look at both the dominance of hydrocarbon energy and the escalating war on hydrocarbon energy.

HYDROCARBON ENERGY DOMINANCE

Driven by efforts to decarbonize, the world has spent almost $4 trillion on renewable energy over the last 15 years.[3] More than 300,000 wind turbines were erected, millions of solar arrays were installed, hundreds of thousands of acres of forest were cut down for biomass, and hundreds of billions of gallons of biofuels were produced to reduce consumption of hydrocarbon fuels. But hydrocarbons continue to dominate energy supplies.

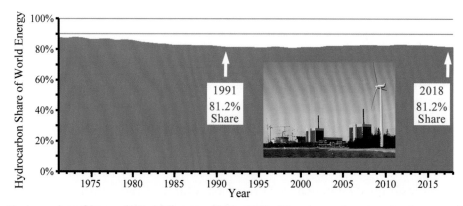

Hydrocarbon Share of World Energy 1971–2018. The share of coal, natural gas, and oil of the total primary energy supply has been relatively stable for 45 years. Hydrocarbons provided 81.2 percent of the world's energy in 1991 and again in 2018. Image of Olkiluoto Nuclear Power Plant and wind turbine in Finland. (International Energy Agency, 2020)[4]

According to the International Energy Agency, in 2018 coal, oil, and natural gas provided 81.2 percent of the world's primary energy supply, the same share as in 1991.[5]

Green Policies Require Coercion

"Sixty percent of our emissions that need to be reduced come from you, the person across the street, the senior on fixed income, right? There is no bad guy left, at least in Massachusetts, to point the finger at, turn the screws on, and, you know, to break their will so they stop emitting. That's you. We have to break your will."
— Massachusetts Undersecretary for Climate Change David Ismay, Jan. 25, 2021[10]

Today, petroleum-based fuels propel 90 percent of US transportation[6] and 95 percent of European transportation.[7] More than 99 percent of aviation fuel comes from oil.[8] More than 99 percent of international shipping fuel comes from oil or natural gas.[9] Green versions of biofuels, hydrogen, and other alternative fuels produce headlines but tend to be significantly more expensive than hydrocarbon fuels, resulting in small production volumes.

Wind and solar have penetrated power markets in Europe and the US. In 2021, renewables provided 39.6 percent of Europe's electricity, including hydroelectric, the leading renewable at 16.1 percent of generation. But coal, oil, and natural gas still produced 36.7 percent of Europe's power, while nuclear generated 21.9 percent.[11] In the US, renewables generated 20 percent of electricity in 2021, including hydroelectric's 5.8 percent share, with coal, oil, and gas providing 61.1 percent, and nuclear providing 18.6 percent of power.[12]

The push for renewable fuels has been less successful in home-heating, cooling, and cooking applications. Wealthy nations in northern latitudes now rely on extensive networks of natural gas distribution lines serving more than 500 million customers. In 2019, about 50 percent of the energy used in European households was from hydrocarbon fuels, with 25 percent from electricity, mostly for lighting, and the last quarter from renewables and other sources. Much of the energy used in homes in the renewable category was biofuels, better known as burning wood. Since 1990, natural gas grew from 25 percent to 36 percent of the energy used in European homes, replacing much of the use of oil, coal, and wood.[13]

Energy use in US homes is similar to that of Europe. In 2020, 49.9 percent of US household energy use came from natural gas, propane, and fuel oil. Renewables provided 6.8 percent, with the majority of that from burning wood. Electricity accounted for 43.3 percent of the energy used in homes.[14]

Hydrocarbon fuels also power the world's industries. Renewable fuels only provide about 15 percent of industrial fuel.[15] Fertilizer, chemical, plastic, steel, cement, and other industries rely heavily on hydrocarbons for fuel and feedstock.

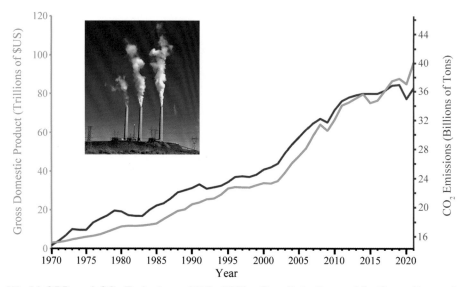

World GDP and CO₂ Emissions 1970–2021. Growth in the world's Gross Domestic Product (GDP) closely tracks the rise in global CO₂ emissions. Image of the coal-fired Navajo Generating Station in Arizona. (World Bank, Global Carbon Project, 2021)[16]

It's interesting to note that the growth in the wealth of modern society, as measured by the rise in global Gross Domestic Product, closely follows the rise in carbon dioxide emissions over the last 50 years. Rising CO_2 emissions, driven by the increasing use of hydrocarbon fuels, may be the best metric for the recent rise in human prosperity.

THE SHALE REVOLUTION

United States production of crude oil peaked in 1970 at 9.6 million barrels per day (bpd) and then began to decline. At that time, the US was importing about 21 percent of its petroleum products, including gasoline, jet fuel, and fuel oils. The 1973 Arab Oil Embargo and the 1979 Oil Crisis, along with the rising ability of the Organization of the Petroleum Exporting Countries (OPEC) to control world prices, boosted oil prices by a factor of 10 by 1980.[17] But US crude oil production continued to fall until 2008 to a level of five million bpd.[18]

Despite US government measures to try to reduce demand, consumption of petroleum products rose from 14.7 million bpd to over 20 million bpd by 2006. The net imports' share rose to 60 percent of US consumption that same year.[19] The US balance of trade in petroleum products reached a negative $386 billion in 2008 when oil prices hit $140 per barrel.[20] Many predicted that world oil production would peak soon after the year 2000.

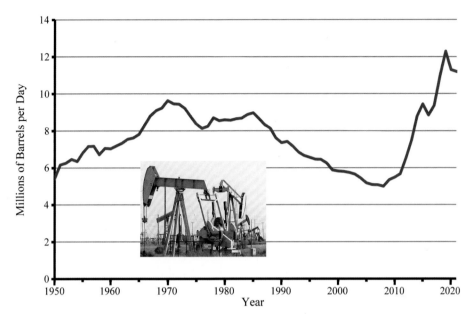

US Crude Oil Production 1950–2021. US annual crude oil production decline and resurgence in millions of barrels per day. Image of Lost Hills Oil Field in California. (Energy Information Administration, 2022)[21]

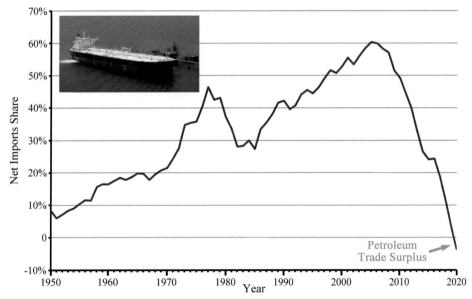

US Imports' Share of Petroleum Products 1950–2021. Net imports' share of petroleum products supplied over the last 70 years. Petroleum products are processed products, such as gasoline, jet fuel, and fuel oils. Exports exceeded imports for the first time in 2020. Image of *AbQaiq* oil tanker in Iraq. (Energy Information Administration, 2022)[22]

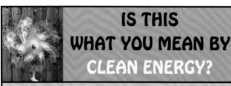

IS THIS WHAT YOU MEAN BY CLEAN ENERGY?

Space Tourism: Rockets Emit 100 Times More CO2 per Passenger than Flights - Imagine a Whole Industry

"The commercial race to get tourists to space is heating up between Virgin Group founder Sir Richard Branson and former Amazon CEO Jeff Bezos."
— *The Conversation*, July 19, 2021[23]

"Climate change threatens life as we know it." — Richard Branson, August 31, 2009[23]

"Climate change is the biggest threat to our planet." — Jeff Bezos, February 17, 2020[23]

But instead of reaching peak oil, the world witnessed an energy miracle in the form of the Shale Revolution. US entrepreneurs and petroleum engineers applied two existing technologies, hydraulic fracturing and horizontal drilling, to extract oil and gas from shale rock.

Hydraulic fracturing, or fracking, uses explosive charges or a pressurized liquid to fracture rock. Fracking had been employed since 1947 to enhance production from oil wells. Early techniques used nitroglycerin or gelled gasoline to fracture rock and increase oil output.[24]

Horizontal drilling was first used in 1971 to drill a shaft underneath a river for a gas line. Before the use of the technique in the oil and gas industry, horizontal drilling was praised by environmental groups as a method to drill underneath rivers without digging damaging trenches to cross rivers. Horizontal drilling continues to be widely used today in river-crossing applications.[25]

In 1981, George Mitchell, one of the leading gas producers in Texas, began efforts to produce natural gas from the Barnett Shale, a deep underground layer of rock spanning thousands of miles in area around Fort Worth, Texas. Shale is known as "tight" rock, with pores so small that oil and natural gas cannot flow through them easily. Mitchell and others had long produced oil and gas from above and below the shale using vertical drilling but were unable to produce oil or gas from the Barnett Shale itself.

For 15 years, Mitchell's team drilled well after well into the shale without success. Skeptics told him it couldn't be done. Finally, in 1997, by the combined use of pressurized water, sand, and a small amount of chemicals, along with horizontal drilling, the team was able to free the trapped natural gas and establish a financially viable well.[26]

Over the next two decades, fracking produced an oil and gas boom in shale fields in Colorado, New Mexico, North Dakota, Pennsylvania, Texas, Wyoming, and other US locations. US crude production rose from five million bpd in 2005 to over 12 million bpd in 2019. Natural gas production rose 74 percent over the same period.[27] The US passed Russia to become the world's leading producer of gas in 2011 and surpassed both Russia and Saudi Arabia as the largest producer of petroleum in 2018. By 2020, fracking operations produced about 65 percent of US petroleum[28] and 78 percent of US natural gas.[29]

With the rapid rise in production, US oil and gas exports exploded. In 2015, the Obama Administration lifted a 40-year ban on US crude exports, which then increased by a factor of nine from 2014 to 2020.[30] The net imports' share of US petroleum products dropped from 60 percent in 2006 to zero in 2020. The US balance of payments in oil products changed from a negative $386 billion in 2008 to a small positive in 2020, the first trade surplus in oil products in more than 70 years.[31]

Prior to 2010, several natural gas terminals were under construction on the US Gulf Coast to import liquefied natural gas (LNG). But the Shale Revolution produced a huge volume of

Casualty in the War on Hydrocarbons

The Gas Stove[32]

gas at one-half of the price of gas in Europe and one-third of the price in Japan. LNG terminals designed to import gas were converted to export liquefied gas, and additional terminals were built.

The Shale Revolution provided a huge positive economic benefit for US citizens. In 2019, the Council of Economic Advisors (CEA) reported that the fracking revolution reduced the domestic price of natural gas by 63 percent and the wholesale price of electricity by 45 percent. The CEA further concluded that the Shale Revolution saved US consumers $203 billion annually, or about $2,500 per year for a family of four.[33]

Back in the summer of 2008, the price of West Texas Intermediate crude was approaching $150 per barrel. OPEC, led by Saudi Arabia, remained firmly in control of world oil prices. The United States, Europe, and other developed nations annually transferred more than half a trillion dollars to OPEC nations in the form of oil purchases. But the Shale Revolution changed the world energy picture.

From 2008 to 2017, more than 10 million bpd of new oil production came online, and the US supplied more than six million bpd, or 60 percent of the new supply.[34] The US frackers broke OPEC's stranglehold on global oil prices. From 2010 to 2020, global petroleum prices trended downward, reversing a 30-year rising trend.

The Shale Revolution had an even greater favorable impact on the price of natural gas. Prior to 2009, the per-barrel price of US petroleum was typically nine times higher than the price of natural gas per million Btu. From 2009 to 2020, the US price of oil was about 25 times the price of gas. The prices of oil and natural gas were closely correlated prior to 2009 but have moved largely independently since 2009.[35] The growth in intercontinental shipments of liquefied natural gas is changing gas pricing from a regional to a global market. In the long run, these trends should mean lower-cost energy for the world.

The US Shale Revolution and rising petroleum production also appears to have brought improved stability to the world economic system. According to the US National Bureau of Economic Research, there have been eight US recessions during the last 50 years, with most of these also causing world economic slowdowns. Of these, high oil prices around the world were the primary cause of three of these slumps, in 1973, 1979, and 1981, with oil-price shock a major contributing factor to recessions in 1990 and 2008. After the recession of 2007–2009, the US enjoyed more than 10 years of economic growth, the longest expansion in modern history, until the recession in 2020 caused by the COVID-19 pandemic.[36]

Despite many economic benefits, fracking has become a primary target of environmental groups in the war on hydrocarbon energy. Fracking is accused of polluting water, using too much water, exposing nearby residents to harmful chemicals, causing earthquakes, and of course, causing global warming. But hydraulic fracturing actually has less environmental impact than conventional oil- and gas-extraction technologies.

According to industry estimates, the average size of a multi-well pad for drilling and fracturing operations is 3.5 acres (0.14 square kilometers), the size of two standard soccer

Natural gas fracking site in Pennsylvania[37]

Is Fracking Environmentally Safe?

Hydraulic fracturing, the latest technology to produce petroleum and natural gas, is under continuous assault from environmental groups and the global warming movement. Like many other industrial processes, fracking potentially can damage the environment. But decades of experience show that fracking can be effectively employed to access petroleum and natural gas while minimizing environmental impact.

The main argument against hydraulic fracturing is that the process can pollute nearby water supplies. The 2010 documentary *Gasland* showed a man lighting the natural gas coming out of his faucet and claimed that this was caused by fracking.[38] But instead, the natural gas escaping from the faucet was caused by seeps of gas from a local reservoir, a common natural process documented in many locations over the last two centuries.

Fracking operations are conducted at depths of 5,000 feet or more, with thousands of feet of impermeable rock between the rock fracturing and the local water supply above. In compliance with state regulations, drilling operators encase well shafts in concrete and steel to prevent chemical and water leakage into nearby surface drinking water reservoirs. By 2010, more than one million wells had been fractured in the United States. EPA Administrator Lisa Jackson stated before Congress in 2011, "I am not aware of any proven case where the fracking process itself affected water."[39]

Opponents charge that fracking uses chemicals that can harm nearby residents. Injected pressurized fracking fluid consists of 85 percent water, 14 percent sand, and less than one percent chemicals.[40] These fluids are injected a mile or more below the surface, far below residents. The chemicals employed maximize the flow of oil or gas from the well. These chemicals consist of substances that are typically used in household products, such as toothpaste, makeup remover, or foodstuffs. Former Colorado Governor John Hickenlooper and others have swallowed the liquid portion of fracking fluid to publicly demonstrate that the chemicals used in hydraulic fracturing are safe.[41]

Opponents also charge that fracking uses too much water. According to the American Petroleum Institute, the average fractured well uses about four million gallons of water.[42] But other industrial processes use large amounts of water as well. Biodiesel vehicle fuel production uses about 268 times more water than gasoline production. Ethanol fuel production uses about 40 times more water than gasoline production.[43] The average US golf course uses about 160 acre-feet of water per year for irrigation, or 52 million gallons per year, more than 12 times the water used in a fracking well.[44] Both fracking sites and golf courses recycle water to reduce the net usage.

Disposal of fracking wastewater is an important issue. Hydraulic fracturing has been blamed for causing earthquakes. But the US Geologic Survey points out that it is "extremely rare" for fracking to cause earthquakes.[45] Instead, disposal of fracking wastewater into deep underground reservoirs has caused minor quakes in Oklahoma and other locations. But in most locations, underground wastewater injection is safe without any earthquake danger. Geologists advise on safe disposal locations.

By 2020, more than two million wells had been fractured in the US. Fracking is underway in more than 20 states.[46] Experience shows that, when proper safeguards are followed, hydraulic fracturing is an environmentally safe operation.

fields.[47] By using horizontal drilling, a frac pad can access oil or gas from a lateral distance of two miles, or an area of more than 12 square miles around the drilling site. The oil or gas is recovered from a depth of 5,000 to 15,000 feet, leaving the surface area around the frac pad relatively undisturbed, when compared to conventional vertical-well technology.

The US is the dominant user of hydraulic fracturing technology, but fracking operations are growing internationally. About 45 countries have shale formations with proven or probable oil reserves. Large commercial fracking operations are underway in Argentina, Canada, and China.[48] More than 200,000 wells have been fracked in Canada, and 80 percent of new wells use fracking.[49] Fracking in Argentina's Vaca Muerta Shale, one of the world's largest shale deposits, reached record levels in 2021.[50] China began fracking in 2012. About 10 percent of China's natural gas production in 2020 came from fracking in shale fields.[51] Fracking operations have begun in Australia, Columbia, India, Mexico, Oman, South Africa, Ukraine, and the United Arab Emirates.

But opposition to hydraulic fracturing is strong. National fracking bans or moratoriums have been established in Bulgaria, France, Germany, Ireland, Italy, Spain, and the UK.[52] Massachusetts, New Jersey, New York, and Vermont have enacted bans in the US, along with a number of local communities. The Canadian provinces of Nova Scotia and Quebec enacted moratoriums on fracking.[53]

At first glance, Europe would appear to be a fertile location for hydraulic fracturing. In 2021, Europe imported about 75 percent of its petroleum and 63 percent of its natural gas from nations outside of Europe, and imports are rising.[54] A 2017 assessment of shale oil and gas resources by the European Commission found 49 shale formations in Europe containing either gas or oil, with major shale potential in Bulgaria, France, Poland, Portugal, Romania, Ukraine, and the United Kingdom.[55]

But Europe has chosen to eliminate petroleum and natural gas production and to pursue a risky transition to renewable energy. If consumers resist adoption of electric vehicles and electric appliances, and if renewables are unable to cost-effectively power heavy industry, the policy of eliminating oil and gas will reduce the economic growth and standard of living for Europeans. As we will discuss in Chapter 10, the global energy crisis in 2022 is closely connected with Europe's drive for renewables.

California Dreamin'?

Carbon-Neutral California Would Save 14,000 Lives a Year, UCLA Study Says
— *City News Service*, May 5, 2020[56]

NOT ON PLANET EARTH: PIPELINES

In the past, protests against oil and gas projects were local and could be characterized as NIMBY, or "not in my backyard." But opposition to hydrocarbon projects is now global and should be labeled NOPE, or "not on planet Earth." Fracking activists and other oil and gas opponents travel between states and countries to target any and all hydrocarbon projects. If there is a fracking operation, a pipeline, a power plant, an export terminal, or even a university investment in hydrocarbons, it's going to be opposed.

Oil and gas pipelines serve as high-visibility targets for the climate movement. Safety, fear of spills, fear of accidents, indigenous peoples' rights, pollution, wetland damage, and even hummingbird nests provide reasons to halt pipeline projects. But the underlying reason for pipeline opposition is fear of human-caused global warming.

Pipeline opponents have scored a number of successes. After six years of protests, the Atlantic Coast Pipeline project was abandoned

The Climatist Empire Strikes Back

Hummingbird Halts Construction of Controversial Oil Pipeline
"Trans Mountain Corp, which is carrying out construction of a US$12.6 billion project that will nearly triple capacity of the pipeline, was ordered to halt work on a section to protect the hummingbird's nests."
— *Independent*, April 29, 2021[57]

in July 2020. Plans had called for the 42-inch pipeline to convey natural gas from the fracking fields of West Virginia to Virginia and North Carolina.[58]

Likewise, the Keystone XL pipeline project had planned for the pipeline to carry 830,000 barrels of oil from the oil sands of Alberta, Canada, and the fracking fields of North Dakota and Montana to US refineries on the Texas Gulf Coast. The Keystone XL would have joined 31 other crude oil pipelines that cross the Canada-US border. But the project became a lighting rod for the climate movement. For 13 years, opponents claimed that the pipeline would damage water supplies, harm indigenous peoples, and even cause cancer. President Barack Obama halted the project in November 2015, but the Trump Administration revived the project in early 2017. Then in January 2021, on his first day in office, President Joe Biden revoked the federal permit for construction of the Keystone XL, stating that the pipeline was not consistent with his administration's "climate imperatives."[59] TC Energy, the developer behind the Keystone XL, abandoned the project in June 2021.[60]

Despite cancellation of the Keystone XL and Atlantic Coast pipelines, the US oil and gas pipeline networks continue to expand. According to the US Department of

Get With The Herd!

"If we use less energy, we can help keep the Earth cooler."
— *The Clubhouse Kids Make a Big Difference*, Teacher's Guide, 2007[61]

Transportation, the US crude oil pipeline network grew from 49,000 miles in 2004 to over 85,000 miles in 2020. The network of gas pipelines grew from 1.9 million to almost 2.3 million miles over the same 16 years.[62] Europe has banned hydraulic fracturing, but European nations are still approving pipeline projects. Prior to the Ukraine invasion by Russia in 2022, this included Nord Stream 2, which connected Germany to Russia to supply natural gas through a route under the Baltic Sea, and the Eastern Mediterranean pipeline, which will connect Israel to Greece. By the summer of 2021, gas pipelines were also planned or under construction in Brazil, China, India, Indonesia, and other countries.[63]

Pipelines are the safest method of transporting crude oil, natural gas, and chemicals. A 2012 study by the Manhattan Institute, using data from the US Pipeline and Hazardous Materials Safety Administration (PHMSA), showed 20 times more incidents involving hazardous materials in the case of rail transportation than for oil and gas pipelines per billion ton-miles. Truck transportation suffered hundreds of times more incidents than pipelines.[64] PHMSA data also shows that the number of incidents and deaths from pipelines in the US have declined since 2000, despite the growth of pipeline networks.[65] As long as people demand oil and gas, pipelines will be needed.

THE CLIMATE-LAWSUIT AVALANCHE

Although 1,800 national laws to combat climate change have been enacted in more than 130 countries, climate advocates fear that these measures are inadequate, so they increasingly pursue litigation to "meet the climate challenge." Energy companies face a rising tide of climate lawsuits. Cities, counties, states, and environmental groups sue the world's leading oil and gas firms for presumed or anticipated damages from rising seas, extreme weather, and even snow disappearance. Non-governmental groups sue local and national governments to demand compliance with existing climate statutes or to force the development of new

It Must Be the Oil Companies

"The $5 billion ski industry is in jeopardy as a result of 'low-snow' winters and shorter seasons."
— County of Boulder, Colorado v. Oil Companies, April 17, 2018[66]

Climate Litigation Legal Issues

Plaintiffs allegedly damaged by climate change face a high bar in efforts to win in suits against oil company defendants. They must first demonstrate to the court that they have "standing" to bring the case. Standing refers to requirements that must be met to successfully bring a claim before the court. For example, in the US, plaintiffs must show that they were injured by climate change, that their injury was caused by defendant actions, and that a remedy exists that the court could order that would compensate for the injury in some way. The question of standing remains less of a barrier in developing nations.

Second, suing parties must show that the court has the authority to render a verdict in their favor. In the US and other nations, separation of powers requires that one branch of government generally cannot act outside the authority granted to it by a constitution or other laws. US courts have generally taken the position that climate change issues are better left to the executive and legislative branches of government.[67]

---

statutes. A 2020 climate litigation report by the United Nations identified 1,550 cases filed in 38 countries, with approximately 1,200 of those filed in the United States. This number was up 75 percent from 884 cases in 2017.[68]

In 2017, Oakland and San Francisco filed separate lawsuits against BP, Chevron, ConocoPhilips, ExxonMobil, and Royal Dutch Shell in California circuit courts. The City of New York filed similar litigation in January 2018 in the Southern District Court of New York.[69] These actions sought billions of dollars in damages for "severe and irreversible harms" from hotter temperatures, severe heat waves, extreme precipitation, rising seas, and other alleged effects.[70]

However, in 2018, these three high-profile lawsuits were thrown out. The judge in each case ruled that the courts should defer to the executive and legislative branches regarding climate issues. After appeal, the Oakland and San Francisco cases were reinstated by the Ninth Circuit Court of Appeals and returned to a federal district court, where they remain today. After appeal, the City of New York case was dismissed by the Second Circuit Court of Appeals, and the city was reprimanded for trying to usurp a federal function.[71] As of August 2021, no court anywhere in the world has awarded a plaintiff monetary damages for injuries suffered as a result of a company's contribution to climate change.[72]

Suits seeking to force governmental action or non-monetary remedies have been more successful. Among the most important was *Massachusetts v. Environmental Protection Agency*, a suit brought by Massachusetts and 10 other states claiming that the EPA should regulate greenhouse gases under the Clean Air Act. The US Supreme Court ruled in favor of the plaintiffs in 2007, stating,

Under the clear terms of the Clean Air Act, EPA can avoid taking further action only if it determines that greenhouse gases do not contribute to climate change or if it provides some reasonable explanation as to why it cannot or will not exercise its discretion to determine whether they do.[73]

As a result of this ruling, the EPA issued an Endangerment Finding on December 7, 2009, concluding that "greenhouse gas pollution … threatens public health and welfare."[74] This finding serves as the basis for all US climate change regulations today.

Some courts appear to be eager to solve the climate crisis. In a case brought against Royal Dutch Shell by seven environmental groups, the Hague District Court in the Netherlands ruled in May 2021 that Shell must reduce its greenhouse gas emissions by 45 percent by 2030, based on 2019 levels.[75] The court apparently believes it now has the authority to establish emissions goals for individual companies. Shell will appeal the decision.

In addition to lawsuit attacks, the governing boards of oil and gas companies are under tremendous pressure. Environmental groups, partnering with financial institutions, seek to place green advocates on the boards of directors of major firms. In May 2021, three independent directors were elected to the board of ExxonMobil. Financial fund managers BlackRock, State Street, and Vanguard, along with pension-fund and advisory-services shareholders, succeeded in electing the new directors, who are expected to push the firm to cut greenhouse gas emissions.[76] That same month, Chevron lost a shareholder vote directing the company to account for the emissions of Chevron customers when planning emissions reductions.[77] These shareholder challenges are regarded by many as a milestone in moving big oil toward greener policies.

NET ZERO BY 2050

"Net Zero," the latest buzz phrase of the climate movement, has become both a goal and a mandate for society. The IPCC *Fifth Assessment Report* of 2014 recommended that "global net emissions of CO_2 eventually decrease to zero."[79] Proponents tell us that Net Zero means a zero balance between the amount of greenhouse gas emitted and the amount removed from the atmosphere. They claim that attaining Net Zero by 2050 is needed to limit the rise in global temperatures to 1.5°C above the

Get With The Herd!

Bank of America Announces Actions to Achieve Net Zero Greenhouse Gas Emissions before 2050
— *Bloomberg*, February 11, 2021[78]

background temperature level of the 1800s. The United Kingdom became the first major nation to establish Net Zero by 2050 into law in 2019.

Reaching Net Zero by 2050 is the latest badge of commitment to fight climate change. According to the Energy & Climate Intelligence Unit, as of August 2021, 134 countries had adopted becoming Net Zero on or before 2050 as national policy, including China, France, Germany, Japan, the UK, and the US, along with the European Union. Twelve countries enacted the goal into law. The goal of net-zero emissions has been adopted in 84 cities across the world and by 34 states or territories, including 10 US states. Alphabet, Amazon, Apple, BP, CVS Health, Daimler, Royal Dutch Shell, Toyota Motor, Volkswagen Group, and Walmart lead a climate-fighting parade of over 400 companies who have adopted the goal.[80]

But virtually nothing our modern society does is "zero emissions." If you build a house, sizeable greenhouse gases are emitted by cutting down trees for producing lumber, mining materials and manufacturing wire and components for electricity, producing plastic or copper for pipes, and manufacturing drywall, roofing, brick, glass, cement for concrete, and many other materials. Manufacturing of household furnishings, such as furniture, appliances, and computers, also emits large quantities of CO_2. Even a grass hut isn't Net Zero.

Nor are solar panels, wind turbines, or electric cars. Producing renewables requires extensive mining for raw materials and intensive energy to fabricate finished components, such as silicon for solar cells, concrete, steel, and carbon polymers for wind turbine towers and blades, and special metals for electric car batteries. Both residences and renewable systems require energy to transport products to markets or to construction sites.

Proponents of Net Zero apparently count on removing carbon dioxide from industrial exhaust streams or from the atmosphere. But effective carbon capture schemes don't currently exist and, if invented, are unlikely to be widely deployed by 2050, as we will discuss in Chapter 9.

DIDN'T YOU GET THE MEMO?

Fatih Birol, Executive Director of the International Energy Agency, announced to the press in May 2021, "If governments are serious about the climate crisis, there can be no new investments in oil, gas, and coal, from now—from this year."[81] Climatists seem to believe that if they can only stop exploration, pipelines, and other investments, the world will stop using hydrocarbons. But it appears that developing nations didn't get the memo.

While wealthy nations pursue draconian emissions cuts, emissions continue to rise from seven-eighths of the world's population. Developing nations continue to adopt hydrocarbons to expand their economies. According to Global Energy Monitor, 941 coal-fired power plants were in planning or under construction in July 2022, including 515 in China, 97 in Indonesia, 85 in India, 29 in Vietnam, 27 in Turkey, 22 in Zimbabwe, 21 in Bangladesh, 15 in Mongolia, and 15 in the Philippines.[82] Poorer nations continue to need coal to provide electricity for their growing populations.

Natural gas consumption in developing nations is skyrocketing. From 2000 to 2020, gas consumption in African countries almost tripled, Brazil's usage tripled, China's increased by 13 times, India's and Mexico's more than doubled, and Vietnam's almost tripled. From 2010 to 2020, natural gas usage rose in all regions around the world except Europe.[83]

Despite emissions cuts in Europe and the US, it is virtually certain that global emissions will continue to rise over the next two decades. From 2010 to 2019, carbon dioxide emissions from Africa rose 19 percent, China rose 20 percent, India rose 56 percent, and Asia (excluding China and India) rose 21 percent. Total global emissions rose 10 percent over the period.[84] These numbers don't include emissions for biofuels and biomass, which should also be counted, as we will discuss in the next chapter. Rising energy demand for transportation, industry, and housing will continue to drive emissions in the near future.

If the world were to stop hydrocarbon investment today, as Fatih Birol urges, an energy disaster would arise that would dwarf the oil price shocks of the 1970s. The price of crude oil would soon rise to over $200 per barrel and the price of gasoline to over $10 per gallon, with similar increases in coal, natural gas, and electricity prices. Humanity would suffer a global depression of historic magnitude. The resultant misery and death in poorer nations from this human-created energy shock would far exceed any forecasted disasters from global warming. The world experienced a taste of this in the 2022 global energy crisis.

But many call for an energy transition from hydrocarbons to renewables by 2050, beginning with the use of renewables for generation of electricity. Let's examine the possibility that global electrical power can be provided by wind and solar and other renewables in the next chapter.

THE FOOL

Poor Prophecy

"As University of California physicist John Holdren has said, it is possible that carbon-dioxide climate-induced famines could kill as many as a billion people before the year 2020."
— *The Machinery of Nature* by Paul Ehrlich, 1986[85]

CHAPTER 5

100 PERCENT RENEWABLE ELECTRICITY?

"Under my plan of a cap-and-trade system, electricity rates would necessarily skyrocket. … Because I'm capping greenhouse gases, … they would have to retrofit their operations. That will cost money. They will pass that money on to consumers."
—PRESIDENTIAL CANDIDATE BARACK OBAMA (JANUARY, 2008)[1]

Electric power has been and remains the primary target of the Climatist movement for their proposed energy transformation. Transition of electricity generation from coal and natural gas to renewable sources tops the list of green-energy efforts. As we stated last chapter, renewables, including hydroelectric power, now provide about 30 percent of Europe's electricity and about 20 percent of the US's electricity. But renewable energy proponents are just getting started. Many governments in wealthy nations now demand a move to 100 percent renewable electricity by 2050 or even sooner.

However, renewables suffer from serious shortcomings in efforts to replace traditional

---

Leaders Pledging 100 Percent Renewable Electricity

"We'll take steps toward my goal of achieving 100-percent carbon pollution-free electric sector by 2035."   — United States President Joe Biden, January 27, 2021[2]

"Our energy policy today includes bringing forward our target to have New Zealand 100 percent renewable electricity generation by 2030."
        — New Zealand Prime Minister Jacinda Ardern, September 11, 2020[3]

"We believe that in 10 years' time, offshore wind will be powering every home in the country."   — United Kingdom Prime Minister Boris Johnson, October 6, 2020[4]

"On electricity, we're committed to phasing out coal-fired electricity by 2030 … and that we have a net-zero grid by 2035."
        — Canada Prime Minister Justin Trudeau, November 2, 2021[5]

---

hydrocarbon electricity. Where renewables are deployed, and coal, nuclear, and natural gas plants are shuttered, we see rising electricity prices and deteriorating electricity reliability.

IT MUST BE WIND AND SOLAR

Efforts to transition to renewable energy must be dominated by wind and solar. According to the International Energy Agency (IEA), coal, oil, and natural gas generated 63.1 percent of the 26,936 terawatt-hours (TWh) of global electricity produced in 2019.[6] Although biomass, geothermal, hydroelectric, solar, wave and tidal, and wind sources meet the generally accepted definition of renewable energy, only wind and solar have the potential to replace hydrocarbon electricity generation on a large scale.

Hydroelectric power is currently the world's leading source of renewable electricity. Although hydropower produces low-cost power with negligible emissions, opportunities to expand this source are limited. Hydropower's share of the world's electricity generation declined from 20.9 percent in 1973 to 15.7 percent in 2019.[7] Dams already span most of the world's major rivers. New dam construction projects face strong opposition from environmental groups and landowners.

Nuclear energy produces insignificant carbon dioxide emissions and could serve as a electricity source to replace coal and natural gas fuels. The world's 437 operating nuclear reactors provided 9.8 percent of the world's electricity in 2021. But nuclear output has plateaued since the end of the last century. Global nuclear output has been flat since 2006, and the number of reactors has grown only slightly from the 435 that were operating that year.[8] The share of nuclear power peaked at 17 percent of the world's electricity in 1996. Atomic power is not regarded as safe by much of the public. Nor is it classified as renewable by environmental groups. Unless public opinion changes, nuclear power will not grow enough to replace hydrocarbon fuels.

Traditional biomass fuel, including wood, charcoal, crop residue, and dung, served as the world's dominant energy source until the late nineteenth century. Biomass remains a major source in poorer nations today. Electricity from biomass grew in the late twentieth century in response to the oil shocks of the 1970s and the quest for alterative energy.

But biomass delivered only 1.9 percent of the world's electricity in 2019.[9] Biomass is considered a renewable electricity fuel, even though combustion of biomass emits more carbon dioxide per unit of electricity produced than combustion of coal. In any case, biomass requires vast amounts of forest harvesting to produce wood chips to generate electrical power. Large areas of forest in Europe are being cleared to feed plants burning wood chips. To replace a significant portion of coal and natural gas fuel for electricity, millions of square miles of the world's forests would need to be cut down. It's unlikely that society will pursue this path on a large scale. We will discuss biomass again.

Sacrificed to Save the Planet

EU Biofuels Goals Behind Deforested Area as Big as the Netherlands — *Independent,* July 5, 2021[10]

Geothermal energy, defined as heat from fluids and rocks in Earth's crust, is regarded as renewable energy. Sub-surface heat from geothermal fields converts water to steam to generate electricity. Nations located around the Pacific Ring of Fire, the ring of volcanic activity around the Pacific Ocean, enjoy good opportunities to generate electricity from geothermal sources. These include Indonesia, Japan, the Philippines, and the western US. The Philippines generates about 11 percent of its electricity from geothermal power plants. Iceland and Turkey also use large amounts of geothermal energy, with Iceland getting over 60 percent of its total energy from geothermal sources.[11]

But overall, geothermal remains a footnote as a global energy source. In 2019, geothermal power produced about 95 TWh, only 0.4 percent of the world's electricity.[12] Without unforeseen technological advances, geothermal electricity is too small to change the world's energy picture.

Wave and tidal electricity remains an experimental power source. Only 45 GWh of electricity was produced by wave and tidal sources in 2019, which is 2,000 times less than geothermal generation.[13] It will likely be decades before wave and tidal output approaches one percent of global electricity generation, if ever.

So if a transition to renewable energy must occur, wind and solar provide the only plausible alternatives. But can the world be powered on wind and solar energy? Let's look at three major shortcomings of these sources.

WIND AND SOLAR ARE DILUTE ENERGY

Energy density is not usually mentioned when comparing alternative sources of electrical power. But renewable energy sources require much more land than the coal and natural gas power plants that they are meant to replace.

Solar arrays have the best power density of any of the renewable electricity generators, but it's still tiny compared to traditional power sources. Solar installations, both solar photovoltaic and concentrating solar power, produce between four and 10 watts of electricity for each square meter of land (W/m^2) that they occupy. But for a stand-alone solar facility, this is 10 to 250 times lower output per square meter than coal plants, even when coal mines, ash waste disposal, cooling ponds, and rail transportation facilities are included in the computation for coal.[14] Roof-top solar reuses land area, but land-intensive stand-alone facilities constitute an increasing global share of solar energy systems.

Biomass plants suffer the poorest energy density per unit of electricity output. The huge area of forest land or agricultural field needed to produce fuel to feed the generating facility dwarfs the area of the generating plant itself. The energy density of a biomass power system is a meagre $0.5–0.6 \ W/m^2$, some 400–4,000 times lower than the density of a natural gas system, the source with the highest power density.[15]

Wind arrays are not much better. The power density of wind systems is only $0.5–1.5 \ W/m^2$, because wind turbine towers must be spaced about 140 meters apart for maximum output. Wind systems occupy about 100–1,000 times as much land as a comparable coal or natural gas system to produce the same average output.[16]

Wind arrays can coexist with farmland, pastureland, or forests on the plains below the wind turbine towers. When only tower pads and roads are included in the area calculation, the wind power density rises to about $50 \ W/m^2$, still roughly an order of magnitude less dense than coal or gas systems. While wind can coexist with agriculture or forest, its huge overall footprint still needs to be considered when massive wind deployments are planned.

To approach 100 percent renewable electricity using primarily wind and solar systems,

Power Density of Electricity Sources[17]

Vaclav Smil, professor emeritus of the University of Manitoba, conducted extensive analysis on the power density of alternative sources used to generate electricity. He defines the power density of an electrical power source as the average flow of electricity generated per unit of horizontal surface (land or sea area). Power density is measured in watts of electricity generated per square meter of surface (W/m^2). The area measurement to estimate power density is complex, encompassing the total-needed footprint to produce the electricity, including plant area, storage yards, mining sites, agricultural fields, pipelines and transportation, and other associated land or sea areas. Power densities of individual systems vary widely depending upon the specific land area required.

Smil's analysis shows that coal, natural gas, and nuclear power plants have the highest power densities, at between 70 and 2,000 W/m^2. Solar photovoltaic (PV) and concentrating solar power (CSP) systems have power densities 10 to 500 times lower. Biomass systems have the lowest power densities, only about 0.5–0.6 W/m^2. Wind system densities range between 0.5–1.5 W/m^2 when the total area is considered, or up to 50 W/m^2 when only the wind turbine pads and roads are included in the area.

Power Source	Power Density (W/m^2)	
	Low	High
Natural Gas	200	2,000
Coal	100	1,000
Nuclear	70	1,600
Hydroelectric	1	10
Solar PV and CSP	4	10
Wind (Total Area)	0.5	1.5
Wind (Only Tower Pads and Roads)		Up to 50
Biomass	0.5	0.6

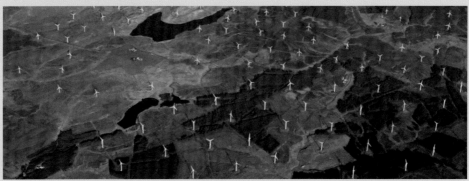

The huge area occupied by the Whitelee Wind Farm, Scotland, UK.[18]

the land requirements are gigantic. "Net-Zero America," a 2020 study published by Princeton University, calls for wind and solar to supply 50 percent of US electricity by 2050, up from about 11 percent today. The study estimates that this expansion would require about 228,000 square miles of new land (590,000 square kilometers).[19] This is an area larger than the combined area of Illinois, Indiana, Iowa, Kentucky, West Virginia, and Wisconsin. This area would be on the order of 100 times as large as the physical footprint of the coal and natural gas power systems that would be replaced.

When power density is considered, hydrocarbon and nuclear power plants are actually the most friendly for Earth's environment. These systems require only a tiny surface-area footprint when compared to currently favored wind and solar systems. Without the misconception that carbon dioxide causes dangerous global warming, deployments of wind, solar, and biomass systems would be regarded as ecologically unfriendly.

Wind and solar are dilute energy. They require massive amounts of land to generate the electricity required by modern society. Net-zero plans for 2050, powered by wind and solar, will encounter obstacles with transmission, zoning, local opposition, and just plain space that are probably insurmountable.

Land Needed for 50 Percent US Wind and Solar Electricity. The additional land required to go from 11 percent wind and solar electricity in 2020 to 50 percent wind and solar by 2050 is estimated at 228,000 square miles, which is larger than the combined area of Illinois, Indiana, Iowa, Kentucky, West Virginia, and Wisconsin. (Princeton University, 2020)[20]

WIND AND SOLAR ARE INTERMITTENT ENERGY

Wind and solar are intermittent energy sources. For example, consider the output from Texas wind turbines for the month of March 2014.[21] Wind electricity output for the entire state varies erratically from over 8,000 MW to near zero over a period of only a few hours. Several days of very low wind output are not uncommon.

Solar insolation is the measurement of the average daily solar radiation, or sunlight, received at a location. Solar insolation varies by location with latitude, time of year, time of day, and cloudiness. In a good location, solar systems can output usable electricity for about 10 hours per day, but often it is less. In the US, solar winter output is usually only one half of summer output or less. Nightfall and snowfall eliminate solar output.

The capacity factor of an electrical power system is defined as the actual power output as a percentage of the system's maximum power output. For the US in 2020, nuclear plants operated at the highest level of utilization, with an average capacity factor of 92.5 percent of full output. US system average capacity factors were natural gas (56.6%), hydroelectric (41.5%), coal (40.2%), wind (35.4%), solar photovoltaic (24.9%), and solar thermal (20.5%).[22] Note that in states with large amounts of wind, solar, and hydro output, coal and natural gas plants are typically scaled back to run at lower utilization rates. Coal and natural gas systems can run at more than 80 percent capacity factors when needed.

Wind capacity factors across the world come in below the US average. In 2019, wind systems in China, the world's largest wind operator, achieved a capacity factor of only 19.6

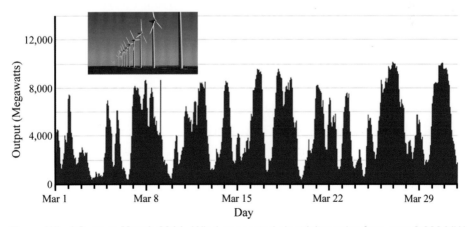

Texas Wind Output, March 2014. Wind-generated electricity varies from over 8,000 MW to almost zero within a few hours. Image of Brazos Wind Array, Fluvanna, TX. (ERCOT, Energy Information Administration, 2014)[23]

percent. Germany, the third-largest wind nation, operated at only 23.7 percent. The world's wind capacity factor for 2019 was estimated at about 28.1 percent by IEA Wind TCP.[24]

Electricity is an always-on system. With hardly a second thought, residents of advanced nations count on electricity for their lights, to run refrigerators and air conditioners, to pump tap water and gasoline, and to power their televisions and computers. The average US annual power interruption totals only about seven hours per year, or about two hours per year if major events are excluded.[25] Outages happen less often in other wealthy countries, including Australia, France, Japan, the Netherlands, and the UK.[26]

Cleaning solar panels on a cloudy day in the UK. Can you feel the solar power?[27]

But advanced nations are sliding down a slope toward unreliable electricity systems, driven by their obsession for wind and solar energy. Wind and solar output depends upon the weather. These sources are good on sunny, windy days. But for much of the year, their intermittent output is fundamentally incompatible with modern always-on electricity demand. Wind and solar should be called "unreliables," instead of renewables.

WIND AND SOLAR ARE COSTLY ENERGY

Stories about low-cost renewables fill today's broadcasts and media websites. Wind and solar are praised as the new lowest-cost sources of energy, beating coal and natural gas. Without a deeper understanding, the average reader could conclude that wind and solar should take over the power grid, with hydrocarbon and nuclear systems exiting.

It's true that the construction cost of wind and solar declined substantially during the last decade. According to the US Energy Information Administration (EIA), the construction costs of solar arrays fell 50 percent since 2013, and the construction costs of onshore wind systems dropped 27 percent. Wind and solar arrays narrowed the construction-cost gap with natural gas plants, whose costs declined 13 percent over the same period.[28] But construction costs comprise only part of the total cost of delivering electrical power.

Europe's wind and solar penetration ranks as the highest in the world. In 2021, wind provided electricity in Denmark (44%), Ireland (31%), Portugal (26%), Spain (24%), and Germany (23%). These penetration numbers far exceeded the share of wind electricity

---

Headlines Touting Low-Cost Renewables

"Wind Power Prices Now Lower than the Cost of Natural Gas"
— *ARS Technica*, August 17, 2019[29]

"Solar and Wind are the Cheapest New Sources of Energy Says BNEF"
— *SMART ENERGY International*, April 29, 2020[30]

"Renewables Increasingly Beat Even Cheapest Coal Competitors on Cost"
— International Renewable Energy Agency, June 2, 2020[31]

---

share in the US (9%) and China (8%).[32] That same year, solar provided almost nine percent of Germany's electricity, amongst the world's highest share of electricity provided by solar.[33] If wind and solar provide the lowest-cost electricity, the nations with the most wind and solar installed should enjoy the lowest prices, right?

But a graph of wind and solar capacity versus electricity prices for the nations of Europe shows exactly the opposite. The nations with the *most* wind and solar capacity deployed experience the *highest* residential electricity prices. Ireland and Spain, with more than double the wind and solar capacity per person than that of Bulgaria and Hungary,

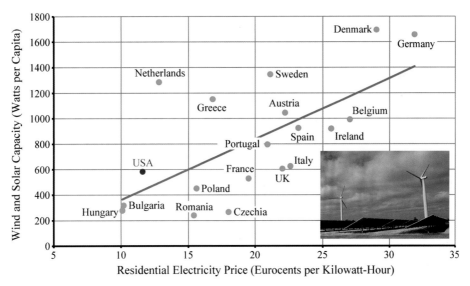

Wind and Solar Capacity and Electricity Prices in Europe, 2021. Installed wind and solar capacity per person and residential electricity prices for nations of Europe and the United States. Higher electricity prices are strongly associated with higher wind and solar capacity. (Eurostat, EurObserv'ER, World Bank, US EIA, 2022)[34]

paid more than double the price for their electricity. The residents of Denmark and Germany, with the highest penetration of wind and solar in the world, paid about 30 euro cents ($0.35) per kWh for electricity in 2021, almost triple the price of US power.[35] We've been plotting this chart for more than six years, with little change in the trend. In Europe, residents in nations with the most wind and solar installed pay the highest electricity prices.

In the US, electricity prices in states with the highest penetration of wind systems are rising faster than the national average. US electricity prices rose on average a total of only 27 percent from 2008 to 2022, lower than the rate of inflation, which rose 36 percent over the 14-year period.[36] But in eight of the top 12 wind states, electricity prices rose between 33 and 73 percent.[37] So the evidence shows that, in both the US and Europe, large deployments of wind systems produce higher electricity prices.

Wind and solar arrays increase the cost of electricity in three ways: 1) they incur higher transmission costs; 2) they lower the utilization of traditional generating plants; and 3) they suffer system intermittency costs. These costs rise with increasing wind and solar penetration of the power system. Let's review some of the basics of power systems to see why adding wind and solar would raise electricity costs.

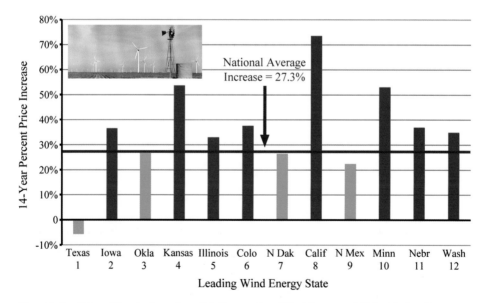

Electricity Price Rise in Leading US States for Wind Usage, 2008–2022. Electricity price increases for the 12 leading US wind states compared to a national electricity price increase of 27 percent over the 14-year period. Prices are average end-user prices, all sectors. Image of wind array in West Texas. (US EIA, 2009, 2023)[38]

Electrical power systems consist of three basic components: generation, transmission, and distribution. Generation consists of the hydrocarbon, renewable, or nuclear power plants that create electricity. The transmission system connects generating plants to the distribution system, transferring large amounts of electricity to population centers. The distribution system divides the electrical power received from the transmission system and routes electricity to individual residential and business customers.

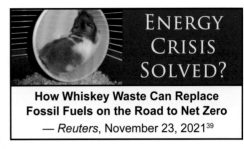

ENERGY CRISIS SOLVED?

How Whiskey Waste Can Replace Fossil Fuels on the Road to Net Zero
— *Reuters*, November 23, 2021[39]

According to the Federal Energy Regulatory System, the North American electric system of the US and Canada "contains more than 211,000 miles of transmission lines operating at 230 kilovolts and greater."[40] The US transmission system was constructed over the last century. Peak system construction occurred in the 1960s and 1970s, when roughly 6,000–8,000 circuit miles were added to the transmission network every year. New construction dropped to under 2,000 circuit miles per year from 1995 to 2010. Since 2010, though, new circuit miles have been constructed to connect to newly installed wind and solar arrays.[41]

Wind and solar typically require longer transmission connections, resulting in higher transmission costs. Because of the large amounts of land required, wind and stand-alone solar systems tend to be scattered on farms, plains, deserts, and hills. Transmission lines are also needed to connect to offshore wind arrays. These renewable energy sites tend to be far from cities, in contrast to coal and natural gas plants, which are usually situated near population centers. As a result, additional high-voltage transmission lines need to be constructed, raising the cost of wind- and solar-delivered electricity.

The addition of intermittent wind and solar generators to a power system results in lower utilization of existing coal and natural gas facilities. Because of regulatory mandates and subsidies, wind and solar output usually receives first priority in the power hierarchy, requiring coal and natural gas output to be scaled back on windy and sunny days. Instead of running at capacity factors of 80 percent as designed, coal and gas plants assume a backup role to wind and solar, dropping their capacity factors to 40 to 60 percent. This makes it difficult for coal and gas plants to produce enough revenue to cover the original costs of plant construction, requiring electricity prices to be raised to cover system costs.

In most regions of the US, electricity is provided each day through the mechanism of electric power markets. In the Northeast, Mid-Atlantic, and Midwest, and in California and Texas, Regional Transmission Organizations (RTO)s operate day-ahead and real-time markets, in which generators offer to sell electricity and power providers bid for that electricity to meet expected customer demand. Supply-side quantities and demand-side bids are ordered from low to high offer price. The market clears when the total amount of electricity that generators offer equals the total that power providers demand for customers. Generators then each receive the highest final bid that clears the market.[42]

The combination of the power market structure and federal and state subsidies favor wind-generated electricity. US wind generators receive a Production Tax Credit (PTC) of about two cents per kilowatt-hour generated. Some states, such as Iowa, add an additional state tax credit for wind energy.

The US PTC allows wind arrays to offer electricity at one or two cents per kWh in RTO auctions, or even at negative prices, and still make a profit. If the market clears at a typical five cents per kWh, wind systems, along with all generators, receive this price. The PTC and power market structure favor displacement of hydrocarbon and nuclear power by wind-generated electricity, forcing traditional plants to run at low capacity factors.

Why Raise Our Energy Prices?

WINTER CRISIS: One MILLION Pensioners Fear They Cannot Afford to Heat Their Homes

"As many as 90 percent of the 2,000 pensioners surveyed … believe the high cost of gas and electricity presents a real health threat to elderly people living in the UK."

— *Express*, January 17, 2017[43]

In Europe, regulations force power companies to prioritize electricity from renewable sources, regardless of price. The European Parliament passed Directive 2001/77/EC in September 2001, requiring nations to adopt legally binding national renewable targets and promote the consumption of renewable electricity. The directive also stated,

> When dispatching generating installations, transmission system operators shall give priority to generating installations using renewable energy sources insofar as the operation of the national electricity system permits.[44]

In other words, utility companies must scale back traditional generator output when wind and solar are available.

Shortfall in wind and solar output due to intermittency is a well-known issue, but too much wind and solar output is also problematic. Excess wind and solar can cause system instability. Depending upon weather and seasonal characteristics, operators with wind or

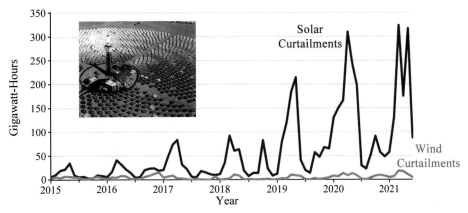

California Curtailments of Solar and Wind, 2015–2021. Monthly curtailments of solar- and wind-generated electricity in California by the California Independent System Operator (CAISO). About five percent of utility-scale solar electricity was curtailed in 2020. Image of Solar One array in California. (CAISO, US EIA, 2021)[45]

solar penetration of 10 percent or more increasingly switch off wind or solar generators when output is too high. Curtailments of wind and solar are rising.

California received about 14 percent of its electricity in 2019 from solar generation. But during spring months, when electricity demand is low and solar output is high, California switches off its solar systems. About five percent of solar output was curtailed in 2020, and 15 percent was curtailed during afternoons in March 2021.[46]

In the United Kingdom, energy prices are skyrocketing due in part to "constraint payments." The UK National Grid makes payments to wind operators for electricity not generated, when turbines are switched off during high-wind periods and output exceeds demand. These payments began in 2011 at £12 million and then increased by a factor of 19 to £230 million in 2020, mostly paid to Scotland wind operators. Constraint payment costs constitute a growing part of consumer electricity bills. Over the last decade, the UK discarded roughly 10 TWh of electricity, enough to power all Scottish residences for a year. Much of the wasted power could not be used because of insufficient transmission resources. Wind electricity output rose to 19.8 percent of UK electricity in 2019, with constraint payments growing exponentially.[47]

An additional intermittency cost is the cost of interventions to balance electricity supply

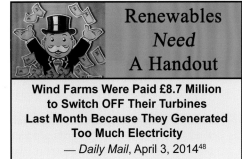

Renewables Need A Handout

Wind Farms Were Paid £8.7 Million to Switch OFF Their Turbines Last Month Because They Generated Too Much Electricity
— *Daily Mail*, April 3, 2014[48]

and demand. When supply diverges from demand, operators must intervene to switch off generators or to bring generators online. Clouds passing over solar resources, sudden changes in wind speeds, and other weather effects require either automatic or manual system changes. Intervention operations can be costly. For example, German grid operator 50Hertz paid 1.5 billion euros for intervention operations in 2017.[49] As intermittent generators are added to a power system, the cost of interventions rises.

APPROACHING 100 PERCENT RENEWABLE ELECTRICITY

Despite the issues of high land usage, intermittency, and cost, most government administrations appear determined to try to move to 100 percent renewable electricity. As we discussed, unless nuclear power is reconsidered as a favored power source, this renewable transition must be dominated by installation of wind and solar systems.

From 2000 to 2020, wind and solar output rose from zero to an 11 percent share of US electricity production as coal-fired output declined. But over the same period, the share of US electricity provided by natural gas rose from 16 percent to 40 percent.[50] Like in the US, natural gas now dominates the electricity supply of many nations.

Because of intermittency, the capacity of wind and solar systems does not equate to the capacity of traditional power plants. Passing clouds interrupt the output of solar arrays, and wind output varies with the whims of zephyrs. Electrical power operators count on only about 10 percent of the rated capacity of wind and solar systems as a reliable contribution

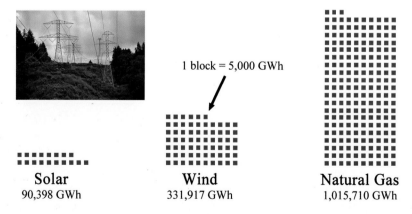

1 block = 5,000 GWh

Solar
90,398 GWh

Wind
331,917 GWh

Natural Gas
1,015,710 GWh

Additions to United States Electricity Production, 2000–2020. Additions to solar, wind, and natural gas electricity production, with one block equal to 5,000 GWh. Image of power lines in Auburn, Washington. (EIA, 2021)[51]

to overall system capacity. This means that, as more and more wind and solar are added to a power system, most traditional power sources *must* remain in service to maintain continuity of electricity supply.

A 2016 study by Stephen Brick and Samuel Thernstrom analyzed electricity systems in California, Germany, and Wisconsin. Their analysis looked at changes to system capacity and cost with increasing penetration of intermittent wind and solar resources. They estimated that, as more and more renewables are added to power systems, 90 percent of traditional power plants must be retained as backup for wind and solar. The traditional power plants are run at lower and lower capacity factors as renewable penetration moves from 50 percent to 80 percent of electricity output. This results in a rising level of system size that must be maintained, as well as rising electricity costs for consumers.

Brick and Thernstrom projected that, in the case of California, overall system capacity would rise by 69 percent with 50 percent renewable penetration, and rise by 130 percent when renewable penetration reached 80 percent. The price of wholesale electricity would rise 85 percent for 50 percent wind and solar penetration, and would rise 269 percent for 80 percent penetration, almost tripling in price. The authors recommended using a more

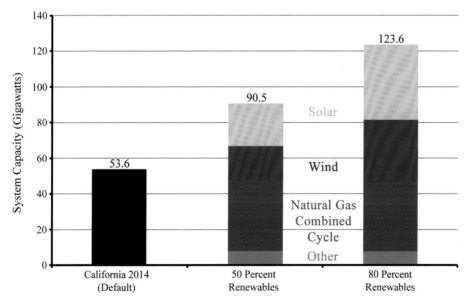

California System Size with Renewables Penetration. Rising California system capacity with 50 percent- and 80 percent-renewable generation of electricity. Ninety percent of the capacity of natural gas and other traditional generating sources must be retained if continuity of electricity supply is to be maintained. (Brick and Thernstrom, 2016)[52]

balanced approach of increasing the use of nuclear power with wind and solar to limit increasing system size and electricity cost.[53]

In the foolish drive to become Net Zero, states and nations may initially try to choose not to retain most of their existing reliable hydrocarbon and nuclear power plants. The disastrous result will be declining grid reliability.

TRAGEDY IN TEXAS

On February 13, 2021, a winter storm brought extreme cold to Texas for more than a week. The cold wave caused a spike in electricity demand along with a drop in supply. The unexpected surge in demand could not be met by generating resources, requiring the system operator, the Electric Reliability Council of Texas (ERCOT), to initiate controlled system outages for about 20 percent of the customers to prevent system collapse. About 4.5 million Texans lost power for more than 70 hours, or about three days. Deaths caused by the storm and power outages numbered 210, with property damage estimated at $130 billion.[54]

Electrical power systems require that generated electricity equal demanded electricity at every instant in time so that system voltage and frequency remain in tight tolerances. If electricity supply cannot be made to equal demand, system instabilities grow, causing generating plants to trip off and eventually shut down.

ERCOT system operators knew the cold weather was coming. CEO Bill Magness led an ERCOT board meeting on February 8, five days before the storm hit, urging generators to be ready. But they underestimated the depth of the cold and the resulting magnitude of customer demand. In their planning process, ERCOT had used the winter storm in 2011 as their worst-case scenario, when Dallas temperatures got down to 13°F. They chose to look at this storm when preparing, even though temperatures in Dallas had reached 4°F or less 16 days since 1899, most recently in 1989.[55]

Sixty-one percent of Texas residents use electricity to heat their home, which resulted in a powerful surge in demand when the storm hit on February 13. The demand peak was estimated at 76.8 GW on February 15, when Dallas temperatures dropped to –2°F. This exceeded ERCOT's worst-case estimated demand of 59 GW by 18 GW.

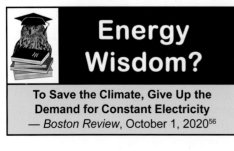

To Save the Climate, Give Up the Demand for Constant Electricity
— *Boston Review*, October 1, 2020[56]

Adding to the problem, when temperatures dropped to single digits on February 15, gas generating facilities began to shut down due to a lack of gas supply from the extreme cold. Texas gas production dropped 45 percent, causing 20 GW of gas generation outages. Gas systems were not weatherized and failed during the event. Texas wind resources, with 31 GW of nameplate capacity, produced only about 2 GW of output during the crisis. All other generators were running flat out, but there wasn't enough supply to meet demand.

The operator in the ERCOT control room began shedding load at 1:23 a.m. on Monday, February 15. By 1:51 a.m., system frequency had dropped to 59.4 Hz. The operator ordered several more load sheds, removing electricity from millions of residents and producing a controlled outage of 10.5 GW. The system was only minutes away from

Electricity Frequency and Voltage Control[57]

Reliable operation of power systems is complex. Today, it is not cost effective to store large quantities of electricity. Therefore, electricity must be produced and used the instant it is needed. Failure to match generation to demand (or load) causes system instability, which can damage equipment or shut down some or all of the system. Special measures must be used to match generation to demand and to control frequency and voltages.

The normal frequency of the AC power system in North America is 60 cycles per second, or 60 Hertz (Hz), with 50 Hz used in Europe. Most residential electricity sockets provide 120 volts in North America, with 230 volts common in Europe. When generation exceeds demand, system frequency rises. When load exceeds the power generated, system frequency falls, a more serious situation that can cause system shutdown. Changes in demand can also cause voltages to increase or decrease. High voltages can exceed the insulation capabilities of equipment and cause dangerous electric arcs. Low voltages can cause damage to motors and electronic equipment and result in system collapse. During the Texas electricity crisis on February 15, 2021, a huge demand for power caused a drop in system frequency from 60 Hz to 59.4 Hz, triggering generator shutdowns and causing 70 hours of blackouts for more than four million Texans.[58]

Many processes help to maintain the frequency and voltage of power systems. Turbine generators of coal, gas, nuclear, and hydroelectric power plants contain inertial energy in the rotating mass of the turbine that resists changes in system frequency. Governors at each plant sense turbine-shaft speed and change the steam input to adjust the speed back to the desired level. A central balancing authority adjusts the output of system generators automatically and manually to maintain system frequency. Voltage is controlled by automatic voltage regulators at each generator and reactors in the system. In cases of very high demand, operators shut down portions of system load with local rolling blackouts to bring generation and demand back into balance.

The intermittent output of wind and solar arrays reduces electrical system stability. The erratic output of these systems must by compensated for by ramping or diminishing the output of backup natural gas or hydroelectric generators. In addition, wind and solar don't have the inherent inertial stability of the rotating turbines of steam generators.

a complete collapse. If this had occurred, it may have taken weeks to restart the system. Deaths as a result of the blackout could have numbered in the thousands.[59]

Many have discussed the causes of the Texas 2021 blackout. One conclusion is certain. The system did not have nearly enough baseload capacity from reliable coal, gas, or nuclear generators. In 2020, Texas got 21.6 percent of its electricity from wind and solar arrays,[60] but these were useless during the storm. From 2010 to 2020, Texas added 20 GW of intermittent wind capacity,[61] while closing 8.5 GW of coal capacity.[62] The results, unfortunately, proved lethal for Texas residents.

Although not widely reported, Oklahoma suffered similar power outages during that same storm. Over the last decade, Oklahoma constructed numerous wind arrays, which provided 35 percent of the state's electricity in 2020.[63] But these systems shut down during the storm, a major factor in four days of statewide blackouts. On February 16, Oklahoma Governor Kevin Stitt commented,

> Basically, right now, wind energy, we are not getting the wind, some of the stuff is frozen, we've got ice on the propellers.[64]

CALIFORNIA FOLLY

California is the epicenter for Climatism in the United States. The state established the first renewable portfolio standard (RPS) in 2002, mandating that 20 percent of electricity be from renewable sources by 2017. Governor Arnold Schwarzenegger accelerated the 20 percent RPS requirement to 2010 and instituted a 33 percent requirement by 2020.[65] Then on September 10, 2018, Governor Jerry Brown signed an executive order mandating 100 percent zero-carbon electricity by 2045.[66]

California achieved its interim renewable goal in 2018, generating 34 percent of its electricity from renewable sources. In 2020, California generated about 276.5 GWh of electricity, with 70 percent produced in-state and 30 percent imported from surrounding states. Of the power generated in-state, natural gas provided 48.3 percent, with the remainder from solar (15.4%), hydroelectric (11.2%), nuclear (8.5%), wind (7.2%), geothermal (5.9%), and biomass and other fuels (3.5%).[68]

The Climate Apocalypse

I Moved My Family Off-Grid in Rural Alaska to Prepare for a Zombie Apocalypse
— *The Sun*, November 8, 2021[67]

The transition from traditional power plants to renewables has been a top priority for the state for 18 years. By November 2020, California's grid contained more than six GW of wind and 13 GW of solar capacity, plus an additional 11 GW of customer-sited solar.[69] The state retired 11 coal-fired power plants and converted the last three coal plants to burn biomass fuel by 2019.[70] Electricity output from natural gas declined 24 percent from 2012 to 2020.[71] The San Onofre Nuclear Generating Station closed in 2013, and the last nuclear plant, the Diablo Canyon Power Plant, is scheduled to close in 2025.[72] But at the current level of 42 percent renewable electricity (including hydropower), California has too much intermittent generation and too little reliable power capacity.

During August 14–19, 2020, California experienced a statewide heat wave with temperatures 10 to 20 degrees above normal. During peak days, the California Independent System Operator (CAISO) usually relies on electricity imports. But in this case, high temperatures in neighboring states, and the derating of a connection to the Pacific Northwest, reduced the available power for import. CAISO issued a Flex Alert warning on August 13, calling for voluntary conservation the afternoon and evening of August 14.[73]

At 2:57 p.m. on August 14, a gas plant generating 475 MW went offline due to plant trouble. Between 3 p.m. and 6 p.m. CAISO struggled to maintain reserve capacity, while solar electricity output declined. On August afternoons, solar arrays provide more than 20 percent of California's electricity, but that output disappears by evening. At 6:38 p.m., CAISO could no longer meet demand and ordered two load sheds totaling about 1 GW, removing power from almost 500,000 California residences and businesses.

On August 15, CAISO again was unable to meet the demand for electricity. Late afternoon storm clouds reduced solar output, and a decline in wind generation reduced system reserves. At 6:13 p.m., CAISO ordered rolling blackouts to allow the system to recover. The widespread blackouts on August 14 and 15 were the first in California since 2001.

The root cause analysis report published by CAISO in January 2021 listed several causes for the blackouts. Among these was the assumption that wind and solar resources would drop by only 80 percent from their average output, which was too optimistic. CAISO also planned for peak demand, which occurred in the late afternoon, which is typical for system planning. But the worst demand-supply imbalance was actually after peak demand and

If You *Like* Your Blackouts, You Can *Keep* Your Blackouts

"Gaps" in Renewable Energy Led to Blackouts for Millions of Californians, Gov Newsom Says
— *Daily Caller*, August 17, 2020[74]

late in the day, when the sun was setting and solar output was quickly dropping.[75]

In any case, with 42 percent of electricity coming from intermittent renewables, California's grid has a shortage of always-on generator capacity. The state announced the opening of five new gas plants in August 2021 to build grid margin. As the Brick and Thernstrom

Gee, Ya Think So?

California to Open 5 Natural Gas Plants to Avoid Blackouts
— *FOX26NEWS*, August 20, 2021[76]

analysis predicts, California must continue to operate most of its traditional natural gas or nuclear plants to maintain power system reliability, raising the amount of capacity to be maintained and forcing electricity costs to rise, with greater renewable penetration.

Indeed, California's electricity prices are rising. From 2008 to 2021, California's electricity prices rose 52 percent, compared to an average US price increase of 14 percent. In 2021, the state's residential electricity price exceeded 22 cents per kWh, almost double the price of other western states and amongst the highest in the US.[77]

Note that recent rolling blackouts happened in the leading wind states. Texas generated the most electricity from wind, with Oklahoma third, and California in sixth place. Reliance on intermittent wind resources increases the risk of rolling blackouts.

ARE GRID-SCALE BATTERIES THE ANSWER?

But renewable energy proponents claim that storage solves the problem of wind and solar intermittency. Advocates propose that if electricity can be stored in grid-scale batteries during periods of high wind and solar output and then discharged during times of low output, wind, solar, and storage may be able to completely replace coal, gas, and nuclear power plants that generate electricity around the clock.

News headlines declare that batteries are rewiring the grid and obsoleting hydrocarbon fuels. Politicians embrace storage, such as US Senator Susan Collins of Maine, who says,

> Next-generation energy storage devices will help enhance the efficiency and reliability of our electric grid, reduce energy costs, and promote the adoption of renewable resources.[78]

Governments are introducing subsidies and mandates to promote electricity storage in an effort to compensate for wind and solar intermittency.

Batteries serve as effective tools in modern electricity systems to balance supply and

Headlines Touting Grid-Scale Batteries

"Giant Batteries and Cheap Solar Power Are Shoving Fossil Fuels Off the Grid"
—*Science*, July 11, 2019[79]

"A Deluge of Batteries is About to Rewire the Power Grid"
—*Bloomberg*, August 2, 2019[80]

"The Batteries that Could Make Fossil Fuels Obsolete"
—*BBC*, December 17, 2021[81]

demand and enhance grid stability. Batteries help maintain grid frequency and voltage within needed limits. They can charge during periods of low demand, when electricity is less expensive, and discharge in periods of high demand. But batteries have not yet been widely used to store excess electricity generated by wind and solar arrays.

Grid-scale batteries are rated for power capacity and energy capacity. Power capacity is the maximum electrical output a battery can deliver at any point in time, measured in megawatts (or gigawatts). Energy capacity is the maximum electrical energy that a battery can deliver from being fully charged to discharged in megawatt-hours (or gigawatt-hours). Duration is the length of time that a battery can discharge. Typical duration times for grid-scale batteries are two to four hours.

In 2021, about 70 percent of US grid storage was provided by pumped storage systems. Pumped storage uses electricity to pump water from a low-elevation reservoir up to a high-elevation reservoir to store energy. When electricity is needed, water is released from the high-elevation reservoir, driving turbines to generate electricity as it cascades back down to the low-elevation reservoir. But special terrain conditions are needed to develop pumped storage systems, which are not available in most locations. Batteries are the leading technology for deployment of grid storage.

Despite the headlines, very little of today's electricity uses storage. In 2021, the electricity system of the US generated 4.1 million GWh of electrical energy. But the amount of electricity stored was only about 32 GWh. The amount stored in grid-scale batteries was only about 9 GWh. Only about two watt-hours in *every million* watt-hours generated was stored

ENERGY CRISIS SOLVED?

"Consider the world's biggest battery factory, the one Tesla built in Nevada. It would take 500 years for that factory to make enough batteries to store just one day's worth of America's electricity needs."
— Mark Mills, September 14, 2020[82]

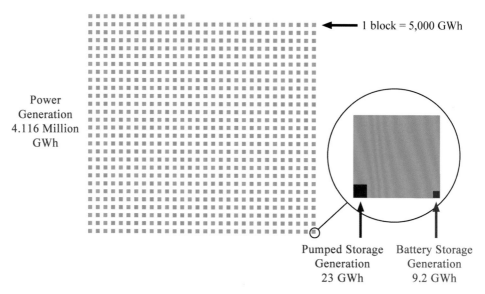

1 block = 5,000 GWh

Power
Generation
4.116 Million
GWh

Pumped Storage   Battery Storage
Generation   Generation
23 GWh   9.2 GWh

2021 US Electricity Generation and Grid-Scale Storage. US electrical energy generation represented as more than 800 blocks of 5,000 gigawatt-hours. The electricity stored by pumped storage and grid-scale batteries in 2021 is approximated as only a tiny portion of one of the blocks. (EIA, National Hydropower Association, 2022)[83]

in batteries.[84] Consulting firm Wood MacKenzie places global grid-scale battery energy-storage capacity at about 28 GWh for 2021, or roughly three times the US total.[85] This means that less than one watt-hour in every million watt-hours of electricity generated globally is stored in grid-scale batteries. But utilities are ramping investment for grid storage, urged on by political leaders.

Neoen, a French renewable energy company, completed the first phase of construction of the Hornsdale Power Reserve in the province of South Australia in November 2017. Hornsdale—a 100 MW power capacity, 129 MWh energy capacity system using Tesla lithium-ion batteries—was hailed as "the world's first big battery." A 50 percent system expansion was completed in September 2020.[86]

California currently leads global efforts to deploy high-capacity batteries. Grid-scale battery projects of 100–300 MW of power capacity were completed or nearing completion in Long Beach, San Diego, San Francisco, and Moss Landing, south of San José, during 2020–2021.[87] As of May 2021, California, Massachusetts, New Jersey, New York, Oregon, and Virginia had set energy-storage targets or requirements. Other states plan to integrate storage into requirements for power systems.[88] Florida Power & Light began construction of the Manatee Storage Center in South Florida in 2020. When completed, this battery system, with 409 MW of power capacity and 900 MWh of energy capacity, would be the world's largest.[89] The Energy Information Administration estimates that US grid-scale battery capacity will increase to about 10 GW of power capacity and 20 GWh of energy capacity by 2023.[91]

GREENHOUSE GAS HORROR!
Electricity Needed to Mine Bitcoin is More than Used by 'Entire Countries'
— *The Guardian*, August 20, 2021[90]

The International Energy Agency reports rapidly rising investment in battery storage around the world, led by the US, China, and Europe. China announced plans for a 10-fold increase in battery capacity by 2025. More than 90 percent of installations over the last five years have been lithium-ion technology, driven by steeply declining costs.[92] But the idea that batteries combined with wind and solar generators can replace traditional power plants to achieve 100-percent zero-carbon electricity faces huge cost, duration, and scale obstacles.

Batteries consume electricity. Only about 85 percent of the original charging electricity returns to the grid after discharge from grid-scale batteries. Batteries also suffer from short lifespans. Wind and solar arrays can operate for about 20 to 25 years, while the lifespans of coal, gas, and nuclear power plants typically exceed 40 years. Grid-scale batteries last only about 10–15 years. Operators will need to buy storage twice to match wind and solar lifespans. These factors raise the cost of electricity from renewable-plus-battery systems.

The short storage duration of today's grid-scale batteries looms as a major cost barrier. Consider the plans of the state of New York for offshore wind and battery storage. The state is moving forward to construct 9,000 MW of wind arrays in the Atlantic Ocean southeast of New York City by 2035 at a cost expected to be over $9 billion.[93] The state hopes to back this up with 3,000 MW of battery power capacity, which, at a cost of $2,500 per kW, will likely cost about $7.5 billion.[94] But this planned battery deployment is not adequate to remove the wind intermittency.

If the capacity factor of the wind system is 33 percent, the planned storage will be able to deliver the average wind output, but only for about two to four hours. To maintain the wind output for a full day when the wind isn't blowing, 36,000 MW of two-hour storage, or 18,000 MW of four-hour storage, would be needed, at a cost of five or 10 times the cost of the wind array itself. Since several days of low wind is common, even a day of battery backup will be unable to maintain power availability.

Seasonality of wind and solar output is also a major issue. Data from the California

Independent System Operator shows that wind and solar generation during December and January produces only about half of the output of the peak summer months.[95] Since batteries that can hold electricity for months do not exist, additional wind and solar capacity must be deployed to operate during winter months of low output, requiring additional infrastructure costs. But remember that during the cold wave in Texas in February 2021, wind and solar only delivered six percent of their rated output.

Above all the cost issues, the scale of investment in batteries to back up wind and solar would be huge. Matt Howell, CEO of Tomago Aluminum of New South Wales, Australia, pointed out that the lauded Tesla batteries of the Hornsdale Power Reserve could power his aluminum smelter for "less than eight minutes."[97] The IEA's *Net Zero by 2050* roadmap calls for 3,100 MW of battery power capacity by 2050 (about 12,400 MWh of energy capacity), an increase of 172 times the world's 2020 deployment.[98] But this huge amount of storage would still be able to store only about one watt-hour in every thousand watt-hours generated globally in 2050, wholly insufficient to make up for wind and solar intermittency.

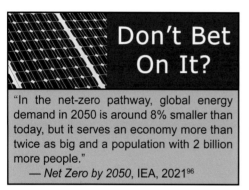

Don't Bet On It?

"In the net-zero pathway, global energy demand in 2050 is around 8% smaller than today, but it serves an economy more than twice as big and a population with 2 billion more people."
— *Net Zero by 2050*, IEA, 2021[96]

EUROPE'S BIOMASS EMISSIONS ERROR

When Thomas Edison established the Pearl Street Station power plant in New York City in 1892, he used coal for fuel, not wood. Wood could not compete with the cost of coal in 1892 and still can't today. But burning biomass is widely regarded as sustainable and promoted as a solution for climate change, particularly in Europe.

In 2018, combustion of biomass, biofuels, and waste provided 59 percent of Europe's renewable energy and 20 percent of Europe's total energy production. Most biomass fuel provided energy for heating applications. About 70 million homes in Europe still use wood fuel for heating.[99] Biomass, biogas, and waste produced about six percent of Europe's electricity. Since 2006, bioenergy production is up 66 percent.[100]

Six percent of Europe's electricity produced by bioenergy is a small share overall, but it is higher in some nations, such as Denmark. Biomass provided 18 percent of Denmark's electricity in 2019. Since 2000, Denmark's coal-fired power decreased 80 percent, but

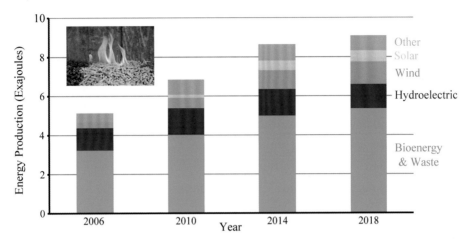

Europe's Energy from Renewable Sources 2006–2018. Bioenergy dominates primary production of energy from renewable sources in Europe. Image of burning wood-pellet biomass. (Eurostat, EurObservER, 2009–2020)[101]

biomass electricity increased by a factor of five, replacing much of the coal output.[102] About three-quarters of the biomass consumed is wood, with most of it imported.

But the sustainability of biomass is questionable, despite the popular notion that "if it grows, it must be sustainable." Burning wood emits more carbon dioxide than burning coal. A 2012 study by Synapse Energy Economics estimated that a typical smokestack of a biomass plant emitted about 1.67 tons of CO_2 per megawatt-hour of electricity generated, or 50 to 85 percent more than emissions from a coal-fired plant. The carbon dioxide emissions from a biomass plant exceed triple the CO_2 emissions from a natural gas plant.[103]

Despite these well-known numbers, neither the US Environmental Protection Agency (EPA) nor the European Commission (EC) counts CO_2 emissions from facilities that burn wood. The EPA stated in 2010,

> However, in the long run, the CO_2 emitted from biomass-based fuels combustion does not increase atmospheric CO_2 concentrations, assuming the biogenic carbon emitted is offset by the uptake of CO_2 resulting from the growth of new biomass.[104]

The EC ruled in 2007, "Biomass is considered as CO_2 neutral. An emission factor of 0 shall be applied to biomass."[105]

The assertion that burning wood is carbon neutral originated from the 1996 Greenhouse Gas Inventory paper from the Intergovernmental Panel on Climate Change (IPCC). The IPCC assumed that, as trees grow, they absorb CO_2 equal to the amount released when burned.[106] If correct, substitution of wood for coal would reduce net emissions.

But a 2011 opinion by the European Environment Agency Scientific Committee warned of a "serious accounting error" in estimates of greenhouse emissions. The carbon-neutral assumption fails to account for CO_2 absorbed by vegetation that grows naturally on land not used for biofuel production.[107] In addition, forests felled to provide wood chips for power plants immediately release large quantities of carbon dioxide, but decades of tree regrowth would be needed to reabsorb released CO_2. Substitution of wood for coal in power plants actually *increases* CO_2 emissions.

One of the largest industrial emitters of carbon dioxide in Europe is the Drax Power Station in North Yorkshire, England. The Drax plant produces 3,900 MW of power, more than six percent of the UK's electricity supply. Until 2013, Drax used coal for fuel.

In the name of cutting CO_2 emissions, four of the six Drax generating units were converted to burn wood over the last seven years, at a cost of £700 million ($833 million).[108] Seventeen trains, with 28 cars each, bring 20,000 tons of wood pellets to Drax each day. Hailed as "the biggest decarbonization project in Europe," Drax now consumes more than seven million tons of wood pellets per year, shipped 3,000 miles from the US and Canada.[109]

Thousands of square miles of forest feed the voracious Drax plant, with acres of forest felled each day. Replanted trees will take 40 to 50 years to grow. Despite the decarbonization claims, the CO_2 emitted from Drax today far exceeds the CO_2 exhausted when coal fuel was burned.

Because it is regarded as zero emitting, burning biomass in Europe is heavily subsidized. Drax received £832 million ($990 million) in renewable subsidies in 2020 from the UK government and received more than £7.4 billion ($8.8 billion) from 2012 to 2020.[111] Coal-to-biomass plant conversions are underway across the continent. Europe now spends more than €6 billion per year for biomass plant subsidies.[112]

As a fuel, wood contains less energy and is usually more expensive than coal or natural gas. According to the EIA, coal produces about 25 percent more energy per ton than wood.[113] Since wood is less dense than coal, more than twice the volume of wood is required to produce the same electrical output.

Back To The Future?

Europe's Renewable Energy Policy is Built on Burning American Trees
— *Vox*, March 4, 2019[110]

As a result of the biomass emissions error, European claims of CO_2 emissions reductions are wrong. Research from the Woodwell Climate Research Center concludes that the 26-percent decline in Europe's CO_2 emissions between 1990 and 2019, reported by the EU, would be only a decline of 15 percent if biomass-combustion emissions were counted.[115]

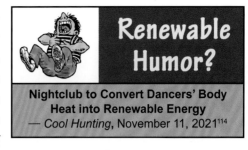

Renewable Humor?

Nightclub to Convert Dancers' Body Heat into Renewable Energy — *Cool Hunting*, November 11, 2021[114]

Nevertheless, Europe continues to expand the use of biomass electricity. EC Executive Vice President for the European Green Deal Frans Timmermans stated in 2021,

> To be perfectly blunt with you, biomass will have to be part of our energy mix if we want to remove our dependency on fossil fuels.[116]

European nations won't acknowledge the obvious emissions error because, without biomass, already tough emissions goals would become impossible to meet.

Led by Europe, more than 60,000 acres of trees are cut down and burned each year worldwide. This quantity is forecasted to double by 2027. Rising biomass combustion cuts down forests and boosts the cost of electricity, without any real reduction in carbon dioxide emissions.

100 PERCENT RENEWABLE: FUTILE QUEST

The world pursues a futile effort to obtain 100 percent of its generated electricity from renewable sources. Since electricity from nuclear is not favored, vast arrays of wind and solar systems, backed up by battery storage, must be deployed to try to achieve the energy transition to renewable generation. But except in locations with abundant hydroelectric power—such as Brazil, Canada, Norway, or Washington State—intermittency, land requirements, and cost will make this goal impossible to achieve.

The intermittency of wind and solar looms as the largest problem. Wind output varies erratically with wind conditions. Solar arrays output electricity for only about 10 hours per day on sunny days. How can always-on electricity systems rely on wind and solar unreliables?

As renewable energy penetration increases, utilities must still maintain about 90 percent of traditional coal, gas, and nuclear power plants, but run them at lower utilization rates to back up wind and solar. Electricity prices will double and triple as renewable penetration

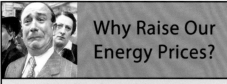

Why Raise Our Energy Prices?

Crippling Cost of Ontario's Obsession with Wind Power: 71% Increase in Power Bills
— *StopTheseThings*, October 2, 2021[117]

increases. Look for rate-payer revolts long before 100 percent is reached.

Batteries are the hope of renewable advocates, but they are decades away from a meaningful contribution. Globally, less than one watt-hour in every million watt-hours of electricity is stored in today's grid-scale batteries. This will remain small by 2050, even with impossibly optimistic build-out projections. Today's grid-scale batteries only store power for about four hours, and wind and solar output drops by 50 percent from summer months to winter months in most nations.

Wind and solar arrays require 50 to 250 times as much land as coal, natural gas, and nuclear systems. Vast amounts of land will be required for wind and solar arrays to supply even 50 percent of electricity output. Transmission lines must be constructed to reach remote renewable locations. Look for rising community opposition to growing land demands for wind, solar, and transmission.

The cost of high penetration of wind, solar, and batteries will become prohibitive. Even without battery deployment, European nations that use the most wind and solar suffer double the electricity costs of neighboring nations. Electricity prices in US states using the most wind are rising much faster than the national average. The short lifespan of wind, solar, and battery systems further adds to their cost disadvantage.

Renewable advocates claim that if we only spend trillions of dollars and euros on wind, solar, and grid-scale batteries, we can stop global warming and "save the planet." But not only must your electricity be green, you need to switch from gas appliances to electric appliances, as we'll discuss in the next chapter.

CHAPTER 6

BUT I'D LIKE TO KEEP MY GAS STOVE

"Every time I go near the stove, the dog howls."
—PHYLLIS DILLER, COMEDIAN[1]

Gas appliances characterize modern society. Gas usage has been rising rapidly in wealthy nations for the last 60 years. Roughly half a billion residences in North America and Europe use stoves, furnaces, and water heaters powered by natural gas, delivered by vast networks of gas pipelines.

Gas usage is also expanding in emerging nations. According to the World Bank, the use of gas fuels reached 37 percent of the population in developing nations in 2019, exceeding the use of biomass from wood, charcoal, and dung for the first time.[2] Canisters of liquid petroleum gas, a fuel composed of primarily propane along with small amounts of butane and propylene, deliver fuel for appliances in developing nations that lack gas lines to homes.

But renewable advocates seek to eliminate the use of gas for residential heating and cooking because of fear of human-caused climate change. People must be "encouraged" to switch from gas appliances to electric appliances, with electricity generated by wind and solar arrays, or else bans must be imposed.

RISING NATURAL GAS USAGE AROUND THE WORLD

During the last 60 years, society adopted gas as a primary fuel for businesses and residences. From 1965 to 2020, global annual consumption of natural gas and other gas fuels increased by a factor of six. Over the 20 years since 2000, gas consumption was flat in Europe but rose in North America (37%) and South America (48%), and it more than doubled in Africa, Asia Pacific, and the Middle East.[3] Natural gas and propane now supply the majority of energy for home heating and cooking in developed nations.

Gas usage is pervasive in Europe and the United States. In Europe in 2019, natural gas provided 38 percent of fuel for heating homes; another 14 percent came from propane and other petroleum fuels for a total of 52 percent. Twenty-eight percent of European home heating came from renewable energy sources, with wood supplying the bulk of this at 22 percent. Heat pumps, solar, and geothermal delivered only about six percent of the energy for residential heating in Europe. Similarly, natural gas and petroleum fuels provided 53 percent of the energy used for water heaters and 44 percent of the energy used for cooking. Electricity supplied 49 percent of Europe's energy for cooking, along with 100 percent of

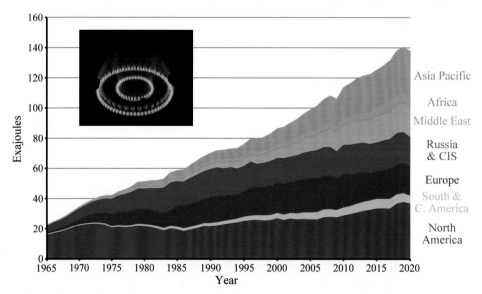

World Natural Gas Consumption 1965–2020. Total world and regional annual gas consumption in exajoules of energy. Image of liquid propane gas flame. (BP, 2021)[4]

the energy for lights and other appliances.[5]

In the US, natural gas and petroleum products (heating oil, kerosene, and propane) delivered 50 percent of the energy for residences in 2020. Natural gas is used in about 58 percent of US homes. Renewable sources, including geothermal energy, solar energy, and wood accounted for seven percent of home-energy consumption. Electricity provided 43 percent, with much of that for lighting and electric appliances.[6]

The use of natural gas has been a tremendous boon to humanity. In the mid-1900s, many US homes burned coal. Every winter, fallen snow in Chicago was blackened within a few days by coal dust exhausted from furnaces. Homeowners employed spring cleaning each year to wash coal dust from inside walls. Gas furnaces soon replaced coal, oil, and wood boilers in homes, vastly reducing pollution and ending the need for spring cleaning. Gas furnaces and stoves continue to replace wood burners around the world, reducing particle emissions by a factor of more than one thousand per unit of energy and at lower cost.[7]

Today, three billion people still do not have access to modern fuels for heating and cooking. Where gas lines do not exist, containers of liquefied petroleum gas (LPG), primarily propane, bring modern energy to households in need. As a result of the Shale Revolution, US propane gas production tripled from 2007 to 2020. In 2020, two-thirds of US propane production was exported, with China, India, and Japan as the biggest importers.[8]

In 2016, Prime Minister Narendra Modi of India announced a program to bring LPG to 50 million low-income families. Eleven thousand LPG gas-canister distribution centers opened across the nation in the last six years. Clean-burning gas has been made available to tens of millions of Indian families.[9]

The adoption of gas has reduced air pollution more than any other energy source. But despite the benefits of low-cost household energy and reduced air pollution, the global obsession with carbon dioxide seeks to eliminate gas fuels for home use.

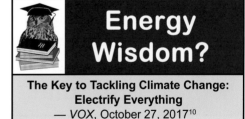

Energy Wisdom?

The Key to Tackling Climate Change: Electrify Everything
— *VOX*, October 27, 2017[10]

THE ELECTRIFICATION MOVEMENT

Historically, the term "electrification" meant extending the electrical grid to rural areas to provide power to homes without electricity. But the renewable-energy movement has redefined electrification to mean electrify everything. Environmental groups demand elimination of all forms of hydrocarbon combustion, such as gasoline- and diesel-fueled vehicles, and gas and propane used for heating and cooking. These would be replaced by plug-in electric vehicles and electric heat pumps, stoves, and water heaters, supplied by a grid that uses wind and solar generators, rather than gas.

But homeowners often prefer gas appliances. Gas furnaces tend cost less than heat pumps in northern regions. Burners on gas stoves boil water faster than electric-coil stoves, and gas-stove heat can be shut off immediately. Propane deliveries by truck provide excellent low-cost energy for rural locations not connected to the gas network. And we all love our propane barbecue grills. So bans will be required to force the electrification of homes.

In 2020, more than 90 percent of California homes used gas, with almost 70 percent using gas stoves.[11] But in July 2019, Berkeley, California, became the first US city to ban natural gas appliances in the construction of new single- and multi-family homes. By the end of 2021, more than 50 California cities had enacted bans or restrictions on gas appliances in new buildings, including the major cities of San Francisco and San Jose. Over 12 percent of the state's population lives in areas restricting gas construction.[12]

California residents can pay significantly more in utility bills for electric appliances. In 2020, the average price of natural gas supplied to homes in California was $13.64 per million British Thermal Units (Btu). For a new 95 percent efficiency natural-gas furnace or water heater, this translates to an actual cost of $14.35 per million Btu. California's 2020 residential electricity price was 20.51 cents per kWh, or a cost of $60.11 per million Btu.[13] So California residents pay over four times as much to operate electric stoves, water heaters, or electric baseboard heaters, compared to gas appliances.

Heat pumps provide lower-cost operation than electric baseboard heaters but still can't

California's Cities Lead the Way to a Gas-Free Future
— *Sierra Club*, December 13, 2021[14]

compare to gas appliances. Heat pumps use a refrigerant to absorb heat from outside air (or below ground) even during cold weather and then transfer the heat to indoor air. But a 2017 study by the New York State Energy Research and Development Authority, a green-energy advocate, concluded that,

At current installed costs and energy prices, only around … 4% of the state's residential/commercial heating, ventilation, and air conditioning (HVAC) load … could cost effectively switch to using heat pumps.[15]

So mandates must be used to force a shift to electric appliances, which will reduce flexibility and significantly raise costs.

A battle rages in the US over gas appliances. Outside of California, more than 25 cities had established bans on new gas hookups by the end of 2021. In December 2021, the New York City council voted to ban natural gas in new buildings.[16] Municipalities in seven states—California, Colorado, Massachusetts, New York, Oregon, Vermont, and Washington—have established bans on gas in new construction. But, in opposition, 19 other states recently established statewide laws preventing local governments from banning natural gas, propane, or "impairing a consumer's ability to choose a utility service."[17] Another four states have proposed legislation that would prohibit bans by local governments.[18]

The electrification movement is growing in cities around the world where government leaders pursue Net Zero. Effective January 1, 2022, Vancouver, Canada, requires space and water heating to be zero emissions in new residential construction, proposing to use expensive heat pumps and renewable natural gas (RNG).[19] RNG comes from landfills or bio-gas facilities but is in limited supply and triple the price of conventional natural gas in Vancouver.[20]

Seven European cities joined together to form the Decarb City Pipes 2050 project to transform residential heating and cooking. Bilbao, Bratislava, Dublin, Munich, Rotterdam, Vienna, and Winterthur pledge to become carbon neutral by 2050.[21] But the largest efforts to eliminate gas usage come from the Netherlands and the United Kingdom, two nations with among the highest penetration of natural gas in homes in the world.

GAS-FREE DUTCH AND BRITISH?

In the Netherlands, 92 percent of homes use gas heat, and 83 percent of heating energy used in buildings comes from natural gas. Only seven percent of energy comes from electricity. UK heating energy in buildings comes from gas (78%) and electric (12%).[22] But both countries now pursue quests to completely transform energy use in buildings.

The UK Parliament established a goal to reach Net Zero by 2050 as a modification of its Climate Change Act in May 2019. The nation intends to remove carbon dioxide emissions

Green Policies Require Coercion

Ban Gas Boilers in New Homes by 2025, Says Committee on Climate Change

"UK homes are not fit for the future."
— *The Guardian*, February 20, 2019[23]

from power generation, transportation, industry, and homes, and to capture CO_2 from the atmosphere as an offset. The UK government expects a cost of 1–2 percent of GDP each year until 2050, as estimated by the UK Climate Change Committee (CCC).[24]

According to the CCC, homes emit 14 percent of UK emissions from heating, with another six percent from electricity use. Of the 29 million homes in the UK today, about one million burn wood or biomass waste for heating. These are considered to be low emissions, even though they emit triple the CO_2 and more than 100 times the particles of gas-heated homes. Almost no homes use heat pumps or district heating.

The CCC recommends that all UK homes shift to heat pumps and district heating, install high levels of insulating material, and favor wood construction over concrete and steel to reduce emissions. The CCC proposes the use of financial incentives for homeowners and government-imposed regulatory standards to achieve the transition. They also recommend that no new homes be connected to the gas grid after 2025.[25]

But the cost of this housing transition will be very high. Michael Kelly, a professor at the University of Cambridge, estimated that the cost to reduce home carbon emissions by 80 percent using heat pumps and extensive insulation would be £75,000 per home. This would total more than £2.1 trillion by 2050 for the nation.[26] It's clear that British residents don't want to pay for this transition. A poll commissioned by Net Zero Watch in 2021 found that 58 percent of UK adults would not pay higher taxes on their energy bills to reach net-zero targets.[27] Elimination of gas heating and a forced transition to electric heating will impose high costs and reduce the standard of living of British residents.

The Netherlands passed the Energy Transition Progress Act in July 2018, mandating that new buildings could no longer be connected to the gas network.[28] In addition to enacting bans on new construction, the nation intends to disconnect gas from eight million homes by 2050. This requires more than 250,000 disconnections each year. Since passage of the 2019 Climate Act, 10,000 homes have been disconnected from gas.[30] In support, in 2020, Amsterdam announced its ambition to become *aardgasvrij*, or gas free, by 2050.

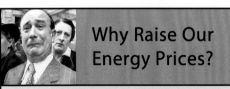

Why Raise Our Energy Prices?

No One Is Being Honest About the Effect of Zero on Britain's Poorest Families

"To replace the gas with electrical power would imply a rise in household bills of 160 percent."

— *Telegraph*, November 4, 2021[29]

The Dutch people appear to be all in for becoming gas-free but don't know how to get there. Installing a heat pump costs up to €20,000 and produces higher heating bills than gas. Geothermal and hydrogen-fueled systems don't exist today.

District heating systems provide heat from a central source through insulated pipe networks to homes and businesses. But only five percent of Dutch homes today use district heating.[31] Converting to district heat will require massive efforts to install both underground pipes and unsightly above-ground pipes, which will mar

District heating pipes in Gelsenkirchen, Germany.[32]

the beauty of Dutch cities. District heating systems also need renewable fuel for the central boiler, which is usually more expensive than gas. There are no cost-effective, large-scale energy sources that can eliminate gas heating in the Netherlands. Like in the UK, gas-free efforts will reduce the standard of living of the Dutch people, all for an undetectable effect on global temperatures.

We'll see if citizens of these countries rebel against net-zero demands. But since climate change fears may not be enough to convince the public of the need to eliminate gas fuel, opponents increasingly raise the spectre that gas appliances generate dangerous pollution.

INDOOR POLLUTION FEARS

An increasing number of papers and articles claim that gas appliances, especially your stove, cause harmful indoor and outdoor air pollution. Green-energy advocates warn that pollution from a gas stove poses an unseen danger to you and your children. They claim that a switch to electric appliances will protect your health and also save the climate.

A 2020 paper from the University of California at Los Angeles (UCLA) argued that gas appliances, including stoves, furnaces, and water heaters, posed a health hazard to residents. The authors warned that gas appliances produce unhealthy levels of indoor carbon monoxide (CO) and nitrogen dioxide (NO_2) pollution, along with dangerous levels of outdoor small particles ($PM_{2.5}$). They recommended that California gas appliances be transitioned to electric, claiming an annual reduction in health costs of $3.5 billion from the switch.[33]

But the evidence provided by the UCLA paper does not support the assertion that gas appliances cause harmful indoor pollution. For example, the paper cites three peer-reviewed studies to support its warnings about NO_2 pollution, but *none* of the studies found evidence of unhealthy emissions from gas stoves.[34] This UCLA paper, along with

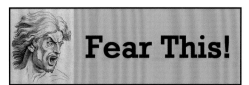

Kill Your Gas Stove

"It's bad for you and the environment. If you can avoid it, you probably should."
— *The Atlantic,* October 15, 2020[35]

other scientific literature, does not support the claim that stove-emitted CO or NO_2 pose a health menace.

Gas furnaces and water heaters should be vented to the outside air, preventing indoor pollution from these sources. Indoor emissions from properly operating gas stoves are in the low parts-per-billion (ppb) levels, below minimum levels for adverse health effects. Despite the headlines, residents should be confident that their gas appliances do not pose a threat to their health.

Weak Claims about Dangerous Pollution from Gas Appliances

A 2020 study by researchers at the University of California at Los Angeles, titled "Effects of Residential Gas Appliances on Indoor and Outdoor Air Quality and Public Health in California," claimed that pollutants produced from gas appliances such as CO, NO_2, and $PM_{2.5}$ "can be detrimental to human health." The study recommended that the state phase out the use of gas appliances.[36]

Regarding indoor air pollution, the state of California requires furnaces and water heaters to use outside vents, making stoves the only appliance that might be a concern for indoor air. But the model results and the references cited by the UCLA paper are not supported by evidence that indoor levels of either CO or NO_2 from stoves are unhealthy, or that emissions of $PM_{2.5}$ from gas appliances to the outside air are significant.

The California paper's own model results do not show that CO emissions exceed either California or EPA standards, despite the claims of the paper. Carbon monoxide poisonings in the US have been declining since 1980, with US gas use rising more than 50 percent. CO detectors are essential for raising an alarm in the case of faulty operation, but residents can have confidence that their gas stoves are not emitting hazardous levels of carbon monoxide.[37]

Nitrous dioxide can be produced by stove burner flames, but the good news is that the NO_2 produced is at low parts-per-billion levels. The study projected that two hours of simultaneous burner and oven use could produce an indoor NO_2 level of 34 ppb. But this level is less that the EPA National Ambient Air Quality Standard level of 53 ppb. EPA states that, for NO_2 levels below 50 ppb, "no health impacts are expected for air quality in this range."[38]

The California paper contends that the elimination of particle emissions ($PM_{2.5}$) from gas appliances into the outdoor air would save 354 lives and $3.5 billion in health costs per year. But these claims are based on the false assertion that low levels of particle pollution cause premature death. Elimination of gas appliances from 13 million California buildings would reduce $PM_{2.5}$ levels by only 0.11 micrograms per cubic meter, or less than one percent of state particulate pollution, a level too small to be measured.[39]

OUTDOOR SMALL-PARTICLE FEARS

In 2011, Environmental Protection Agency (EPA) Administrator Lisa Jackson testified before the US House of Representatives, stating,

> Particulate matter causes premature death. It doesn't make you sick. It's directly causal to dying sooner than you should.[40]

The EPA classifies particulate pollution as $PM_{2.5}$ and PM_{10}, for particles less than 2.5 microns in diameter and 10 microns in diameter, respectively. The EPA is primarily concerned with outdoor particle pollution, which is a mixture of airborne dust, metals, pollen, nitrates and sulfates, and organic chemicals. $PM_{2.5}$ particles are smaller than the eye can see.[41]

The EPA claims that any level of small particles can cause premature death. The agency warns that inhalation of $PM_{2.5}$ may cause death within a few hours or after long-term inhalation over decades. Suppose Frank is a senior citizen with a weak heart, who dies days before his seventieth birthday. According to the EPA, Frank's death may be "premature" and caused by particle pollution. The American Heart Association, American Lung Association, British Heart Foundation, European Environment Agency, and World Health Organization (WHO) join the EPA to warn that particle pollution causes premature death.

Bangladesh, India, Pakistan, the nations of Africa, and other developing countries suffer the world's worst outdoor $PM_{2.5}$ pollution levels. Outdoor particulate levels in poor nations average 5–10 times the levels in Europe and the US.[42] But an even more serious problem is indoor air pollution in these countries.

According to the WHO, about 2.6 billion people in the developing world cook over open fires or simple stoves fueled by wood, animal dung, crop waste, or charcoal. An estimated 3.8 million die each year from illnesses attributable to household air pollution.[43]

Particle levels from indoor air smoke in homes fueled by biomass can be 100 to 500 times higher than levels in homes using modern gas fuels. Dr. Christopher Olopade of the University of Chicago tested air quality in 100 homes in Nigeria that cooked with indoor fires. He measured average airborne $PM_{2.5}$ levels of 1,800 micrograms per cubic meter ($\mu g/m^3$).[44] This is 150 times the EPA's outdoor average $PM_{2.5}$ limit of 12 $\mu g/m^3$.[45]

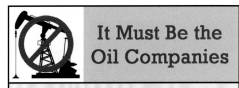

It Must Be the Oil Companies

Fossil Fuel Air Pollution Kills One in Five People

"The global toll of premature deaths attributed to burning coal, gasoline, and diesel is breathtakingly high, with new research doubling previous estimates."
— NRDC, February 19, 2021[46]

Today, air quality in Australia, Canada, Europe, the US, and other developed nations is excellent. According to the EPA, US ambient air pollution is down by 78 percent since 1970.[47] Particulate levels are down 30–40 percent since data was first recorded in 1990, but levels are probably down 90 percent since the coal-furnace days of 1950. This vast improvement in air quality in wealthy nations remains a great untold story of our modern era.

While indoor air and possibly outdoor air remains a serious health issue in developing nations, the size of the dose makes the poison. The medical evidence for particulate-caused death from the low airborne-particulate levels in advanced nations is highly questionable.

The US $PM_{2.5}$ limit of 12 micrograms per cubic meter isn't very much. Dr. James Enstrom, a retired epidemiologist of the UCLA School of Public Health, points out that, at this level, the average person would breathe in less than one teaspoon of microscopic small particles over an 80-year lifetime.[48] The EPA's claim that this tiny dose of particles causes premature death is not credible.

How does the EPA conclude that these low levels of particles cause tens of thousands of premature deaths annually? Further, how does the EPA conclude that inhalation of small particles can cause death within hours? No coroner ever attributes the cause of death to small particles unless someone is caught in a fire. Instead, the EPA relies on epidemiological

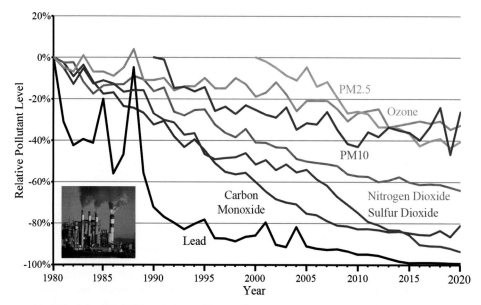

Air Pollution in the United States 1980–2020. Declining concentration levels of lead (Pb), carbon monoxide (CO), sulfur dioxide (SO_2), nitrogen dioxide (NO_2), ozone (O_3), and particulates ($PM_{2.5}$ and PM_{10}), which are deemed criteria pollutants by the EPA. Image of North Platte River power plant in 1973. (EPA, 2021)[49]

observational studies that associate particulate pollution with death.

Epidemiological studies analyze statistical associations between exposure to an agent and appearance of disease in a population. An example is the study in the 1950s, conducted by Richard Doll and Austin Bradford Hill, that found that cigarette smoking caused lung cancer in a population of 41,000 British medical doctors.[50] The EPA concludes that associations found by epidemiological studies show that breathing small particles causes premature death.

At the EPA standard of 12 micrograms per cubic meter, a person inhales less than one teaspoon full of small particles over an 80-year lifespan.[51]

The Harvard Six Cities study of 1993[52] and the American Cancer Society study of 1995[53] form the basis of the EPA's small-particle science. These studies found an increase in relative risk of less than 20 percent (RR=1.2), which is almost statistically indistinguishable from zero. By comparison, the Doll and Hill study found that smokers had 10 times the rate of lung cancer of non-smokers, a relative risk of RR=10.[54] The weak association (small relative risk) between death and particle pollution that the EPA judges to be causal could be due to other factors in measured populations, or even random chance. The underlying data from the Harvard study and the American Cancer Society study have never been released. As a result, outside scientists are unable to replicate and verify the results of these studies.

Other studies find no causal association between particle pollution and death. For example, a 2017 study by risk analysis expert Anthony Cox analyzed particulates and death of persons 75 years or older in Boston and Los Angeles from 2007 to 2013. The study found that ambient $PM_{2.5}$ concentrations did not predict elderly mortality rates in either city.[55]

The EPA uses "prevention" of premature deaths from particles to justify tighter pollution regulations. For example, the Clean Power Plan (CPP), which was proposed in 2015 and then eventually abandoned, would have forced closure of US coal-fired plants. The EPA claimed the CPP would prevent up to 3,600 premature deaths each year and provide $26–45 billion in climate and health benefits.[56] But most of the claimed benefits came from an EPA calculation of savings from avoidance of premature death from particles. In the UCLA paper previously discussed, the $3.5 billion in reduced health costs due to a transition from

Smoking a single tobacco or marijuana cigarette delivers more small particles than breathing ambient air in the US for a year.[57]

gas to electric appliances was estimated savings from prevention of premature death.

Those raising alarm about premature death from particles need some perspective. On January 1, 2018, California legalized recreational use of marijuana. That very same day, a California law regulating particle emissions from leaf blowers and lawn mowers went into effect. But smokers inhale thousands of times more particles than people breathing ambient air. A 2011 study by chemists Stephen Alderman and Bradley Ingrebrethsen determined that smokers inhale more than a billion small particles per cubic centimeter of air.[58] A single tobacco cigarette or marijuana joint delivers more than 100 billion particles to the user, which is more than a *year* of breathing California air.

In 2017, California experienced some of the worst wild fires in history. During only two October days, fires in Napa Valley produced an estimated 10,000 tons of $PM_{2.5}$. This is about the same amount that the 35 million California vehicles produce in a year.[59]

ELECTRIFICATION MADNESS

Natural gas, propane, and liquid propane gas fuels have done more to reduce air pollution than any other energy source. The world continues its transition from the age of coal furnaces and biomass stoves to clean-burning gas. But we still have 70 million wood stoves in Europe. Particle emissions from gas stoves are roughly 1,000 times lower than emissions from a wood stove.

Modern gas fuels provide the best opportunity to reduce the estimated 3.8 million deaths each year associated with indoor combustion of coal, charcoal, wood, and dung. People of Africa and Asia need gas fuels as the primary solution to this problem. But the electrification advocates seek to ban the use of gas fuels because of their obsession with carbon dioxide. They have the pollution issue exactly wrong.

As gas appliances are banned and disconnected, consumers in the Netherlands, the UK, and other nations will face rising energy costs and a reduced standard of living. Time will tell if we see a trend toward electrification revolts. In the next chapter we'll look at electric vehicles, another side of the madness around electrification.

CHAPTER 7

TRADE MY GASOLINE PICKUP TRUCK FOR AN ELECTRIC CAR?

"I believe that ultimately the electric motor will be universally used for trucking in all large cities, and that the electric automobile will be the family carriage of the future."
—THOMAS EDISON (1914)[1]

Today's world marches ahead to adopt electric vehicles (EVs). Electric car companies successfully portray EVs as the latest thing in transportation. A Tesla sedan is the new status symbol for the wealthy. Stock prices of EV start-up companies soar to dizzying heights. Old-time auto makers join the party, announcing plans for a transition to all-electric manufacturing. Big corporations vow to convert their fleets to battery-powered vehicles. Governments establish EV incentives and mandates, driven by the obsession to reduce greenhouse gas emissions. Media sources tell us that electric cars are best for us and best for the planet. Even oil companies invest in EV charging networks.

127

But a global transition to EVs faces several hurdles. EVs are heavier and have a shorter driving range. They cost more and will likely remain more costly than cars with an internal combustion engine (ICE) for years to come. Charging your EV at home can be inexpensive, but public charging is problematic. And as we will discuss, environmental impacts from widespread adoption of EVs, particularly those associated with mining and waste disposal, will become major issues. Let's look at the history, the status, and the pros and cons of EVs.

PATH TO A NEW AGE OF ELECTRIC CARS

Electric vehicles are nothing new. At the dawn of the age of automobiles in the early 1900s, EVs held a majority of the car market. But as the industry developed, gasoline- and diesel-powered vehicles soon left electric cars in the dust. Improving road systems connected cities, establishing a need for longer-range vehicles. The growing US oil industry dropped the price of fuel, making it affordable for the average consumer. In 1912, Charles Kettering invented the electric starter for gasoline cars, replacing the hard-to-use hand-crank starter. But what might have been the biggest factor in favor of ICE cars was the introduction of their mass production by Henry Ford in 1908, eventually dropping their price to one-third of the price of electric cars. By the mid-1930s, EVs had all but disappeared from the US market.[2]

From the 1930s to the 1970s, the use of EVs was confined to special applications or locations where fuel was expensive or hard to get. In England, electric vehicles called milk floats delivered milk and bread to customers from the 1930s until late last century.[3] After World War II in Japan, when gasoline was scarce, the Tama provided taxi service in Tokyo. It attained speeds of 20 mph with a range of 40 miles using lead-acid batteries.[4]

The oil shocks of the 1970s encouraged a new look at electric vehicles to reduce dependence on petroleum and gasoline. The US Congress passed the Electric and Hybrid Vehicle Research, Development, and Demonstration Act in 1976, authorizing support for research and development for electric vehicles.[6]

Automakers introduced several experimental electric cars during the 1960s–1970s. General Motors (GM) developed the Electrovair I, followed by the Electrovair II in 1966. The Electrovair used silver-zinc batteries and a Corvair chassis. The car could attain 80 mph and had a range of 40-80 miles, but the battery

It's Time to Admit It:
We Are Addicted to Cars
"The saddest thing about this epidemic is that individuals get hooked not because they want, but because society leads them to use the cars." — *Humankind*, June 9, 2018[5]

pack cost $160,000 and could survive only 100 recharge cycles. None were ever sold.[7]

Sebring-Vanguard Inc. of Florida, later Commuter Vehicles Inc., developed and introduced the golf-cart-sized Citicar in 1974. Later versions reached a speed of 38 mph and a range of almost 40 miles. Citicar and later versions sold 4,444 cars in the 1970s, the largest plug-in electric car production in America since World War II, a record held until 2013.[9]

Slow is the New Green

Motorway Speed Limits Cut to 60 mph in Bid to Reduce Carbon Emissions

"Highways England has kicked off a 12-month trial on sections of motorway in England."

— *Confused.com*, October 29, 2020[8]

In 1980, John Goodenough and his collegues at Oxford University invented a lithium battery with a cathode of cobalt oxide. Today, this battery powers a wide range of consumer electronic devices and provides the foundation for electric cars with ranges of hundreds of miles. Goodenough and two other researchers received the 2019 Nobel Prize in Chemistry for the development of lithium-ion batteries.[10]

California's Zero Emissions Vehicle (ZEV) program was established in 1990. The ZEV required major auto manufacturers to sell electric or fuel-cell vehicles in California, beginning in 1998, and to ramp up EVs to 10 percent of total vehicle sales in the state by 2003. The original goal of the ZEV program aimed to reduce nitrogen oxides and hydrocarbon tailpipe emissions, but the program later shifted to target greenhouse gas emissions.[11]

The early goals of the ZEV program were far too optimistic. Electric car and battery technology did not yet allow commercialization of cars that consumers would buy. Six major changes were made to the ZEV program from 1996 to 2012, including postponing mandates regarding percentage of sales, establishing EV sales credits and allowing trading of credits between automakers, and providing credits for hybrid electric vehicles and low-emission ICE cars.[12]

But the ZEV program succeeded in its efforts to drive development of EV technology. At the same time that major auto manufacturers were suing California to relax the ZEV sales requirements, they were also working to develop new EV designs to meet state ZEV mandates. If California was a country, it would rank as the seventh-largest auto market in the world, a market too large for auto companies to ignore.

In reaction to ZEV mandates, General Motors developed the EV1 during the 1990s. The EV1 was developed from the ground up as an all-electric vehicle. Later versions used an advanced nickel-metal-hydride (NiMH) battery, which provided a 140-mile range on a single charge. But because of high production costs, the EV1 was never offered for sale. About 800 were leased from 1996–2003.[13]

Toyota introduced the Prius to Japan in 1997 and to world markets in 2000. The car became the world's first mass-produced hybrid electric vehicle, achieving cumulative global sales of one million units in 2008. The car contained both a gasoline engine and an electric motor with a NiMH battery pack. Early Prius models were not plug-in hybrids but used regenerative braking and the internal combustion engine to charge the battery.[14]

Martin Eberhardt and Marc Tarpenning incorporated Tesla Motors in 2003. They used an electric prototype, called tzero, developed in the 1990s by startup AC Propulsion to pitch Silicon Valley venture capitalists on the idea of a high-end luxury electric car. The tzero used lithium-ion batteries, which were just becoming available thanks to basic research by industry and government. Eberhardt and Tarpenning approached investor Elon Musk, who wound up pouring money into Tesla and becoming Tesla's chief executive officer.[15]

Tesla Motors initiated production in 2008 with the Roadster. The Roadster was the first commercial car to use lithium-ion batteries and the first to demonstrate a 200-mile driving range. The Roadster cost buyers just under $100,000 and could accelerate to 60 mph in about four seconds. Unlike almost all prior EVs, the Roadster was sporty, fast, and cool.[16]

Nissan began delivering the LEAF in 2010, the world's first practical electric car for daily travel. The LEAF cost just over $25,000 after the US plug-in electric car tax credit and had a range of 73 miles between charges.[17] The LEAF became the world's best-selling electric car, with almost 450,000 units sold by the end of 2019. It was surpassed by the Tesla Model 3, which became the new cumulative global leader in early 2020.[18]

In 2016, GM introduced the Chevrolet Bolt, the first affordable longer-range electric car. The Bolt cost about $30,000 after the federal tax credit. It could go 238 miles on a single charge.[19]

A major enabler during this period of new model introductions was the rapid drop in the cost of vehicle batteries, which went from about $1,500 per kilowatt-hour in 2008 to under $200 per kWh in 2018.[21] As the result of government incentives and mandates, the perception of EVs as a status symbol, and the supposed environmental benefits, EVs became the hot new transportation technology by 2020.

Tesla Roadster in San Diego, 2010.[20]

ELECTRIC VEHICLES HAVE ARRIVED

Of course, EVs are now regarded as more than a new vehicle technology. They're branded as an essential tool in the fight against human-caused global warming. In reality, EVs are not zero emissions but produce about one-half of the greenhouse gases that conventional vehicles produce over their life cycle.[22] The International Energy Agency (IEA) states,

> For EVs to unleash their full potential to combat climate change, the 2020s will need to be the decade of mass adoption of electric light-duty vehicles.[23]

The electrification movement that seeks to eliminate your gas stove also demands replacement of your gasoline car or pickup truck. Administrations across the world have lined up to force EV adoption.

A growing array of national policies promote electric vehicles and restrict internal combustion engine vehicles, especially in Canada, Chile, China, India, Japan, New Zealand, the US, and the nations of Europe. City, state, and provincial authorities add additional regulations. EV promotional policies include purchase subsidies, vehicle tax exclusions or rebates, and free toll-road travel. EVs enjoy free access to low-emissions zones in city centers and unfettered use of highway high-occupancy vehicle lanes. Tightening national greenhouse-gas tailpipe regulations force auto sales toward zero-emissions cars. More than 20 nations have announced plans for outright bans of ICE vehicles.[24]

The EV's market share reached 8.3 percent of 81 million new light vehicles sold worldwide in 2021.[25] EV sales include battery electric vehicle (BEV) and plug-in hybrid electric

---

Electric Vehicle Plans and Pledges

"We need a motivational goal: make France Europe's top producer of clean vehicles by bringing output to more than one million electric and hybrid cars per year over the next five years." — French President Emmanuel Macron, May 26, 2020[26]

"It shall be the goal of the State that 100 percent of in-state sales of new passenger cars and trucks will be zero-emission by 2035."
 — California Governor Gavin Newsom, Executive Order N-79-20, Sep. 23, 2020[27]

"In 2030, we are ending the market for hydrocarbon ICEs, internal combustion engine vehicles." — British Prime Minister Boris Johnson, November 22, 2021[28]

"Climate change is real, and we want to be part of the solution by putting everyone in an electric vehicle."
 — General Motors Corporation Chair and CEO Mary Barra, July 20, 2021[29]

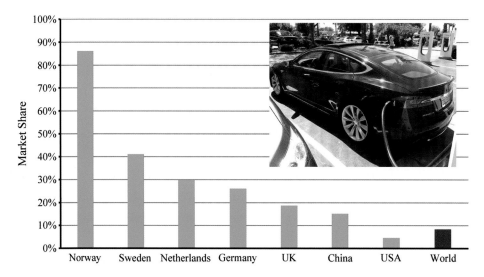

Electric Vehicle Share of 2021 Sales. EV share of new light-vehicle sales in 2021 for the world and selected nations. EVs include battery electric vehicles and plug-in hybrid electric vehicles. Image of Tesla Model S. (*EVVolumes*, other sources, 2022)[30]

vehicle (PHEV) versions. BEVs are all-electric vehicles powered by electric motors and batteries. PHEVs are plug-in vehicles that house batteries, an electric motor, and also a fuel-powered internal combustion engine. Seventy-one percent of 2021 global sales of electric vehicles were BEVs.[31]

Hybrid electric vehicles (HEVs), like the Toyota Prius, contain both an electric and an ICE engine, but they don't use a power plug. But HEVs are not considered true EVs by leading organizations and the media. For this reason, we will also exclude non-plug-in HEVs from our EV numbers. However, it must be said that the volume of HEV sales can't be ignored. HEVs outsold plug-in EVs in Europe, Japan, and the US in 2021 and held about a six percent share of global light-vehicle sales, just below the 8.3 percent EV share.[32]

Europe ranks as the world leader in EV adoption. In 2021, the EV share of new light vehicles sold reached new highs in several European countries, including Norway (86%), Sweden (41%), the Netherlands (30%), Germany (26%), and the UK (19%). About 18 percent of Europe's 2021 new light-vehicle sales were plug-in electric models.[33]

Subsidies and mandates play a major role in EV adoption in Europe. Germany provides direct-purchase subsidies of over $10,000 for BEVs and almost $8,000 for PHEV models. France provides a direct-purchase subsidy of about $8,000 for a BEV. ICE sales bans have been announced with effective dates in Norway (2025), Denmark, Ireland, the Netherlands, Slovenia, Sweden, and the UK (2030), France and Spain (2040), and Germany (2050).[34]

Norway is the poster child for EV incentives. Norway's EV purchasers do not pay the 25 percent value-added tax or the large additional tax on vehicle weight and CO_2 emissions, both of which are paid by owners of gasoline and diesel cars. The elimination of these taxes makes EVs less expensive than ICE vehicles in Norway. EVs also cost less to drive in Norway. Norway's gasoline taxes are among the highest in the world, while the nation's hydropower provides one of the lowest electricity prices in Europe. EVs enjoy exemption from payments in the Oslo Low Emissions Zone and travel toll roads for free. In addition, with Norway's announced plan to ban ICE vehicle sales in 2025, buyers of new cars fear that used fuel vehicles will soon be hard to sell.[35]

China leads the world in light-vehicle sales and also EV sales. In 2021, 22.6 million new light vehicles were sold in China, 15 percent of which were EV models. This amounts to about half of the world's EV sales.[36] China's government uses a New Electric Vehicle subsidy program for buyers, and a New Electric Vehicle mandate for manufacturers. These programs incentivize consumers and force automakers to adopt EVs. The New Energy Automobile Industry Plan aims to see zero-emissions cars comprise 20 percent of sales by 2025.[37]

In the US, sales of electric vehicles reached 4.5 percent of almost 15 million new light vehicles sold in 2021.[38] In 2009, the federal government established a plug-in electric vehicle credit of $2,500 to $7,500, depending upon battery size, for EV purchasers starting in 2010. The credit was phased out when manufacturer sales exceeded 200,000 units, which Tesla and GM reached in 2018.[39] The administration of President Joe Biden passed the Inflation Reduction Act in 2022, which extended and expanded the credit with restrictions on vehicle price and manufacturing location. Lower incentives account in part for lower EV penetration in US markets, compared to other countries.

Electric vehicle sales are growing rapidly but still remain a tiny part of the world's vehicle fleet. The number of plug-in EVs grew by 6.6 million in 2021, to a little over 16 million worldwide.[40] By the end of 2021, EVs accounted for just over one percent of the world's 1.4 billion vehicles.[41] An additional one percent of the world's vehicles were HEVs.

Car manufacturers appear to be all in for electric transport. Eighteen of the top 20 automakers intend to boost production of electric vehicles. Announcements include: GM will only sell zero-emission cars and trucks by 2035; Honda will phase out all gasoline cars by 2040; Mercedes' new-vehicle platforms will only be

THE FOOL

Poor Prophecy

"Battery technology will be ubiquitous. … All new vehicles in 2020 will have some level of hybridization." — IBM, 2008[42]

Green Policies Require Coercion

It's Time to Ban the Sale of Pickup Trucks

"Reducing further climate destruction and harm from needlessly fatal road accidents is more important than corporate or consumer freedom."

— *Passage*, July 13, 2021[43]

EVs starting in 2025; Volkswagen targets 70 percent of Europe sales to be BEVs by 2030, along with 50 percent in the US and China; and Volvo will be totally electric by 2030.[44]

But automakers have no choice. National emissions and mileage regulations may soon make it impossible to sell ICE vehicles. Early emissions regulations established in developed countries from 1960–1990 sought to reduce carbon monoxide, oxides of nitrogen and sulfur, and volatile organic compounds from vehicle exhaust. These efforts succeeded. As we discussed in Chapter 6, US ambient air pollution has fallen 78 percent since 1980. And we discussed in Chapter 2 that volatile organic compounds exhausted from US vehicles declined 98 percent since 1970. European nations and other developed countries achieved similar dramatic successes. But global emissions regulations now target tailpipe carbon dioxide emissions because of fears of human-caused climate change.

According to the Environmental Protection Agency, a typical ICE car with a 22 mpg fuel economy emits about 404 grams of CO_2 per mile, or 250 grams per kilometer.[45] But these levels already exceed emissions regulations in China (117g CO_2/km), Europe (95g CO_2/km), and the US (114g CO_2/km).[46] Manufacturers continue to produce ICE vehicles by using exemptions and a fleet mix of high-mileage economy cars and hybrid EVs, but this is increasingly difficult. Tightening regulations are forcing automakers to switch to EVs.

Electric vehicle ownership serves as the latest status symbol for the rich and famous. Celebrities who drive a Tesla include Cameron Diaz, Morgan Freeman, Demi Moore, Brad Pitt, and Will Smith. Celebrities who drive other high-end EVs include Justin Bieber, George Clooney, Prince Harry, Tom Hanks, and Arnold Schwarzenegger.[47] Not only can you drive a cool EV, but you can stop global warming as well.

Electric vehicle mania has captured global financial markets. From 2019 to the end of 2021, stock prices of EV companies soared to dizzying heights. Traditional automaker Volkswagen's $291 billion in sales for year 2021 led the world. At the end of the year, investors valued Volkswagen at $129 billion, for a market capitalization-to-sales ratio of 0.44. Toyota, the second largest auto seller, posted 2021 revenue of $272 billion. Toyota's year-end stock valuation was $253 billion, for a market cap-to-sales ratio of 0.93. Equity markets value traditional auto firms at about one-half to one times the sales revenue.[48]

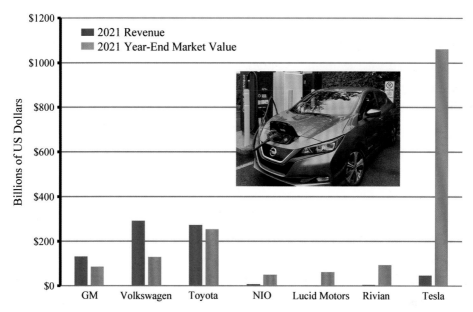

2021 Auto Company Sales and Valuation. Year-end 2021 revenue and stock market valuation for selected auto companies. The four EV manufacturers on the right enjoy astronomical stock valuations despite low annual sales compared to the three traditional auto firms on the left. Image of 2019 Nissan LEAF. (*CompaniesMarketCap.com*, 2022)[49]

In contrast, from the start of 2019 to the end of 2021, Tesla stock soared from $67 per share to over $1,000 per share, a rise of 15 times. Tesla's 2021 revenue was about $47 billion, but the market placed Tesla's market capitalization at $1.061 trillion, a value-to-sales ratio of 22.6. At the end of 2021, Tesla was worth more than Toyota, Volkswagen, Mercedes-Benz, General Motors, Ford, BMW, and Honda combined.[50]

The valuations of China EV-makers NIO, Lucid Motors, and Rivian were sky high. Luxury automaker NIO's market value fell in 2021 but was still at 10 times annual sales at year's end. Rivian and Lucid Motors completed initial public stock offerings in 2021 despite almost no vehicle shipments. Year-end 2021 valuations for these two firms were huge, with Rivian at $95 billion and Lucid at $63 billion, but both had only tiny sales, with Rivian having sold $1 million and Lucid $0.6 million.[51] Welcome to the EV stock market bubble.

EV PROS AND CONS

Electric vehicle demand is being driven by got-to-have status, government money, and save-the-planet ideology. Now that we've discussed the growing demand for EVs, let's see how they actually stack up against traditional fuel-powered vehicles.

Tesla's business plan was excellent. They targeted the luxury car market with sporty, futuristic automobile designs. The EV's fast acceleration and quiet ride give it leadership features in the luxury car segment. The high cost of batteries was only a small disadvantage in high-priced luxury markets.

The Tesla Model 3 Performance model can accelerate from zero to 100 kilometers per hour (62.1 mph) in a lightning-fast 3.3 seconds.[52] But, on average, the 0-to-60 mph acceleration of EVs and gasoline cars is about the same, six seconds, according to *Car and Driver*. This same source measured the EV's interior sound to be slightly lower than in ICE cars when cruising at 70 mph, and significantly lower (8 dB) when in maximum acceleration.[53]

Because electric vehicles and hybrid vehicles (when using the electric motor) are quieter than fuel-powered vehicles, they pose a danger to pedestrians and cyclists that may be unaware of their approach. In 2018, the US National Highway Transportation Administration enacted rules requiring automakers to add sound to "quiet cars." The regulation requires EVs to generate artificial sound at speeds below 18.6 mph (30 km/hr).[54]

A big advantage of electric cars is the ability to charge at home. The Nissan LEAF was designed as a charge-at-home commuter car. Charging your vehicle at home and eliminating fuel stops is attractive to many EV buyers. EV owners can use a traditional wall plug to charge at home but most upgrade to a Level 2 charger for faster charging.

Electric cars cost more than traditional fuel-powered cars. The 2022 Toyota Corolla gasoline car lists at a Manufacturer Suggested Retail Price (MSRP) of $20,075. The MSRP of a comparable 2022 Chevrolet Bolt EV is $31,000, 54 percent more than the Corolla.[55]

Electric cars also cost more to drive. A number of studies claim that EVs are cheaper to operate, but they typically fail to include the direct costs of commercial charging, highway taxes, and the purchase and installation of a home charger, as well as the indirect costs of longer fueling times and time expended to reach a charging station. A study by the Anderson Economic Group in 2021 estimated that, when all direct costs and indirect costs of operation are included, EVs cost $6–$10 more per 100 miles to drive than a comparable ICE car.[57] This study was completed prior to higher gasoline prices in the 2021–2022 energy crisis.

The big disadvantage for electric vehicles can be summed up in one word: battery. Lithium-ion batteries provide a specific energy

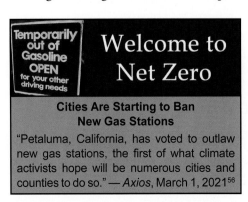

Cities Are Starting to Ban New Gas Stations

"Petaluma, California, has voted to outlaw new gas stations, the first of what climate activists hope will be numerous cities and counties to do so." — *Axios*, March 1, 2021[56]

Electric Vehicles: Higher Cost to Operate

Electric vehicles are often presumed to be less expensive to operate than gasoline- or diesel-powered vehicles. Automaker and government incentives currently favor EVs. Failure to consider indirect costs, such as fueling time, can distort the full picture.

A study by the Anderson Economic Group (AEG) compared the real-world cost of fueling six categories of EVs and ICE vehicles in the US Midwest in 2021. The study looked at electricity costs, road and registration taxes, home-charger costs, costs associated with extra driving miles to find a charger, and the time costs of charging. AEG found that, for both direct and indirect costs, "EVs often cost more to fuel than similar ICE vehicles."[58]

The AEG study found that the direct monetary costs of fueling were higher for EVs. Direct cost for ICE vehicles is captured in the retail price of gasoline, which is inclusive of road taxes and the cost of operating the pump. Direct costs for EVs include the cost of electricity at residential and commercial chargers, highway and registration taxes, and the cost of purchasing and installing a home charger.

The AEG study found that Midwest US charging costs were between 15¢ and 25¢ per kWh for residential chargers. Commercial chargers cost 30¢ to 43¢ per kWh without Time-of-Use (ToU) charging rates, but they were as high as 33¢ to 66¢ per kWh for commercial charging where ToU rates are used. The study estimated the purchase cost and installation of a home 240V charger to be $1,600. The study found that, in Michigan, the direct monetary cost to drive an ICE vehicle 100 miles is between $8 and $12, while the cost to drive an EV 100 miles is between $12 to $15.

Charging at home incurs no time costs, but drivers of electric vehicles expend significant time charging at commercial chargers. The study estimated that an EV owner makes about eight trips per month to a commercial charger if mostly commercial charging is used, or four trips per month if mostly home charging is used. These trips are in addition to 25 home charging sessions per month in each case. Setup at a commercial charger takes five minutes to connect and disconnect, and to use a mobile app to prepare the car for charging. Charging itself takes about 30 minutes using a 50 kWh fast DC charger to increase the charge by about a third of total capacity. In comparison, a typical ICE car makes four trips to the gas station per month and spends only five minutes per stop, including time to fill the tank, to make a credit card payment, and to enter and leave the station.

In addition to charging time, EV drivers incur additional miles driving to reach a commercial EV charging station. This amounts to between 480 and 960 miles per year, or one to two additional hours of driving time per month, compared to an ICE vehicle driver.

Using these estimates, the AEG study concluded that, for vehicles that drive 12,000 miles per year, an ICE vehicle spends about one hour per month to refuel the vehicle compared to 4.5 hours for an EV that uses mostly home charging, or seven hours for an EV that uses mostly commercial charging. This means an additional cost for time when driving EVs of $405–$695 per year, when valued at the Michigan minimum wage of $9.65 per hour, or $1,386–$2,376 at an hourly wage rate for a salary of $70,000 per year.

In summary, to operate an EV costs $3–4 more per 100 miles in direct costs and an additional $3–6 more per 100 miles in indirect time costs, when valued at Michigan minimum wage, compared to a comparable ICE vehicle.[59]

density of 100–265 Wh/kg, or a volumetric energy density of 250–670 Wh/L, one of the highest energy densities of any battery technology today. This is about 50 percent greater than nickel-metal-hydride batteries and double the density of nickel-cadmium batteries. But Li-ion batteries are still about 100 times less energy dense than gasoline, which contains 12,700 Wh/kg by mass or 8,760 Wh/L by volume.[60] Electric motors are about four times as efficient as internal combustion engines, but this still gives ICE vehicles almost a 20-to-1 energy advantage over EVs. This affects vehicle driving range and weight.

For example, a 2020 Honda Civic can travel 360 miles on a full 12.4-gallon gas tank, containing fuel that weighs 77.5 pounds. But a comparable Chevy Bolt could only travel 21 miles on a 77.5-pound battery. To achieve a driving range equal to a gasoline car, the battery of the electric car would need to be scaled-up by a factor of 17.[61] This means that, because of the weight of the battery, an electric car will need to be about 50 percent heavier to achieve a driving range equal to that of a gasoline car.

In addition to the push for electrification of light vehicles, net-zero advocates call for heavy trucks to switch to electric drive over the next few decades. But a heavy truck with a 500-mile range would be burdened with 10,000 pounds of additional battery weight, compared to a diesel-fueled rig. This would be a significant disadvantage in many US states that limit truck maximum-gross vehicle weight to as to low as 80,000 pounds.[62]

Batteries also suffer disadvantages in terms of operating in cold and hot weather, as well as operating life. Cold weather increases battery charging times and causes a temporary loss of EV driving range. In 2020, the Norwegian Automobile Federation tested 20 of the leading EVs during winter temperatures of 21–37 degrees Fahrenheit. The tests found an average loss of 18.5 percent from EV official driving ranges. Cold-weather charging times also increased to up to 50 percent longer.[64] Worse than that, experience in the US and Canada shows that Tesla and other EVs *will not charge* when temperatures drop to 0°F.

Electric vehicle owners should enjoy lower maintenance costs than owners of ICE vehicles. The battery and electric motor of EVs require little regular maintenance. EVs need fewer fluids, such as engine oil, and use fewer moving parts. The regenerative braking of EVs reduces

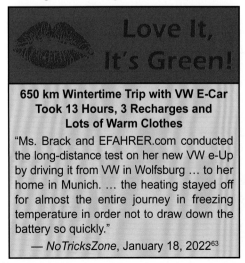

650 km Wintertime Trip with VW E-Car Took 13 Hours, 3 Recharges and Lots of Warm Clothes

"Ms. Brack and EFAHRER.com conducted the long-distance test on her new VW e-Up by driving it from VW in Wolfsburg … to her home in Munich. … the heating stayed off for almost the entire journey in freezing temperature in order not to draw down the battery so quickly."

— NoTricksZone, January 18, 2022[63]

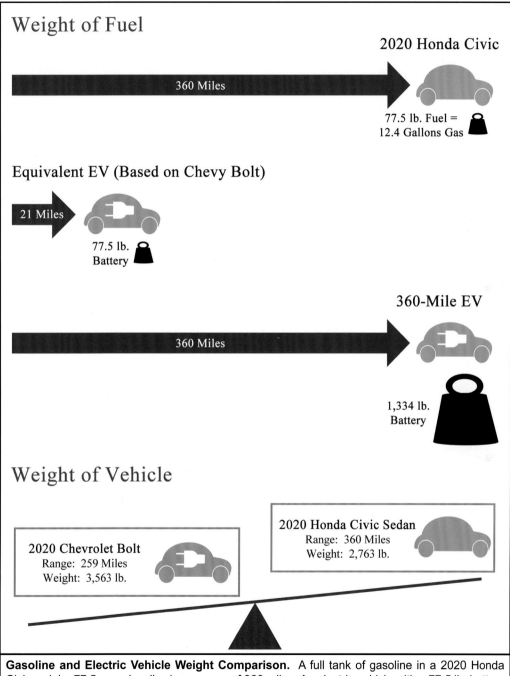

Weight of Fuel

2020 Honda Civic

360 Miles

77.5 lb. Fuel = 12.4 Gallons Gas

Equivalent EV (Based on Chevy Bolt)

21 Miles

77.5 lb. Battery

360-Mile EV

360 Miles

1,334 lb. Battery

Weight of Vehicle

2020 Chevrolet Bolt
Range: 259 Miles
Weight: 3,563 lb.

2020 Honda Civic Sedan
Range: 360 Miles
Weight: 2,763 lb.

Gasoline and Electric Vehicle Weight Comparison. A full tank of gasoline in a 2020 Honda Civic weighs 77.5 pounds, allowing a range of 360 miles. An electric vehicle with a 77.5 lb. battery can go only 21 miles. The battery needed for an EV range of 360 miles would weigh 1,334 lb. An EV with a range equal to that of a gas vehicle will be about 50 percent heavier. (Brookings, 2020)[65]

brake wear.[66] Current EV maintenance costs are high because of few service locations, but these costs will decline with more EVs on the road. The only exception is EV tire maintenance, which will be higher because of vehicle weight.

The adoption of electric vehicles can reduce air pollution in China, India, and developing nations, where auto emissions control systems are not yet widely used. In these locations, the adoption of EVs provides a path to eliminating carbon monoxide, oxides of nitrogen and sulfur, and volatile organic compounds from vehicle exhaust. But in Europe, the US, and developed countries, where emissions control systems are already standard practice, a transition to EVs will provide a significant reduction in only CO_2 emissions.

In summary, electric vehicles may offer faster acceleration, a quieter ride, lower maintenance, and the convenience of charging at home. But they are usually more expensive to buy and more expensive to fuel except when heavily subsidized by governments. EVs are heavier vehicles with a shorter driving range and degraded performance in cold weather. But the biggest EV issue may be the commercial-charging problem.

THE CHARGING PROBLEM

For traditional gasoline or diesel cars, refueling at a filling station is easy. It's just a five-minute stop on the way to work or the grocery store. For electric car owners, charging at home is convenient, but charging on the road is difficult.

Most EV charging happens at home. Home charging accounts for about 80 percent of the US's charging, 72 percent of the UK's charging, and 80 percent of Europe's charging. A Level 1 charger, also known as a wall plug, will charge an EV to 100 kilometers (62 miles) of driving range in six to eight hours. Upgrading a home charger to a 10 kilowatt, three-phase AC charger provides a charge good for 100 km in two to three hours.[67] Overnight charging can be effective for homeowners who use their vehicle for short daily commutes.

Commercial charging stations can be either public or private, but they are not located in homes. Most of these are 240 volt, 7.4 kW or 22 kW AC chargers. The 22 kW chargers provide 100 kilometers of range in one to two hours of charge time. Chargers with 22 kW or more of charging power are considered "fast chargers." By the end of 2020, about 1.3 million chargers were installed worldwide, or about one charger for every eight EVs. But 70 percent of commercial chargers are slow chargers, below 22 kW of power.[68]

China leads with about 800,000 charging outlets installed at the end of 2020, or about 60 percent of the world's total. This means that there is about one charger for every five

	POWER		LOCATION
Fast **DC Chargers** 480-600V 50+ kilowatts	120 kilowatts	10 Minutes	Motorway, Urban Charging Stations (Future Standard)
	50 kilowatts	20-30 Minutes	Motorway, Urban Charging Stations (Current Standard)
Level 2 **AC Chargers** 240V 7.4-22 kilowatts	22 kilowatts	1-2 Hours	Public Charging Stations
	10 kilowatts	2-3 Hours	House, Workplace Wall Box
	7.4 kilowatts	3-4 Hours	Public Charging Stations
Level 1 **AC Charger** 120V 3.3 kilowatts	3.3 kilowatts	6-8 Hours	House, Workplace Wall Box

EV Charger Types and Charging Times. A comparison of charger types and times to charge to 100 kilometers (62 miles) of driving range. (LaMonaca and Ryan, 2021)[69]

EVs on the road in China. The government currently heavily promotes adoption of EVs and discourages the use of ICE cars. China is building out charging infrastructure ahead of demand, preparing for high levels of EV penetration.[70]

About 224,000 commercial chargers were installed in Europe at the end of 2020. Three nations dominated the continent's share of chargers: the Netherlands (29.7%), France (20.4%), and Germany (19.9%). One charger operates for each 11 EVs on the road today in Europe.[71] Only one in nine chargers is a fast charger.[72]

US commercial chargers totaled 107,000 at the end of 2020, in 31,000 locations. Thirty percent of these were fast chargers, with 16 percent 50 kW or higher fast DC chargers. The number of commercial chargers grew 20 percent in 2021. About 1.6 million plug-in vehicles were on the road in the US at the end of 2020, with about one charger for every 15 EVs. About 32 percent of US commercial chargers were located in California.[73]

Slow chargers fall far short of meeting public needs. A car can easily travel 100 km (62 mi) in an hour. But it's a significant problem when the driver then needs to charge for two or more hours to drive for an additional hour, which is the situation with slow chargers.

Tesla recognized the charging problem early on and opened its Supercharger network in 2012. The network uses 90 kW or 250 kW chargers, allowing Tesla EVs to charge up to 200 miles of range in 15 minutes on the highest power stations. The company also offers a period of free charging as part of the purchase price of a Tesla. Tesla built the network over the last decade and now offers more than 30,000 connections at over 3,000 locations in Australia, Asia, Europe, the Middle East, New Zealand, and North America. Network costs are paid for by revenue from the sale of cars, along with charging fees. The network has been usable only by Tesla vehicles, but recently the firm signed agreements to establish compatibility with other car lines and charging networks.[74]

But except for the 30,000 Tesla charging outlets, the other million and a half commercial chargers suffer from serious problems in most countries. Trying to find a working charging station closely resembles a scavenger hunt. Chargers sometimes don't work or are in use when drivers pull up. Reports say that as many as 30 percent of chargers in some regions of China are defective or at parking spaces blocked by ICE cars.[75] Maintaining working stations can be problematic. The thick cables at unsupervised Tesla Supercharging stations are now being cut off by thieves for sale in copper scrap markets.[76]

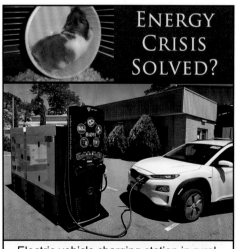

Electric vehicle charging station in rural Australia fueled by waste-fryer oil.[77]

When a driver finds a working outlet, the price can vary widely. Commercial charging rates are usually double or triple the price to charge at home. Rates at a single outlet change by 50 percent due to Time-of-Use charges. In mid-2020, Germany's 30,000 charging points used 288 different tariffs.[78] Users pay by price per kilowatt-hour, charger Time-of-Use, rate of charge, and other metrics. In comparison, gasoline and diesel fuel are paid for in local currency by gallon or liter, the price of which is posted on signs for drivers to survey and which varies locally by as little as 10 percent.

Payment methods for EV charging can also be fragmented. In the US, EV drivers may need to use one of a dozen different apps, and provide their birthday, email address, and name to charge up. None of this is needed for a gasoline car.[79]

Renewables Need A Handout

Biden Makes a $174 Billion Commitment to Electric Cars
"He proposed $174 billion 'to win the EV market,' including point-of-sale rebates and tax incentives, and a national network of half a million EV chargers by 2030."
— *Autoweek*, April 1, 2021[80]

Homeowners can charge overnight, but US residents who live in multi-unit housing (about 32 percent of the population) are out of luck. Only one-half of one percent of US public chargers, less than 600 chargers nationwide, serve multi-unit dwellings.[81] Forty-six percent of Europeans have apartments.[82] The large majority of EV owners own stand-alone houses.

The business case for providing charging service is poor. EV owners prefer to charge at home but need a network of commercial chargers for long-distance driving. This means that utilization rates for commercial chargers will be low. Most travelers don't want to sit at an AC charger for an hour or more but want to charge quickly at a fast DC charger. But a 50 kW DC charger, including charger, transformer, cables, and "make-ready" infrastructure, costs between $80,000 and $110,000.[83] Most studies find that charging points can't pay for themselves over a 10-year period.[84]

To compare, a $100,000 50 kW DC charger can charge an EV in 30 minutes and serve a maximum of 24 customers in a 12-hour day. A $20,000 gas station fuel pump can serve a driver in fewer than six minutes, or about 120 customers in a 12-hour day. The gas pump can serve five times the number of customers each day and costs one-fifth of the investment cost of a fast DC charger. As a result, most gas station owners are not very interested in providing EV chargers.

But governments are determined to force a transition to EVs. Funding for chargers was a major part of COVID-19 recovery plans in many nations during 2020 and 2021. On November 15, 2021, President Biden signed a US $1.2 trillion infrastructure bill into law, including $7.5 billion to subsidize construction of chargers and alternative fuel stations across the nation. An additional $7.5 billion was provided for low-emissions buses and ferries.[85] Europe's €672.5 billion Recovery and Resilience Facility fund included support for charging stations, along with additional funding at a county level by many nations. China announced a $1.4 trillion digital infrastructure spending program, including funding for EV charging stations.[86]

DARK CLOUDS FOR THE EV REVOLUTION

So will the majority of vehicles on the road be electric vehicles by 2050, as many have predicted? Are consumers going to change their driving habits to include a 30-minute stop to recharge their vehicle? Or will they choose to drive less than in the past?

Global electric vehicle sales are rapidly rising, but there are warning signs as well. The University of Chicago looked at a large sample of California EV drivers and found that, on average, they drive about 5,300 miles per year, only half of the annual miles driven by gasoline cars.[87] Could it be that EVs are mostly second-car toys for the rich? A study by the University of California, Davis, found that 18 percent of owners of battery electric vehicles and 20 percent of owners of plug-in hybrid electric vehicles returned to ICE vehicles for their next purchase. Dissatisfaction with charging was the primary reason for their return.[88]

Modern electric vehicles with high-capacity batteries are a new technology that is rapidly gaining market acceptance, but their growth is still at risk for derailment by some unexpected factor. Automakers compete to continue to increase EV range by introducing larger and more powerful batteries. But battery fires may threaten the EV revolution.

Lithium batteries in cell phones and other portable electronic devices are banned from commercial airline baggage compartments because of fire risk. Lithium batteries in electric cars contain graphite, metals, and other materials bathed in flammable electrolytes with thousands of times more energy than your cell phone battery. If they ignite, they can burn for hours with a very high heat and are extremely difficult to extinguish.

BMW, Ford, General Motors, Hyundai, and Tesla electric cars have experienced problems with battery fires.[89] In the most visible case, GM recalled all 141,000 Chevrolet Bolts produced between 2016 and late 2021.[91] In total, the number of EV fires per car does not exceed the fire rate for ICE cars. But EV fires can ignite unexpectedly when charging overnight in the garage or even when just parked in the driveway, locations where gasoline-powered cars typically don't catch fire.

Widespread adoption of EVs may overload the electrical grid in many locations. DC fast chargers require new transformers and additional equipment. Even the common use of home chargers may overload the grid.

If You *Like* Your Blackouts, You Can *Keep* Your Blackouts

Government Mulls Emergency Measures that Would Enable Networks to Switch Off Your Electricity without Warning or Compensation

"Electricity networks in Great Britain were not designed to accommodate the significant additional demand that certain consumer devices, such as electric vehicle chargers, presents."

— *Daily Mail*, September 17, 2020[90]

The Chevrolet Bolt Debacle

Jesus Damien's Bolt exploded into flames when parked in a parking lot while he was sleeping nearby in his apartment. The car wasn't plugged in or running when the fire started. Several nearby cars were also damaged before firefighters were able to extinguish the flames. Mr. Damien had already taken the car in to General Motors as part of a recall and received fixes intended to prevent fire problems.[92]

In November 2020, GM recalled 50,000 Chevrolet Bolt EVs from model years 2017 to 2019 to correct battery cell defects. The batteries were sourced from LG Energy Solutions and produced at either a Korean or a Michigan facility. In mid-2021, GM engineers found additional battery defects. The company again recalled some of the same cars in the earlier recall for additional fire safety problems.

The company warned Bolt owners without battery corrections not to fully charge or discharge their vehicles, not to charge overnight, and to park their vehicles outside after charging. Signs went up around the nation prohibiting Bolts from parking in commercial parking facilities.

The defects involved torn anode contacts or folded separators, the thin sheets of material that separate the battery anode and cathode. Small defects in a single battery module could result in a runaway condition that spread to other battery modules, resulting in combustion of the entire car battery. Fourteen Bolt fires had been publicly identified by the end of 2021.

By this time, GM had recalled 141,000 Bolts over six model years and suspended car production. The recalls were expected to cost GM about $1.8 billion.[93]

Electric Cars Are Hot!

For customer safety:

CHEVROLET BOLT EVs are STRICTLY PROHIBITED from parking at this facility.

Thank you for your compliance!

Sign at outdoor parking lot in San Francisco, California
— *InsideEVs*, September 8, 2021[94]

In the UK, homes typically use 2 kW of power on average per day, rising to 7 kW in the winter. An additional 7 kW will be needed to charge an EV overnight, which is about double the power an average home uses today. Neighborhood grid upgrades may be needed.[95]

The high price of electric vehicles compared to gasoline- or diesel-fueled cars may slow the uptake of EVs. In November 2021, the average US electric vehicle cost $56,437, which was 22 percent higher than the average light-vehicle price of $46,329, and more than double the price of the average compact car.[96] This price gap may be slow to close.

Prices for cobalt, copper, lithium, and nickel are surging, driven by the demand for batteries. A typical 1,000 lb. EV battery requires mining operations to move about 500,000 lb. of earth. Mining of these key metals will need to increase by as much as *five or 10 times* globally to supply enough metals for broad adoption of EVs.[97] Metal shortages could

Sacrificed to
Save the
Planet

**More Western Leaders Call for the End
of Private Vehicle Ownership"**
— *The TruthAboutCars*, Dec. 29, 2021[98]

halt the decline in battery prices and keep the price of EVs high. We will discuss this further in Chapter 10.

Almost all automakers announced plans for a transition to electric vehicles, but it won't be easy. Changing factories from manufacturing internal combustion engines to electric-drive engines will cost billions. It took Tesla over a decade to make a profit. Most competing automakers will lose money on every EV sold for the next five to 10 years. Look for car companies to delay their EV goals as their losses grow.

The electric vehicle revolution points toward more government control and less freedom for the individual driver. Because of the poor business case for private owner-ship of charging networks, these networks probably will be owned by governments or government-subsidized utility companies. In an EV world, driving will cost more and people will drive less. Many leaders now call for the end of private vehicle ownership. In addition to traditional mass transit and private ride-sharing services, such as Uber and Lyft, look for a rise in government-sponsored ride-sharing operations. Beware of the movement underway to take away your gasoline pickup truck.

IT'S GOING TO BE INTERESTING

Electric vehicles are here to stay. EV sales are rising rapidly. Automakers profess to be disciples of the revolution, promising new electric models and an end to traditional fuel vehicles. Governments rush to subsidize EVs and build global charging networks, announcing policies and plans to retard and eventually ban ICE vehicles. The IEA predicts that 145 million EVs will be on the roads by 2030.[99] Others predict an all-electric vehicle future by 2050.

But this sounds like the old business quip about the company that spent millions promoting a new dog food but eventually found out that the dogs wouldn't eat it. Many drivers will not want to change their habits to drive EVs. Consumer preferences, EV prices, cost of ownership, and charging issues will be joined by a huge need for additional mining and rising amounts of battery waste. These problems point to a shared future for ICE and electric cars, rather than a transition to all EVs. But it's sure going to be interesting. The next chapter covers prospects to power your plane, ship, and train with green energy.

CHAPTER 8

GREEN LEAFY SHIPS, PLANES, AND TRAINS?

"To travel is to live."
—HANS CHRISTIAN ANDERSON[1]

Global exports of goods have grown 2,000 times since 1900. Modern ships use fuel from petroleum to ferry the bulk of these goods across the oceans. Trucks and trains dominate freight transport on land, carrying people and goods from city to city and nation to nation, primarily powered by diesel fuel. Aviation is the fastest-growing form of transportation, energized mostly by jet fuel derived from crude oil.

But like efforts to convert automobiles to electric drive, efforts are also underway to transform ships, planes, trucks, and trains in the energy revolution. Despite serious deficiencies in renewable fuels regarding distance, cost, availability, and practicality, advocates demand that we switch from hydrocarbons to biofuels, battery-powered transport, and even hydrogen fuel within the next three decades. Let's look at these issues.

PROBLEMS WITH BIOFUELS

Biofuels remain the favored energy source to decarbonize heavy transportation industries. Biofuels primarily consist of ethanol, which is blended with gasoline, and biodiesel, which is blended with diesel fuel. Ethanol is produced primarily from corn, sugar cane, sugar beets, wheat, or barley. Biodiesel is produced from the oil of rapeseed, sunflower, soybean, and palm. Agricultural waste and used cooking oil also produce small quantities of biofuels.

Biofuels have played a minor supporting role as a vehicle fuel in the age of modern transportation. German engineer Nikolaus Otto developed an internal combustion engine that ran on an ethanol blend in 1860. Rudolph Diesel, another German engineer, considered pure vegetable oil to be a possible fuel for his compression-ignited diesel engine in 1893. Henry Ford stated in 1906 that carburetors on his Model T cars could use gasoline or alcohol. Ethanol and methanol were used as alternative fuels during World War I and II due to petroleum-based fuel shortages. But the low prices and high energy content of gasoline and diesel overwhelmingly dominated fuel markets during the twentieth century.[2]

The modern age of biofuel use for transportation began with the oil shocks of the 1970s. Nations started efforts to develop renewable vehicle fuels to reduce dependence upon foreign oil. In 1979, the first bioethanol plant with a distillation column was established at South Dakota State University. Production of biodiesel from rapeseed began in 1989 at the world's first industrial-scale biodiesel plant in Asperhofen, Austria.[3]

Until the late 1970s, Tetraethyllead (TEL) was used as an additive to gasoline in US markets as an oxygenate to improve gasoline combustion, increase octane rating, and reduce engine knocking. To reduce harmful air pollution, the US Environmental Protection Agency (EPA) directed a phase-out of leaded gasoline in 1979, requiring the replacement of TEL with the oxygenate Methyl Tertiary-Butyl Ether (MTBE). TEL and MTBE are produced in oil and gas refineries. In 2000, the EPA began a phase-out of MTBE in vehicle fuel due to water pollution issues from spillage, replacing it with ethanol, also a fuel oxygenate.[5] The blending of up to 10 percent ethanol in gasoline created a massive rise in the number of US ethanol production facilities since 2002.

Since 1975, governments have used subsidies and mandates to encourage and force the

ENERGY CRISIS SOLVED?

Surgeon Uses Human Fat to Run His Cars

"A leading Beverly Hills plastic surgeon … claims to be able to power both his Ford Explorer and his girlfriend's Lincoln Navigator on biofuel converted from excess flesh from human tums, bums, and thighs."
— *Independent*, December 26, 2008[4]

Cheerleaders for Biofuels

"I set a goal to replace oil from around the world. The best way and the fastest way to do so is to expand the use of ethanol."	— US President George W. Bush, April 26, 2006[6]

"I am determined that we use biofuel, from palm and rape oil to soya and sugar, and then eventually use cellulosic biofuels, and potentially even hydrogen, to replace petrol and diesel with low- or no-carbon alternatives."
	— UK Minister of Parliament Gordon Brown, October 30, 2006[7]

"I am convinced that one of the greatest challenges of our time is climate change. ... Therefore we have developed a common framework—which includes biofuels. ... The Americans have an ambitious goal of introducing 20 percent biofuels. The European Union has set itself the goal of 15 percent."
	— German Chancellor Angela Merkel, April 30, 2007[8]

growth of biofuels, as we discussed in Chapter 2. The International Institute for Sustainable Development estimated that global subsidies given to biofuel producers was $22 billion in 2011, more than 25 percent of the $83 billion value of the world biofuel market.[9] By 2019, four decades of incentives had boosted biofuel consumption in the US and Europe to nine and eight percent of the total vehicle fuel used, respectively. The Americas (mostly Brazil and the US) and Europe consume 73 percent of the world's transportation biofuels.[10] But today, biofuels provide only about three percent of the vehicle fuels used globally, while

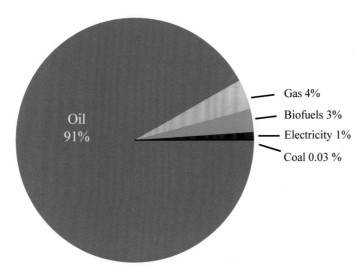

Oil
91%

Gas 4%
Biofuels 3%
Electricity 1%
Coal 0.03 %

World Transportation Fuel Used in 2019. Oil continues to hold a dominant share of the world's transportation fuel. (World Bioenergy Association, 2021)[11]

oil and gas provide 95 percent. A close look at biofuels uncovers serious issues regarding land use, water use, and cost. In addition, it's questionable whether using them really helps reduce emissions of carbon dioxide (CO_2).

Just like biomass fuels used for electricity, biofuels produced from harvests suffer from very low power density (power output per square meter of land), therefore requiring huge amounts of land for volume production. Vaclav Smil estimated the power density of US ethanol production to be only 0.26 watts per square meter. This is 500 times less than the average output of US oil fields and thousands of times less than the best oil fields in the Middle East.[12] As a result, biofuels now consume three percent of the world's agricultural land to produce three percent of the world's vehicle fuel.

Europe's Renewable Energy Directive of 2009 mandated that member states achieve a 10 percent renewable-energy share of transportation fuel by 2020. This caused a huge increase in the demand for soy and palm oil to produce biodiesel. An estimated 8.8 million hectares (34,000 square miles) of land has been used over the last decade for feedstock farms in Europe, South America, and Southeast Asia, an area larger than the size of Austria.[13] Soy oil was shipped 8,000 miles from Brazil, and palm oil was shipped 10,000 miles from Indonesia, to feed Europe's biofuel plants in the name of sustainability. It is estimated that Europe's drive for biofuels contributed heavily to Amazon deforestation and destroyed 10 percent of orangutan habitats in Indonesia.[14]

Biofuel production also consumes huge amounts of water. A 2009 study by the University of Twente in the Netherlands found that, while production of a gallon of gasoline requires about 7 gallons of water, production of a gallon of ethanol requires about 268 gallons of water. Production of a gallon of biodiesel requires a huge 1,989 gallons of water.[15] Since production of biofuels requires roughly a thousand times more land and vastly more water, how can biofuels be regarded as sustainable?

In fact, burning biofuels, like burning biomass, doesn't reduce CO_2 emissions when compared to burning hydrocarbon fuels. Biofuel production causes both direct and indirect land-use changes. Direct land-use change occurs when new cropland is created for growing biofuel feedstock. Indirect land-use change

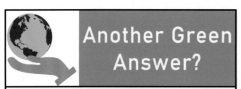

Another Green Answer?

Poo-Powered Bus Hits the Road in the UK

"In the U.K., the country's first ever bus powered on food waste and human poo has taken to the road, which engineers believe could provide a sustainable way of fueling public transport."

— *The Digest*, Nov. 20, 2014[16]

occurs when existing cropland is converted to biofuel production, forcing food and feed to be grown on new land elsewhere.

A 2015 study funded by the European Commission found that high emissions were produced from land-use change for the production of palm oil, rapeseed oil, soy oil, and sunflower oil, which provide about 80 percent of Europe's feedstock for biodiesel fuel.[17] Transport & Environment (T&E), a non-governmental organization based in Brussels, pointed out that, when land-use changes are considered, "all vegetable oil-based biodiesel has more emissions than fossil diesel." They also concluded that fuels based on soy and palm oil emit *two and three times more* CO_2 than hydrocarbon diesel fuel, respectively. T&E calls for a phase-out of all crop-based biofuels in Europe by 2030, with the substitution of electric vehicles for road transport and hydrogen fuels for shipping and aviation.[18]

The cost of biofuels does not compare well with the cost of diesel and gasoline. The energy content of ethanol is 76,000 British Thermal Units (Btu) per gallon, which is only 66 percent of the 115,000 Btu content of gasoline. Reduced mileage isn't apparent with a 10 percent ethanol blend, but a car that gets 30 mpg on pure gasoline will only get 21.4 mpg when fueled by E85, the 85 percent ethanol blend. The price of E85 in the US is usually lower than gasoline but more expensive per gallon when the mileage reduction is considered. Biodiesel gets only 91 percent of the mileage of pure diesel fuel.[19] Ethanol and biodiesel are poor mileage fuels.

An indirect cost of biofuels is the increased cost of food production. More than 90 million acres of land in the US are planted annually with corn, and 10 to 20 percent of the crop is exported. Land for ethanol production for fuel has grown to almost 40 percent of the land planted with corn in the US.[20] Each bushel of corn produces about 2.7 gallons of ethanol. A sport utility vehicle using E85 consumes about 25 gallons of ethanol per tank. Therefore, a single tank of E85 uses over nine bushels of corn, which, according to some estimates, can provide most of the annual diet for a person in the developing world.[21]

Despite major cost, land-use, and water-use problems, biofuels still remain the favored fuel of green advocates, particularly for shipping and aviation. It appears that no other solution can "decarbonize" these industries.

College Courses We Expect to See?[22]

Transportation 278
Sailboats and Blimps to Save the Planet

TRANSFORMATION OF SHIPPING?

Today, almost 100 percent of maritime fuel comes from hydrocarbons. In 2020, about 79 percent of ship fuel, or bunker fuel, was fuel oil, which included Heavy Fuel Oil (HFO) and a small portion known as Low Sulfur Fuel Oil. HFO is a high-sulfur residual fuel that resembles tar until heated. Marine diesel oil and a small amount of liquefied natural gas provided the other 21 percent of maritime fuels.[23]

Ships transport more than 70 percent of goods globally. In 2020, about 100,000 ships, weighing 100 gross tons or more, transported 10.7 billion metric tons of freight. This freight total was down about 3.8 percent from 2019 due to the COVID-19 pandemic. Tankers carried 27 percent of maritime freight, including crude oil, refined petroleum products, gas, and chemicals. The other 73 percent of maritime freight was dry cargo.[24]

According to the International Maritime Organization (IMO), a United Nations agency responsible for regulating the world maritime industry, shipping emitted about 2.9 percent of global greenhouse gases (GHG) in 2018. Shipping's share of the world's emissions has been growing slowly for several decades. The IMO projects that, without reduction measures, CO_2 emissions from shipping will continue to grow as trade volumes expand.[25]

Until 2020, the maritime industry had not been subject to CO_2-emissions regulations, but that is changing. In July 2021, the European Union announced emissions regulations for ships of 5,000 gross tons and above operating in the European Economic Area (EEA). The new regulations would include GHG-intensity standards for ship fuels and taxes on bunker fuel sold in the EEA.[26]

The IMO established goals in 2018, calling for a 50 percent reduction in GHG emissions from shipping by 2050. The organization proposes "carbon pricing mechanisms," which include the use of low-carbon fuels, energy efficiency standards for ships, and even mandates to reduce ship speed. The shipping industry appears ready to comply.[27]

Ships and aircraft are the most difficult transportation vehicles to decarbonize. Powering ships and planes with electricity is practically impossible because of long-distance and high drive-power requirements. Ships powered by liquified natural gas may be an alternative, but the IMO is concerned with possible global warming caused by gas leaks. Improved ship efficiency and low-carbon fuels appear to be the only alternatives.

Slow **is the New Green**

Climate Change: Speed Limits for Ships Can Have 'Massive' Benefits
— *BBC*, November 11, 2019[28]

The Great Green Fleet Debacle

The US military is the largest institutional consumer of petroleum-derived fuel in the world. Observers estimate that the US Department of Defense (DoD) consumes about 4.6 billion gallons of fuel each year, with 70 percent used for operational purposes. The US Navy uses about 1.6 billion gallons of that fuel.[29]

Under the administration of President Barack Obama, the US Navy announced plans to reduce the use of hydrocarbon fuels in 2009. In 2011, US Secretary of the Navy Ray Mabus stated, "By no later than 2020, at least half of all energy that the navy uses, both afloat and ashore, will come from non-fossil fuel sources."[30] The Great Green Fleet initiative was a major part of this effort.

The Great Green Fleet program sought to use a drop-in blend of biofuels to replace diesel fuel in ships. In the summer of 2012, the DoD paid about $27 per gallon for small quantities of biodiesel, later to be mixed with diesel at a 50 percent blend. After purchasing 77 million gallons of biodiesel made from beef fat in 2016, the navy deployed a carrier task force using a fuel mixture of 90 percent diesel and 10 percent biodiesel.[31] After subsidies, the fuel blend cost just over $2 per gallon, competitive with hydrocarbon diesel fuel. However, the 10 percent biofuel portion still cost about $14 per gallon.[32] The navy also proposed to install hybrid electric-drive engines in 34 "green destroyers" to allow them to run on either fuel or electric power generated from fuel.[33]

But Great Green Fleet efforts to date have been a dismal failure. In addition to high costs, biofuels were not available around the world, requiring the use of traditional diesel fuel at overseas ports. Hybrid electric-drive destroyers could not keep up with nuclear-powered carriers when using electric engines. By the end of 2017, the navy had spent $57 billion on green programs.[34] The electric-drive destroyer program was cancelled in 2018. Two biofuel facilities are under construction, which will provide about five percent of the navy's fuel beginning in 2022.[35] But at the start of 2022, with the exception of nuclear-powered ships, more than 99 percent of US Navy's fuel still came from petroleum.

The IMO states, "The easiest and cheapest way to reduce emissions is to reduce ship speed." The group calls for a 2.8 percent reduction in average ship speed by 2030, which it estimates will increase shipping costs by 1.5 percent. This is probably an underestimate. The IMO acknowledges that slower speeds will require more ships.[36] A study by European consultancy CE Delft called for a 20 percent reduction in ship speeds to lower CO_2 emissions by 24 percent, requiring a 22 percent growth in the number of ships.[37]

Adoption of these proposals would be very expensive. The value of the world's shipping fleet at the end of 2021 was $985 billion.[38] The cost of a 20 percent increase in the number of ships would approach $200 billion, with additional costs for training new crews. Shipping cycle times would increase. It would take 20 percent longer to deliver cargo to the same location, requiring crews to be paid for longer voyages.

Today, corporations practice cycle-time reduction as a key business process. Apple, the world's most valuable company, calls it "reducing time to value."[39] Retailing giant Amazon implemented one-day delivery for many products. Footwear and apparel producer Nike announced a goal to reduce supply chain lead times by 83 percent.[40] But slow is the new green for shipping.

The IMO and other groups promote low-carbon fuels as the primary solution to decarbonize shipping and air travel. But today's biofuels cost roughly twice as much as bunker fuel, making the use of biofuels uneconomic for most shipping. Fuel is the single largest voyage cost for most carriers.[41] Biofuels are not available in many ports around the world. In addition, as in the case of biofuels used in land vehicles, the combustion of ship biofuels produces carbon dioxide. Only by ignoring the data can one conclude that biofuels emit less carbon dioxide than traditional petroleum-based fuels. Hydrogen fuels remain experimental for maritime applications.

Maritime operations certainly need to reduce harmful exhaust and discharges of waste into the oceans. It's smart environmental policy to reduce sulfur dioxide emissions by adoption of low-sulfur fuels and to regulate other harmful pollutants, but measures to reduce CO_2 emissions will be costly and won't achieve any measurable environmental benefits.

PROBLEMS WITH SUSTAINABLE AIRCRAFT

More than 99.9 percent of aircraft fuel today is derived from petroleum. In 2019, the world consumed 106 billion gallons of jet fuel, which was 99 percent of the aviation fuel used. Jet fuel consumption is expected to more than double to 230 billion gallons per year by 2050. Commercial aviation accounts for about 13 percent of transportation greenhouse gas emissions and over two percent of global CO_2 emissions.[42]

Today's jet aircraft can't be replaced with electric planes. The energy density of jet fuel is a minimum of 43 megajoules per kilogram (MJ/kg), while the best lithium battery energy densities are 0.7 MJ/kg.[44] Electric engines are more efficient, but jet fuel engines still have about a 20-to-one energy advantage compared to batteries. Battery-powered aircraft will remain commercially impractical for decades to come.

France Moves to Ban Short-Haul Domestic Flights

"French lawmakers have moved to ban short-haul internal flights where train alternatives exist, in a bid to reduce carbon emissions." — *BBC News*, April 12, 2021[43]

An agency of the UN, the International Civil Aviation Organization (ICAO), and the International Aviation Transportation Association (IATA) pin their decarbonization hopes on sustainable aviation fuel (SAF). According to the ICAO, SAF is an environmentally sustainable fuel that achieves a GHG reduction by using a production process that has lower

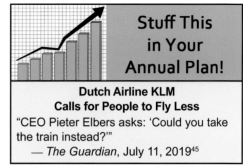

Stuff This in Your Annual Plan!

Dutch Airline KLM Calls for People to Fly Less
"CEO Pieter Elbers asks: 'Could you take the train instead?'"
— *The Guardian*, July 11, 2019[45]

emissions, also called "on a life-cycle basis." Production of SAF should use marginal land or other methods to not compete with food sources. SAF is meant to be a drop-in fuel that can be used in total or blended with jet fuel for existing aircraft.[46]

In 2009, the IATA established a goal of a 50 percent reduction in aviation emissions by 2050.[47] In 2021, they established a new target of net-zero emissions by 2050, probably an impossible goal. The organization projects that 65 percent of the emissions reduction will come from the use of SAF, 19 percent from new technologies, 13 percent from carbon offsets or carbon capture, and three percent from improved infrastructure and operations.[48]

Combustion of aviation fuel emits 3.16 metric tons of carbon dioxide for each metric ton of fuel burned.[49] Sustainable aviation fuel consists of an identical mix of the same hydrocarbon molecules as jet fuel. When you burn SAF, 3.16 tons of CO_2 are created for each ton of fuel, just like regular jet fuel. So where's the emissions reduction?

IATA claims that SAF reduces CO_2 emissions "by up to 80 percent"[50] on a life-cycle basis,

---

Jet Fuel and Sustainable Aviation Fuel

Jet fuel consists of a blend of n-alkanes, iso-alkanes, cycloalkanes, and aromatics. This blend is a mix of hydrocarbon molecules, which are composed of a chain of between 7–18 carbon atoms and about double the number of hydrogen atoms. The average molecule in jet fuel has 11 or 12 carbon atoms. When jet fuel is burned in engines, oxygen is taken from the air and 3.16 tons of CO_2 are exhausted for each ton of fuel burned.

Like regular jet fuel, SAF is a refined product. SAF is primarily produced by breaking down (or cracking) large lipids (fatty acids). As in the case of biofuels, lipids come primarily from oilseed crops with a small portion from waste oils. SAF can also be refined by building up molecules in small-molecule feedstock, such as from ethanol.

Because aircraft and aircraft engines can be in service for decades, SAF must be a drop-in fuel, essentially identical to jet fuel. SAF blends must perform the same as traditional jet fuel in terms of energy density, thermal stability, viscosity, freezing point, flash point, surface tension, and other properties. Because of identical specifications, SAF produces the same amount of carbon dioxide as jet fuel when burned.[51]

These Hybrid Airships Are the Low-Carbon Future of Air Travel
— *Euronews.Green*, September 15, 2021[52]

but it's hard to understand how this is possible. Oil seed crops must be planted, fertilized with chemicals produced from hydrocarbons, and then refined to make SAF. These crops suffer the same issues related to land-use-change emissions as biofuels for land vehicles.

SAF advocates say that waste oil, such as used cooking oil, can be refined to produce SAF. If waste oil were the primary SAF feedstock, this would indeed reduce emissions because waste oil emits CO_2 as it decays anyway. But there is not enough waste oil available. Most waste oil collected today is already used to provide biofuel feedstock used for land vehicles.

Fuel represents 20 to 30 percent of the operating cost of an airline, a cost only exceeded by labor. SAF is expensive. The Finnish company Neste is a leading producer of SAF, having begun production in 2011. Neste produces fuel from recycled cooking oil. But recycled oil is expensive to gather. As a result, Neste SAF is three or four times the price of typical fuel.[53] Airlines will be slow to take on this cost burden.

If sustainable aviation fuels are adopted, the scale of the capacity required will be huge. In 2018, only two million gallons of SAF were produced. Compare that to the 230 billion gallons that would be needed each year by 2050. According to the ICAO, about 170 new large SAF refineries need to be built *every year* until 2050, at a cost of up to $60 billion per year, to replace traditional jet fuel.[54] A wholesale transition to SAF is unlikely, but if it's somehow accomplished, actual CO_2 emissions reductions will be tiny.

GREEN TRAINS

Railroads provided about eight percent of passenger travel and nine percent of freight transport globally in 2020, according to the International Energy Agency (IEA).[55] Of train activity around the world, 60 percent carries passengers and 40 percent carries freight. Passenger-rail traffic rose 91 percent from 1996 to 2016 to over four trillion passenger-kilometers per year. Freight-rail activity rose by about two-thirds over the same period. Rail-traffic growth was similar to the growth in car, truck, and aviation transportation over the last two decades, almost maintaining its share at just under 10 percent of transportation.[56]

The IEA is a big fan of trains. It points out that rail "requires 12 times less energy and emits 7–11 times less greenhouse gases per passenger-kilometer traveled than private vehicles and airplanes."[57] The friction of steel train wheels on steel tracks causes 85–95 percent less energy loss than the friction of truck tires on roads. Railways use only three percent of the world's transport energy to carry almost 10 percent of the world's passengers and freight.[58]

Rail is the only mode of transportation that is widely electrified today. Electrified trains receive power from overhead lines or third rails. Globally, electricity powers three-quarters of passenger railways and almost half of freight railways, with the remaining trains powered by diesel fuel. Rail traffic produces only about three percent of the CO_2 emissions of the transportation sector.[59]

Types of railways and their drive power sources vary by region and continent. Europe built the first international train network, which was the largest in the world until surpassed by China in 2015. In Europe, more than 80 percent of the railways are traveled by passenger trains, and more than 80 percent of these are powered by electricity.[60]

In contrast, in North America freight transportation dominates rail networks. More than 90 percent of railroad mileage is traveled by freight trains. Currently, 100 percent of freight trains are pulled by diesel engines, and less than 30 percent of passenger-miles traveled are powered by electricity.[61]

High-speed rail is the fastest-growing segment of the rail industry. The Shinkansen, also known as the bullet train, began operation in Japan in 1964 as the world's first high-speed rail system (HSR). It remains the world's busiest HSR network, carrying more than 420,000 passengers on a typical weekday. High-speed rail networks, which carry only passenger traffic, have grown by a factor of more than seven since 2000, now accounting for about five percent of railroad tracks around the world. HSR trains whisk passengers along at a minimum of 200 km/h (120 mph), with newer HSR trains reaching speeds as high as 430 km/h (270 mph), attained by China's maglev train near Shanghai.[62] Unlike the growth of HSR systems seen in Europe and China, the US is without a single high-speed train. Lower population density in cities, stronger private property rights, and America's car culture act to make HSR projects tough to justify financially.

China's deployment of HSR is one of the

most amazing transportation stories of the twenty-first century. China began HSR service in 2008 between Beijing and Tianjin at speeds of up to 350 km/h (217 mph). The nation invested more than $200 billion over the next decade, installing more than 40,000 kilometers of track, and, in doing so, had laid down more than 60 percent of the world's total HSR track by 2017. As a result, China's regional airlines were forced to cut airfares and cancel short intercity routes.[64]

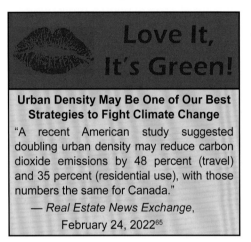

Urban Density May Be One of Our Best Strategies to Fight Climate Change

"A recent American study suggested doubling urban density may reduce carbon dioxide emissions by 48 percent (travel) and 35 percent (residential use), with those numbers the same for Canada."

— *Real Estate News Exchange,*
February 24, 2022[65]

Green-energy advocates call for people to switch from car, truck, and plane transportation to lower-emissions trains. The IEA laments that, if trends continue, railway traffic will lose share to other transportation by 2050. They call for taxes on aviation fuels, parking fees and road tolls, and "policies that promote high-density living" to boost use of rail networks.[66]

Advocates also call for the further decarbonization of rail systems. The IEA proposes a 100 percent decarbonization of railways by 2050, using a combination of electrification and hydrogen-fueled trains, and nations are following their lead. The UK Department of Transportation has set a goal to eliminate all diesel-only trains by 2040.[67]

The US will be a tough nut to crack, however. Privately owned US rail companies use diesel-fueled freight trains to carry more than 90 percent of rail traffic.[68] US rail companies tout their lower-energy use and low emissions, while at the same time requesting government support to build rail transport market share. But a CO_2 target is on their back. Renewable-energy advocates will soon be demanding the elimination of diesel trains, which will require hundreds of billions in capital investment to switch to electric or hydrogen systems. In Europe, China, and other regions, governments provide the majority of the capital investment funds for rail infrastructure. Free-market US train systems may need to become government financed or owned to make such a transition.

PROPOSED HYDROGEN SOLUTIONS

Today there is a high level of international enthusiasm for hydrogen as a possible low-emissions fuel for transportation and industrial uses. When hydrogen burns, the only combustion product is water vapor. Too reactive to exist naturally, it must be created and stored. Hydrogen is currently almost entirely produced by hydrocarbon sources that exhaust carbon dioxide. Globally, about six percent of natural gas and two percent of coal is used for production of hydrogen.[69] But advocates propose that "green hydrogen" be produced by electrolysis of water, using electricity from wind and solar facilities, to minimize CO_2 emissions. Green-hydrogen fuel could then become a solution for difficult-to-decarbonize ship, plane, and train transportation.

During the Gaslight Era of the early- to mid-1800s, town gas, as it was called, was manufactured from coal, pitch, whale oil, or petroleum. It was piped to cities in Europe and the US for use in streetlights, commercial buildings, and homes. Town gas consisted of a mix of methane and 30–50 percent hydrogen. Over the next 100 years, town gas was replaced with lower-cost natural gas (almost all methane) produced from gas wells. The last US gas manufacturing plant in New York closed in the early 1950s.[70]

Hydrogen has been of interest as a transportation fuel since the oil shocks of the 1970s, driven by unfounded concerns about reaching peak oil and climate change. Spending on hydrogen research and development rose to about $1 billion per year by 2008, mostly centered in Europe, Japan, and the US. Annual spending then fell to about $600 million per year in 2012 and recently began rising again as a proposed fuel in net-zero plans.[71]

But transportation fueled by hydrogen remains experimental. There were only about 11,000 hydrogen-fueled cars and light-duty vehicles in operation globally in 2019, mostly in California, Europe, and Japan. About 25,000 factory forklifts and 2,000 buses and trucks were operating in demonstration markets, along with two hydrogen trains in Germany. These vehicles use hydrogen almost entirely produced from natural gas. Maritime and aviation use of hydrogen is currently limited to small hydrogen demonstration projects, and the infrastructure needed to refuel hydrogen vehicles remains almost non-existent at ports, airports, and on vehicle routes.[72]

Hydrogen-fueled transportation faces larger obstacles than those encountered by electric vehicles. Hydrogen (H_2) is the smallest element in the chemical environment, which means that it leaks easily from storage containers

Your Renewables Ain't Makin' It

BC Transit's $90M Hydrogen Bus Fleet to Be Sold Off, Converted to Diesel

"The 20 vehicles were part of a $90-million plan to showcase hydrogen power during the 2010 Winter Olympic Games. ... Hydrogen buses cost $1.34 per kilometre to maintain, versus 65 cents per kilometre for diesel-powered buses. ... The hydrogen fuel had to be trucked in from Quebec."
— *CBC News*, December 4, 2014[73]

and pipeline systems, causing corrosion at seams. Hydrogen has low volumetric density, requiring either compression and storage at high pressures or cooling to liquid form to almost absolute zero for use in practical applications. In addition, hydrogen gas is highly flammable and ignites more easily than natural gas.[74] Safety measures for the broad use of hydrogen as a transportation fuel will be challenging to develop and costly to implement. We will discuss hydrogen fuel again in the next chapter.

DIFFICULT ROUTE FOR GREEN TRANSPORTATION

Today, 91 percent of global transportation is fueled by oil, and another four percent is fueled by natural gas. Biofuels provide only three percent of transport fuel, while electricity provides one percent, both with questionable effectiveness in reducing CO_2 emissions. Almost 100 percent of maritime and aviation fuel comes from hydrocarbons, with the vast majority from petroleum. Only rail systems use a high degree of electric propulsion, but trains are slowly losing transportation share to aircraft, ships, and motor vehicles.

"United continues to lead from the front when it comes to climate change action," said United CEO Scott Kirby. "Today's SAF flight is not only a significant milestone for efforts to decarbonize our industry, but when combined with the surge in commitments to produce and purchase alternative fuels, we're demonstrating the scalable and impactful way companies can join together and play a role in addressing the biggest challenge of our lifetimes."
— *PR Newswire*, December 1, 2021[75]

Decarbonization of heavy transportation will be difficult and economically impossible in some sectors. With hydrogen fuel in the experimental stage, biofuels are considered the only feasible option for decarbonizing ships and aircraft. But maritime biofuels are twice as expensive as traditional bunker fuel and do not reduce carbon dioxide emissions when taking land-use changes into account. Sustainable aviation fuel is chemically identical to standard jet fuel and emits the same amount of CO_2 when burned. There isn't enough waste oil in the world to power even a small part of global aviation. Nevertheless, the maritime and aviation industries have jumped on board to pursue the mirage of Net Zero, because there is no other alternative.

But global industries that use vast amounts of hydrocarbon fuels and feedstock face similar demands to decarbonize. Let's look at efforts to power heavy industry with renewable energy in the next chapter.

CHAPTER 9

CAN RENEWABLES POWER HEAVY INDUSTRY?

"We are a fossil-fueled civilization whose technical and scientific advances, quality of life, and prosperity rest on the combustion of huge quantities of fossil carbon, and we cannot simply walk away from this critical determinant of our fortunes in a few decades, never mind years." —VACLAV SMIL (2022)[1]

After 150 years of growth and evolution, hydrocarbon-using industries span the globe, producing billions of tons of materials every year. These industries provide components for manufacturing vehicles, appliances, and other consumer goods. They produce materials for buildings, factories, houses, and roads, as well as wind turbines and solar facilities. They supply essential ingredients for agriculture, medicine, and science. Today's heavy industry provides the basis for the flourishing of modern society.

Four big industries—ammonia, cement, plastics, and steel—are powered by hydrocarbons. The world's ammonia industry produced almost 200 million tons of ammonia in 2020, primarily for agricultural fertilizer, using natural gas as fuel and feedstock. About

4.3 billion tons of cement, the essential material for concrete, were output that same year, while exhausting carbon dioxide (CO_2) and burning hydrocarbons in furnaces. Over 300 million tons of plastic are produced each year using gas for feedstock and fuel. The steel industry produces 1.9 billion tons of steel each year by using coal and gas.[2]

Although small compared to the amount of (CO_2) naturally emitted from the oceans and land areas, the quantity of CO_2 exhausted from heavy industry is still large. Green advocates seek to transform industry to either use renewable energy or to capture emissions when using renewables is not feasible. Let's look first at carbon capture and storage, and then we'll look at the proposed transition of the four big industries to renewable energy. Finally, we'll discuss the prospects for an economy based on hydrogen fuel.

CARBON CAPTURE AND STORAGE

Carbon capture and storage (CCS) is the process of capturing CO_2 from an industrial operation before it enters the atmosphere, transporting it, and storing it for centuries to millenia. For more than a decade, government and industry leaders have proposed that CCS could be the solution for eliminating CO_2 emissions from hard-to-decarbonize heavy industry. The International Energy Agency (IEA) calls for nine percent of emissions worldwide to be captured by 2050 in the agency's Sustainable Development Scenario.[3]

But CCS has been slow to take off, since it's expensive and has a product that is not very salable. As of July 2021, the 27 large-scale CCS facilities operating around the world had an annual carbon dioxide capture capacity of about 40 million tons per year, or only about 0.1 percent of the man-made emissions produced globally.[4]

Sixteen of the operating CCS facilities reside in the US and Canada, which is more than half of the world's total. Fourteen of these use captured CO_2 for enhanced oil recovery. Captured CO_2 is injected into oil wells to boost well output. In fact, 22 of the world's 27 large-scale CCS facilities use captured CO_2 for this purpose.[5] Environmental groups attack this use of captured CO_2, pointing out that this process stimulates increased petroleum production. In any case, there are not enough opportunities to use CO_2 to recover oil on the huge scale envisioned for CCS.

Governments now offer a wide array of incentives to boost CCS. The US federal government offers CCS projects a 45Q tax credit

of \$50 per ton of CO_2 captured and stored, or \$35 per ton for CO_2 captured and used in applications such as enhanced oil recovery.[7] Other nations, such as Australia, provide direct investment in CCS projects to accelerate deployment.

In Europe, CCS operations accrue carbon permits, which can then be sold on the European Emissions Trading System (ETS). By early 2022, the price of a carbon permit on the ETS had risen to more than €80.[8] The Norwegian state-owned oil company Equinor stores about one million tons of CO_2 per year in the Sleipner field, a saline formation one kilometer below the seabed in the North Sea. For the Sleipner operation, Equinor receives permits from the government worth about €80 million per year on the ETS. The company is also planning a new project, called Northern Lights, to gather liquefied CO_2 from a number of industrial customers and store it 8,500 feet below the sea floor. Norway's government will pay for 80 percent of the first phase of the Northern Lights project.[9]

CCS activity is rising, supported by tax credits, carbon permits, and direct subsidies. Close to \$18 billion has been committed by industry across the world for 120 new CCS projects since early 2020. Almost 50 new US projects were announced between January 2020 and August 2021. With these new projects, the IEA estimates that global CCS capacity will double by 2030.[10]

But the economics for carbon capture and storage remain poor. As an example, in 2020 Wyoming passed a statute requiring CCS equipment to be added to existing coal-fired power plants by 2030. Analysis by Wyoming power companies found that the costs of moving to CCS were too high to be economically feasible.

Carbon Capture and Storage and Wyoming Utilities

Wyoming is the leading US coal state, mining 41 percent of US coal in 2020 and producing 85 percent of the state's electricity from coal-fired power plants. With abundant coal resources and good opportunities to store carbon dioxide underground, Wyoming appeared to be in an excellent position to equip power plants with CCS. In support of its coal industry, Wyoming passed House Bill 200 in March 2020, directing utilities to produce 20 percent of electricity from coal plants fitted with CCS by 2030.[11] In response to the statute, Rocky Mountain Power and Black Hills Energy, Wyoming's two major power companies, analyzed CCS alternatives for their coal operations and provided comments to the Wyoming Public Service Commission in March 2022.

But the comments were not favorable for CCS. Black Hills Energy determined that adding CCS to two existing coal plants would cost an estimated \$506 million and \$474 million. This was three times the cost to build the plants.[12] Rocky Mountain Power stated that adding CCS to its existing plants was "not economically feasible at this time."[13]

Beyond cost, the amount of CO_2 that proponents say must be captured crushes any ideas about feasibility. As we discussed in Chapter 3, the amount of CO_2 produced by industry is only about five percent of what nature releases into and absorbs from the atmosphere every day. But the amount of industrial CO_2 produced is still huge in human terms.

The Drax Power Station in North Yorkshire, England, which has been converted to using two-thirds biomass fuel, is experimenting with CCS for biomass operations. Each day, the plant uses about 20,000 tons of wood pellets delivered by 475 railroad cars. When the fuel is burned, two oxygen atoms from the atmosphere join with each carbon atom to produce the exhausted CO_2. Picture the volume that these 475 railroad cars would carry and then more than double it to get an idea of the amount of CO_2 to be captured and stored *each day*. The Global CCS Institute estimates that 70 to 100 major CCS facilities will need to be built *each year* until 2050 to meet IEA goals, at a total cost of about $1 trillion.[14]

CCS also faces major logistical issues. The huge underground storage areas needed might be far from fuel-combustion sites. A vast network of pipelines would need to be built for CO_2 storage. CO_2 leaks will present major liability issues, which may decrease participation by private industry. Water availability for CCS can also be a limiting factor. The addition of CCS technology to a coal-fired power plant can boost water usage by 35–40 percent.[16]

The huge obstacles against carbon capture and storage preclude success on a large scale. Efforts to pursue CCS will be a foolish episode in human history, along with other green efforts to control global temperatures. Every dollar spent on CCS is a dollar not available to provide clean water, a healthy diet, and a rising standard of living for billions in need.

Double the coal burned in a large power plant to estimate the CO_2 volume that needs to be stored. Image of a coal train in Wyoming.[15]

AMMONIA: ESSENTIAL FOR AGRICULTURE

The ammonia industry, the first of the four big industries we'll look at, produces one of the world's largest-volume synthetic chemicals. About 70 percent of the 186 million metric tons of ammonia (NH_3) delivered in 2020 was used to make fertilizers for agriculture. Almost half of all nitrogen atoms in human food come from synthetic ammonia. The remaining ammonia output is used to produce plastics, explosives, and synthetic fibers.

The industry consumes about two percent of the world's energy and exhausts about 1.3 percent of CO_2 emissions.[17]

Most natural nitrogen is nitrogen gas, which comprises 78 percent of our atmosphere. But nitrogen gas consists of the molecule N_2, in which two atoms are held together chemically by a strong triple bond. Most plants cannot get nitrogen directly from the air. In the early 1900s, German chemists Fritz Haber and Karl Bosch invented a process to produce nitrogen-containing ammonia from air and methane (natural gas) under high temperatures and pressures. Improved versions of this process today provide nitrogen for agriculture.

Production of ammonia begins with the production of hydrogen. Methane feedstock is first cleaned of sulfur impurities. It's then reacted with steam and oxygen under high pressure to produce hydrogen gas, carbon monoxide, and CO_2, a process called steam methane reforming (SMR). Water vapor is then used to convert the carbon monoxide to additional CO_2 and H_2. In 2020, 72 percent of hydrogen used for ammonia production came from the SMR process. Almost all of the remaining hydrogen for ammonia comes from coal gasification, which is used in China to produce most of the world's coal-produced ammonia.[18]

After the production of hydrogen, ammonia is created by reacting the hydrogen gas with nitrogen from the air in the presence of iron or another metal catalyst at high temperatures (400–650°C) and high pressures (150–200 atmospheres). Only two percent of ammonia is directly applied to crops. Instead, ammonia is converted into urea, nitric acid, and ammonium nitrate fertilizer.[19] Urea, the largest derivative of ammonia, uses carbon dioxide captured from ammonia production at collocated facilities on a large scale.

Ammonia production is energy and emissions intensive. The most efficient facilities produce a metric ton of ammonia using 28 gigajoules of energy, about equal to the energy contained in 212 gallons of gasoline.[20] Production of a ton of ammonia exhausts 2.4 tons of CO_2, almost twice the emissions released in steel production and four times the emissions released in cement production.[21]

GREENHOUSE GAS HORROR!
How Fertilizer in Farming is Pushing Climate Change Past "Worst Case Scenarios"
— *Global News*, October 7, 2020[22]

The International Energy Agency and other groups say that the fertilizer industry's current trajectory is unsustainable. Ammonia production is projected to increase by 40 percent by 2050, driven by economic and population growth. They propose that CCS be used for SMR and coal-gasification processes, or that the fertilizer industry make a complete switch to green hydrogen for feedstock and fuel.

But a switch to green energy faces major issues related to cost, logistics, and scale. Today, more than 99 percent of the hydrogen used for ammonia production comes from SMR or coal gasification. Less than one percent of hydrogen comes from "green" electrolysis of water, which is a very expensive process. In April 2021, the world's largest electrolyzer, with a capacity of 30 MW, began production in Baofeng, China. The IEA estimates that ten 30 MW electrolysers must begin production *each month*, along with one large CCS project *every four months*, between now and 2050 just to serve the global ammonia industry.[23]

CEMENT: ESSENTIAL FOR CONSTRUCTION

Concrete is the world's most-used material that is manufactured. Each year, construction industries deploy about 14 billion cubic meters of concrete by volume to build roads, bridges, buildings, and structures of every kind.[24] Cement, the second of the four big industries, is the essential ingredient of concrete, the glue that binds it together. Cement is mixed with water, sand, and small stones (aggregate) on a construction site to form concrete. Cement reacts with water in a process called hydration, a chemical reaction that makes concrete extremely strong. The industry produced 4.3 billion tons of cement in 2020, exhausting about seven percent of global CO_2 emissions. China produces 55 percent of the world's cement, with India a distant second at eight percent.[25]

Cement production is a complex three-stage process. First, heavy-duty machines mine materials containing calcium carbonate, such as limestone, marl, or chalk, from quarries. The quarried materials are crushed and mixed with small amounts of iron ore, bauxite, shale, clay, or sand to provide the iron oxide, alumina, and silica needed to meet process and product requirements. The crushed material is then milled to a fine powder called raw meal.[26]

In the second stage, the raw meal powder passes through a series of three or more rotating kilns, which heat the powder to 900°C and then 1450°C. During this process, the limestone in the raw meal is melted and calcinated into lime. The resulting small, grey lumps, called clinker, are 3–25 millimeters (mm) in diameter.

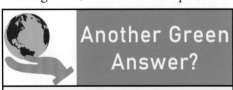

Engineers Create World's First Carbon-Neutral Cement Out of Algae

"It's currently unclear how cost-effective the method would be compared to traditional cement production."

— *Freethink*, July 3, 2022[27]

In the third stage, the clinker is blended with gypsum and ground into a fine powder, known as Portland cement, or ground with other materials to make blended cement.[28]

Cement production exhausts large quantities of carbon dioxide, which is about 0.59 tons of CO_2 for each ton of cement output. Limestone is mostly calcium carbonate ($CaCO_3$). When limestone is reduced to lime to order to form clinker, CO_2 is exhausted, which is about 60–70 percent of the CO_2 expended in making cement. The other 30–40 percent is from fuel used to heat cement kilns.[29]

The IEA and the World Business Council for Sustainable Development call for the cement industry to reduce CO_2 emissions "by 24 percent below current levels by 2050." In addition to calling for an improvement in the efficiency of production, they propose a shift towards alternative fuels, "with biomass and waste increasing to 30% globally as a share of thermal energy by 2050." They also propose that the CO_2 exhausted from creating clinker be captured by CCS processes.[30] But we've heard this before. Again, biomass combustion does not reduce CO_2 emissions, and there isn't enough waste to power transportation, let alone heavy industry. CCS is expensive and captures less than 0.1 percent of the emissions produced by the cement industry today.

Concrete and cement have served as essential building materials throughout history. The ancient Romans developed a form of hydraulic cement that set up underwater. Many of their concrete structures still exist today after 2,000 years.

But some want to curtail, or even end, concrete use. The UN and environmental groups want to see cement production decline from 2020 to 2050.[31] This is despite the fact that world cement production has more than tripled in recent years, from 1.2 billion tons in 1990 to 4.3 billion tons in 2020.[32] The average US home today uses 120,000 pounds of concrete, 15,000 pounds of concrete block, and 75,000 pounds of sand, gravel, and bricks.[33] While American homes tend to be larger and contain more materials than those in other nations, concrete remains an essential material to raise the standard of living for billions of people across the globe.

Save our planet

Kill yourself

Planet Over People?

Three Reasons Why We Should Stop Using Concrete

"We can't continue destroying the environment to create living spaces for ourselves."
— *Climate Conscious*, May 15, 2020[34]

CHEMICALS AND PLASTICS

We live in a world dependent on chemicals. Food, clothing, medicine, cell phones, toys, and materials for packaging, automobiles, buildings, and industry are derived from petrochemicals and fundamental to modern society. Plastics, the third big industry, are the largest portion of the chemical industry, which also includes ammonia, methanol, and specialty chemical products. Global plastics consumption has increased by a factor of 10 since 1970, and plastics remain the fastest-growing group of bulk materials in the world.

Petrochemicals are made from oil and gas. The manufacture of petrochemicals uses 14 percent and eight percent of the world's primary demand for oil and gas, respectively, and these totals are increasing. Oil and gas provide about 90 percent of the feedstock for the chemical industry, with the rest coming from coal and biomass. Chemical industries emit about five percent of CO_2 emissions, including 1.3 percent from ammonia production.[35]

Over 300 million tons of plastics are produced and consumed each year. Most plastics are derivatives of ethylene or propylene, reactive petrochemical compounds that are used to produce polymers to make plastics. Over 250 million tons of ethylene and propylene are produced worldwide each year and then used to manufacture polyethylene (PE), polypropylene (PP), polyvinylchloride (PVC), polystyrene (PS), and other plastics.[36]

Packaging constitutes about 36 percent of global demand for plastics, by far the largest end-user segment. Drink bottles made of polyethylene terephthalate (PET), other food packaging, and general industry packaging make up this segment. PVC is a leading product for the construction industry and totals 16 percent of global consumption. PVC is used for window and door frames and underground pipes, due to its stiffness and durability.

About 15 percent of plastics production goes toward making textiles. Synthetic textile products are made primarily from PET and PP for rope, carpet, clothing, and specialized applications such as Kevlar bullet-proof body armor. Polyester fiber recently surpassed cotton as the largest-volume fiber used, now accounting for about 60 percent of global fiber production. Consumer products, including toys and utensils, are the next largest market segment, making up about 10 percent of plastics production. PE, PP, PS, and other compounds serve consumer markets and other smaller specialty segments.[38]

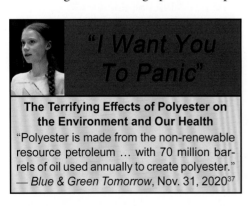

The Terrifying Effects of Polyester on the Environment and Our Health
"Polyester is made from the non-renewable resource petroleum ... with 70 million barrels of oil used annually to create polyester."
— *Blue & Green Tomorrow*, Nov. 31, 2020[37]

Based on current trends, the International Energy Agency projects that by 2050 chemical consumption will grow 60 percent and CO_2 emissions will rise by about 30 percent, if the industry does not transition to using renewable energy. Plastics will be the key driver of demand. Today, developed nations use up to

20 times as much plastic as underdeveloped nations use on a per-person basis, pointing to a huge rise in demand for plastics from developing economies in the coming years.

The IEA calls for a 60 percent reduction in CO_2 emissions from the chemical industry by 2050, even as it grows by 60 percent in that same period. They assert that this reduction can be achieved by widespread deployment of CCS, a transition from coal fuel to gas (primarily in China), better plastics recycling, and the use of hydrogen and biofuels for fuel and feedstocks.[39] But like in other industries, the chemical industry's use of CCS is in its infancy, and hydrogen and biofuels are expensive with limited available quantities.

Rather than spending up to a trillion dollars to transition the chemical and plastics industry to renewable energy to reduce CO_2 emissions, suppose we pursue a solution to a different and very real environmental problem. The world's oceans contain about 100 million tons of plastic waste, with an additional 10 million tons entering the oceans every year.[40] Let's put efforts toward the development and widespread adoption of biodegradable plastics, rather than trying to eliminate CO_2, a gas that is actually great for the biosphere.

IRON AND STEEL

Steel, the last of the four big industries, is the third-most abundant human-made material on Earth, after concrete and timber. The high strength, durability, and low cost of steel makes it a key material for buildings, infrastructure, transportation, machinery, and consumer goods. The steel industry consumes about eight percent of the world's energy and exhausts seven percent of CO_2 emissions.[41]

About 80 percent of steel is produced from iron ore with small amounts of scrap. Iron ore is primarily oxides of iron. The oxygen must be removed in the steel-making process.

Like cement production, steel production is also a complex three-step process. First, ore is surface mined and crushed in preparation for production of iron. Fine particles are partially melted in a process called sintering to increase particle size. Ore with low iron concentration is agglomerated and pelletized in a furnace to increase concentration. The prepared ore consists of particles 10–15 mm in diameter with a 50–60 percent iron concentration.[42]

In the second step of the process, carbon monoxide is used to cleave the oxygen atoms from the iron ore to make iron. Coal is heated to 1100°C in an oven to create coke, a pure-carbon version of coal. The combustion of coke then provides carbon monoxide for the reduction of iron oxide in iron making.

The blast furnace-basic oxygen furnace (BF-BOF) process enables about 70 percent of the world's steel and 90 percent of iron production. Iron ore and coke are fed into the top of the blast furnace, and air and oxygen gas are injected at the bottom. As it descends, coke burns with oxygen, creating carbon monoxide (CO). The CO reacts with the descending iron ore oxide, producing pure iron and exhausting CO_2. Lime and other additives reduce impurities and control temperature. Molten pig iron, at temperatures of up to 1500°C, is tapped from the bottom of the furnace, along with slag impurities, which float on top of the iron.

In the third step, liquid iron is fed into a basic oxygen furnace, which uses oxygen to lower the metal carbon content from 4–5 percent to the 0.25 percent needed for steel. Nickel or chromium are added to produce stainless steel or other metals for other steel alloys.[44]

An alternative, less-productive method is the direct reduction of iron (DRI), which uses gaseous reducing agents, usually natural gas, to produce iron from ore, followed by the use of an electric furnace (EF) to produce steel. The DRI-EF process produces about five percent of steel from ore globally and another 20 percent from scrap. This process requires pellets with a higher iron concentration, but it consumes about half of the energy of when a blast furnace is used. An additional five percent of the world's steel is produced in electric furnaces directly from scrap.[45]

To reduce emissions produced by the industry, the IEA calls for both a decline in the growth of steel production and a transition to renewable energy. World steel production grew about four percent per year from 2000 to 2020, more than doubling the amount produced from 850 million tons to 1.9 billion tons.[47] The IEA projects that the world's population will rise from 7.7 billion to 9.7 billion and that GDP will rise by 2.5 times by 2050. But they also project that steel production will only rise 1.1 percent annually over the same period, assuming a reduction in demand in ways such as "extending the lifetime of buildings" and shifting "away from private vehicles."[48]

The IEA's Net Zero 2050 scenario calls for

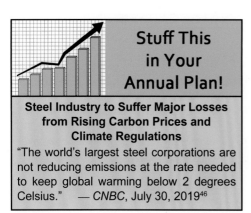

Stuff This in Your Annual Plan!

Steel Industry to Suffer Major Losses from Rising Carbon Prices and Climate Regulations

"The world's largest steel corporations are not reducing emissions at the rate needed to keep global warming below 2 degrees Celsius." — *CNBC*, July 30, 2019[46]

a technology shift from BF-BOF to DRI-EF production, in which DRI-EF usage will increase from about 25 percent to over 50 percent of production by 2050. The scenario calls for hydrogen produced from electrolysis of water to fuel about 15 percent of DRI production. CCS would be used for 15 percent of the steel produced from traditional blast furnaces. The industry's coal usage would drop by 40 percent, and electricity usage would double. If implemented, steel CO_2 emissions would fall by over 50 percent by 2050.[49]

Under pressure from governments and world organizations, the industry has adopted plans to pursue low-emissions steel production. The World Steel Association, the American Iron and Steel Institute, and other organizations have signed up to a version of Net Zero by 2050. Because of the costs of such a transition, they look toward large government subsidies and partnerships to help out. But major obstacles stand in their way.

Many emissions-reduction proposals are experimental and very costly. Consulting firm McKinsey & Company points out that carbon capture from BF-BOF and hydrogen-fueled DRI are technologies still in infancy. Only one steel facility using CCS operates today, the gas-fueled DRI plant of Emirates Steel in the United Arab Emirates, providing CO_2 for enhanced oil recovery. McKinsey is optimistic about a green steel industry, but they point out that green steel will be 20−25 percent more expensive and will need hydrogen and CO_2 production, transport, and storage facilities, which don't exist today.[50]

The average age of an iron- and steel-making facility is about 12 years, which is less than one-third of a typical plant lifetime. China, home to most of the facilities, produced 53 percent of the world's steel in 2021, primarily using BF-BOF technology.[51] Steel makers will likely oppose the early retirement of these plants. It's also doubtful that CCS pipelines and storage and hydrogen electrolytic capacity will be available to support this industry by 2050, even with massive government subsidies. Decarbonization goals for the steel industry appear to be beyond aggressive, more likely a wish and a prayer.

Port Talbot Steel Works and Tata Steel

Indian conglomerate Tata Steel has threatened to close the Port Talbot Steel Works in South Wales without financial support from the UK government. UK Tata Steel currently employs 8,000 workers to operate two blast furnaces to produce steel from iron ore. The company proposes replacing the blast furnaces with electric arc furnaces and using recycled steel. The firm wants a subsidy of £1.5 billion, half of the cost of the transition, to continue operations. Natarajan Chandrasekaran, chairman of the Tata Group, stated,

"A transition to a greener steel plant is the intention that we have. ... But this is only possible with financial help from the government."[52]

HYDROGEN FUEL FOR HEAVY INDUSTRY?

World leaders call for a new hydrogen economy to reduce emissions and fight global warming. Energy-poor nations hope that hydrogen can provide a measure of energy security. Like hydrogen is proposed as a transportation fuel, as we discussed in Chapter 8, it is also increasingly touted as a replacement for natural gas and coal in heavy industry. But tall barriers must be leaped for hydrogen to become a major fuel in the twenty-first century.

Hydrogen does not freely exist in nature, yet it is not expensive. Today, industrial hydrogen costs only about $1 per kilogram. About 99 percent of the world's 70 million tons of annual production comes from gas, using steam methane reforming, or from coal, using coal gasification, as we have discussed. Advocates propose to produce green hydrogen from electrolysis of water, using electricity from wind, solar, and other renewable sources.[53]

Electrolysis uses electricity to decompose water into hydrogen and oxygen gas. Industrial hydrogen electrolyzers use complex cell structures, catalysts, and electrolytes to maximize efficiency and reduce cost. But few electrolyzers operate today because the hydrogen they produce is very expensive. Hydrogen from electrolysis costs about $5 per kilogram, which is five times as much as hydrogen from natural gas.[54] Proposals for green hydrogen count on the grid to provide electricity from renewables to power the electrolyzers.

In addition, electrolysis uses huge quantities of electricity. Production of a single kilogram of hydrogen from electrolysis requires between 50–55 kWh, approaching double the daily power consumed by a US home.[55] For hydrogen to be green, it must be produced only from renewables. But the majority of electricity in most nations isn't produced from renewables. For hydrogen from electrolysis to become a significant energy source, disadvantages regarding cost, efficiency, transport, storage, intermittency, and scale must be overcome.

The top three nations pursuing a hydrogen economy—India, Japan, and Germany—don't have enough renewable electricity to produce green hydrogen. In 2021, India Prime Minister Narendra Modi announced a national hydrogen mission for his country; to make India a hub for hydrogen production and export. But 74 percent of India's electricity comes from coal.[57] So India's hydrogen producers must erect their own wind and solar facilities, rather than use grid electricity, multiplying the cost of green hydrogen.

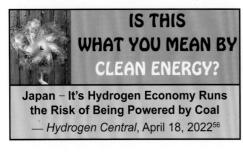

IS THIS WHAT YOU MEAN BY CLEAN ENERGY?

Japan – It's Hydrogen Economy Runs the Risk of Being Powered by Coal
— *Hydrogen Central*, April 18, 2022[56]

Japan was first to announce a nationwide program for hydrogen production in 2017.

Hydrogen Fuel Advocates

"Because green hydrogen is not just a huge commercial opportunity. Green hydrogen is good for the planet. Green hydrogen is good for energy security. And energy security is an important pillar of our European independence."
— President of the European Commission Ursula von der Leyen, May 17, 2022[58]

"Not only will green hydrogen be the basis of green growth through green jobs, but it will also set an example for the world towards clean energy transition."
— India Prime Minister Narendra Modi, August 15, 2021[59]

"Through innovation, hydrogen energy will become a trump card to solve the issues of energy security and global warming. ... Japan will lead the world in materializing a hydrogen society." — Japan Prime Minister Shinzo Abe, December 26, 2017[60]

Germany announced a hydrogen strategy in 2020. But since the 2011 Fukushima nuclear disaster, Germany and Japan closed most of their nuclear plants. Japan still gets 65 percent of its electricity from coal, gas, and oil. In 2021, Germany produced 40 percent of its power from wind, solar, and hydropower, but coal-fired electricity increased 21 percent to generate 28 percent of the nation's power, largely due to low-wind conditions during the summer.[61] Few nations have enough renewable electricity to electrolyze hydrogen in large quantities.

Intermittency will be a problem for electrolyzers. Wind and solar facilities output maximum power only 15–40 percent of the time. On cloudy or windless days, electrolysis output must be curtailed. Try to run a plant only on intermittent electricity from renewables.

Electrolysis uses huge amounts of water. About nine liters (2.4 gallons) of water are used to produce one kilogram of hydrogen. Currently, electrolytic production of the world's demand for hydrogen would consume 617 million cubic meters of water annually. Large electrolysis operations may not be possible in water-short regions, such as the Southwest US.

Today, most hydrogen is used on site. For hydrogen to power industry, it must be transported to plant sites and stored until needed. Distribution today relies on trucks carrying hydrogen as either a compressed gas or a supercooled liquid. Hydrogen can be stored in salt caverns or in tanks as gas or liquid, like natural gas. But hydrogen storage is more expensive because of lower volumetric density. For example, hydrogen at 700 atmospheres of pressure at a vehicle refueling station requires seven times the storage volume of gasoline.[62]

Advocates propose that the world's three million kilometers of gas pipelines be used to transport hydrogen. But hydrogen degrades metal by a process known as hydrogen embrittlement. Embrittlement can cause cracks, leaks, and even explosions in metal pipelines.[63] The US National Renewable Energy Laboratory recommends that blends be less than 20 percent hydrogen to minimize embrittlement.[64] Since the energy density of hydrogen is only one-third that of natural gas, a 20 percent blend of hydrogen would reduce the energy a pipeline transports by 13 percent. In addition, some industries today cannot use hydrogen blends. Control systems and seals of chemical pipelines can tolerate blends of only five percent hydrogen without the need to replace equipment, which can be costly.[65]

India and other nations plan to export hydrogen, but transport of hydrogen by ship is also costly. Liquefaction of hydrogen to −253°C requires energy equal to about 25–35 percent of the hydrogen itself, compared to the 10 percent needed to liquify natural gas. Hydrogen can be transported by ship in the form of ammonia, which liquifies at 35°C, making it much cheaper to transport than hydrogen. But conversion to and from ammonia requires the energy equivalent of up to 30 percent of the hydrogen itself.[66]

Finally, the scale of electricity needed to produce hydrogen to power industry is *gigantic*. The IEA estimates that producing all primary chemicals from electrolytic hydrogen in 2050 would require between 12,000–17,500 TWh of renewable electricity.[67] This is 3.2–4.7 times the total renewable electricity generated globally in 2021.[68]

INDUSTRY TRANSFORMATION FANTASY

Renewable advocates propose that the heavy industries of the world be transformed to use CCS and green hydrogen fuel to eliminate CO_2 emissions. They view this as a goal for 2050, but it is better classified as a fantasy. To decarbonize the ammonia, cement, plastics, and steel industries, more than 3,000 large-scale carbon-capture facilities would need to be built, compared to the 27 small-scale facilities that struggle to operate currently. Thousands of large-scale electrolyzers would need to be erected to produce green hydrogen, compared to the dozens of small-scale plants today. These electrolyzers would require more than five times the electricity output from renewable facilities than the total of the world's renewable electricity output today. Massive regional pipeline networks would need to be constructed to transport captured CO_2, along with huge additional networks for hydrogen. We have not discussed other industries that use large amounts of natural gas, including aluminum, metal smelting, glass, mining, paper, and food processing. Green hydrogen and CCS can serve only a small fraction of these industries' fuel needs by 2050.

As we will discuss in the next chapter, a number of trends are emerging that will stunt the growth of renewable energy and lead to the failure of plans for a global energy transition.

CHAPTER 10

ENERGY CRISIS AND
THE SEEDS OF FAILURE

"All renewables thus require a material throughput—from mining to processing to installing to disposing of the materials later as waste—that is orders of magnitude larger than for non-renewable energy sources."
—MICHAEL SHELLENBERGER (2018)[1]

To some, the green-energy wave appears to be irresistible. Political leaders, university scholars, Fortune 500 CEOs, the United Nations, and the media tout the need for an energy transition to save the planet. Nations, provinces, states, cities, companies, and associations announce net-zero goals. The world is spending more than $500 billion per year on renewable energy and electric vehicles (EVs), including tens of billions in renewable subsidies. Advocates tell us that if we all work together, we can get there.

But a closer look reveals that the renewable energy movement is in trouble. Countries and states with rising renewable electricity penetration suffer an increasing burden of higher electricity prices and declining power reliability. Escalating metal costs threaten to stunt the growth of EVs. Accumulating waste from old wind turbine blades, solar panels, and EV batteries increasingly clogs landfill sites. Local opposition to land-intensive renewable projects rises across the world. Carbon capture and storage (CCS) and hydrogen fuel plans falter beneath the vast scale of emissions by heavy industry. Global CO_2 emissions continue to rise, driven by developing economies. And the global energy crisis of 2022 may be the first of a series of energy crises resulting from renewable energy adoption.

COVID-19 AND THE GLOBAL ENERGY CRISIS OF 2022

The first official cases of the human coronavirus disease COVID-19 were recorded on December 31, 2019, in Wuhan, China. The World Health Organization (WHO) declared the outbreak a "public health emergency" in January 2020 and a "pandemic" in March 2020.[2] By midyear of 2022, more than half a billion cases of COVID-19 and over six million deaths had been confirmed globally.[3]

Governments reacted to the pandemic in early 2020 with travel bans, lockdowns, and forced business closures. At one point, more than 80 nations had closed their borders, and schools worldwide were closed to an estimated 1.6 billion children. In the second quarter of 2020, the Gross Domestic Product (GDP) fell more than 10 percent in Europe, and US GDP dropped 8.9 percent. Global GDP declined 3.2 percent for the year.[4]

Demand for oil products crashed. Americans drove 40 percent less than normal in April 2020—levels not seen since before 1950.[5] World exports dropped by double digits that same month. Demand for petroleum also declined, with the price of Brent Crude Oil down to $20 per barrel on April 20. OPEC oil producers agreed in April to reduce production by 10 percent. The number of US drilling rigs in operation had been slowly declining from more than 800 in April 2019 to just under 700 in March 2020, but then they dropped sharply to less than 200 in operation by June.[7]

Oil and gas exploration and drilling had been declining for the last six years. Investment in exploration and drilling peaked at $779 billion in 2014 but declined to only $328 billion during 2020.[8] Oil and gas opponents were pleased with the reduction in hydrocarbon

Fear This!

Bill Gates Issued a Stark Warning for the World: "As Awful as This Pandemic Is, Climate Change Could be Worse"

— *Business Insider*, August 5, 2020[6]

demand and the low level of investment. They called for the world to build back without hydrocarbons and solve the climate crisis. Secretary General of the United Nations Antonio Guterres stated,

> The upheaval of this pandemic presents an opportunity to chart a new course, one that can address every aspect of the climate crisis head on.[9]

Global economies began to recover in the third quarter of 2020, with energy demand growing again. To stimulate lagging economies, governments adopted almost $17 trillion in spending and revenue measures by September 2021.[10] The International Monetary Fund estimated that global GDP rose 6.1 percent in 2021 and was projected to rise 3.2 percent in 2022.[11] World crude oil prices rose from a low of $20 per barrel in April 2020 to $80 per barrel by October 2021.[12] The combination of rising global oil prices and soon-to-explode European natural gas prices initiated the 2022 world energy crisis.

For the last two decades, closures of traditional power plants and rising numbers of wind and solar installations increased Europe's reliance on weather-dependent sources of electricity. Then in the summer of 2021, winds were light in much of Europe. Both onshore and offshore wind output in France, Germany, and the UK was down 20–30

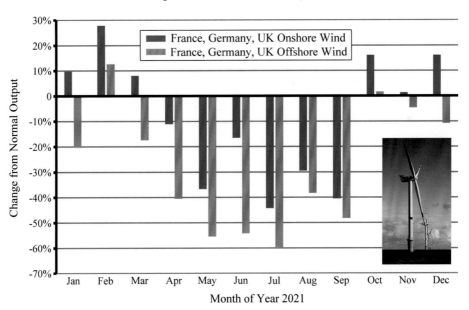

Europe's 2021 Wind Shortfall. Monthly change in combined wind output for onshore and offshore wind installations in France, Germany, and the United Kingdom for 2021, compared to average long-term output. Wind output was low for much of 2021. Image of offshore wind turbines on the Thornton Bank, Belgium. (Hoskins, 2022)[13]

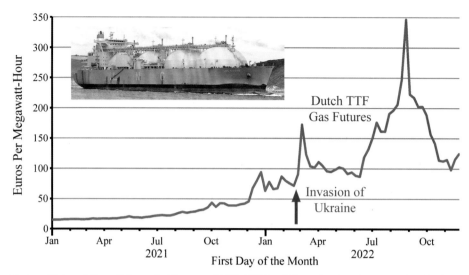

Rising Natural Gas Prices in Europe 2021–2022. Price of natural gas at the Netherlands Title Transfer Facility in euros per megawatt-hour. Gas prices increased by a factor of five prior to Russia's invasion of Ukraine and increased again after the invasion. Image of LNG tanker. (Intercontinental Exchange, 2022)[14]

percent at that time from long-term trends.[15] As a result, most of Europe burned more natural gas to generate electricity throughout the year. Gas storage remained at low levels by the fall of 2021, multiplying natural gas prices.

Throughout 2019 and 2020, the price of natural gas in Europe ranged from 13–18 euros per megawatt-hour. With economic recovery and the decrease in wind electricity output, Europe's gas prices rocketed to 80 €/MWh by December 2021.[16] By February 2022, 31 UK suppliers of natural gas, serving two million customers, had gone out of business. Price controls had forced these firms to sell gas at prices below their wholesale purchase price.[17]

In 2000, Europe had produced 56 percent of its natural gas and 44 percent of its petroleum. But the region chose to invest in wind and solar, instead of using hydraulic fracturing to boost oil and gas production. By 2021, Europe was producing only 37 percent of its own natural gas and 25 percent of its petroleum.[19] Concurrently, rising imports from Russia created a serious dependency. Russia provided Europe with 27 percent of its natural gas, 17 percent of its crude oil, and 38 percent of its coal in 2021.[20] At the same time, 23 European nations announced that they would phase out

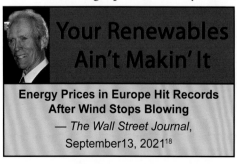

Your Renewables Ain't Makin' It

Energy Prices in Europe Hit Records After Wind Stops Blowing
— *The Wall Street Journal,*
September 13, 2021[18]

coal.[21] Also, more than 100 nuclear plants had closed or were scheduled to close, including 30 in Germany and 34 in the UK.[22] By closing coal and nuclear plants and failing to develop shale resources, Europe had increased its dependency on imported natural gas.

Rising natural gas prices triggered a parallel rise in Europe's electricity prices months before Russia invaded Ukraine. For much of 2020, average monthly wholesale power prices in France and Germany varied between about €15 to €35 per MWh, with UK prices around £25–35/MWh. But with low wind output in 2021 and rising natural gas prices, wholesale electricity prices skyrocketed to over €200 and £200 per megawatt-hour by December 2021, an increase of more than six times.[23]

When Russia invaded Ukraine on February 24, 2022, it drove the world's energy markets into a full-blown crisis. The price of natural gas in Europe immediately jumped to over 100 €/MWh, and the price of crude oil rose to over $100 per barrel. Russian energy exports to Europe began to fall. In April, the European Union agreed to ban coal imports from Russia. Russian flows of natural gas had been running at 400 million cubic meters (mcm) per day in early 2021 but dropped to less than 80 mcm per day by July 2022.[24] Natural gas prices soared to over 200 €/MWh by August.

Also by August 2022, monthly average electricity prices had doubled again. Electricity

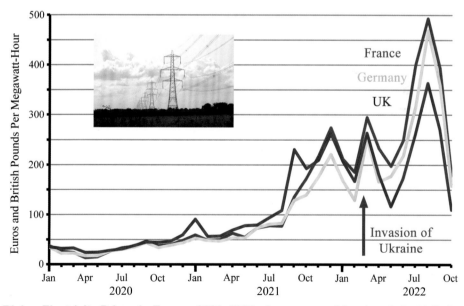

Rising Electricity Prices in Europe 2020–2022. Average monthly price of electricity in euros per megawatt-hour for France and Germany, and British pounds per MWh for the UK. Power prices rose by a factor of six by the end of 2021, prior to the Russian invasion of Ukraine. Image of powerlines near Laytham, England. (Statista, Ofgem, 2022)[25]

prices for the next year in France and Germany exceeded €1,000/MWh before falling back. These prices were all-time records, more than 10 times higher than average power prices in the first half of 2020.[26]

US shipments of liquefied natural gas (LNG) to Europe began rising in 2021 in response to higher prices. The US became Europe's largest LNG source in 2021, providing 26 percent of its imports. LNG suppliers shifted cargo destinations from Asia to Europe to take advantage of high prices in Europe. During the first four months of 2022, 74 percent of US LNG went to Europe, compared to only 34 percent in 2021. This provided a daily increase of 144 mcm, replacing about half of the decline in Russian gas supply.[27] With so much being exported, US domestic gas prices more than doubled, from $3 per million Btu to over $7 per million Btu by September, but this was still less than one-fifth of Europe's price. With US shipments diverted to Europe, gas prices rose in China, Japan, and South Korea.

Rising petroleum prices caused the world energy crises of 1973 and 1979, and exacerbated the recessions of 1990 and 2008. But during the twenty-first century, nations increasingly turned to natural gas as a cleaner-burning fuel to replace coal for electricity and wood for heating homes. Expansion of LNG shipments worldwide found 44 nations importing gas in 2021, twice as many as a decade ago. Nations importing more than 20 percent of their gas included Germany, Greece, Italy, Japan, Mexico, Spain and Turkey. Natural gas became the hottest commodity in the world in 2022, driving the energy crisis, inflation, and geopolitics. As gas prices exploded in Europe, prices in Asia rose at almost the same rate. Gas had become the new petroleum.[28]

Despite net-zero goals, the world embarked on an accelerated program to build LNG terminals and tankers. In China, the world's largest importer of LNG, 10 new import terminals were scheduled to come online in 2023 to double import capacity by 2025. South Korea, the world's leading builder of LNG tankers, saw a surge in shipyard orders and a shortage of skilled workers.[30]

In Europe, 25 LNG import facilities were in process or planning by the fall of 2022, located in Germany (7), Greece (5), Italy (4), Ireland (2), the Netherlands (2), Cyprus (1), Estonia (1), Finland (1), France (1), and Poland (1).[31] Most of these were Floating Storage Regasification Units, which could be operational within

Temporarily out of Gasoline OPEN for your other driving needs

Welcome to Net Zero

Britons Advised to Stop Showering to Conserve Energy

"Water utilities in the UK are advising customers to save water and energy by using damp towels or spray bottles instead of taking showers during a heatwave and drought this summer."

— *OilPrice.com*, August 8, 2022[29]

The Destruction of European Industry

By late summer of 2022, Europe's natural gas and electricity prices were more than five times higher than levels in 2020. It appeared that high prices would continue throughout 2023 and into 2024. Europe's pursuit of weather-dependent wind and solar, the shutdown of coal and nuclear power plants, and their dependence on natural gas imports, along with the Russian embargo, created conditions that could destroy European industry.

Uniper SE, Germany's largest natural gas provider, lost €12 billion in the first half of 2022.[32] Uniper was forced to buy gas at exorbitant prices after Russian giant Gazprom halted shipments on long-term contracts due to the war in Ukraine. In July, the German government purchased 30 percent of Uniper for €15 billion. In September, the government spent an additional €8 billion to nationalize the company.[33]

Utility companies were scrambling to get loans from governments. Finland announced plans to offer €10 billion in liquidity guarantees to utilities, with €2.35 billion to go to Fortum Oyj.[34] Sweden announced it would provide up to 250 billion crowns (€23 billion). Switzerland's Axpo received a line of credit worth four billion francs from the government. Centrica plc, the owner of British Gas, pursued billions of pounds of additional credit from UK banks.[35] Power prices threatened utilities with financial failure across the continent.

Natural gas is essential for production of ammonia, which is used to make urea and ammonium nitrate fertilizer. Europe's fertilizer producers without long-term gas contracts lost money on every ton of fertilizer produced. Norwegian giant Yara International cut ammonia output by two-thirds. CF Industries (UK), Achema (Lithuania), and Nitrogen-muvek (Hungary) all halted ammonia production. More than half of Europe's ammonia production, and 33 percent of its nitrogen fertilizer production, disappeared in 2022.[36]

Skyrocketing power prices pose a special problem for electricity-intensive metal production, such as aluminum and zinc smelting. One metric ton of aluminum requires about 15 MWh of power, costing €7,000 at August 2022 prices, but could only be sold for less than €2,500.[37] By August, the Norsk Hydro aluminum plant in Slovakia and the Nyrstar zinc smelter in the Netherlands had closed. Half of Europe's aluminum and zinc output had been lost from production curtailments or plant closures.[38] Strategic industries, such as defense, aerospace, and automaking, were forced to turn to imports for metal parts.

ArcelorMittal SA, one of the world's largest steelmakers, planned to close a blast furnace in Bremen and a direct-reduction plant in Hamburg. The firm has reduced gas demand by 40 percent since the start of 2022. Steel firms increasingly bought iron from US plants because they could not afford to produce it locally.[39]

Chemical companies suffered a double whammy of high prices for gas feedstock and high prices for the gas fuel and electricity needed for chemical processing. BASF, Germany's largest chemical producer, began buying ammonia rather than producing it. German chemical production fell more than 40 percent, and imports rose 40 percent, from the end of 2020 to the first half of 2022.[40]

With most futures contracts for natural gas and electricity ending in December 2022, hundreds of companies in chemicals, fertilizer, energy, metals, steel, glass, paper, and food processing faced the prospect of business shutdown. Europe's energy policies appear to have set the table for a new era of deindustrialization in Europe.

two years, more quickly than permanent onshore terminals. Environmental groups fear these LNG projects will lock in gas consumption for the next two decades.

Weather also contributed to the energy crisis in Europe. Continental rainfall totals were below normal for January through March 2022. Then a series of heat waves in May, June, and July caused drought conditions throughout the region. In August, the Joint Research Centre of the European Commission estimated that 47 percent of Europe was in "drought warning" condition and 17 percent was in the more severe "drought watch" condition.[41]

River and reservoir levels fell across the continent, reducing hydroelectric power output. More than 100 municipalities in France suffered shortages of fresh water, requiring water delivery by truck in many locations. The water in the Rhine River dropped to extremely low levels, which prevented coal barges from delivering fuel to restarting the coal power plants needed to offset the natural gas shortage. Low river levels and high water temperatures impacted cooling systems at nuclear plants in France, forcing a reduction in power output. The hot, dry conditions increased wildfire incidents and the size of burned areas.[42]

European nations agreed to cut energy consumption by 15 percent and adopted a variety of measures to do so. Citizens and businesses were limited to a maximum indoor temperature of 19°C (66.2°F) during the fall and winter and a minimum indoor temperature of 27°C (80.6°F) in summer. Lights on monuments, fountains, and public buildings were switched off. Showers were limited to no longer than five minutes, and hot water was limited to certain hours of the day. Shop lights went out at 10 p.m.[43] Countries were stockpiling gas reserves for winter but also developing plans for rationing gas.

Faced with looming gas shortages, Europe had no choice but to roll back a number of energy policies and green initiatives. On July 6, the European Parliament voted to classify nuclear and natural gas projects as "environmentally sustainable."[44] Along with Europe's building spree for LNG import terminals, the Netherlands resumed drilling for gas, and Denmark, Italy, and Norway announced plans to increase gas production. Germany postponed closure of three nuclear power plants. Across the continent, coal-fired plants restarted.

Governments used energy price caps to try to shield homes and businesses from wholesale price increases. UK home-energy prices,

Why Raise Our Energy Prices?

A Third of Brits Face Poverty with Energy Bills Set to Hit $5,000

"Nearly one-third of households in the United Kingdom will face poverty this winter after paying energy bills that are set to soar again in January."

— *CNN Business*, August 9, 2022[45]

The Coal Comeback

Plans for a global transition to renewable electrical power call for natural gas to replace coal in the short term, followed by the widespread use of wind and solar with battery storage by 2050. But the 2022 energy crisis interrupted these plans in a major way. Coal consumption surged across the world in response to skyrocketing natural gas prices.

As economies rebounded from the recession caused by COVID-19 in 2021, world electricity generation grew by a record 1,577 terawatt-hours, an increase of 6.2 percent over 2020. Coal consumption grew six percent, higher growth than natural gas or oil. Coal provided 51 percent of the increase in demand for power globally in 2021. China and India accounted for 70 percent of the coal increase, which together contributed more energy than the 2021 growth in renewables.[46]

With soaring natural gas prices in 2022, the coal resurgence continued. Power generation from coal in France, Germany, Italy, the Netherlands, Spain, and the UK grew more than 20 percent from 2021 combined.[47] This increased consumption of coal ran counter to national pledges to phase out coal. Germany announced it would stick to its plan to eliminate coal by 2030 but then restarted 27 coal-fired power plants. In the first half of 2022, Germany's power produced from coal rose 17.2 percent above 2021, to provide 31.4 percent of the nation's electricity.[48]

Drought conditions in China caused a severe electricity shortage in 2022. China's coal consumption was down due to the COVID-19 lockdowns, but the nation announced measures to boost coal production to offset lower coal imports and high gas prices.[49] Similarly, India announced plans to boost coal-fired electricity capacity by year 2032.[50]

Coal prices rose to a record high of over $450 per metric ton. This was more than four times higher than prices in 2018 and 2019 but was still less expensive than gas.[51]

already controlled prior to the 2022 crisis, jumped 54 percent in April 2022, the largest rise ever recorded. Prices were due to rise another 80 percent in October but were limited to an additional 27 percent rise, with the UK government to pay the difference between homeowner bills and market prices, an estimated £100 billion.[52] The UK and other European nations committed together to spend over €500 billion in subsidies to homes and businesses and to pay for caps on energy prices.[53]

Even with government actions to reduce prices, the impact on Europe's residents was severe. After measures announced by the government, UK citizens spent almost 10 percent of their income on home and vehicle energy, which was more than during the oil crises of the 1970s. UK residents cooked less often, took fewer showers, and turned down the heating in their homes. Household gas bills in Germany more than doubled from 2021 to 2022, and oil-heating bills were up by three-quarters. Germans showered and shaved at work when possible. And energy bills for Italian families were the highest in 25 years.[54]

Like in Europe, economies around the world were impacted by the energy crisis. Natural

gas prices in Asia rose to almost keep pace with those in Europe. Nations boosted their use of coal, now cheaper than gas, to produce power. Record-high prices for natural gas and coal, along with high prices for oil and vehicle fuel, triggered worldwide inflation.

From 2020 to 2021, global consumption of coal, gas, and oil *each* increased more than consumption of renewables.[56] Some leaders claim the energy crisis and the new pursuit of coal, gas, and oil is only temporary. But others are concerned that the crisis will not be short. Belgian Prime Minister Alexander De Croo warns, "The next five to 10 winters will be difficult."[57] It appears that the irresistible force of the green-energy transition has collided with the immovable object of energy reality and come to a grinding halt, at least in Europe.

RISING ELECTRICITY COSTS AND FALLING RELIABILITY

Five of six states in the northeastern US—Connecticut, Massachusetts, Maine, Rhode Island, and Vermont—mandated an economy-wide reduction in carbon dioxide emissions of 80 percent or more from levels found in 1990 or 2001. In 2021, New England's power generation came from natural gas (43%), nuclear (21%), imports (17%), hydroelectric (6%), renewables (12%), and other generators (1%). About half of the electricity generated from renewables was from wind systems.[58]

The Integrated System Operator New England (ISO) is responsible for reliable operation of the New England power system and for planning future system operation. The ISO issued a report in 2022 that looked at four scenarios to decarbonize the future New England power grid by 2040. The report included government efforts to electrify home and business heating and transition from conventional cars to electric vehicles.

Today, most homes and businesses in New England heat with natural gas, propane, and oil. In August 2022, Boston Mayor Michelle Wu announced plans to ban gas and oil in new building construction and renovation.[59] The ISO projects a transition to heat pumps, with the demand for electricity for heating increasing by 340 times to over 23 GW by 2040. The ISO also projects that EVs will increase the demand for power by more than 10 GW.[60]

Of the four scenarios in the ISO report, only one could meet the decarbonization goals set by member states when including the additional power demand from heating and EVs. That scenario called for 84 GW of new wind, solar, and storage, to comprise 56 percent of generated electricity by 2040. Imports (16%), natural gas (13%), nuclear (12%), and hydroelectric (3%) would provide the remainder.[61]

But the New England ISO concluded that such a wind-, solar-, and battery-dominated system *would not be reliable*. The report stated,

Climate Change Magic?

The Solar Panel That Generates Power at Night!
"Sadly this technology has one huge problem. Current experiments have infrared solar panels at 1.8% efficiency and only produce about 2.26 mW per square meter. That is about 0.00023% of the power an average solar panel makes per square meter." — *Predict*, November 19, 2022[62]

> The variable energy resources in the future grid scenarios lack the controllability and predictability of the region's current dispatchable resources. … Modeling showed that by large margins, available resources were repeatedly unable to match their aggregate output to system demand.[63]

In other words, the wind-, solar-, and battery-powered system would suffer repeated failures, requiring imposed blackouts to avoid total shutdown. The analysis showed that even by installing 2,400 GWh of battery-energy capacity and boosting system reserve margins from 15 percent to 300 percent, the system would fail during 15 days, and be at risk for failure during an additional 36 days, each year.[64] Note that increasing reserve margins to 300 percent would mean building *three times as much* capacity as is needed to serve usual demand.

The ISO's proposed transition to getting 56 percent of its electricity from renewables, much of it offshore wind, would be hugely expensive. The average construction cost for onshore wind in the US is about $1,300 per kilowatt.[65] Offshore wind and batteries are more expensive. The cost of adding 84 GW of new renewable generators would be over $125 billion. Additional large costs will be needed to build transmission. In 2021, residential power prices for the New England states were already all in the top 10 in the nation, at between 17.03 and 22.91 cents per kilowatt-hour.[66] Look for these prices to double or triple if the electricity decarbonization plan is pursued, accompanied by rising power outages.

Transmission systems constitute a major roadblock to deploying renewable energy. Wind and solar installation sites tend to be far from population centers and spread out over wider areas than coal, gas, or nuclear plants. Renewables therefore require more and longer transmission lines, incurring higher costs. California will need to spend more than

What's Wrong with This Picture???

California Asks Residents Not to Charge Electric Vehicles, Days After Announcing Gas Car Ban

"With California's power grid under strain due to extreme heat and high demand, the utility grid operator is asking residents to avoid charging their electric vehicles. This comes days after the state announced a plan to ban the sale of gas-powered cars by 2035."
— *MyStateLine.com*, August 31, 2022[67]

$30 billion for new transmission systems over the next 20 years to support its plan to utilize renewables.[68] A study by Berkeley National Laboratories in 2021 estimated that 660 GW of wind and solar projects await transmission interconnection in the US.[69] Transmission shortages also stall wind deployment in Germany, the UK, and other nations.

It's clear that the reliability of the US electricity system is declining. Data from the Energy Information Administration shows that the number of hours of interruptions per customer more than doubled from 2013 to 2021. Outages without major events have risen by 13 percent over that period, and event-driven outages have roughly tripled.[70] Rising outages due to storms and other events show that grid margin is shrinking.

In fact, weather events have become the preferred excuse for electricity failure in the US. Heat waves and cold snaps are labeled "extreme" and blamed on human-caused climate change. Utilities whine that they aren't responsible for providing continuous power output

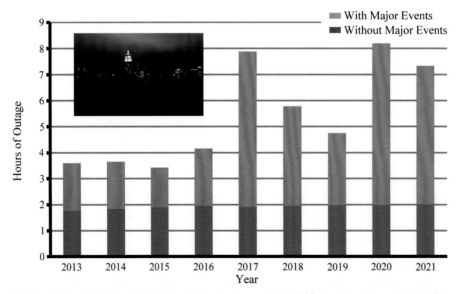

US Electric Power Outages 2013–2021. Average annual US electric power interruptions in hours per customer. Image of the New York City blackout caused by Hurricane Sandy in 2012. (Energy Information Administration, 2022)[71]

during extreme weather events. California and Texas utility companies repeatedly ask customers to cut back their electricity usage to keep the system from failing. But the frequency of these public service messages indicates a shortage of dispatchable coal, gas, and nuclear power.

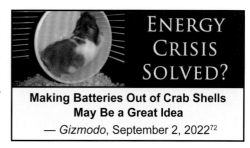

ENERGY CRISIS SOLVED?

Making Batteries Out of Crab Shells May Be a Great Idea
— *Gizmodo*, September 2, 2022[72]

Offshore wind will add additional possibilities for system failure in eastern US states. Connecticut, Massachusetts, Maryland, New Jersey, New York, North Carolina, Rhode Island, and Virginia had all announced offshore wind plans by early 2022, totalling over 35 GW of capacity.[73] By the end of 2020, Europe had already installed about 25 GW of offshore wind.[74] But weather along the US Atlantic Coast can be more severe than in Europe, and US wind systems may not be able to survive.

The Great New England Hurricane of 1938 brought Category 3 winds (111-129 mph) to New York, Connecticut, and Rhode Island. The Great Atlantic Hurricane of 1944 delivered Category 2 winds (96-110 mph) along the coast from North Carolina to Maine. Likewise, Hurricane Carol in 1954 and Hurricane Gloria in 1985 brought Category 3 winds to the shores of eastern states.[75] Offshore wind arrays will be hurricane targets, adding to system outages, with consumers footing the bill to rebuild damaged wind arrays.

The New England ISO study typifies the problem facing utility companies around the world. Intermittent electricity sources remain fundamentally incompatible with the always-on power needs of homes and businesses. We can't turn up the wind and solar energy when demand spikes or a weather event occurs. Battery systems remain far too expensive to solve this problem. Power systems dependent on wind and solar sources suffer rising system costs and declining system reliability as renewable penetration increases. At some point, people will want to return to reliable and low-cost power. Power systems will fail to even come close to using renewables 100 percent of the time, except possibly in the case of nations blessed with large amounts of hydroelectric power.

RISING MINING AND METAL COSTS

Electric vehicles and renewable energy systems require huge amounts of minerals to be mined and refined. A transition from conventional vehicles and coal, gas, and nuclear power plants to EVs and wind and solar generators, should it occur, would be a transition from a fuel-intensive to a materials-intensive energy system. Like the scale challenges of other green-energy initiatives, the quantity of needed materials would be vast.

Wind and solar systems require enormous amounts of steel from iron ore, concrete, plastics, and glass. A 100 MW wind system uses about 30,000 tons of iron ore in the form of steel, 50,000 tons of concrete, and 900 tons of non-recyclable plastics for the turbine blades. The amount of bulk materials needed for solar installations—concrete, steel, and glass—is 150 percent larger than that used by wind systems for the same energy output.[76]

Renewables use such huge quantities of materials because of the low energy density and huge footprint of wind and solar installations. Energy expert Mark Mills observes,

> Replacing the energy output from a single 100-MW natural gas-fired turbine, itself the size of a residential house ... requires at least 20 wind turbines, each one about the size of the Washington Monument, occupying some 10 square miles of land.[77]

Renewable systems also require large amounts of special metals. Vehicle and grid-scale batteries need cobalt, nickel, and lithium to achieve high energy density and performance. Magnets in wind turbines require rare earth elements, such as neodymium and dysprosium. Large quantities of copper are essential for EV engines, batteries, and wind and solar arrays, as well as for building electricity transmission systems to connect to remote wind and solar sites. And hydrogen electrolyzers and fuel cells use nickel and platinum.

According to the International Energy Agency (IEA), an EV uses about 207 kilograms (kg), or 455 pounds (lb.), of special metals, more than six times as much as the 34 kg (75 lb.) used in a conventional car. These numbers do not include the aluminum and steel used in the car. An EV typically contains about 66 kg of graphite, 53 kg of copper, 40 kg of nickel, 25 kg of manganese, 13 kg of cobalt, and 9 kg of lithium.[78] In addition to special metals, EVs usually contain more than twice the aluminum of conventional cars.

A typical offshore wind system uses more than 15,000 kg of special metals for each megawatt of capacity, with an onshore wind system using over 10,000 kg of metals per megawatt. On a capacity basis, an onshore wind system uses almost nine times the metals of a natural gas plant, again excluding aluminum and steel.[80] But conventional power plants typically operate at higher capacity factors (utilization levels) than wind systems. In the US in 2020, the average capacity factor for intermittent wind systems was 35.4 percent, which is less than the 56.6 percent average for

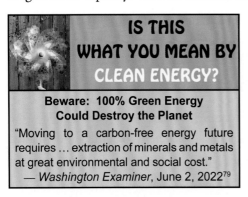

IS THIS WHAT YOU MEAN BY CLEAN ENERGY?

Beware: 100% Green Energy Could Destroy the Planet

"Moving to a carbon-free energy future requires ... extraction of minerals and metals at great environmental and social cost."
— *Washington Examiner*, June 2, 2022[79]

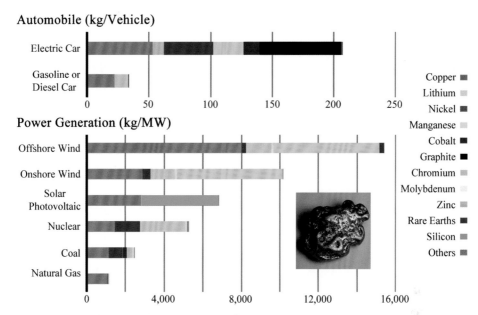

Metals Used in Automobiles and Power Generation. Metals used in cars in kilograms per vehicle and in power generation in kilograms per megawatt of capacity (not including aluminum and steel). Image of copper. (International Energy Agency, 2022)[81]

gas plants.[82] When utilization is considered, onshore wind generators require 14 times the special metals used in natural gas plants.

A huge portion of the projected demand for metals is for EVs. Global banking firm ING projects that the EV's share of the passenger-vehicle fleets will grow globally to nine percent by 2030 and 39 percent by 2040. ING analysis estimates that, should this occur, the demand for aluminum for vehicles will double by 2040, rising to about a 20 percent share of the world demand.[83] Needs for special metals will be even higher. The IEA projects that the demand for copper will grow by about 50 percent by 2040, with copper for EVs and renewables rising to half of the world demand. In addition, the IEA estimates that the global demand for nickel will increase by 2.5 times by 2040, the demand for cobalt will quadruple, and the demand for lithium will increase by more than 10 times—all driven by the need for special materials for EV batteries, storage, and renewable energy.[84]

Multiplying global mining output for cobalt, copper, nickel, lithium, and rare earth elements will have a serious impact on the environment. Mining typically requires changes to land areas that can hurt biodiversity, and mining and mineral-refining processes require huge volumes of water, especially for copper and lithium. They generate large amounts of waste in the form of wastewater, acid drainage, tailings, and waste rock. Environmental groups have long opposed new mining operations but are now promoting a transition to

Lithium mine at Salinas Grandes salt desert, Jujuy Province, Argentina.[85]

metal-intensive EVs and renewables.

Mining for special metals takes place mostly in developing nations. Almost 70 percent of the world's cobalt is mined in the Democratic Republic of the Congo (DRC). More than 30 percent of the nickel comes from Indonesia. Chile produces 28 percent of the copper. China produces 60 percent of the rare earth elements. Australia produces more than half of the world's lithium; Chile, China, and Argentina are also major producers.

China is the world's leading refiner of special metals, with large processing shares of cobalt (65%), copper (40%), lithium (55%), nickel (35%), and rare earths (85%).[86] The United States and European nations risk building a serious dependence on China for special metals by continuing efforts to deploy EVs and renewable energy systems.

Developing nations struggle to contain environmental and social impacts as mining volumes grow. DRC cobalt mines suffer from poor working conditions and the use of forced and child labor. Dumping of tailings from copper and nickel mines into the ocean near Indonesia causes contamination of marine environments. A huge waste lake in China, nicknamed "rare earth lake," is infamous for soils that are highly polluted with rare earths.

Lithium, the most important metal for batteries in EVs, uses the most water and has the highest potential for causing water pollution of any special metal. Lithium is produced in huge evaporation ponds, called brine ponds, using solar evaporation over hundreds of days. Each ton produced requires approximately half a million gallons of water.[87] By 2040, lithium used in EVs is projected to have increased by a factor of more than 40 since 2020.[88]

The world has plenty of special metal reserves, but it is unlikely that mining output can keep up with demands for a net-zero transition to EVs, renewable energy, and grid-scale batteries by 2050. Establishing a large-scale mining operation takes 16.5 years on average from discovery to production.[89] Local opposition, environmental issues, and just the sheer volume of minerals needed will not allow global production to meet the expected demand.

The result will be rising metal prices, particularly for the battery metals of cobalt, copper, lithium, and nickel. We have already seen this in 2022, with cobalt and nickel up more than 50 percent and lithium up by 10 times over 2020.[90] As a result, the total cost of EV raw materials increased by 144 percent from 2020 to 2022.[91] General Motors, Tesla and other manufacturers hiked EV prices in 2022. Look for high metal prices to keep EV prices higher than conventional car prices during the next two decades, slowing EV penetration.

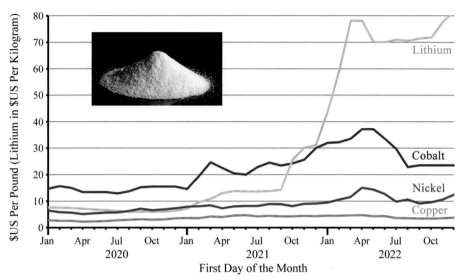

Battery Metal Price Trends 2020–2022. Trends of metal spot-market prices for cobalt, copper, and nickel in dollars per pound and for lithium in dollars per kilogram. Image of lithium hydroxide. (Daily Metal Prices, 2022)[92]

THE AGE OF RENEWABLE WASTE

We appear to be entering the Age of Renewable Waste. Demand for renewable energy, batteries, and electric vehicles in unprecedented quantities, all to be installed by 2050, is on track to produce gigantic volumes of waste. Most of this waste is not recyclable today.

Wind turbines, solar panels, batteries, and EVs have shorter operating lives than conventional power plants and vehicles. While coal and gas plants can operate for about 40 years, and nuclear plants can operate for 60 years or more,[93] wind and solar arrays only have operating lifetimes of 20–25 years and 25–30 years, respectively.[94] Grid-scale batteries must be replaced after 10–15 years.[95] A typical US gasoline or diesel automobile stays on the road for about 12 years, but EV lifetimes will be less. The average EV battery life is about eight years, and the cost to replace it can range from $6,000–$20,000, depending upon the battery size. Because of shorter life spans, renewables and EVs produce more waste than their conventional counterparts.

About 80 percent of a wind tower—the steel, copper, and aluminum—can be recycled, but the blades pose a special problem. Wind turbine blades are primarily composed of glass- or carbon-reinforced polymers. Blades as long as 100 meters (330 feet), almost a football field in length, are strong, lightweight, and durable, making disposal difficult.

Most blades today go to landfills. Wind turbine waste is already piling up in the US

Wind turbine-blade waste near Bath, New York.[96]

and other nations. Used turbine blades in Iowa are too big for local landfill sites, so they are shipped to Nebraska or Kansas for burial. Ten metric tons of turbine-blade waste results from every megawatt of wind capacity installed. It is estimated that blade waste will exceed two million tons annually by 2050, with cumulative waste estimated at 43 million tons by 2050.[97]

Blade recycling is immature and expensive. Some blades are chopped up, requiring heavy machinery, and then incinerated. Germany uses a small amount of blade waste as clinker in cement. Austria, Finland, Germany, and the Netherlands prohibit disposal in landfills. WindEurope, an advocate group, called for a landfill ban for decommissioned blades by 2025.[98]

Projections for the amount of waste from solar panels almost doubles the projections for wind turbine waste. The IEA estimates there will be a cumulative global total of 78 million tons by 2050.[99] This number will be even larger if homeowners with rooftop solar panels upgrade the panels before the end of their product life. After 20 years of incentives in California, worn-out panels from more than 1.3 million rooftop installations are now arriving at landfills. Fewer than one in every 10 panels is recycled. Solar panels contain small amounts of cadmium, lead, and selenium, which are sometimes classified as hazardous waste.[100]

Recycling solar panels is difficult and costly. Specialized equipment must be used to remove the aluminum frame without shattering the panel. Only about $2–4 worth of materials can be recovered from each panel. It costs about $20–30 to recycle each panel, compared to $1–2 to send it to a landfill.[101]

But the biggest renewable-waste issue promises to be electric vehicle batteries. Less than five percent of EV batteries are recycled today. The European Commission plans to classify lithium as hazardous waste, which will hamper recycling efforts.

The IEA predicts that 145 million EVs will be on the road by 2030.[102] If this happens, about 50,000 EV batteries will reach the end of their life each day. The average battery weighs 1,000 pounds and has a useful life of about eight years. With these numbers, it means that nine million tons of battery waste will be produced each year by 2035. If EVs penetrate just 15 percent of world light-vehicle markets by 2050, this number will triple to about 27 million tons of EV battery waste each year.

NO RENEWABLES IN OUR BACKYARD

Arrays of wind turbines as far as the eye can see, acres and acres of solar panels, and thousands of miles of transmission towers loom over us in a net-zero future. As we discussed in Chapter 5, for the US to obtain 50 percent of its electricity from wind and solar, it would require more additional land area than six Midwest states. Other nations face the same voracious renewable land gobble.

But renewables face a rising tide of opposition. Opponents decry wind array impacts on aesthetics, health, property values, and wildlife. Rural residents in more than 30 US states have opposed the erection of new wind systems, pushing for setbacks from property lines, noise limits, tower height limits, and outright bans.[103] The European Platform Against Windfarms (EPAW) was founded in 2008 and has grown to 1,615 member organizations from 31 countries. The EPAW calls for a moratorium on European wind energy projects.[104]

Turbines are usually placed atop ridge lines and hills. Here these 500-foot, 50-story-tall structures interrupt skylines and scenery for miles around. Turbine-top obstruction lights blink in concert every night to alert aircraft, annoying local residents. Many people just don't want the beautiful scenery interrupted by wind towers and service roads.

A growing amount of medical research raises concern about adverse health effects caused by the noise created by wind turbines. Turbines generate low-frequency audible noise between 20 and 200 hertz and inaudible noise below 20 hertz. Residents in Europe, New Zealand, the US, and other nations complain about noise and resulting sleep disturbance, especially when living close to turbines operating at noise levels above 35 decibels.[105] Dr. Carl Phillips of the Populi Health Institute in Pennsylvania observes,

> There is overwhelming evidence that electricity-generating wind turbines cause serious health problems in a non-trivial fraction of residents living near them.[106]

If your neighbor permits wind turbines on his land, it can also hurt your property value. Stephen Gibbons at the London School of Economics looked at more than one million property sales in England and Wales, finding a 12-percent loss in sale price for homes within two kilometers of a large turbine.[107] A 2016 study by economists Sunak and Madlener found that prices for properties in Germany were 9–14 percent lower near turbines.[108]

Wind turbines also kill numerous birds and bats. A study by biologist K. Shawn Smallwood

Planet Over People?

Is Having a Baby in 2021 Pure Environmental Vandalism?
— *Vogue*, April 25, 2021[109]

Sacrificed to Save the Planet

Windfarms Kill 10–20 Times More than Previously Thought
"Wind turbines are actually slaughtering millions of birds and bats annually."
— St. Francis Arboreal & Wildlife Assn., 2022[110]

estimated that in 2012 US wind turbines killed 888,000 bats and 573,000 birds, including 83,000 raptors.[111] These numbers have likely more than doubled to over one million birds a year by 2021, since the number of turbines more than doubled in that time. There is also evidence that studies undercount these numbers, missing injured birds and bats outside of the search area, as well as those taken by predators.

Like wind arrays, solar arrays are very land intensive. In California, the Ivanpah Solar Electric Generating System, sitting on 3,500 acres, uses 20 times as much land as the Diablo Canyon Nuclear Power Plant to produce only one-fifth of the average output, or 100 times the land for the same electricity output. Solar systems blanket the land and change the sunlight, moisture, and rainfall runoff where they are placed. This alteration of plant and wildlife habitats will grow as more arrays are deployed.

Electricity transmission systems also pose a big issue. The National Renewable Energy Laboratory estimated that the current 240,000 miles of transmission lines would need to double to support a move to using 90 percent wind and solar electricity in the US.[112] Like wind towers, 200-foot-high electrical towers face strong opposition from local communities. Wind towers, wide-area solar installations, and the expansion of transmission systems are increasingly being opposed by communities around the world.

CARBON CAPTURE, HYDROGEN, AND EVS

Green advocates tout carbon capture and storage (CCS), hydrogen fuel, and electric vehicles as the means to decarbonize heavy industry and transportation. But a specter of failure looms over these methods. CCS, hydrogen, and EVs require endless billions in government subsidies for market penetration. They will fall far short of the hoped-for revolutionary transition of the global economy.

CCS is expensive and wholly dependent on government subsidies. There are few carbon dioxide pipelines and few places to store CO_2. After decades of government support, only 27 capture plants existed in 2021. The IEA calls for the capture of nine percent of the world's emissions by 2050, which would require 70 to 100 major CCS plants to come online *each year* until 2050. We will likely see only a tiny fraction of this amount.

A hydrogen economy would require staggering amounts of electricity from renewable sources to drive the electrolyzers. For example, the average European steel plant produces about four million tons of crude steel per year. Hydrogen Europe, a hydrogen advocacy group, estimates that running this one plant on hydrogen requires about five GW of solar-array capacity to drive the electrolyzers. This is more than 13 times the output of California's

Ivanpah solar facility in California. More than 13 Ivanpahs would be needed to power hydrogen electrolyzers for a single average-sized steel plant.[113]

Ivanpah solar facility, and it would cover an area of over 70 square miles. A capital investment of more than €7 billion would also be needed.[114] To convert the world's steel industry to run on hydrogen and renewable electricity, these numbers would need to be scaled up by 500 times, to 2,500 GW and over 5,000 TWh. This is more than *the world's total output* of renewable electricity today. A solar-powered steel industry using hydrogen fuel would need more than 35,000 square miles of land just for the solar arrays.

Alternatively, the world would need to build an incremental 600 nuclear plants, added to the 437 nuclear plants operating today, just to power electrolyzers for the steel industry. There just won't be enough renewables to power hydrogen electrolyzers for heavy industry.

The clouds of reality darken for EVs as well. For the last several years, EV sales in Europe have skyrocketed. But the 2022 energy crisis produced a new factor. UK petrol prices rose to about 150 pence per litre in the first half of 2022, up 14 percent from 131 pence per litre in 2020.[115] But electricity prices rose much faster. At the start of 2022, it cost only £13.69 to charge a 64 kWh EV, such as the Kia e-Niro, at home. But by October, the price had risen to £22.31, up 63 percent since the start of the year. If not for the UK price freeze on home energy prices, October prices would have been an additional 50 percent higher.[116] Both charging at home and in public are now more expensive than buying petrol in the UK. Across Europe it may soon cost more to drive an EV than a petrol car.

RICH NATIONS AND THE DEVELOPING WORLD

The transition to green energy serves rich nations and their wealthy residents. Massive agriculture projects in South America and Southeast Asia provide feedstock that is shipped thousands of miles so that Europe's diesel cars can run on "green" biomass. Electric vehicles are overwhelmingly purchased by wealthy people, and often as pricey second cars. But lower-income apartment dwellers without a garage can't charge an EV at home. The

Food to Save The Planet?

Utah School Gives Kids "Disgusting" Insects to Eat in Class for Climate Assignment on Cows Killing Earth

"There's only one right answer to this essay. And it's that Americans should be eating bugs," a teacher said.

— *Fox News*, March 16, 2023[75]

average citizen pays higher power bills so that wealthy homeowners can mount solar cells on their roofs, paid for by favorable net metering or feed-in tariff programs. And wealthy nations seek huge increases in mining output from poorer nations to provide metals for luxury EVs, often produced by forced or child labor.

Meanwhile, developed nations are urging poorer nations to skip hydrocarbon fuels, and instead to use unreliable wind and solar. In exchange, they dangle the prospect of billions in reparations payments to poorer nations for what they say is for climate change loss and damage. But developing nations want to grow and prosper, and renewables aren't the answer. Renewables favor the world's elites, and developing nations will likely eventually oppose further green-energy expansion.

THE SPROUTING SEEDS OF FAILURE

Output from nuclear power grew rapidly from 1956 to 1980. Leaders projected that nuclear would become the dominant source of global electricity. But the nuclear industry ran into cost, safety, and waste concerns as it grew larger. Similarly, wind, solar, and EVs have grown quickly and are projected to dominate the world's energy systems. When energy sources are small, they can grow rapidly with little negative effect on the overall energy system. But as they grow larger, negative side effects can slow and then halt penetration.

Wind and solar now face mounting problems with poor electrical power reliability from intermittency, local opposition to vast land requirements, transmission infrastructure shortages, and rising electricity bills for rate payers. Electric vehicles encounter rising battery metal costs and charging issues. Biofuels require increasing amounts of land and provide negligible emissions reductions. Accelerating demands for mined metals and rising end-of-life wastes for wind, solar, and EVs sprout as major cost and environmental issues. The push for carbon capture and hydrogen fuel faces insurmountable cost, transport, and scale barriers. With all these problems and the negative side effects, the transition to renewable energy is headed for failure.

CHAPTER 11

GREEN BREAKDOWN AND THE FUTURE

"It's tough to make predictions, especially about the future."
—YOGI BERRA, NEW YORK YANKEES CATCHER[1]

Green energy is headed for a breakdown. The Europe-centered global energy crisis of 2022 appears to be the first in a series of coming renewable energy shocks. Several transnational energy crises are likely to happen during the 2020s and 2030s, each driven by forced efforts to transition to green energy. People will learn the hard way with escalating energy prices, fuel shortages, and electricity blackouts. It will take decades for governments to step back from the powerful ideology that humans are causing climate change and seeking solutions in renewable energy, and instead return to sensible policies based on reliable and low-cost hydrocarbon energy sources. Let's look at some of the impacts of the coming renewable energy failure, the resulting shock and recovery from climate superstition, and a better plan for the future.

197

DOWN THE RENEWABLE PRIMROSE PATH

Hydrocarbon energy is the foundation of modern society. The Hydrocarbon Revolution of the 1800s and 1900s captured the power of low-cost coal, oil, and natural gas fuels, bringing unprecedented advances in mechanization, transportation, and electricity. Hydrocarbons paved the way for advances in agriculture, medicine, and science, generating huge growth in personal incomes, food production, education levels, life spans, and overall prosperity.

During the second half of the twentieth and into the twenty-first century, society increasingly pursued renewable energy sources. Fears of reaching peak oil and rising air pollution drove demand for wind, solar, and biofuel alternatives. But the Shale Revolution showed that vast quantities of oil and natural gas were available from the world's shale fields, pushing concerns about reaching peak oil into the distant future. Pollution was vastly reduced by smokestack scrubbers, catalytic converters, unleaded gasoline, and other methods. Air and water pollution continue to fall in developed nations, with developing nations to follow the same path to pollution reduction.

But in the early twenty-first century, public opinion around the world was captured by the fear of human-caused global warming. The United Nations and scientists using climate models convinced humanity that coal, oil, and natural gas must be eliminated to avoid worldwide catastrophe. Fighting climate change became the reason for existence for environmental groups and the driving force for global adoption of renewable energy.

DEVELOPING NATIONS WILL PURSUE HYDROCARBONS

Renewable energy remains almost nonexistent in most developing nations. In 2021, non-hydroelectric renewables provided only tiny shares of energy in Africa (2.3%), Central America (8.2%), the Middle East (0.5%), South America without Brazil (6.0%), Southeast Asia (5.3%), and Russia and the Commonwealth of Independent States (0.2%). Non-hydroelectric renewables supplied only 6.7 percent of the world's total energy in 2021.[3]

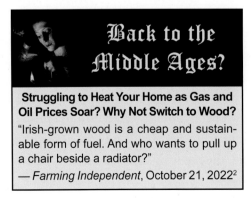

Back to the Middle Ages?

Struggling to Heat Your Home as Gas and Oil Prices Soar? Why Not Switch to Wood?

"Irish-grown wood is a cheap and sustainable form of fuel. And who wants to pull up a chair beside a radiator?"

— *Farming Independent*, October 21, 2022[2]

Developing countries appear to be all in for world decarbonization, with high levels of participation at annual UN climate conferences. Why shouldn't they be? Poorer nations seek billions in wealth transfers from richer nations in the name of climate change. Prior to the COP26 conference in Scotland in 2021, India demanded $1 trillion per year from wealthy countries to help it reach Net Zero by 2070.[4] About 25 percent of all financial aid to the developing world now goes to fund climate-related projects, up from only four percent in 2005.[5]

Despite decarbonization lip service, developing nations continue to aggressively pursue the expansion of hydrocarbon energy. Nations in Africa are building more than $400 billion worth of new natural gas wells, pipelines, processing facilities, and gas-fired power plants, for completion by 2030. Africa still has hundreds of millions of people without access to electricity and almost a billion without modern cooking fuels.[6]

These efforts run counter to the directives of the International Energy Agency (IEA), which says that no new oil or gas fields should be developed. Leaders in Europe have long called for African countries to skip oil and gas development in favor of wind and solar. But these same leaders now seek increased natural gas imports from Algeria, Nigeria, and other African nations to ease Europe's current natural gas shortage. Andrew Kamau, principal secretary at the Kenyan Ministry of Petroleum and Mining, observes,

> Oil producing countries in Africa are feeling the hypocrisy. "All of a sudden" after Russia's invasion there is money to develop oil and gas assets, "but for me, not for you."[7]

More than 900 new coal-fired power plants are in planning or under construction across the world, with growth led by China, India, and Indonesia.[8] As another example, 60 million tons of new steel capacity is planned for or under construction in Southeast Asia, financed by Chinese investment. Eighty percent of these steel investments consist of blast furnace-basic oxygen furnace technology, using coal- and natural gas-intensive processes.[9] These new coal and steel plants will emit large quantities of carbon dioxide (CO_2).

Developing nations seek to continue increasing the prosperity of their peoples. Over 700 million people lack electricity. Another two billion suffer power outages each day. Intermittent wind and solar cannot solve this problem. Always-on hydrocarbon or nuclear plants are needed. Richer nations enjoy one vehicle for every two persons, while many poorer nations have only one vehicle for every 20 persons. Electric cars remain decades away as a possible

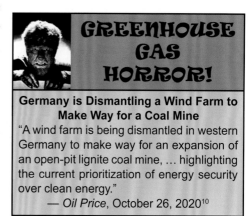

GREENHOUSE GAS HORROR!

Germany is Dismantling a Wind Farm to Make Way for a Coal Mine

"A wind farm is being dismantled in western Germany to make way for an expansion of an open-pit lignite coal mine, ... highlighting the current prioritization of energy security over clean energy."
— *Oil Price*, October 26, 2020[10]

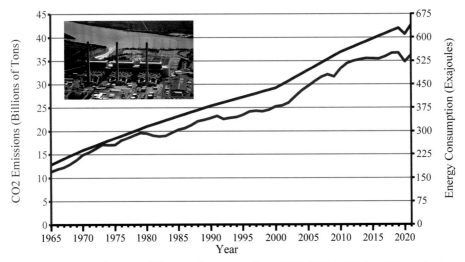

Global CO$_2$ Emissions and Energy Consumption 1965–2021. Rising CO$_2$ emissions in billions of tons and energy consumption in exajoules. Image of the Gladstone Power Station in Queensland, Australia. (Global Carbon Project, 2022; Smil, 2010; BP, 2022)[11]

solution. Those in poorer nations use only one twentieth of the plastic used by people in developed nations. To raise standards of living, developing nations need huge quantities of concrete, steel, plastics, and chemicals, all of which exhaust CO$_2$ when produced.

The UN, the IEA, and green leaders call for an eight percent reduction in world energy consumption by 2050. But energy consumption increased 47 percent from 2000 to 2021. They call for a 40 percent reduction in CO$_2$ emissions by 2030. But global CO$_2$ emissions increased by 44 percent from 2000 to 2021.[12] Green demands run counter to history and common sense. Forcing developing nations to forego hydrocarbon energy would be tragic but, in any case, will not occur. Driven by the needs of 80 percent of the world, energy consumption and CO$_2$ emissions will continue to rise for many years to come.

THE LOOMING RENEWABLE ENERGY FAILURE

Advanced nations should prepare for the coming renewable energy failure. Where wind and solar systems have been extensively deployed, renewable weaknesses are becoming increasingly apparent. The longer leaders try to force a transition from traditional energy to renewables, the greater the damage will be to current energy systems.

Europe passed its Green Deal in 2020, which has been considered a landmark climate package. Just two years later, Europeans were restarting dozens of coal plants, putting in place 25 natural gas import terminals, and boosting drilling for gas production. Europe faces a decade of energy disaster. Europeans now depend upon intermittent wind and solar and imports of high-priced liquefied gas. For many years, France and Germany provided surplus electricity to neighboring countries, but that excess power has disappeared. In the last decade, Germany shut down almost all of its nuclear plants. France's nuclear plants now suffer from corrosion and years of poor maintenance, reducing output.[13] Europe's green policies, along with nuclear retirement, produced fragile and expensive national energy systems with damaging consequences for homes and businesses.

Nevertheless, European leaders still appear determined to double down on commitments to drastically reduce CO_2 emissions. The European Commission proposed the Fit for 55 program in 2021, which set a goal to reduce emissions by 55 percent by 2030. Efforts underway at the end of 2022 pushed to enact Fit for 55 into law in all 27 European states.[14] This initiative still continues with electricity prices up by five times and widespread blackouts possible in the case of cold winters. Many believe the solution to the crisis is even more reliance on renewables. Commissioner for Energy Kadri Simson spelled out the plan,

> Our response to the twin climate and energy challenge is a plan called REPowerEU. …
> Our energy system cannot become renewables-based overnight, but we can accelerate the process.[15]

As a specific example, the United Kingdom continues to march to the renewables drumbeat. In 2021, natural gas generated 40 percent of the nation's electricity.[16] The UK plans to replace all gas-generated power with wind systems by 2035. The result may be hundreds of deaths during blackouts in severe winter cold when the wind doesn't blow.

Australia may be next for a renewable crisis. The nation's leaders pursued an aggressive wind and solar build-out between 2000 and 2021. Wind and solar provided 22 percent of Australia's electricity in 2021, compared to coal and natural gas, which provided 51 and 18 percent, respectively. But also, over the same period, Australia's electricity prices climbed at roughly twice the rate of inflation, rising from amongst the lowest in the world in 2000 to amongst the highest by 2020.[17]

Australia's power reliability in 2020 was better than that of the US, with only about half of the annual hours of outage. But Australia intends to phase out coal and natural gas

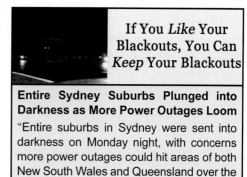

If You *Like* Your Blackouts, You Can *Keep* Your Blackouts

Entire Sydney Suburbs Plunged into Darkness as More Power Outages Loom
"Entire suburbs in Sydney were sent into darkness on Monday night, with concerns more power outages could hit areas of both New South Wales and Queensland over the next 24 hours." — *7 News*, June 13, 2020[18]

generators. The country has no nuclear plants and gets only six percent of its power from hydroelectric systems.[19] When coal and gas generators are replaced by intermittent wind and solar, system reliability will rapidly decline.

US New England states may soon join California and Texas as candidates for energy shock. Over 80 percent of homes in the Northeast use natural gas, propane, or fuel oil for heating, and gas supplies more than half of the electricity.[20] But for years the state of New York blocked gas pipeline construction to the Northeast in favor of following Climatist ideology. Nuclear capacity was also retired. Protests blocked new transmission lines from Canada. As a result, New England needs imports of liquefied natural gas to meet demand.

In 2020, Boston received 60 percent of US shipborne natural gas imports, some of it from Russia. New Englanders now pay more than $20 per million Btu for gas, triple the price of most of the continental US. This price is higher because they must pay more than $30 per million Btu for the liquified gas that is imported.[21] During the next severe winter, the region may run out of gas and need to force rolling blackouts. In any case, residents now pay the highest prices for natural gas and fuel oil in more than 25 years.

Net Zero will not be achieved. People will increasingly push back against high electricity prices, vehicle bans, rising power outages, and mandates to eliminate gas stoves. There won't be enough batteries to compensate for wind and solar intermittency or enough renewable electricity to create green hydrogen to decarbonize heavy industry. There won't be enough used cooking oil to produce sustainable aviation fuel for airlines. Biofuels won't become competitive for use by the shipping industry. Carbon capture systems will capture only a negligible part of industrial emissions, despite billions of dollars in subsidies. CO_2 pipelines will be opposed and halted by local residents. Electricity prices will rise faster than gasoline- and diesel-fuel prices in most decarbonizing nations, making charging electric vehicles (EVs) more expensive. EVs will penetrate world markets, but internal combustion engine (ICE) vehicles will hold the majority for decades to come. Developing nations will continue to adopt hydrocarbon energy, the only sensible path to economic growth. Net Zero will become a hated phrase, associated with mandates, high prices, and energy shortages.

The world will fall far short of obtaining 100 percent, or even 50 percent, of its energy from renewable sources by 2050. It probably won't even reach 50 percent by 2100. The twenty-first century will be a period of mixed hydrocarbon

Spanish Shops and Restaurants Banned from Setting Air-Conditioners Below 27C Amid Energy Crisis
— *ABC News*, August 2, 2022[22]

and renewables use, with renewables delivering at best only the smaller share of the world's energy. More than \$15 trillion will be wasted in efforts to switch to zero-carbon processes, with little gained in energy-system performance, reliability, or reduction of real pollutants.

THE GREAT NEWS

The great news is that human carbon dioxide emissions are not causing dangerous global warming. Earth has warmed only about one degree Celsius in 140 years. Average global temperatures today are lower than temperatures during many multi-century-long periods that occurred naturally during the last 10,000 years. Water vapor, not CO_2 or methane, is Earth's dominant greenhouse gas. Human industry causes only about 1–2 percent of Earth's greenhouse effect. Climate change is dominated by natural, not man-made factors.

Contrary to headlines, data shows that storms are neither more frequent nor stronger than in past ages. Droughts and floods are neither more numerous nor more severe. Oceans continue to rise at 7–8 inches per century, and the rise is not accelerating. The gentle warming over the last century is good for humanity, and CO_2 emissions are great for plant life.

White Spruce Stump. This stump is from a white spruce tree carbon-dated to have died about 4,900 years ago. It's located 100 kilometers north of the tree line in northern Canada, evidence of naturally warmer past temperatures. (Ritchie, 1962)[23]

Future global temperatures are difficult to predict, but some scientists forecast that Earth will experience a period of cooling for the next few decades. Satellite data indicates that surface temperatures have been slightly declining since 2016. In any case, it will become apparent by the second half of the twenty-first century at the latest that humans cannot control global temperatures. The theory of human-caused climate change will rank high on the list of historical superstitions, alongside past beliefs that the Earth was flat, that witches caused crop failures, and that matter was composed of air, earth, fire, and water.

RECOVERY FROM RENEWABLE DEMANDS

Recovery after the attempted shift to renewable energy will be long and painful. Green industries will be forced to downsize. Organizations based on the shaky foundation of a climate-driven energy transition will disappear. Young people will need to find new causes to pursue and new reasons to fear the future.

As we have discussed, clean-energy solutions suffer from critical weaknesses compared to traditional energy sources. Wind and solar intermittency and their huge land requirements remain major disadvantages for electricity generation. Billions of dollars in subsidies, tax breaks, and mandates have driven the growth of wind and solar industries. Look for these industries to shrink without the benefit of subsidies and mandates, confined to operating in windy and sunny locations where reliable backup electricity sources are available.

Biofuels require much more land, water, fertilizer, and insecticides to produce than fuel from oil. They produce less energy when burned and cost more than gasoline and diesel fuel. Without subsidies and mandates and their green-energy designation, biofuels and their industries are set for a decline as well. People will choose not to cut down forests for biomass fuel for electricity.

"Green" hydrogen produced from electrolysis, powered by intermittent wind and solar electricity, will penetrate only a tiny share of global fuel markets. High production costs, high transportation costs, and a shortage of renewable electricity to drive electrolyzers will limit this fuel source for many decades to come. Nations that eliminate coal, gas, and nuclear generators will struggle to keep the lights on, unable to build capacity to produce hydrogen.

Carbon dioxide has uses in industry, but huge captured quantities will have little value. Carbon capture and storage (CCS) projects exist only with government subsidies and payments from companies subjected to emissions trading markets. When these transfer payments decline, CCS will be discarded into the wastebasket of failed human efforts.

Today, climate change initiatives and the quest for a global energy transition provide livelihood for millions of people. When climate fear subsides, thousands of professors in university climate and energy departments, thousands of green consultants, and endless numbers of people employed to provide Environmental, Social, and Governance certification, carbon-footprint analysis, sustainability certification, LEED certification for green buildings, and carbon credits will be looking for new jobs. Scientists from more than 30 climate modeling teams will move on to better projects. These millions of people may find positions where they can make valuable contributions to society, instead of wasting their efforts on a false theory and an unneeded energy transition.

Save our planet

Planet Over People?

Kill yourself

Should We Be Having Kids in the Age of Climate Change?
— *NPR*, August 18, 2016[24]

Likewise, world leaders must find another cause to replace their quest to "fight climate change." Thousands of laws will need to be rewritten or revoked. Emissions restrictions on cars, trucks, ships, planes, trains, stoves, air conditioners, light bulbs, houses, factories, power plants, farms, and food will be lifted. A fresh wind of freedom will blow throughout the global economic system.

Climate strike in Melbourne, Australia, March 15, 2019.[25]

For most of three decades, young people have been bombarded by sustainable-energy ideology and climate fear in schools, colleges, and the media. Hundreds of thousands of students marched during the global climate strike in 2019. It's now common for climate protesters to throw chemicals or food on works of art to protest the climate emergency. Members of advocacy groups like the Extinction Rebellion and Letzte Generation block streets, occupy restaurants, and glue themselves to airport runways, driven by the delusion that time is running out to avoid catastrophe.

But failure of the theory of human-caused warming will awaken Greta Thunberg and countless others from their climate nightmares. Millions will be wandering around thinking "What do we do now?" Our current generation of youths will need to be deprogramed. Freed from climate fear, young people may decide to have children after all. A new generation will grow up and drive new environmental efforts. Like initiatives to remove river dams, demolishing wind turbines may become a favored trend to restore natural landscapes.

A BETTER PLAN FOR THE FUTURE

Instead of forcing the adoption of renewable energy and trying to eliminate carbon dioxide emissions, humanity should pursue a better plan. Initiatives for the future should be based on: 1) adaptation to climate change, 2) sensible energy choices, 3) technological development of new energy sources, and 4) reduction of harmful air and water pollution (not CO_2). These elements will minimize the frequency and impact of energy shocks, provide low-cost energy to billions, enable an improving environment, and support the highest levels of human growth and flourishing for both developed and developing nations.

Adaptation to climate change is far more effective than attempting to control global temperatures. Building local sea walls to counter flooding from rising oceans, as the

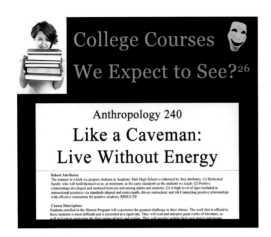

College Courses We Expect to See?[26]

Anthropology 240

Like a Caveman: Live Without Energy

School Attributes
The manner in which we prepare students at Academy Park High School is informed by four attributes: (1) Dedicated faculty who will hold themselves to, at minimum, to the same standards as the students we teach; (2) Positive relationships developed and nurtured between and among adults and students; (3) A high level of rigor included in instructional practices via standards aligned and contextually driven instruction; and (4) Connecting positive relationships with effective instruction for positive academy RESULTS!

Course Description:
Students enrolled in the Honors Program will experience the greatest challenge in their classes. The work that is offered to these students is most difficult and is presented at a rapid rate. They will read and interpret great works of literature, as well as learn to appreciate the finer points of style and writing. They will practice writing their own stories and poems.

Netherlands has done for centuries, is targeted and cost effective. Erecting wind turbines and solar arrays to reduce CO_2 emissions, in order to try to stop rising temperatures, reduce icecap melting, slow ocean rise, and stop flooding, will take decades with only an uncertain chance of improvement. Effective forest management will reduce the danger of California wildfires, but forced adoption of EVs will have no effect on fires. Access to low-cost electrical power from hydrocarbons, along with fans and air conditioners, can reduce heat wave mortality in developing nations, but eliminating gas stoves and forcing the use of transportation biofuels will do nothing about heat waves. Boosting the wealth of developing nations and constructing sturdy housing are real solutions that reduce the death and disaster resulting from hurricanes. But switching heavy industry to hydrogen fuel will never make storms less frequent or less severe. Humans have adapted to rising seas, droughts, floods, storms, and heat waves for thousands of years. Adaptation to climate change remains the only rational option.

Sensible energy choices based on performance, reliability, cost, and real environmental impact should guide future policy. Coal and natural gas remain the highest-performing, most-reliable, and lowest-cost fuels for providing electrical power. Coal has an edge in reliability, since coal can be stored at the plant site. Coal-fired plants require pollution-control systems, such as scrubbers, to reduce emitted pollutants. Natural gas has the smallest land footprint, is the cleanest-burning fuel, and has historically been the lowest-cost fuel. Output from gas-fired plants can also be ramped up quickly in times of need. When nations begin to boost exploration and drilling for natural gas again, world prices will fall, and gas will once more become the cheapest power source in gas-producing countries.

Hydroelectric power remains an excellent low-cost electricity source, which can also be ramped up quickly, as long as reservoir water levels remain high. Nuclear power is also an excellent source, but its capital costs remain high compared to those of coal and natural gas. The nuclear industry needs technological breakthroughs to reduce costs and become a favored power source again.

Wind and solar have their place in the energy picture. In windy and sunny locations, such as Hawaii, wind and solar can be useful electricity sources. Rooftop solar panels can provide benefits to homeowners in the Sun Belt. But intermittent sources cannot replace always-on systems if power-system reliability is to be maintained.

California Dreamin'?

California Looks to Ban Diesel Trucks at Ports by 2035
— *The Wall Street Journal*, Nov. 20, 2022[27]

Transportation will remain overwhelmingly powered by hydrocarbon fuels for decades. Electric vehicles have the advantages of a quiet ride, fast acceleration, and home charging, compared to traditional gasoline and diesel vehicles. In developing nations, where auto-emissions-control devices are not yet widely used, EVs may provide a shortcut to reduce harmful emissions. EVs will penetrate world markets, but users should purchase them based on performance, reliability, and cost. Governments should not seek to force a switch to EVs with bans and subsidies in the belief that eliminating CO_2 emissions will improve the environment.

About two billion people still lack modern fuels for cooking and heating their homes; instead they burn charcoal, wood, biomass, and dung. This practice causes high levels of indoor pollution, along with respiratory disease and death. The use of natural gas, liquid petroleum gas, and propane should be extended to people across the world. The adoption of these fuels for cooking and heating has done more to reduce indoor air pollution than any other method. Electric appliances are typically more expensive per unit of energy, without any significant advantage in pollution reduction compared to gas appliances.

Technological development will provide new energy sources long before we run out of hydrocarbons. Society should invest in efforts to achieve energy breakthroughs instead of efforts to reduce CO_2 emissions. Advancements in nuclear reactor technology may have the largest potential. Developments in small modular reactors and molten salt reactors may be able to lower capital and operating costs and eliminate the possibility of reactor meltdowns. These advances should make nuclear power competitive with gas and coal again. They may also enable small nuclear reactors to compete for new applications, such as in commercial ships or industrial plants. Fusion research efforts continue, but fusion reactors still struggle to reach energy breakeven, with a long road to becoming cost competitive after breakeven is achieved. Geothermal energy from deep wells has potential if production costs can be substantially reduced.

Continuing advances in battery technology should reduce EV cost and range disadvantages, which will increase EV market penetration. Hybrid cars, with both gasoline and electric engines, will probably become market winners, once mainstream opinion shifts

Gee, Ya Think So?

New York Times Essay Says You Should Mate with Short People to Save the Planet
— *Fox News*, January 3, 2023[28]

away from the notion that all ICE vehicles must be eliminated. Electric motors in hybrids provide superior miles-per-gallon performance for everyday travel, with the use of the gasoline engine for long-distance trips. Improved battery technology will increase the use of grid-scale batteries, but their cost and the size of power systems means it will be many decades before they can compensate for wind and solar intermittency on a large scale, if ever.

Reduction of harmful air and water pollution should continue to be a priority. Pollution levels continue to fall in developed nations, including Australia, Canada, Japan, New Zealand, the US, and European countries. In 2013, particulate air pollution peaked in China and has been declining for the last seven years.[29] Today, the nations that use the most energy per person have the lowest levels of air pollution, including carbon monoxide, lead, nitrous oxides, ozone, sulfur oxides, and particulates. CO_2 is great for the biosphere and should not be considered a pollutant. Instead of focusing on CO_2, we should accelerate efforts to find solutions for treating wastewater in developing nations and reducing the amount of plastic litter entering our oceans.

A FINAL WORD

The world has arrived at a crossroads. The 2022 global energy crisis and an increasing frequency of energy shocks will force nations to reconsider their pursuit of green energy policies. The value of low-cost, always-on hydrocarbon energy, combined with nuclear power, will again become the focus of world energy policy.

Today, one in 10 people suffer from hunger, and one in three lack regular access to adequate food. More than 600 million people try to survive on under $2 per day. A billion people lack access to clean drinking water, 700 million don't have electricity, and 2.4 billion lack modern cooking fuels. Tropical diseases plague more than 1.5 billion people each year. HIV and malaria each kill more than 600,000 people a year, and more than one million die from tuberculosis.[30]

The real tragedy of renewable energy polices is the vast misallocation of global resources in efforts to reduce emissions of CO_2, a harmless, invisible gas we all exhale. Let's take the trillions spent on pursuing green energy and instead use it to solve real-world problems.

RECOMMENDED READING

Meredith Angwin, *Shorting the Grid: The Hidden Fragility of Our Electric Grid* (Carnot Communications, 2020)

Robert Bryce, *A Question of Power: Electricity and the Wealth of Nations* (Public Affairs, 2020)

Roger Bezdek, Craig D. Idso, David R. Legates, and S. Fred Singer, *Climate Change Reconsidered II: Fossil Fuels* (The Heartland Institute, 2019)

Jerome R. Corsi, *The Truth About Energy, Global Warming, and Climate Change: Exposing Climate Lies in an Age of Disinformation* (Post Hill Press, 2022)

Donn Dears, *Clean Energy Crisis: The Challenge of Replacing Fossil Fuels* (Donn Dears LLC, 2023)

Alex Epstein, *Fossil Future: Why Global Human Flourishing Requires More Oil, Coal, and Natural Gas—Not Less* (Portfolio/Penguin, 2022)

Steve Goreham, *Outside the Green Box: Rethinking Sustainable Development* (New Lenox Books, 2017)

Steve Goreham, *The Mad, Mad, Mad World of Climatism: Mankind and Climate Change Mania* (New Lenox Books, 2012)

Steven Koonin, *Unsettled: What Climate Science Tells Us, What it Doesn't and Why it Matters* (BenBella Books, 2021)

Bjorn Lomborg, *False Alarm: How Climate Change Panic Costs Us Trillions, Hurts the Poor, and Fails to Fix the Planet* (Basic Books, 2020)

Patrick Moore, *Fake Invisible Catastrophes and Threats of Doom* (Independently published, 2021)

Robert R. Nordhaus and Sam Kalen, *Energy Follies: Missteps, Fiascos, and Successes of America's Energy Policy* (Cambridge University Press, 2018)

Norman Rogers, *Dumb Energy: A Critique of Wind and Solar Energy* (Dumb Energy Publishing, 2019)

Michael Shellenberger, *Apocalypse Never: Why Environmental Alarmism Hurts Us All* (Harper, 2020)

S. Fred Singer and Dennis Avery, *Unstoppable Global Warming Every 1500 Years,* (Rowman & Littlefield, 2007)

Vaclav Smil, *Energy and Civilization: A History* (The MIT Press, 2017)

Vaclav Smil, *Power Density: A Key to Understanding Energy Sources and Uses* (The MIT Press, 2015)

Anthony Watts and James Taylor, *Climate at a Glance for Teachers and Students: Facts on 30 Prominent Climate Topics* (The Heartland Institute, 2022)

NOTES

Introduction

1. Francis Menton, "Without Any Demonstration Project or Feasibility Study," *Manhattan Contrarian*, Oct. 2, 2022, https://www.manhattancontrarian.com/blog/2022-10-2-without-a-demonstration-project-or-feasibility-study
2. Nick Wood, "Save Energy by Showering Together, Swiss Told," *WalesonLine*, Sep. 19, 2022, https://www.walesonline.co.uk/news/world-news/save-energy-showering-together-swiss-25050641
3. Paresh Dave, "Google Aims to Run on Carbon-Free Energy by 2030," *Reuters*, Sep. 14, 2020, https://www.reuters.com/article/idUSKBN2651EP?utm_campaign=Hot%20News&utm_medium=email&_hsmi=95274590&_hsenc=p2ANqtz-_wawHrFfZL82yj3NuvJ6LWfjYu-vW5LqvYyPtuClXDdCx-_Wba1Fw3rStlF5pv8f7CBt6KobMRWJKAEU1bnUhjnp5U5rA&utm_content=95274590&utm_source=hs_email; Angus cattle image from US Department of Agriculture
4. Veronica Henze, "Global Investment in Low-Carbon Transition Hit $755 Billion in 2021," *BloombergNEF*, Jan. 27, 2022, https://about.bnef.com/blog/global-investment-in-low-carbon-energy-transition-hit-755-billion-in-2021/
5. Ibid.
6. "Auto Makers Grapple with Battery Fire Risks in Electric Vehicles," *The Wall Street Journal*, Oct. 19, 2020, https://www.google.com/search?as_q=automakers+grapple+with+battery-fire+risks+in+electric+vehicles&as_epq=&as_oq=&as_eq=&as_nlo=&as_nhi=&lr=&cr=&as_qdr=all&as_sitesearch=&as_occt=any&safe=images&as_filetype=&tbs=; Burning Tesla image by Baltimore County Fire Department, public domain
7. Emma Newburger, "New York City is Banning Gas Hookups for New Buildings to Fight Climate Change," *CNBC*, Dec. 15, 2021, https://www.cnbc.com/2021/12/15/new-york-city-is-banning-natural-gas-hookups-for-new-buildings.html; Guillotine image by Mball93 under Creative Commons License 4.0
8. Hetzmann Mercedesz, "Energy Crisis: Will Hungarian Schools be Heated with Wood?" *Daily News Hungary*, Jul. 7, 2022, https://dailynewshungary.com/energy-crisis-will-hungarian-schools-be-heated-with-wood/?mc_cid=47e339901f&mc_eid=5c20d5e304; "Out of Gas" sign image from 1973 by David Falconer, U.S. National Archives

Chapter 1: Energy Abundance and Need

1. Robert Bryce talk, Manhattan Institute, May 18, 2014, https://www.c-span.org/video/?319523-1/smaller-faster-lighter-denser-cheaper
2. "Access to Energy," *Our World in Data*, 2020, https://ourworldindata.org/energy-access
3. *Energy Transitions: History, Requirements, Prospects* by Vaclav Smil, (Praeger, 2010), appendix; BP Statistical Review of World Energy, June, 2022, https://www.bp.com/en/global/corporate/energy-economics/statistical-review-of-world-energy.html; "Key World Energy Statistics 2020, International Energy Agency, https://www.iea.org/reports/key-world-energy-statistics-2020; Hoover Dam image by snakefisch
4. Ibid.
5. Ibid.
6. Andrea Zuvich, "Stuart Britain: What Was Life Like for Ordinary People?," *History Extra*, May 23, 2018, https://www.historyextra.com/period/stuart/stuart-britain-what-was-life-like-for-ordinary-people/
7. Tim Lambert, "Life in 17th Century England," *Local Histories*, 2020, http://www.localhistories.org/stuart.html
8. Ibid.
9. "What Was the Future of Rail Travel at High Speed." *FortuneTeller*, 2010, http://foresightinhindsight.com/article/show/2172; Locomotive image by GDJ
10. *The Miner's Friend; An Engine to Raise Water by Fire* by Thomas Savory, 1829, https://archive.org/details/minersfriendora00savegoog/page/n4/mode/2up
11. "Thomas Newcomen (1663–1729)," *BBC History*, 2014, http://www.bbc.co.uk/history/historic_figures/newcomen_thomas.shtml
12. "Energy Units," American Physical Society, 2020, https://www.aps.org/policy/reports/popa-reports/energy/units.cfm
13. "Energy," *Wikipedia*, 2020, https://en.wikipedia.org/wiki/Energy
14. American Physical Society, (See no. 12)
15. "How Much Electricity Does an American Home Use?," US Energy Information Administration, Oct. 2, 2019, https://www.eia.gov/tools/faqs/faq.php?id=97&t=3#:~:text=In%202018%2C%20the%20average%20annual,about%20914%20kWh%20per%20month.
16. Carl Lira, "Biography of James Watt," MSU College of Engineering, May 21, 2013, https://www.egr.msu.edu/~lira/supp/steam/wattbio.html#:~:text=James%20Watt%20was%20born%20in,suffered%20from%20migraines%20and%20toothaches.&text=Watt%20learned%20about%20the%20navigational,to%20become%20an%20instrument%20maker.
17. Ibid.
18. Carl Lira, "Watt Atmospheric Engine Description," MSU, May 21, 2013, https://www.egr.msu.edu/~lira/supp/steam/wattengine.htm
19. "Rotative Steam Engine by Boulton and Watt, 1788," Science Museum Group, 2020, under Creative Commons 4.0 Licence, https://collection.sciencemuseumgroup.org.uk/objects/co50948/rotative-steam-engine-by-boulton-and-watt-1788-beam-engine-steam-engine
20. Richard S. Hartenberg, "Robert Fulton, American Inventor," *Britannica*, Feb. 20, 2020, https://www.britannica.com/biography/Robert-Fulton-American-inventor
21. "Stockton and Darlington Railway," Head of Steam Darlington Railway Museum, 2020, https://www.head-of-steam.co.uk/about-us/stockton-and-darlington-railway/
22. Frederick N. Rasmussen, "Riding the B&O; for 175 Years," *The Baltimore Sun*, Feb. 28, 2002, https://www.baltimoresun.com/news/bs-xpm-2002-02-28-0202280278-story.html
23. "Powering the Engines," The University of Vermont, 2011, https://www.uvm.edu/landscape/dating/railroads/fuels.php
24. Henry C. Adams, "Report on Transportation Business of The United States at the Eleventh Census: 1890," US Dept. of the Interior, https://catalog.hathitrust.org/Record/001347987
25. Caleb Johnson, "Voyage of the Mayflower," MayflowerHistory.com, 2020, http://mayflowerhistory.com/voyage
26. Matthew Rozsa, "Climate Activist Greta Thunberg Completes Three-Week Catamaran Voyage across Atlantic," *Salon*, Dec. 6, 2019, https://www.salon.com/2019/12/05/climate-activist-greta-thunberg-successfully-completes-a-three-week-voyage-across-the-atlantic-ocean/; Tortoise image by Moise Nicu under Creative Commons Attribution 3.0
27. International Air Transport Association, 2020, https://www.iata.org/
28. "Oregon Trail," *Wikipedia*, 2020, https://en.wikipedia.org/wiki/Oregon_Trail

29. "First American Oil Well," American Oil & Gas Historical Society, 2020, https://www.aoghs.org/petroleum-pioneers/american-oil-history/
30. Ibid.
31. Ibid.
32. Derek Thompson, "The Spectacular Rise and Fall of U.S. Whaling: An Innovation Story," *The Atlantic*, Feb. 22, 2012, https://www.theatlantic.com/business/archive/2012/02/the-spectacular-rise-and-fall-of-us-whaling-an-innovation-story/253355/
33. Quote from *Oil and Gas News*, October 23, 1919 provided by Matt Novak, *Gizmodo*, https://paleofuture.gizmodo.com/weve-been-incorrectly-predicting-peak-oil-for-over-a-ce-1668986354; Tarot card image by Countakeshi under Creative Commons License 4.0
34. "Internal Combustion Engine," New World Encyclopedia, 2020, https://www.newworldencyclopedia.org/entry/Internal_combustion_engine
35. Richard Muller et al., "Energy and Power," Princeton Physics, 2005, http://wwwphy.princeton.edu/~steinh/ph115/Chapter01D.pdf
36. Joel Havens, "A Brief History of the Internal Combustion Engine," *New World Encyclopedia*, Jan. 15, 2012, https://www.newworldencyclopedia.org/entry/Internal_combustion_engine
37. Internal Combustion Engine, (See no. 34)
38. Image of 1885 gasoline car of Carl Benz by Alonso de Mendoza
39. "History of the Automobile," *Britannica*, 2020, https://www.britannica.com/technology/automobile/History-of-the-automobile
40. "Monthly Energy Review," US Energy Information Administration, Dec. 2020, https://www.eia.gov/totalenergy/data/monthly/pdf/mer.pdf
41. "World Development Indicators," World Bank, 2020, https://datacatalog.worldbank.org/dataset/world-development-indicators; "World Electricity Consumption," US Energy Information Administration, 2020, https://www.eia.gov/international/data/world#/?; Power lines in New Zealand image by Kent Murrill under Creative Commons License 3.0
42. Nancy Gupton, "Benjamin Franklin and the Kite Experiment," The Franklin Institute, Jun. 12, 2017, https://www.fi.edu/benjamin-franklin/kite-key-experiment
43. "Alessandro Volta," Famous Scientists, Jul. 28, 2014, https://www.famousscientists.org/alessandro-volta/#:~:text=Alessandro%20Volta%20was%20a%20physicist,voltaic%20pile%E2%80%9D%20%E2%80%93%20in%201800.
44. L. Pierce Williams, "Michael Faraday," *Britannica*, Sep. 18, 2020, https://www.britannica.com/biography/Michael-Faraday
45. Ibid.
46. "Electricity Explained," US Energy Information Administration, Mar. 20, 2020, https://www.eia.gov/energyexplained/electricity/
47. Douglas Brooks, "Propagation Times," *CMP Media*, Aug. 2000, https://www.ultracad.com/articles/propagationtime.pdf
48. "Voltage and Current," *All About Circuits*, 2020, https://www.allaboutcircuits.com/textbook/direct-current/chpt-1/voltage-current/
49. Akash Peshin, "How Much Current Can the Human Body Withstand?," *ScienceABC*, Oct. 10, 2019, https://www.scienceabc.com/humans/how-many-volts-amps-kill-you-human.html
50. "Basic Electronics: Voltage, Current, & Resistance," Electrical Engineering & Arduino Resources for Makers, 2020, https://idyl.io/electronics/basics/voltage-current-resistance/
51. "Thomas A. Edison Papers," Rutgers School of Arts and Sciences, Oct. 28, 2016, https://edison.rutgers.edu/list.htm#:~:text=General%20Electric%20Company.-,Edison%20General%20Electric%20Company,company%2C%20Edison%20Electric%20Light%20Company.
52. Tom Hodgkinson, "Shakespeare Had No Blackberry and Aristotle Managed without an iPhone," *Guardian*, Nov. 10, 2009, https://www.theguardian.com/environment/2009/nov/10/ethical-living-waste; Owl and books image by Yamachem
53. "Pearl Street Power Station," *Energy Story*, Aug. 10, 2015, https://energystory.org/pearl-street-power-station/
54. "Thomas Edison Biography," *Biography*, Aug. 26, 2019, https://www.biography.com/inventor/thomas-edison
55. Gary Hoover, "George Westinghouse: Servant Leader, Inventor, Captain of Industry," Archbridge Institute, Feb., 27, 2019, https://www.archbridgeinstitute.org/2019/02/27/george-westinghouse-servant-leader-inventor-captain-of-industry/
56. Ibid.
57. John Wilkes, "Edison, Westinghouse and Tesla: the History behind The Current War," *BBC History*, Mar. 2019, https://www.historyextra.com/period/victorian/edison-westinghouse-tesla-real-history-behind-the-current-war-film/
58. Matt Rosenberg, "U.S. Population throughout History," *ThoughtCo.*, Dec. 13, 2019, https://www.thoughtco.com/us-population-through-history-1435268
59. "The United States in 1900," Digital History, 2019, https://www.digitalhistory.uh.edu/disp_textbook.cfm?smtID=2&psid=3175
60. Max Roser et al., "World Population from 10,000 BC to Today," *OurWorldinData*, 2020, https://ourworldindata.org/world-population-growth
61. *Bulletin of the Bureau of Labor*, US Department of Commerce and Labor, No 59, July 1905, p. 164, https://fraser.stlouisfed.org/title/bulletin-united-states-bureau-labor-3943/july-1905-477618/retail-prices-food-498513?start_page=179
62. Digital History, (See no. 59)
63. "Real Median Family Income in the US," Fed. Res. Bank of St. Louis, Sep. 16, 2020, https://fred.stlouisfed.org/series/MEFAINUSA672N
64. Maddison Project Database, University of Groningen, 2018, https://www.rug.nl/ggdc/historicaldevelopment/maddison/releases/maddison-project-database-2018?lang=en
65. *Bulletin of the Bureau of Labor*, (See no. 61)
66. Digital History, (See no. 59)
67. "How Much Did Things Cost in 1900?" *Reference.com*, Apr. 12, 2020, https://www.reference.com/history/much-did-things-cost-1900-9e40559daa251473
68. N.J. Hagens, "Economics for the Future—Beyond the Superorganism," *Ecological Economics*, No. 169, Nov. 20, 2019, https://www.sciencedirect.com/science/article/pii/S0921800919310067
69. Clayton Aldrich, "19 Facts and Photos that Show How Brutal Life Was in the Early 1900s," *BoredomTherapy*, 2020, https://boredomtherapy.com/facts-about-1900s-america/
70. Robert Barro and Jong-Wha Lee, "A New Data Set of Educational Attainment in the World, 1950-2010," *Journal of Development Economics*, Vol. 104, p. 185-198, https://www.nber.org/papers/w15902; Christian Morrisson and Fabrice Murtin, "The Century of Education," Centre for Economics Education, London School of Economics, Sep. 2009, https://eric.ed.gov/?id=ED530031
71. Maddison, (See no. 64); Money pot image by Gnokii
72. "Battle of New Orleans," *History.com*, Sep. 26, 2019, https://www.history.com/topics/war-of-1812/battle-of-new-orleans
73. "Morse Code & the Telegraph," History.com, Jun. 6, 2019, https://www.history.com/topics/inventions/telegraph
74. Johnson Hur, "History of the Telephone," *Bebusinessed.com*, 2020, https://bebusinessed.com/history/history-of-the-telephone/
75. "13 Future Predictions That Were So Wrong People Would Probably Regret Saying Them," *Bored Panda*, 2018, https://www.boredpanda.com/bad-future-predictions-timeline-history/?utm_source=google&utm_medium=organic&utm_campaign=organic; Telephone image by j4p4n
76. Digital History, (See no. 59)
77. "1900: A Year in the Life of America," *Genealogy.com*, 2020, https://www.genealogy.com/articles/research/76_life1900.html
78. "Henry Ford," *History.com*, Mar. 26, 2020, https://www.history.com/topics/inventions/henry-ford
79. Aldrich, (See no. 69)
80. Digital History, (See no. 59)
81. Aldrich, (See no. 69)
82. "Clothes Washing Machines," Edison Tech Center, 2020, https://edisontechcenter.org/WashingMachines.html

83. "Kitchen Stoves 1900–1919," *Weebly.com*, 2020, https://evolutionhomeappliances.weebly.com/kitchen-stoves-1900-1919-steel-gas--electricity.html

84. "Residential Energy Consumption Survey," US Energy Information Administration, May, 2018, https://www.eia.gov/consumption/residential/reports/2015/methodology/pdf/RECSmethodology2015.pdf

85. Emma Grahn, "Keeping Your Food Cool: From Ice Harvesting to Electric Refrigeration," National Museum of American History, Apr. 29, 2015, https://americanhistory.si.edu/blog/ice-harvesting-electric-refrigeration

86. Paul Lester, "History of Air Conditioning," *Energy.gov*, Jul. 20, 2015, https://www.energy.gov/articles/history-air-conditioning

87. *Outside the Green Box: Rethinking Sustainable Development* by Steve Goreham, (New Lenox Books, 2017) p. 34–35

88. Max Roser et al., "Life Expectancy," *Our World in Data*, Oct., 2019, https://ourworldindata.org/life-expectancy

89. Ibid.; Infant in Zimbabwe image by Jzsj under Creative Commons 4.0 License

90. 13 Future Predictions, (See no. 75); Old car image by j4p4n

91. Collin Smith et al., "Current and Future Role of Haber-Bosch Ammonia in a Carbon-Free Energy Landscape," *Energy Environmental Sciences*, 2020, no. 13, p. 331–334

92. "Food Production Index," World Bank, 2020, https://data.worldbank.org/indicator/AG.PRD.FOOD.XD

93. William C. Roberts, "At the Mercy of Oil," Baylor Univ. Medical Center, Apr. 2010, https://www.ncbi.nlm.nih.gov/pmc/articles/PMC2848100/

94. Caterina Clerici et al., "Dumsor: The Electricity Outages Leaving Ghana in the Dark," *Aljazeera*, 2016, https://interactive.aljazeera.com/aje/2016/ghana-electricity-outage-dumsor/index.html

95. "Africa Energy Outlook 2019," IEA, Nov. 2019, p. 228-229, https://www.iea.org/reports/africa-energy-outlook-2019

96. Ibid.

97. Caterina Clerici, (See no. 94)

98. Todd Moss, "Ending Global Poverty-How Can We do Better?" World Economic Forum, Nov. 5, 2019, https://www.weforum.org/agenda/2019/11/energy-poverty-africa-sdg7/

99. "World Energy Outlook 2020," International Energy Agency, 2020, https://www.iea.org/reports/sdg7-data-and-projections/access-to-electricity

100. Todd Moss, (See no. 98)

101. "Least Developed Countries," United Nations Department of Economic and Social Affairs, 2020, https://www.un.org/development/desa/dpad/least-developed-country-category/ldc-data-retrieval.html

102. "World Development Indicators," World Bank, Enterprise Surveys, 2020, https://data.worldbank.org/indicator/IC.ELC.OUTG

103. Shefali Khanna and Kevin Rowe, "The Value of Electricity Reliability in India," International Growth Centre, Feb. 8, 2020, https://www.theigc.org/blog/the-value-of-electricity-reliability-in-india/

104. Students studying in Mumbai, India image by one-11 under Creative Commons License 2.0, Flickr.com

105. World Bank, (See no. 41); "Air Conditioner Power Consumption: Deciphering the Label," Kompulsa, 2020, http://www.kompulsa.com/much-power-air-conditioners-consume/#:~:text=The%20power%20consumption%20of%20air%20conditioners%20averages%20318%20watts%20(hourly,2%2C500%20watts%20in%20most%20cases.; "Energy Use of Some Typical Home Appliances," US Dept. of Energy, Sep. 16, 2020, http://sites.science.oregonstate.edu/~hetheriw/energy/quick/eff/EREC_Brief_Energy_Use_of_Some_Typical_Home_Appliances.htm

106. Africa Energy Outlook, p. 84 (See no. 95)

107. Three sources, (See no. 105); Refrigerator image by W.carter under Creative Commons License 4.0

108. "Vehicles per Capita: Other Regions/Countries Compared to the United States," *Energy.gov*, Jan. 30, 2017, https://www.energy.gov/eere/vehicles/fact-962-january-30-2017-vehicles-capita-other-regionscountries-compared-united-states

109. Tony Swan, "Fast Facts: The 47,000-Plus-Mile U.S. Interstate System, *Car and Driver*, Dec. 27, 2017, https://www.caranddriver.com/features/a14499092/fast-facts-the-47000-plus-mile-us-interstate-system-feature/

110. Ajay Pillarisetti et al., "Household Energy Interventions and Health and Finances in Haryana, India: An Extended Cost-Effectiveness Analysis," Injury Prevention and Environmental Health," The World Bank, 2017, https://www.ncbi.nlm.nih.gov/books/NBK525217/

111. Dhwani Pandya and Debjit Chakraborty, "PM Narendra Modi's Push to Make Kitchens Safer Makes India No. 2 LPG Importer," *The Economic Times*, Apr. 24, 2017, https://economictimes.indiatimes.com/news/economy/policy/pm-narendra-modi-push-to-make-kitchens-safer-makes-india-no-2-lpg-importer/articleshow/58335383.cms?from=mdr

112. Leia Larson, "As Climate Change Tightens its Grip, Are Golf Courses a Luxury We Can No Longer Afford?" *The Salt Lake Tribune*, Jul. 23, 2021, https://www.sltrib.com/news/environment/2021/07/23/with-climate-change/; Skulls image by Antony Stanley under Creative Commons License 2.0; Golf putting on green image by Woodypino under Creative Commons License 4.0

Chapter 2: The Rise of Renewable Energy

1. Arnold Schwarzenegger interview, *BBC News*, Apr. 26, 2012; https://www.bbc.com/news/av/world-us-canada-17863391

2. "Transition to Solar Energy This Summer with Solarize Chicagoland," Sustainable Evanston, City of Evanston, Jun. 15, 2020, https://content.govdelivery.com/accounts/ILEVANSTON/bulletins/290c8f0

3. *Energy Transitions: History, Requirements, Prospects* by Vaclav Smil, (Praeger, 2010), appendix; BP Statistical Review of World Energy, June, 2020, https://www.bp.com/en/global/corporate/energy-economics/statistical-review-of-world-energy.html; "Key World Energy Statistics 2020, International Energy Agency, https://www.iea.org/reports/key-world-energy-statistics-2020

4. "Crude Oil Prices 70-Year Historical Chart," *Macrotrends*, Oct. 27, 2020, https://www.macrotrends.net/1369/crude-oil-price-history-chart

5. "Fact #915: March 7, 2016 Average Historical Annual Gasoline Pump Price, 1929–2015," *Energy.gov*, Mar. 7, 2016, https://www.energy.gov/eere/vehicles/fact-915-march-7-2016-average-historical-annual-gasoline-pump-price-1929-2015

6. "Oil Embargo, 1973–1974," Office of the Historian, US Dept. of State, Apr. 8, 2018, https://history.state.gov/milestones/1969-1976/oil-embargo#:~:text=During%20the%201973%20Arab%2DIsraeli,the%20post%2Dwar%20peace%20negotiations.

7. Crude Oil Prices, (See no. 4)

8. Energy.gov, (See no. 5)

9. "Drink Beer, Save the Planet! NZ Company Introduces World's First Beer-Based Fuel," *t.com*, Jul. 11, 2015, https://www.rt.com/news/273106-new-zealand-beer-fuel/; Laughing boy cartoon by hotta

10. "Monthly Energy Review," EIA, US Dept. of Energy, May, 2020, Table 3.1, https://www.eia.gov/totalenergy/data/monthly/

11. *Energy Follies: Missteps, Fiascos, and Successes of America's Energy Policy* by Robert R. Nordhaus and Sam Kalen, (Cambridge University Press, 2018), p. 107–119

12. Monthly Energy Review, (See no. 10)

13. Jag Bhalla and Eliza Barclay, "How Affluent People Can End Their Mindless Overconsumption," *Vox*, Nov. 20, 2020, https://www.vox.com/21450911/climate-change-coronavirus-greta-thunberg-flying-degrowth; Owl and books image by Yamachem

14. "Relations with the Middle East and the Oil Crises," *CVCE.eu*, Jul. 8, 2016, https://www.cvce.eu/en/collections/unit-content/-/unit/df06517b-babc-451d-baf6-a2d4b19c1c88/548d2b44-a4f0-460e-a26d-999028832012

15. Energy Follies, (See no. 11)

16. Samantha Gross, "What Iran's Revolution Meant for US and Global Oil Markets," *Brookings*, Mar. 5, 2019, https://www.brookings.edu/blog/

order-from-chaos/2019/03/05/what-irans-1979-revolution-meant-for-us-and-global-oil-markets/

17.   Tim Sablik, "Recession of 1981–1982," *Federal Reserve History*, Nov. 22, 2013, https://www.federalreservehistory.org/essays/recession_of_1981_82

18.   Energy Follies, (See no. 11)

19.   M. King Hubbert presentation to the American Petroleum Institute, March, 1956, http://www.energycrisis.com/Hubbert/1956/1956.pdf

20.   "International Data," US EIA, 2020, https://www.eia.gov/international/data/world; Oil pump image by Galya Malanchuk under Creative Commons License 4.0, https://commons.wikimedia.org/wiki/File:Deep_well_pumping_unit_for_oil_extraction._Borehole._05.jpg

21.   President Jimmy Carter, address to the nation, Apr. 18, 1977, https://www.youtube.com/watch?v=zl7BL1DRuwE

22.   "History," California Air Resources Board, 2020, https://ww2.arb.ca.gov/about/history

23.   "Killer Smog Claims Elderly Victims," A&E Television Networks, Nov. 13, 2009, https://www.history.com/this-day-in-history/killer-smog-claims-elderly-victims

24.   Christopher Klein, "The Great Smog of 1952," *History.com*, Aug. 22, 2018, https://www.history.com/news/the-killer-fog-that-blanketed-london-60-years-ago

25.   Arthur C. Stern, "History of Air Pollution Legislation in the United States," *Journal of the Air Pollution Control Association*, 1982, https://www.tandfonline.com/doi/pdf/10.1080/00022470.1982.10465369

26.   "The Modern Environmental Movement," *pbs.org*, 2020, https://www.pbs.org/wgbh/americanexperience/features/earth-days-modern-environmental-movement/

27.   Ibid.

28.   "A Cause Becomes a Mass Movement," *Life Magazine*, Jan. 30, 1970, https://oldlifemagazine.com/january-30-1970-life-magazine.html; Image of nuclear explosion, Apr. 18, 1953, at Nevada test site by National Nuclear Security Administration

29.   "Why Europe Responded Differently from the United States," *Environment & Society Portal*, 2020, http://www.environmentandsociety.org/exhibitions/rachel-carsons-silent-spring/why-europe-responded-differently-united-states

30.   Michael Ray, "The Greens," Britannica.com, 2020, https://www.britannica.com/topic/the-Greens-politics

31.   Vaclav Smil, "'Too Cheap to Meter' Nuclear Power Revisited," *IEEE Spectrum*, Sep. 26, 2016, https://spectrum.ieee.org/energy/nuclear/too-cheap-to-meter-nuclear-power-revisited

32.   Rod Adams, "Why Did Richard Nixon So Strongly Endorse Nuclear Energy in April, 1973," *Atomic Insights*, Sep. 22, 2015, https://atomicinsights.com/why-did-richard-nixon-so-strongly-endorse-nuclear-energy-in-april-1973/; Tarot card image by Countakeshi under Creative Commons License 4.0

33.   Smil, (See no. 31)

34.   "Glenn Responds to 1970s Energy Crisis," NASA, Apr. 10, 2008, https://www.nasa.gov/centers/glenn/about/history/70s_energy.html

35.   "U.S Wind Energy Grows in California, Then Stagnates Nationwide in the 1980s," American Wind Energy Association, 2020, https://www.awea.org/wind-101/history-of-wind/1980s

36.   Richard Bowers, "U.S Wind Energy Production Tax Credit Extended through 2021, US Energy Information Administration, Jan. 28, 2021, https://www.eia.gov/todayinenergy/detail.php?id=46576; Monopoly image by Mike Mozart under Creative Commons License 2.0

37.   "History of Europe's Wind Industry," Wind Europe, 2020, https://windeurope.org/about-wind/history/

38.   *Energy: The Solar Prospect* by Denis Hayes, (Worldwatch Institute, 1977), p. 5

39.   "From 'Beyond Coal' to 'Beyond Gas' Already," *Charleston Gazette-Mail*, Nov. 21, 2017, https://www.wvgazettemail.com/opinion/from-beyond-coal-to-beyond-gas-already/article_157972bf-493f-545a-a5b1-e4b42a0329c3.html

40.   Jackson Kelly, "Sierra Club Launches 'Beyond Natural Gas' Campaign," *Oil and Gas Update*, May 29, 2012, https://oilandgas.jacksonkelly.com/2012/05/sierra-club-launches-beyond-natural-gas-campaign.html

41.   "Decline of aggregation of common pollutants," US EPA, 2020, https://www.epa.gov/air-trends; Volatile organic compounds emissions from EPA National Emissions Inventory Trends Data, https://www.epa.gov/air-emissions-inventories/air-pollutant-emissions-trends-data; Vehicle miles traveled from US Federal Highway Administration, 2020, https://www.fhwa.dot.gov/policyinformation/travel_monitoring/tvt.cfm

42.   Wolfgang Schöpp et al., "Long-term development of acid deposition (1880-2030) in sensitive freshwater regions in Europe," *Hydrology and Earth System Sciences*, 7(4), p. 436-446, 2003, https://www.researchgate.net/publication/250396843_Long-term_development_of_acid_deposition_1880-2030_in_sensitive_freshwater_regions_in_Europe

43.   US EPA, (See no. 41); Image of pollution over Louisville, Kentucky by Bill Strode, EPA, Dec. 2, 1970

44.   Panel presentation by Greta Thunberg, World Economic Forum, Jan. 25, 2019, https://commons.wikimedia.org/wiki/File:Greta_Thunberg-_Our_House_Is_On_Fire.webm

45.   Ibid.

46.   Syukuro Manabe and Richard T. Wetherald, "Thermal Equilibrium of the Atmosphere with a Given Distribution of Relative Humidity," *Journal of the Atmospheric Sciences*, Vol. 24, No. 3, May 1967, https://journals.ametsoc.org/jas/article/24/3/241/17328/Thermal-Equilibrium-of-the-Atmosphere-with-a-Given

47.   J. Hansen et al., "Climate Impact of Increasing Atmospheric Carbon Dioxide," *Science*, Aug. 28, 1981, Vol. 213, No. 4511, http://www.sealevel.info/1981_Hansen_etal_1.pdf

48.   "Congress. Testimony of James Hansen," sealevel.info, Jun. 23, 1988, https://www.sealevel.info/1988_Hansen_Senate_Testimony.html

49.   "The Intergovernmental Panel on Climate Change," 2020, https://www.ipcc.ch/

50.   Patrick Barkham, "'We're Doomed': Mayer Hillman on the Climate Reality No One Else Will Dare Mention," *The Guardian*, Apr. 26, 2018, https://www.theguardian.com/environment/2018/apr/26/were-doomed-mayer-hillman-on-the-climate-reality-no-one-else-will-dare-mention; Image of Greta Thunberg by European Parliament under Creative Commons Attribution License 2.0

51.   "United Nations Framework Convention on Climate Change," United Nations, 1992, https://unfccc.int/resource/docs/convkp/conveng.pdf

52.   "Statement by Atmospheric Scientists on Greenhouse Warming," Feb. 27, 1992, https://borderlandsciences.org/oldsite/newstuff/research/dec7/statemen.htm

53.   Damian Carrington, "UN Environment Chief Resigns Amid 'CO2 Hypocrisy,'" *The Guardian*, Nov. 21, 2018, https://www.euractiv.com/section/energy-environment/news/un-environment-chief-resigns-amid-co2-hypocrisy/; Emoji image by Emoji One under Creative Commons License 4.0

54.   "Kyoto Protocol to the United Nations Framework Convention on Climate Change," UN, Dec. 10, 1997, https://unfccc.int/documents/2409

55.   *Apocalypse Never: Why Environmental Alarmism Hurts Us All* by Michael Shellenberger, (Harper, 2020), p. x

56.   L. Bird et al., "Policies and Market Factors Driving Wind Power Development in the United States," National Renewable Energy Laboratory, Jul. 2003, https://www.nrel.gov/docs/fy03osti/34599.pdf

57.   Michael Lotker, "Barriers to Commercialization of Large-Scale Solar Electricity: Lessons Learned from the LUZ Experience," Sandia National Laboratories, Nov. 1991, https://www.osti.gov/servlets/purl/10108287

58.   Mike Chino, "PARK SPARK: Public Park Converts Dog Poo to Energy," *Inhabitat*, Oct. 6, 2010, https://inhabitat.com/park-spark-public-park-converts-dog-poo-to-energy/; Hamster on wheel image by Aaron Denunzio

59.   Jens Vestergaard et al., "Industry Formation and State Intervention: The Case of the Wind Industry in Denmark and the United States," *Academy of Intl. Bus.*, Nov. 2004, http://www.energybc.ca/cache/denmarkwind/old-hha.asb.dk/man/cmsdocs/publications/windmill_paper2.pdf

60.   "Energy Statistics 2018," Danish Energy Agency, Sep. 2020, https://ens.dk/en/our-services/statistics-data-key-figures-and-energy-maps/

annual-and-monthly-statistics

61.   "Household Energy Prices in the EU Increased Compared with 2018," Eurostat, May, 7, 2020, https://ec.europa.eu/eurostat/documents/2995521/10826603/8-07052020-AP-EN.pdf/2c418ef5-7307-5217-43a6-4bd063bf7f44

62.   "Energy Concept for an Environmentally Sound, Reliable, and Affordable Energy Supply," German Federal Ministry of Economics and Technology, Oct. 2011, https://cleanenergyaction.files.wordpress.com/2012/10/german-federal-governments-energy-concept1.pdf

63.   Paul Hockenos, "Energiewende - The First Four Decades," *Clean Energy Wire*, Jun. 22, 2015, https://www.cleanenergywire.org/dossiers/history-energiewende

64.   Christoph M. Schmidt et al., "Economic Impacts from the Promotion of Renewable Energies: The German Experience," Rheinisch-Westfälisches Institute für Wirtschaftsforschung, Nov. 2009, https://www.rwi-essen.de/media/content/pages/publikationen/ruhr-economic-papers/REP_09_156.pdf

65.   IEA Wind 2011 Annual Report, Jul. 2012, https://community.ieawind.org/viewdocument/iea-wind-2012-annual-report

66.   Benjamin Wehrmann, "Solar Power in Germany—Output, Business & Perspectives," *Clean Energy Wire*, Apr. 16, 2020, https://www.cleanenergywire.org/factsheets/solar-power-germany-output-business-perspectives#:~:text=At%20about%20noon%2C%20when%20both,into%20the%20grid%20in%202019.

67.   "The Nobel Peace Prize 2007," Nobelprize.org, 2020, https://www.nobelprize.org/prizes/peace/2007/summary/

68.   Amy DuFault, "Fashion Meets Renewable Energy—Clothes that Charge Your Smartphone, *The Guardian*, Aug. 4, 2014, https://www.theguardian.com/sustainable-business/sustainable-fashion-blog/fashion-technology-renewable-energy-solar-charge-smartphone; Model image by Pimentel94 under Creative Commons Licence 4.0

69.   L. Bird et al., (See no. 56)

70.   Girl with books image by Timothy Takemoto under Creative Commons License 2.0

71.   "EU Emissions Trading System," European Commission, 2020, https://ec.europa.eu/clima/policies/ets_en

72.   David Molloy, "Climate Change: Can Sending Fewer Emails Really Save the Planet?" *BBC News*, Nov. 19, 2020, https://www.bbc.com/news/technology-55002423; Witch image by uroesch

73.   "Renewables 2020 Global Status Report," REN21, Jun. 16, 2020, https://www.ren21.net/gsr-2020/

74.   Wallace E. Tyner, "The US Ethanol and Biofuels Boom: Its Origins, Current Status, and Future Prospects, *BioScience*, Jul/Aug, 2008, https://academic.oup.com/bioscience/article/58/7/646/237138

75.   "Monthly Energy Review," US Energy Information Administration, May, 2020, https://www.eia.gov/totalenergy/data/monthly/

76.   "EU: Fuels: Biofuel Policy," TransportPolicy.net, 2020, https://www.transportpolicy.net/standard/eu-fuels-biofuel-policy/

77.   "10 Years of EU Fuels Policy Increased EU's Reliance on Unsustainable Biofuels," *Transport & Environment*, Jul. 2021, https://www.transportenvironment.org/wp-content/uploads/2021/07/Biofuels-briefing-072021.pdf

78.   "Biofuels Annual—Brazil," US Department of Agriculture, Sep. 4, 2020, https://apps.fas.usda.gov/newgainapi/api/Report/DownloadReportByFileName?fileName=Biofuels%20Annual_Sao%20Paulo%20ATO_Brazil_08-03-2020

79.   REN21, (See no. 73)

80.   "World Bioenergy Stats. 2017," World Bioenergy Assc., Jun. 26, 2017, https://worldbioenergy.org/uploads/WBA%20GBS%202017_hq.pdf

81.   "Statistical Review of World Energy," BP, Jun. 2022, https://www.bp.com/en/global/corporate/energy-economics/statistical-review-of-world-energy.html

82.   Ibid.

83.   "Hoover Dam, Freq. Asked Questions and Answers," US Bureau of Reclamation, 2020, https://www.usbr.gov/lc/hooverdam/faqs/faqs.html

84.   "Statistical Review of World Energy," (See no. 81); Wind and solar image by Gerry Machen under Creative Commons License 2.0

85.   *Energy Transitions: History, Requirements, Prospects* by Vaclav Smil, (Praeger, 2010), appendix; BP Statistical Review of World Energy, June, 2022, https://www.bp.com/en/global/corporate/energy-economics/statistical-review-of-world-energy.html; "Key World Energy Statistics 2021, International Energy Agency, https://www.iea.org/reports/key-world-energy-statistics-2021; Orapa gas-fired power plant in Botswana by Pro-Per Energy Services under Creative Commons License 4.0

86.   Ibid.

87.   Shaikh M.S.U. Eskander and Sam Fankhauser, "Reduction in Greenhouse Gas Emissions from National Climate Legislation," *Nature Climate Change*, Jul. 13, 2020, https://www.researchgate.net/publication/342909839_Reduction_in_greenhouse_gas_emissions_from_national_climate_legislation

88.   Peter Fricke, "Report: Apple CEO Says Fighting Climate Change More Important than Profits," *Daily Caller*, Mar. 10, 2015, https://dailycaller.com/2015/03/10/apple-ceo-sides-with-liberal-lemmings-while-disparaging-profits/; Profit chart image by *simpletutorials.net*

89.   "Climate Ambition Alliance: New Zero 2050," NAZCA, 2020, https://climateaction.unfccc.int/views/cooperative-initiative-details.html?id=94

90.   Kyle Peterdy, "ESG (Environmental, Social and Governance)," *CorporateFinanceInstitute.com*, Jul. 7, 2022, https://corporatefinanceinstitute.com/resources/knowledge/other/esg-environmental-social-governance/

91.   Gary Gastelu, "California Gov. Newsom Executive Order Bans Gas, Diesel Cars by 2035," *FoxNews*, Sep. 23, 2020, https://www.foxnews.com/auto/california-gov-newsom-order-bans-gas-diesel-cars-by-2034; Guillotine image by Mball93 under Creative Commons License 4.0

Chapter 3: Climate Change Fact and Fiction

1.   Milton Friedman, lecture at Utah State University, Oct. 13, 1977, https://www.youtube.com/watch?v=OOZxMjo14pw&t=171s

2.   Veronika Henze, "Energy Transition Investment Hit $500 Billion in 2020 — For First Time," *BloombergNEF*, Jan. 19, 2021, https://about.bnef.com/blog/energy-transition-investment-hit-500-billion-in-2020-for-first-time/

3.   "Global Temperature Record," Climatic Research Unit, University of East Anglia, 2021, https://lr1.uea.ac.uk/cru/cruhome

4.   Ibid.

5.   "Summary for Policymakers," Intergovernmental Panel on Climate Change, Third Assessment Report, Working Group I, 2001, p. 2, https://www.ipcc.ch/site/assets/uploads/2018/07/WG1_TAR_SPM.pdf

6.   "Climate Change 2014 Synthesis Report Summary for Policymakers," Intergovernmental Panel on Climate Change, 2014, p. 5, https://www.ipcc.ch/site/assets/uploads/2018/02/AR5_SYR_FINAL_SPM.pdf

7.   "The Early Keeling Curve," Scripps Inst. of Oceanography, 2021, https://scrippsco2.ucsd.edu/history_legacy/early_keeling_curve.html

8.   "Trends in Atmospheric Carbon Dioxide," National Oceanic & Atmospheric Admin., 2022, https://www.esrl.noaa.gov/gmd/ccgg/trends/

9.   Ibid.

10. Cara Anna, "Leaders to UN: If Virus Doesn't Kill Us, Climate Change Will," *Associated Press*, Sep. 27, 2020, https://apnews.com/article/climate-climate-change-oceans-environment-united-nations-general-assembly-d073896990db973a3e45db26787d6a18; Image of Greta Thunberg by European Parliament under Creative Commons Attribution License 2.0

11. Image of Domino Sugar is public domain.

12. *Climate Change 2014 Synthesis Report*, IPCC, Fifth Assessment Report, p.10, https://www.ipcc.ch/report/ar5/syr/

13. "Chicago Daily Records," National Weather Service, 2021, https://w2.weather.gov/climate/local_data.php?wfo=lot

14. "Chicago, IL Temperature Records," National Weather Service, 2021, https://www.weather.gov/lot/Chicago_Temperature_Records

15. "This Vodka Helps Fight Climate Change," CNN, Jul. 20, 2021, https://www.cnn.com/videos/tv/2021/07/09/eco-solutions-carbon-negative-vodka-air-company-spc-intl-hnk.cnn; Earth in hand image by elconomeno, OpenClipart

16. *The Mad, Mad, Mad World of Climatism* by Steve Goreham, (New Lenox Books, 2012), pp. 58–62

17. Luc Sorel, "Climatic Changes, the Norsemen and the Modern Man," 2001, http://www.lucsorel.com/media/research/2001_ClimaticChanges-NorsemenAndTheModernMan_Sorel.pdf

18. "What are 'Proxy' Data?" National Oceanic and Atmospheric Administration, 2021, https://www.ncdc.noaa.gov/news/what-are-proxy-data

19. Robert Mulvaney, "How Are Past Temperatures Determined from an Ice Core?" *Scientific American*, Sep. 20, 2004, https://www.scientificamerican.com/article/how-are-past-temperatures/

20. D. Dahl-Jensen et al., "Past Temperatures Directly from the Greenland Ice Sheet," *Science*, Vol. 282, Oct. 9, 1998, https://science.sciencemag.org/content/282/5387/268; Image of ice core machine by K Makinson under GNU Free Documentation License,

21. "Greenland Ice Core Project," British Antarctic Survey, Feb. 14, 2000, http://www.nerc-bas.ac.uk/public/icd/grip/griplist.html

22. Craig Idso, "The Medieval Warm Period Project," 2021, http://www.co2science.org/data/mwp/mwpp.php

23. "Mount Tambora," *Encyclopaedia Britannica*, May 27, 2020, https://www.britannica.com/place/Mount-Tambora

24. Hannah Devlin, "Cows 'Potty-Trained' in Experiment to Reduce Greenhouse Gas Emissions," *The Guardian*, Sep. 13, 2021, https://www.theguardian.com/environment/2021/sep/13/cows-potty-trained-in-experiment-to-reduce-greenhouse-gas-emissions; Earth in hand image by elconomeno, OpenClipart

25. "Bill Gates Pushes Carbon Tax and Lectures on Energy Efficiency While Living in a 66,000 Square Foot Mansion with 30,000 a Month Electric Bill," *Climate Depot*, Sep. 2, 2010, https://www.climatedepot.com/2010/09/02/bill-gates-pushes-carbon-tax-and-lectures-on-energy-efficiency-while-living-in-a-66000-square-foot-mansion-with-30000-a-month-electric-bill/; Image by Emoji One under Creative Commons License 4.0

26. *Unstoppable Global Warming Every 1500 Years* by S. Fred Singer and Dennis Avery, (Rowman & Littlefield, 2007), p. 239

27. Alan Buis, "Milankovitch (Orbital) Cycles and Their Role in Earth's Climate," NASA's Jet Propulsion Laboratory, Feb. 27, 2020, https://climate.nasa.gov/news/2948/milankovitch-orbital-cycles-and-their-role-in-earths-climate/#:~:text=The%20Milankovitch%20cycles%20include%3A,is%20pointed%2C%20known%20as%20precession.

28. Unstoppable Global Warming, (See no. 26)

29. Mike Acalowicz and Stephanie Schollaert Uz, "El Niño," NASA, Feb., 14, 2017, https://earthobservatory.nasa.gov/features/ElNino

30. "Pacific Decadal Oscillation," NOAA, 2021, https://www.ncdc.noaa.gov/teleconnections/pdo/; Image of ocean wave in public domain

31. Ibid.

32. James Taylor, "Chris Christie Exposes His Right Flank on Global Warming," *Forbes*, Jun. 1, 2011, https://www.forbes.com/sites/jamestaylor/2011/06/01/chris-christie-exposes-his-right-flank-on-global-warming/?sh=125ae6472155

33. John Tyndall, "Heat, a Mode of Motion", p. 359, 1875

34. "Tutorial on the Greenhouse Effect," University of Arizona, 2021; https://www.lpl.arizona.edu/~showman/greenhouse.html

35. "Feeding Cattle Seaweed Reduces Their Greenhouse Gas Emissions 82 Percent," University of California at Davis, Mar. 17, 2021, https://www.ucdavis.edu/news/feeding-cattle-seaweed-reduces-their-greenhouse-gas-emissions-82-percent; Laughing face by GDI

36. W. A. van Wijngaarden and W. Happer, "Dependence of Earth's Thermal Radiation on Five Most Abundant Greenhouse Gases," arXiv: 2006.03098, Jun 4, 2020; https://arxiv.org/pdf/2006.03098.pdf

37. Ibid.

38. Syukuro Manabe and Richard T. Wetherald, "Thermal Equilibrium of the Atmosphere with a Given Distribution of Relative Humidity," *Journal of the Atmospheric Sciences*, Vol. 24, No. 3, May 1967, https://journals.ametsoc.org/jas/article/24/3/241/17328/Thermal-Equilibrium-of-the-Atmosphere-with-a-Given

39. *Climate Change 2013: The Physical Science Basis*, IPCC, 5th Assessment Rpt., WG 1, 2014, p. 16, https://www.ipcc.ch/report/ar5/wg1/

40. Bob Henson, "Why the 2020 Atlantic Hurricane Season has Spun Out of Control," *The Washington Post*, Sep. 24, 2020, https://www.washingtonpost.com/weather/2020/09/23/atlantic-hurricanes-record-2020/; Image of hurricane winds at Key West by U.S Navy

41. Lindzen et al., "Does the Earth Have an Adaptive Infrared Iris?", *Bulletin of the American Meteorological Society*, Mar. 1, 2001, https://journals.ametsoc.org/view/journals/bams/82/3/1520-0477_2001_082_0417_dtehaa_2_3_co_2.xml

42. Garth Partridge et al., "Trends in Middle- and Upper-Level Tropospheric Humidity from NCEP Reanalysis Data," *Theory of Applied Climatology*, Feb. 26. 2009, https://citeseerx.ist.psu.edu/viewdoc/download?doi=10.1.1.175.4343&rep=rep1&type=pdf

43. J.T. Houghton et al., "Climate Change: The IPCC Scientific Assessment," IPCC Working Group I, 1990, p. XXII

44. John Kerry presentation at the Massachusetts Institute of Technology, January 9, 2017, https://www.youtube.com/watch?v=k9zVFY86IuA

45. Climate Change, (See no. 43); Temperature data from University of Alabama Huntsville, Apr. 2021, https://www.nsstc.uah.edu/data/msu/v6.0/tlt/uahncdc_lt_6.0.txt; Thermometer image by Erkaha under Creative Commons License 4.0

46. James Hansen, "Climate Change: on the Edge," *Independent*, Feb. 17, 2006; https://www.independent.co.uk/climate-change/news/climate-change-on-the-edge-6108869.html

47. Vivien Gornitz, "Sea Level Rise, After the Ice Melted and Today," *NASA Science Briefs*, Jan. 2007, https://www.giss.nasa.gov/research/briefs/2007_gornitz_09/

48. Arthur B. Robinson, et al., "Environmental Effects of Increased Atmospheric Carbon Dioxide," *Journal of American Physicians and Surgeons*, v. 12, pp. 79-90, 2007

49. President Obama speech to the U.S. Coast Guard, May 20, 2015, https://obamawhitehouse.archives.gov/the-press-office/2015/05/20/remarks-president-united-states-coast-guard-academy-commencement; Emoji image by Emoji One under Creative Commons License 4.0

50. Eric Worrall, "Sea Level Rise? President Obama Just Bought a Beachside Property," *WattsUpWithThat*, Aug. 24, 2019, https://wattsupwiththat.com/2019/08/24/sea-level-rise-president-obama-just-bought-a-beachside-property/

51. "Most Recent GMSL Release," Sea Level Research Group, University of Colorado, 2020; https://sealevel.colorado.edu/

52. Fifth Assessment Report, (See no. 39), p. 124

53. William V. Sweet, et al., "Global and Regional Sea Level Rise Scenarios for the United States," NOAA Technical Report NOS CO-OPS 83, Jan. 2017, https://tidesandcurrents.noaa.gov/publications/techrpt83_Global_and_Regional_SLR_Scenarios_for_the_US_final.pdf

54. Craig D. Idso, "Global Sea-Level Rise: An Evaluation of Data," The Heartland Institute, May, 2019, https://www.heartland.org/publications-resources/publications/global-sea-level-rise-an-evaluation-of-the-data

55. Global and Regional Sea Level Rise, (See no. 53); Image of Juneau, Alaska tide guage by Gillfoto under Creative Commons License 4.0

56. Image of ocean waves from CSIRO under Creative Commons License 3.0

57. Patricia Chambers, "Chasing the World's Highest Tides," *Ocean Conservancy*, Nov. 8, 2018, https://oceanconservancy.org/blog/2018/11/08/chasing-worlds-highest-tides/?ea.tracking.id=20HPXGJAXX&gclid=Cj0KCQjw2NyFBhDoARIsAMtHtZ4xb7yRUbPzLf0Lce8mAsrSNTTfG4UweYwP8yqjy38hADQTegRBCx8aArsjEALw_wcB

58. Willie Soon, presentation to the Doctors for Disaster Preparedness, Aug. 1, 2013, https://www.youtube.com/watch?v=1gmW9GEUYvA

59. Tadea Veng and Ole B. Andersen, "Consolidating Sea Level Acceleration Estimates from Satellite Altimetry," *ScienceDirect*, Jan. 16, 2020, https://www.sciencedirect.com/science/article/pii/S027311772030034X

60. Carl Wunsch, et al., "Decadal Trends in Sea Level Patterns: 1993-2004," *Journal of Climate*, Dec. 15, 2007, https://journals.ametsoc.org/view/journals/clim/20/24/2007jcli1840.1.xml

61. Albert Parker and Clifford D. Ollier, "California Sea Level Rise: Evidence Based Forecasts vs. Model Predictions," *ScienceDirect*, Nov. 2017, https://www.sciencedirect.com/science/article/abs/pii/S0964569117303071
62. "Sea Ice and Snow Cover Extent," Natl. Centers for Env. Information, NOAA, 2021, https://www.ncdc.noaa.gov/snow-and-ice/extent/
63. William Chapman, "Why the Arctic is Climate Change's Canary in the Coal Mine," *TEDEd*, 2021, https://ed.ted.com/lessons/why-the-arctic-is-climate-change-s-canary-in-the-coal-mine-william-chapman
64. Sea Ice and Snow Cover Extent, (See no. 62)
65. Al Gore presentation at the United Nations Climate Conference in Copenhagen, Dec. 14, 2009, https://www.youtube.com/watch?v=Msiolw4bvzI; Tarot card image by Countakeshi under Creative Commons License 4.0
66. Sea Ice and Snow Cover Extent, (See no. 62)
67. Peter West, "U.S. South Pole Station," Nat. Sci. Found., 2021, https://www.nsf.gov/news/special_reports/livingsouthpole/station_new.jsp
68. Adapted from "Temperature in Polar Regions: Arctic and Antarctic," *Climate4You*, 2021, http://www.climate4you.com/, data from University of Alabama Huntsville, https://www.nsstc.uah.edu/data/msu/t2lt/uahncdc.lt
69. Christina Hulbe, "How Close is the West Antarctic Ice Sheet to a "Tipping Point," *CarbonBrief*, Feb. 14, 2020, https://www.carbonbrief.org/guest-post-how-close-is-the-west-antarctic-ice-sheet-to-a-tipping-point
70. "Previously Unsuspected Volcanic Activity Confirmed under West Antarctic Ice Sheet at Pine Island Glacier," National Science Foundation, June 27, 2018, https://www.nsf.gov/news/news_summ.jsp?cntn_id=295861
71. "Understanding the Greenland Ice Sheet," Polar Portal, the Danish Arctic research institutions, 2020, http://polarportal.dk/en/groenlands-indlandsis/nbsp/viden-om-groenlands-indlandsis/
72. "Greenland Ice Loss 2002-2020," NASA, 2021, https://grace.jpl.nasa.gov/resources/30/greenland-ice-loss-2002-2020/
73. David Suzuki video, YouTube, Jan. 31, 2014, https://www.youtube.com/watch?v=E73Tu52livM&t=57s
74. "Fourth National Climate Assessment," U.S. Global Change Research Program, 2018, https://nca2018.globalchange.gov/
75. Paul Ratner, "Swedish Scientist Advocates Eating Humans to Combat Climate Change," *Big Think*, Sep. 8, 2019, https://bigthink.com/surprising-science/swedish-scientist-eating-humans-climate-change; Chef image by GDJ under Creative Commons Public Domain Dedication
76. "Continental United States Hurricane Impacts/Landfalls, 1851–2019," NOAA, 2021, https://www.aoml.noaa.gov/hrd/hurdat/All_U.S._Hurricanes.html; Jeff Masters, "A Look Back at the Horrific 2020 Atlantic Hurricane Season," *Yale Climate Connections*, Dec, 1, 2020, https://yaleclimateconnections.org/2020/12/a-look-back-at-the-horrific-2020-atlantic-hurricane-center/#:~:text=An%20unprecedented%20battering%20of%20the,for%20most%20U.S.%20hurricane%20landfalls.; Image of Hurricane Katrina on Aug. 28, 2005 by NOAA
77. Ibid.
78. "Scatterometry," NASA Jet Propulsion Laboratory, 2021, https://winds.jpl.nasa.gov/aboutscatterometry/history/
79. Yasemin Saplakoglu, "Zombie Storms Are Rising from the Dead Thanks to Climate Change," *LiveScience*, Sep. 25, 2020, https://www.livescience.com/zombie-storms-climate-change.html; *Night of the Living Dead* image public domain
80. Ryan Maue, "Accumulated Cyclone Energy, 2021," http://climatlas.com/tropical/; Image of Tropical Storm Isaac in the Gulf of Mexico, Aug. 28, 2012 by NASA
81. Ibid.
82. Hanna Richie, "OFDA/CRED Intl. Disaster Data, *Our World in Data*, 2021, https://ourworldindata.org/ofdacred-international-disaster-data
83. Ciara Lavelle, "Global Warming Makes Couples Cheat, Says Dating Website," *Miami New Times*, May 28, 2014, https://www.miaminewtimes.com/arts/global-warming-makes-couples-cheat-says-dating-website-6511134; Guilty image in public domain
84. "Running Out of Water -and Time," *The Sydney Morning Herald*," Apr. 25, 2005, https://www.smh.com.au/national/running-out-of-water-and-time-20050425-gdl6xe.html
85. Girl with books image by Timothy Takemoto under Creative Commons License 2.0
86. "NSW Flooding: Extreme Rain Wreaks Havoc in NSW in Once-in-a-Century Event," *The Guardian*, Mar. 21, 2021, https://www.theguardian.com/australia-news/2021/mar/21/nsw-flooding-people-flee-their-homes-overnight-as-extreme-rain-wreaks-havoc
87. Rosie Frost, "Flooding in Australia Triggers Fresh Concerns about the Impacts of Climate Change," *euronews.green*, Mar. 22, 2021, https://www.euronews.com/green/2021/03/22/flooding-in-australia-triggers-fresh-concerns-about-the-impacts-of-climate-change
88. Fourth National Climate Assessment, (See no. 74)
89. "U.S Percentage Areas (Very Warm/Cold, Very Wet/Dry)," National Centers for Environmental Information, NOAA, Feb. 8, 2021, https://www.ncdc.noaa.gov/temp-and-precip/uspa/wet-dry/0
90. Ibid.
91. Henry F. Lamb, et al., "Oxygen and Carbon Isotope Composition of Authigenic Carbonate from an Ethiopian Lake: A Climate Record of the Last 2000 Years," *The Holocene*, May 1, 2007, https://journals.sagepub.com/doi/abs/10.1177/0959683607076452
92. Masaki Sano et al., "Tree-ring Based Hydroclimate Reconstruction over Northern Vietnam from *Fokienia Hodginsii*: Eighteenth Century Mega-Drought and Tropical Pacific Influence," *Climate Dynamics*, Aug. 23, 2008, https://link.springer.com/article/10.1007/s00382-008-0454-y
93. Fourth National Climate Assessment, (See no. 74)
94. Sarah Ruiz-Grossman, "Gov. Gavin Newsom: 'If Anyone Is Wondering if Climate Change Is Real, Come to California," *Huffington Post*, Apr. 12, 2019, https://www.huffpost.com/entry/california-governor-wildfires-climate-change_n_5cb0e185e4b098b9a2d38c95
95. Ray Sanchez and Brandon Miller, "California's New Normal: How the Climate Crisis is Fueling Wildfires and Changing Life in the Golden State," *CNN*, Oct. 30, 2019, https://www.cnn.com/2019/10/29/weather/california-us-wildfires-climate-change/index.html
96. "Top 20 Most Destructive California Wildfires," *Cal Fire*, Apr. 28, 2021, https://www.fire.ca.gov/media/4jandlhh/top20_acres.pdf
97. "Fire on the Mountain: Rethinking Forest Management in the Sierra Nevada," Little Hoover Commission, Feb., 2018, https://lhc.ca.gov/sites/lhc.ca.gov/files/Reports/242/Report242.pdf
98. "California Timber Harvest," Bureau of Bus. and Econ. Research, Univ. of Montana, 2021, http://www.bber.umt.edu/fir/HarvestCA.aspx
99. Todd Morgan, et al., "California's Forest Products Industry and Timber Harvest, 2006,"US Department of Agriculture, Aug. 2012, https://www.fs.fed.us/pnw/pubs/pnw_gtr866.pdf
100. Tom Stienstra, "With 147 Million Dead Trees, Californians Brace for Fire," *San Francisco Chronicle*, Jul. 7, 2019, https://www.sfchronicle.com/outdoors/stienstra/article/With-147-million-dead-trees-Californians-brace-14072558.php
101. Adam Voiland, "Building a Long-Term Record of Fire, NASA Earth Observatory, Aug. 20, 2019, https://earthobservatory.nasa.gov/images/145421/building-a-long-term-record-of-fire; Image of 2013 Stanislaus National Forest fire in California by U.S. Dept. of Agriculture
102. Ibid.
103. Gina McCarthy interview Sep. 14, 2018, https://www.youtube.com/watch?v=92JfmyKE39w
104. Rachapudi Sreeharsha et al., "Delayed Flowering is Associated with Lack of Photosynthetic Acclimation in Pigeon Pea (Cajanus Cajan L.) Grown under Elevated CO2," *Plant Science*, Dec. 3, 2019, https://www.researchgate.net/publication/270255313_Delayed_flowering_is_associated_with_lack_of_photosynthetic_acclimation_in_Pigeon_pea_Cajanus_cajan_L_grown_under_elevated_CO2
105. "Release of Carbon Dioxide by Individual Humans," *The Globe Program Scientists' Blog*, Aug. 11, 2008, https://www.globe.gov/explore-science/scientists-blog/archived-posts/sciblog/2008/08/11/release-of-carbon-dioxide-by-individual-humans/comment-page-1/index.html
106. "The Positive Externalities of Carbon Dioxide: Estimating the Monetary Benefits of Rising Atmospheric CO2 Concentrations on Global Food Production," *CO2Science.org*, Oct., 2013, http://www.co2science.org/education/reports/co2benefits/data.php

107. Randall Donohue, "Deserts 'Greening' from Rising CO2," CSIRO, Jul. 3, 2013, https://www.csiro.au/en/news/news-releases/2013/deserts-greening-from-rising-co2
108. Ibid.
109. Vanessa Haverd et al., "Yes, More Carbon Dioxide in the Atmosphere Helps Plants Grow, But It's Excuse to Downplay Climate Change," *CSIROScope*, Feb. 11, 2020, https://blog.csiro.au/yes-more-carbon-dioxide-in-the-atmosphere-helps-plants-grow-but-its-no-excuse-to-downplay-climate-change/

Chapter 4: The War on Hydrocarbon Energy

1. James Buchan, "Oil: We're Addicted," *NewStatesman*, July. 17, 2006, https://www.newstatesman.com/node/164761#:~:text=A%20century%20ago%2C%20petroleum%20%2D%20what,cosmetics%2C%20CDs%20and%20car%20tyres.
2. Seattle protest image by Daniella Beccaria, taken May 16, 2015 in Seattle Harbor, under Creative Commons License 2.0
3. "Global Trends in Renewable Energy Investment 2020," Frankfurt School FS-UNEP Collaborating Centre for Climate & Sustainability Energy Finance, 2020, https://www.fs-unep-centre.org/wp-content/uploads/2020/06/GTR_2020.pdf
4. "World Energy Balances: Overview," International Energy Agency, 2020, https://www.iea.org/reports/world-energy-balances-overview; Image of Olkiluoto nuclear power station and wind turbine in Finland by kallerma.
5. Ibid.
6. "Energy Use for Transportation," US EIA, May 17, 2021, https://www.eia.gov/energyexplained/use-of-energy/transportation.php
7. "Transport: Increasing Oil Consumption and Greenhouse Gas Emissions Hamper EU Progress toward Environment and Climate Objectives," European Environment Agency, Jul. 14, 2021, https://www.eea.europa.eu/publications/transport-increasing-oil-consumption-and-ghg
8. "Sustainable Aviation Fuel: Review of Technical Pathways," US Dept. of Energy, Sep. 9, 2020, https://www.energy.gov/eere/bioenergy/downloads/sustainable-aviation-fuel-review-technical-pathways-report
9. "Summary for Policymakers and Industry: Charting a Course for Decarbonizing Maritime Transport," The World Bank, 2021, https://openknowledge.worldbank.org/handle/10986/35436
10. Joe Dwinell, "Charlie Baker Climate Official Blasted for Comments to 'Break Your Will' Over Emissions," *Boston Herald*, Feb. 11, 2021, https://www.bostonherald.com/2021/02/05/baker-climate-official-blasted-for-comments-to-break-your-will-over-emissionsvideo/; Guillotine image by Mball93 under Creative Commons License 4.0
11. "Stat. Rev. of World Energy," BP, 2022, https://www.bp.com/en/global/corporate/energy-economics/statistical-review-of-world-energy.html
12. Ibid.
13. "Final Energy Consumption in Households by Fuel," Eurostat Data Browser, Jun. 6, 2021, https://ec.europa.eu/eurostat/databrowser/view/t2020_rk210/default/table?lang=en
14. "Monthly Energy Review," US Energy Information Administration, Mar. 2021, https://www.eia.gov/totalenergy/data/monthly/
15. "Renewables 2021 Global Stat. Rpt," REN 21, Jun. 2021, https://www.ren21.net/wp-content/uploads/2019/05/GSR2021_Full_Report.pdf
16. "GDP (Current US$)," The World Bank, 2021, https://data.worldbank.org/indicator/NY.GDP.MKTP.CD; "Global Carbon Budget Data," Global Carbon Project, 2021, https://www.globalcarbonproject.org/carbonbudget/20/data.htm; Image of Navajo coal-fired generating plant by Matthew Dillion under Creative Commons License 2.0
17. "Crude Oil Prices 70-Year Historical Chart," *Macrotrends*, Jul. 21, 2021, https://www.macrotrends.net/1369/crude-oil-price-history-chart
18. Monthly Energy Review, (See no. 14)
19. Monthly Energy Review, (See no. 14)
20. "U.S. Imports of Petroleum," Census Bureau, July 2, 2021, https://www.census.gov/foreign-trade/statistics/graphs/PetroleumImports.html
21. Monthly Energy Review, (See no. 14); Image of Lost Hills Oil Field by Richard Masoner under Creative Commons License 2.0
22. Monthly Energy Review, (See no. 14), Image of AbQaiq oil tanker at Iraqi oil installation by US Navy
23. Eloise Marais, "Space Tourism: Rockets Emit 100 Times More CO2 per Passenger than Flights - Imagine a Whole Industry," *The Conversation*, Jul. 19, 2021, https://theconversation.com/amp/space-tourism-rockets-emit-100-times-more-co-per-passenger-than-flights-imagine-a-whole-industry-164601; Richard Branson quote, YouTube, Aug. 31, 2009, https://www.youtube.com/watch?v=8YhUVIoanX0; Jeff Bezos quote, *Business Insider*, Feb. 17, 2020, https://www.businessinsider.com/jeff-bezos-giving-10-billion-to-fight-climate-change-2020-2; Pinwheel image by Kgredi76 under Creative Commons License 4
24. John Manfreds, "The Origin of Fracking Actually Dates Back to the Civil War," *Business Insider*, Apr. 14, 2015, https://www.businessinsider.com/the-history-of-fracking-2015-4
25. Andrew Farr, "A Brief History of Directional Drilling: The Birth and Development of the HDD Market," *Trenchless Technology*, Jul. 4, 2012, https://trenchlesstechnology.com/brief-history-horizontal-directional-drilling/
26. Jon Gertner, "George Mitchell," *The New York Times Magazine*, Dec. 21, 2013, https://www.nytimes.com/news/the-lives-they-lived/2013/12/21/george-mitchell/
27. Monthly Energy Review, (See no. 14)
28. "How Much Shale (Tight) Oil is Produced in the United States?", EIA, Mar. 31, 2021, https://www.eia.gov/tools/faqs/faq.php?id=847&t=6
29. "How Much Shale Gas is Produced in the United States/", US EIA, Mar. 31, 2021, https://www.eia.gov/tools/faqs/faq.php?id=907&t=8
30. Monthly Energy Review, (See no. 14)
31. US Imports of Petroleum, (See no 20)
32. Gas stove image by Steven-L-Johnson under Creative Commons License 2.0; Skulls image by Antony Stanley under Creative Commons License 2.0
33. "The Value of U.S. Energy Innovation and Policies Supporting the Shale Revolution," Council of Econ. Advisers, Oct. 2019, https://trumpwhitehouse.archives.gov/wp-content/uploads/2019/10/The-Value-of-U.S.-Energy-Innovation-and-Policies-Supporting-the-Shale-Revolution.pdf
34. Robert Rapier, "How the Fracking Revolution Broke OPEC's Hold on Oil Prices," *Forbes*, Jul. 22, 2018, https://www.forbes.com/sites/rrapier/2018/07/22/how-the-fracking-revolution-broke-opecs-hold-on-oil-prices/?sh=96cd91d48efd
35. Jude Clemente, "Shale Has Delinked US Oil and Gas Prices," *Rigzone*, Dec. 6, 2019, https://www.rigzone.com/news/shale_has_delinked_us_oil_and_gas_prices-06-dec-2019-160504-article/
36. Steve Goreham, "Fewer Recessions Thanks to the Shale Revolution," *WorldNetDaily*, Jan. 31, 2020, https://www.wnd.com/2020/01/fewer-recessions-thanks-shale-revolution/
37. Image of gas fracking site in Pennsylvania by Nicholas A Tonelli, https://commons.wikimedia.org/wiki/File:Flickr_-_Nicholas_T_-_Rig.jpg
38. "Sparks Fly Over 'Gasland' Drilling Documentary," *NPR*, Feb. 24, 2011, https://www.npr.org/2011/02/24/134031183/Gasland-Takes-On-Natural-Gas-Drilling-Industry
39. "EPA Administrator Lisa Jackson Tells Congress 'No Proven Cases Where Fracking Has Affected Water," *YouTube*, May 24, 2011, https://www.youtube.com/watch?v=L4RLzlcox5c
40. "Fracturing Fluid Contents," *FracFocus*, 2021, https://www.fracfocus.org/learn/what-is-fracturing-fluid-made-of
41. Jim Hill, "What's In The Fracking Fluid Hickenlooper Drank?," KUNC, Feb. 15, 2013, https://www.kunc.org/business/2013-02-15/whats-in-the-fracking-fluid-hickenlooper-drank

42.   "How Much Water Does Hydraulic Fracturing Use?", American Petroleum Institute, 2021, https://www.api.org/oil-and-natural-gas/energy-primers/hydraulic-fracturing/how-much-water-does-hydraulic-fracturing-use-2

43.   *The Mad, Mad, Mad World of Climatism* by Steve Goreham, (New Lenox Books, 2012), p. 208

44.   Gregory T. Lyman, "How Much Water Does Golf Use and Where Does It Come From?", US Golf Association, 2012, https://www.usga.org/content/dam/usga/pdf/Water%20Resource%20Center/how-much-water-does-golf-use.pdf

45.   "How is Hydraulic Fracturing Related to Earthquakes and Tremors?", US Geological Survey, 2021, https://www.usgs.gov/faqs/how-hydraulic-fracturing-related-earthquakes-and-tremors?qt-news_science_products=0#qt-news_science_products

46.   "Map: The Fracking Boom, State by State," *Inside Climate News*, Jan. 20, 2015, https://insideclimatenews.org/news/20012015/map-fracking-boom-state-state/

47.   "The Basics - Operations," Shale Gas Information Platform, Helmholtz Centre, Potsdam, 2021, https://www.shale-gas-information-platform.org/ship/categories/operations/the-basics/index.html

48.   "In What Countries is Fracking Done?," *SGK Planet*, Feb. 28, 2021, https://sgkplanet.com/en/in-what-countries-is-fracking-done/#:~:text=According%20to%20the%20publication%20of,shale%20oil%20to%20market%20them.

49.   David Minkow, "What You Need to Know About Fracking in Canada," *The Narwhal*, Apr. 6, 2017, https://thenarwhal.ca/what-is-fracking-in-canada/

50.   Charles Newbery, "Argentina's Vaca Muerta Fracking Activity Rises to Record High in March," *S&P Global Platts*, Apr. 5, 2021, https://www.spglobal.com/platts/en/market-insights/latest-news/natural-gas/040521-argentinas-vaca-muerta-fracking-activity-rises-to-record-high-in-march

51.   Chen Aizhu, "Analysis: Chinese Majors to Struggle to Extend Shale Gas Boom beyond 2025," Reuters, Jan. 26, 2021, https://www.reuters.com/article/us-china-shalegas/analysis-chinese-majors-to-struggle-to-extend-shale-gas-boom-beyond-2025-idUSKBN29V0ZE

52.   "In Which Countries is Fracking Prohibited?" *SGK Planet*, Feb. 28, 2021, https://sgkplanet.com/en/in-which-countries-is-fracking-prohibited/

53.   Fracking in Canada, (See no. 49)

54.   "Stat. Rev. of World Energy," BP, 2022, https://www.bp.com/en/global/corporate/energy-economics/statistical-review-of-world-energy.html

55.   "European Unconventional Oil and Gas Assessment," European Commission, March, 2017, https://ec.europa.eu/jrc/sites/default/files/t8_review_of_results_and_recommendations.pdf

56.   "Carbon-Neutral California Would Save 14,000 Lives a Year, UCLA Study Says," *City News Service*, May 5, 2020, https://www.nbclosangeles.com/news/local/ucla-study-carbon-neutral-california-would-save-14000-lives-a-year/2357598/; Girl surfer image by Daniel Torbekov

57.   Kate Ng, "Hummingbird Halts Construction of Controversial Oil Pipeline," *Independent*, Apr. 29, 2021, https://www.independent.co.uk/news/world/americas/hummingbird-causes-oil-pipeline-disruption-b1839932.html;Darth Vader image is public domain

58.   "Dominion Energy and Duke Energy Cancel the Atlantic Coast Pipeline," Duke Energy, July 5, 2021, https://news.duke-energy.com/releases/dominion-energy-and-duke-energy-cancel-the-atlantic-coast-pipeline

59.   Rob Gillies, "Keystone XL Pipeline Halted as Biden Revokes Permit," *Associated Press*, Jan. 20, 2021, https://apnews.com/article/joe-biden-alberta-2fbcce48372f5c29c3ae6f6f93907a6d

60.   Jeff Brady and Neela Banerjee, "Developer Abandons Keystone XL Pipeline Project, Ending Decade-Long Battle, *NPR*, June. 9, 2021, https://www.npr.org/2021/06/09/1004908006/developer-abandons-keystone-xl-pipeline-project-ending-decade-long-battle

61.   *The Clubhouse Kids Make a Big Difference Teacher's Manual*, (Culver Company, 2007), https://www.mnpower.com/Content/Community/Education/Materials/clubhouse-kids-manual.pdf; Angus cattle image by Scott Bauer, US Department of Agriculture

62.   Annual Report Mileage Summary Statistics," Pipeline and Hazardous Materials Safety Administration, US Dept. of Transportation, Sep. 1, 2020, https://www.phmsa.dot.gov/data-and-statistics/pipeline/annual-report-mileage-summary-statistics

63.   Nick Ferris, "Exclusive Natural Gas Data Reveals Trillions of Dollars of Upcoming Projects," *Energy Monitor*, Jul. 27, 2021, https://energymonitor.ai/finance/risk-management/exclusive-natural-gas-data-reveals-trillions-of-dollars-of-upcoming-gas-projects

64.   Diana Furchtgott-Roth, "Pipelines Are Safest for Transportation of Oil and Gas," Manhattan Institute, Jun., 2013, https://media4.manhattan-institute.org/pdf/ib_23.pdf

65.   "PHMSA Pipeline Incidents: (2001-2020)," US Dept. of Transportation Pipeline and Hazardous Materials Safety Administration, Aug. 17, 2021, https://portal.phmsa.dot.gov/analytics/saw.dll?Portalpages&PortalPath=%2Fshared%2FPDM%20Public%20Website%2F_portal%2FSC%20Incident%20Trend&Page=Serious

66.   "Board of County Commissioners of Boulder County et al. v. Suncor Energy (U.S.A.) et al.," District Court , County of Boulder State of Colorado, Apr. 17, 2018, https://www.sanmiguelcountyco.gov/DocumentCenter/View/3508/Filed-Colorado-Complaint-PDF; Oil pump image by j4n and OpenClipart

67.   "Global Climate Litigation Report, 2020 Status Review," United Nations Environment Programme, 2020, https://www.unep.org/resources/report/global-climate-litigation-report-2020-status-review

68.   Ibid.

69.   David Hasemyer, "Fossil Fuels on Trial: Where the Major Climate Change Lawsuits Stand," *Inside Climate News*, Jan. 17, 2020, https://insideclimatenews.org/news/17012020/climate-change-fossil-fuel-company-lawsuits-timeline-exxon-children-california-cities-attorney-general/

70.   "City of New York against BP PLC, Chevron Corporation, ConocoPhillips, ExxonMobil Corporation, and Royal Dutch Shell PLC," US District Court Southern District of New York, Jan. 9, 2018, https://www.courthousenews.com/wp-content/uploads/2018/01/NYC-fossil-fuels.pdf

71.   Daniel Markind, "Climate Lawsuits Face Setbacks as They Raise Major Public Policy Issues," *Forbes*, May 25, 2021, https://www.forbes.com/sites/danielmarkind/2021/05/25/climate-lawsuits-face-setbacks-as-they-raise-major-public-policy-issues/?sh=206d26b91c1e

72.   Global Climate Litigation Report, (See no. 67)

73.   "Massachusetts et al. v. Environmental Protection Agency et al.," Supreme Court of the United States, Apr. 2, 2007, https://www.supremecourt.gov/opinions/06pdf/05-1120.pdf

74.   "Endangerment and Cause or Contribute Findings for Greenhouse Gases under the Section 202(a) of the Clear Air Act," US EPA, 2021, https://www.epa.gov/ghgemissions/endangerment-and-cause-or-contribute-findings-greenhouse-gases-under-section-202a-clean

75.   Jeff Brady, "In a Landmark Case, A Dutch Court Orders Shell to Cut Its Carbon Emissions Faster," *NPR*, May 26, 2021, https://www.npr.org/2021/05/26/1000475878/in-landmark-case-dutch-court-orders-shell-to-cut-its-carbon-emissions-faster

76.   Steven Mufson, "A Bad Day for Big Oil," The Washington Post, May 26, 2021, https://www.washingtonpost.com/climate-environment/2021/05/26/exxonmobil-rebel-shareholders-win-board-seats/

77.   Ibid.

78.   "Bank of America Announces Actions to Achieve Net Zero Greenhouse Gas Emissions before 2050," Bloomberg, Feb. 11, 2021, https://www.bloomberg.com/press-releases/2021-02-11/bank-of-america-announces-actions-to-achieve-net-zero-greenhouse-gas-emissions-before-2050; Angus cattle image by Scott Bauer, US Department of Agriculture

79.   "Climate Change 2014 Synthesis Report Summary for Policymakers," IPCC, 2014, https://www.ipcc.ch/report/ar5/syr/

80.   "Net Zero: The Scorecard," Energy & Climate Intelligence Unit, 2021, https://eciu.net/analysis/briefings/net-zero/net-zero-the-scorecard

81.   Fiona Harvey, "No New Oil, Gas, or Coal Development if World is to Reach Net Zero by 2050, Says World Energy Body, May 21, 2021, https://www.theguardian.com/environment/2021/may/18/no-new-investment-in-fossil-fuels-demands-top-energy-economist

82.   "Captive Coal Plants," *Glob. Energy Monitor*, July, 2022, https://globalenergymonitor.org/projects/global-coal-plant-tracker/summary-data/

83. "Stat. Rev. of World Energy," BP, 2021, https://www.bp.com/en/global/corporate/energy-economics/statistical-review-of-world-energy.html

84. "Global Emissions Have Not Yet Peaked," *OurWorldinData*, Aug. 2021, https://ourworldindata.org/co2-and-other-greenhouse-gas-emissions

85. *The Machinery of Nature* by Paul Ehrlich, (Simon & Schuster, 1986), p. 274; Tarot card image by Countakeshi under Creative Commons License 4.0

Chapter 5: 100 Percent Renewable Electricity?

1. Barack Obama interview with the *San Francisco Chronicle*, Jan. 2008, *YouTube*, https://www.youtube.com/watch?v=HlTxGHn4sH4

2. "Biden Delivers Remarks on Climate Change," NBC News, Jan. 27, 2021, https://www.youtube.com/watch?v=iAavDmyXY44&t

3. "Jacinda Ardern on 100% Renewable Electricity Generation by 2030," https://www.youtube.com/watch?v=KNIrcGGbxGE

4. "Wind Energy Will Power Every UK Home by 2030, Says Boris Johnson," Oct. 6, 2020, https://www.youtube.com/watch?v=dwgMHWGSW20

5. Canada Prime Minister Justin Trudeau address to COP 26, Nov. 2, 2021, https://www.youtube.com/watch?v=Uqys-68Djrw

6. "Key World Energy Statistics 2021," International Energy Agency, 2021, https://www.iea.org/reports/key-world-energy-statistics-2021

7. Ibid.

8. "Nuclear Power in the World Today," World Nuclear Association, June. 2021, https://world-nuclear.org/information-library/current-and-future-generation/nuclear-power-in-the-world-today.aspx

9. "Renewables 2020 Global Status Report," REN21, 2020, https://www.ren21.net/wp-content/uploads/2019/05/gsr_2020_full_report_en.pdf

10. Arthur Neslen, "EU BNioofuels Goals Behind Deforested Area as Big as the Netherlands," *Independent*, Jul. 5, 2021, https://www.independent.co.uk/climate-change/news/eu-biofuels-deforestation-asia-america-b1878174.html; Image of ox head sacrifice by Deeporaj under Creative Commons 3.0 License

11. Gerald W. Huttrer, "Geothermal Power Generation in the World 2015-2020 Update," Proceedings World Geothermal Congress, 2020, https://www.geothermal-energy.org/pdf/IGAstandard/WGC/2020/01017.pdf

12. Renewables 2020, (See no. 9)

13. Renewables 2020, (See no. 9)

14. *Power Density: A Key to Understanding Energy Sources and Uses* by Vaclav Smil, (The MIT Press, 2016); Vaclav Smil, "Power Density Primer: Understanding the Spatial Dimension of the Unfolding Transition to Renewable Electricity Generation," https://vaclavsmil.com/wp-content/uploads/docs/smil-article-power-density-primer.pdf

15. Ibid.

16. Power Density, (See no. 14)

17. Power Density, (See no. 14)

18. Image of Whitelee wind farm in Scotland, UK by Thomas Nuget under Creative Commons License 2.0

19. Eric Larson, et al., "Net-Zero America: Potential Pathways, Infrastructure, and Impacts," Princeton University, Dec. 15, 2020, https://netzero-america.princeton.edu/the-report

20. Ibid.

21. April Lee, "Texas Hits New Peak Wind Output," US EIA, Jun. 23, 2014, https://www.eia.gov/todayinenergy/detail.php?id=16811

22. "Electric Power Monthly, February, 2021," Energy Information Administration, Feb. 2021, https://www.eia.gov/electricity/monthly/

23. "Wind Output," (See no. 21); Image of Green Mountain wind array in Texas by Leaflet under Creative Commons Licence 3.0

24. "IEA Wind Annual Report, 2019," IEA Wind, Aug. 2020, https://iea-wind.org/

25. "Annual Electric Power Industry Report," US Energy Information Administration, Nov. 2022, https://www.eia.gov/electricity/annual/

26. "U.S. Power Reliability: Are We Kidding Ourselves?" *T&D World*, Jan. 14, 2015, https://www.tdworld.com/grid-innovations/article/20966117/us-power-reliability-are-we-kidding-ourselves

27. Image of girl cleaning solar panels in UK by Gregor Hagedorn under Creative Commons License 2.0

28. Alex Mey, "Average U.S. Construction Costs for Solar and Wind Generation Continue to Fall," Energy Information Administration, Sep. 16, 2020, https://www.eia.gov/todayinenergy/detail.php?id=45136

29. John Timmer, "Wind Power Prices Now Lower than the Cost of Natural Gas," *ARSTechnica*, Aug. 17, 2019, https://arstechnica.com/science/2019/08/wind-power-prices-now-lower-than-the-cost-of-natural-gas/

30. Philip Gordon, "Solar and Wind are the Cheapest New Sources of Energy Says BNEF," SMART Energy International, Apr. 29, 2020, https://www.smart-energy.com/industry-sectors/energy-grid-management/solar-and-wind-are-the-cheapest-new-sources-of-energy-says-bnef/

31. "Renewables Increasingly Beat Even Cheapest Coal Competitors on Cost," International Renewable Energy Agency, June. 2, 2020, https://www.irena.org/newsroom/pressreleases/2020/Jun/Renewables-Increasingly-Beat-Even-Cheapest-Coal-Competitors-on-Cost

32. "IEA Wind Annual Report 2021," IEA Wind TCP, Dec. 2022, https://iea-wind.org/category/annual-reports/; "Wind Energy Penetration in Leading Wind Markets in 2021," Statista, Aug. 2021, https://www.statista.com/statistics/217804/wind-energy-penetration-by-country/

33. "Development of Renewable Energy Sources in Germany in the Year 2021," Federal Ministry for Economic Affairs and Energy (BMWi), Sep. 2020, https://www.erneuerbare-energien.de/EE/Redaktion/DE/Downloads/development-of-renewable-energy-sources-in-germany-2020.pdf?__blob=publicationFile&v=31

34. Population data for nations from World Bank, 2022, https://data.worldbank.org/; Wind and solar capacity data for nations from EuroObserver, 2022, https://www.eurobserv-er.org/; Residential price of electricity for European nations for 2022 from Eurostat, https://ec.europa.eu/eurostat/data/database; US wind and solar capacity residential price of electricity from EIA ElectricPower Monthly, Feb. 2022, https://www.eia.gov/electricity/monthly/; Exchange rate data for 2021 from exchangerates.org.uk; Wind and solar image by Juwi Renewable Energies, Ltd. under Creative Commons License 2.0

35. Ibid.

36. "US Inflation Calculator," https://www.usinflationcalculator.com/

37. "Electric Power Monthly," US Energy Information Administration, 2009–2022; https://www.eia.gov/electricity/monthly/

38. Ibid; Image of Roscoe wind array in West Texas by Matthew T Rader under Creative Commons License 4.0

39. "How Whiskey Waste Can Replace Fossil Fuels on Road to Net Zero," *Reuters*, Nov. 3, 2021, https://nypost.com/2021/11/03/how-whisky-waste-can-replace-fossil-fuels-on-road-to-net-zero/; Hamster on wheel image by Aaron Denunzio, public domain

40. "Reliability Primer," Fed. Energy Reg. Commission," Apr. 2020, https://www.ferc.gov/sites/default/files/2020-04/reliability-primer_1.pdf

41. "Modernizing Our Transmission Infrastructure and Driving the Development of Clean Energy," The White House, Jul. 2015, https://obamawhitehouse.archives.gov/sites/default/files/docs/modernizingourelectrictransmission.pdf

42. Kathryne Cleary and Karen Palmer, "US Electricity Markets 101," Resources for the Future, Mar. 3, 2020, https://www.rff.org/publications/explainers/us-electricity-markets-101/

43. Sarah O'Grady, "WINTER CRISIS: One MILLION Pensioners Fear They Cannot Afford to Heat Their Homes," *Express*, Jan. 17, 2017, https://www.express.co.uk/news/uk/754900/energy-prices-winter-pensioners-heat-homes-expensive-bills; Weeping Parisian public domain

44. "Directive 2001/77/EC of the European Parliament and of the Council," *Official Journal of the European Communities*, Sep. 27, 2001, http://

extwprlegs1.fao.org/docs/pdf/eur40867.pdf

45. Lori Aniti, "California's Curtailments of Solar Electricity Generation Continue to Increase," US Energy Information Administration, Aug. 24, 2021, https://www.eia.gov/todayinenergy/detail.php?id=49276#:~:text=Curtailments%20of%20solar%2Dpowered%20electricity,its%20utility%2Dscale%20solar%20production.; Image of Solar One array by U.S. Department of Energy, 1993

46. Ibid.

47. "A Decade of Constraint Payments," Renewable Energy Foundation, Dec. 30, 2019, https://www.ref.org.uk/ref-blog/354-a-decade-of-constraint-payments

48. Jonathan O'Callaghan, "Wind Farms Were Paid £8.7 Million to Switch OFF Their Turbines Last Month Because They Generated Too Much Electricity," DailyMail, Apr. 3, 2014, https://www.dailymail.co.uk/sciencetech/article-2595902/Wind-farms-paid-millions-switch-OFF-turbines-generate-electricity.html; Monopoly image by Mike Mozart under Creative Commons License 2.0

49. "Fewer Grid Interventions, More Renewables," En:Former, May 12, 2020, https://www.en-former.com/en/fewer-grid-interventions-more-renewables/

50. "Electric Power Monthly," US Energy Information Administration, Mar. 2011, Feb. 2021; https://www.eia.gov/electricity/monthly/

51. Ibid.; Image of power lines in Auburn, Washington by Joe Mabel under Creative Commons License 4.0

52. Stephen Brick and Samuel Thernstrom, "Renewables and Decarbonization: Studies of California, Wisconsin, and Germany," The Electricity Journal, Mar. 22, 2016, https://core.ac.uk/download/pdf/82637221.pdf

53. Ibid.

54. Peter Cramton, "Lessons from the 2021 Texas Electricity Crisis," University of Maryland, Sep. 6, 2021, http://www.cramton.umd.edu/papers2020-2024/cramton-lessons-from-the-2021-texas-electricity-crisis.pdf

55. "DFW - Temperature Extremes," National Weather Service, 2021, https://www.weather.gov/fwd/dgr8mxmn

56. David Hughes, "To Save the Climate, Give Up the Demand for Constant Energy," Boston Review, Oct. 1, 2020, https://bostonreview.net/articles/david-mcdermott-hughes-battery-trap/#:~:text=Image%3A%20Flickr-,To%20Save%20the%20Climate%2C%20Give%20Up%20the%20Demand%20for%20Constant,time%E2%80%94and%20too%20many%20lives.; Owl and books image by Yamachem

57. Reliability Primer, (See no. 40)

58. Peter Cramton, (See no. 54)

59. Peter Cramton, (See no. 54)

60. Electric Power Monthly, (See no. 22)

61. Fred Mayes and Elesia Fasching, "Wind is a Growing Part of the Electricity Mix in Texas," Energy Information Administration, Oct. 15, 2020, https://www.eia.gov/todayinenergy/detail.php?id=45476

62. Mark Watson, "Place, Price, Alternatives Playing Roles in Coal-Fired Generation Retirements," S&P Global Platts, Feb. 1, 2021, https://www.spglobal.com/platts/en/market-insights/latest-news/coal/020121-feature-place-prices-alternatives-playing-roles-in-coal-fired-generation-retirements

63. Electric Power Monthly, (See no. 22)

64. Jason Hackett, "Gov. Stitt Urges Oklahomans to Conserve Electricity, Gives Update on Rolling Power Outages," KOCO News 5, Feb. 16, 2021, https://www.koco.com/article/gov-stitt-urges-oklahomans-to-conserve-electricity-gives-update-on-rolling-power-outages/35520891

65. "RPS Program Overview," California Public Utilities Commission, 2021, https://www.cpuc.ca.gov/industries-and-topics/electrical-energy/electric-power-procurement/rps/rps-program-overview

66. Camila Domonoske, "California Sets Goal of 100 Percent Clean Electric Power by 2045," NPR, Sep. 10, 2018, https://www.npr.org/2018/09/10/646373423/california-sets-goal-of-100-percent-renewable-electric-power-by-2045

67. Carly Bass, "I Moved My Family Off-Grid in Rural Alaska to Prepare for a Zombie Apocalypse," The Sun, Nov. 8, 2021, https://nypost.com/2021/11/08/i-moved-my-family-off-grid-in-rural-alaska-to-prepare-for-a-zombie-apocalypse/; Night of the Living Dead image public

68. "California Electrical Energy Generation," California Energy Commission, Jun. 2021, https://www.energy.ca.gov/data-reports/energy-almanac/california-electricity-data/california-electrical-energy-generation

69. "California," Energy Information Administration, Feb. 18, 2021, https://www.eia.gov/state/analysis.php?sid=CA

70. "California's Declining Reliance on Coal," California Energy Commission, Oct., 2018, https://www.energy.ca.gov/sites/default/files/2019-12/declining_reliance_coal_ada.pdf

71. California Electrical Energy Generation, (See no. 68)

72. David L. Chandler, "Q&A: Options for the Diablo Canyon Nuclear Plant," MIT News, Nov. 8, 2021, https://news.mit.edu/2021/diablo-canyon-nuclear-plant-1108

73. "Root Cause Analysis," California ISO, Jan. 13, 2021, http://www.caiso.com/Documents/Final-Root-Cause-Analysis-Mid-August-2020-Extreme-Heat-Wave.pdf

74. Chris White, "'Gaps' in Renewable Energy Led to Blackouts for Millions of Californians, Gov Newsom Says," Daily Caller, Aug. 17, 2020, https://dailycaller.com/2020/08/17/california-blackouts-renewable-energy-california-gavin-newsom/; Image of Bellingham, WA power outage by Robert Ashworth under Creative Commons License 2.0

75. Root Cause Analysis, (See no. 73)

76. Shelby Bracho, "California to Open 5 Natural Gas Plants to Avoid Blackouts," FOX26NEWS, Aug. 20, 2021, https://kmph.com/news/local/california-to-open-5-natural-gas-plants-to-avoid-blackouts; Question guy image by Scout, Open Clip Art

77. Electric Power Monthly, (See no. 37)

78. Josh Siegel, "Susan Collins Unveils $300M Energy Storage Bill to Combat Climate Change," Washington Examiner, May 22, 2019, https://www.washingtonexaminer.com/policy/energy/susan-collins-unveils-300m-energy-storage-bill-to-combat-climate-change

79. Robert F. Service, "Giant Batteries and Cheap Solar Power are Shoving Fossil Fuels Off the Grid," Science, Jul. 11, 2019, https://www.science.org/content/article/giant-batteries-and-cheap-solar-power-are-shoving-fossil-fuels-grid

80. David Stringer, "A Deluge of Batteries Is About to Rewire the Power Grid," Bloomberg, Aug. 4, 2019, https://www.bloomberg.com/news/features/2019-08-03/a-deluge-of-batteries-is-about-to-rewire-the-power-grid

81. Cheryl Katz, "The Batteries that Could Make Fossil Fuels Obsolete," BBC, Dec. 17, 2020, https://www.bbc.com/future/article/20201217-renewable-power-the-worlds-largest-battery

82. Mark Mills, "What's Wrong with Wind and Solar?" YouTube, Sep. 14, 2020, https://www.youtube.com/watch?v=RqppRC37OgI; Hamster on wheel image by Aaron Denunzio, public domain

83. Robert Walton, "US Energy Storage Capacity Tripled in 2021: EIA," Utility Dive, Jul. 12, 2022, https://www.utilitydive.com/news/energy-storage-capacity-eia-2021-report/627028/#:~:text=Battery%20storage%20capacity%20in%20the,July%205%20Electricity%20Monthly%20Update.; "Electric Power Monthly," Energy Information Admin., Feb. 2022, https://www.eia.gov/electricity/monthly/; "Pumped Storage Report," National Hydropower Association, 2021, https://www.hydro.org/wp-content/uploads/2021/09/2021-Pumped-Storage-Report-NHA.pdf

84. Ibid.

85. Jason Plautz, "Global Energy Storage Set to Nearly Triple in 2021: Wood Mackenzie Forecast," Utility Dive, Oct. 8, 2021, https://www.utilitydive.com/news/global-energy-storage-set-to-nearly-triple-in-2021-wood-mackenzie-forecast/607905/

86. "South Australia's Big Battery," Hornsdale Power Reserve, Neoen, 2021, https://hornsdalepowerreserve.com.au/

87. "Battery Storage in the United States: An Update on Market Trends," Energy Information Administration, Aug. 16, 2021, https://www.eia.gov/analysis/studies/electricity/batterystorage/pdf/battery_storage_2021.pdf

88. Ibid.

89. "Manatee Energy Storage Center: World's Largest Solar-Powered Battery 75% Complete," *Energy Industry Review*, Aug. 17, 2021, https://energyindustryreview.com/renewables/manatee-energy-storage-center-worlds-largest-solar-powered-battery-75-complete/

90. Lauren Aratani, "Electricity Needed to Mine Bitcoin is More than Used by 'Entire Countries,'" *The Guardian*, Feb. 27, 2021, https://www.theguardian.com/technology/2021/feb/27/bitcoin-mining-electricity-use-environmental-impact; Wolfman image by Horror Monsters

91. Battery Storage, (See no. 87)

92. George Kamiya, "Energy Storage," International Energy Agency, Nov. 1, 2021, https://www.iea.org/reports/energy-storage

93. "White Paper on Clean Energy Standard Procurements to Implement New York's Climate Leadership and Community Protection Act," NYSERDA, Jun. 18, 2020, file:///C:/Users/goreh/Downloads/%7BE6A3B524-6617-4506-A076-62526F8EC4CB%7D%20(2).pdf

94. Battery Storage, (See no. 87)

95. "Annual Report on Market Issues & Performance," California ISO, Aug. 2020, http://www.caiso.com/Documents/2020-Annual-Report-on-Market-Issues-and-Performance.pdf

96. "Net Zero by 2050," International Energy Agency, Oct. 2021, https://www.iea.org/reports/net-zero-by-2050; Solar panel image by j4p4n

97. Matt Kelly, "Tomago Aluminium Executive Confirms the Smelter's Output is Down Due to the High Cost of Power," *Newcastle Herald News*, Nov. 27, 2019, https://www.newcastleherald.com.au/story/6514639/tomago-aluminium-feeling-the-squeeze-from-high-power-prices/

98. Net Zero by 2050, (See no 96)

99. "Residential Wood Burning," *Clean Heat*, Mar., 2016, https://www.clean-heat.eu/en/actions/info-material/download/background-paper-residential-wood-burning-3.html

100. "Energy, Transport, and Env. Stats.," Eurostat, 2009–2020, https://op.europa.eu/en/publication-detail/-/publication/cabb084a-32bb-11eb-b27b-01aa75ed71a1/language-en; "The State of Renewable Energies in Europe," EurObservER, 2015-2020, https://www.eurobserv-er.org/

101. Ibid; Image of burning wood-pellet biomass by American Heritage Biomass, under Creative Commons 4.0 License

102. "Energy Statistics 2019," Danish Energy Agency, Apr. 2021, https://ens.dk/en/our-services/statistics-data-key-figures-and-energy-maps/annual-and-monthly-statistics

103. Jeremy Fisher et al., "The Carbon Footprint of Electricity from Biomass," Synapse Energy Economics, Jun. 11, 2012, https://www.synapse-energy.com/project/carbon-footprint-electricity-biomass

104. "Inventory of U.S. Greenhouse Gas Emissions and Sinks: 1990–2008," US EPA, Apr. 15, 2010, https://rosap.ntl.bts.gov/view/dot/4876

105. "Establishing Guidelines for the Monitoring and Reporting of Greenhouse Gas Emissions Pursuant to Directive 2003/87/EC of the European Parliament and of the Council," European Commission, Jul. 18, 2007; https://eur-lex.europa.eu/LexUriServ/LexUriServ.do?uri=CONSLEG:2007D0589:20100622:EN:PDF

106. "Revised 1996 IPCC Guidelines for National GHG Inventories, Reference Manual (Volume 3)," Intergovernmental Panel on Climate Change, 2021, https://www.ipcc-nggip.iges.or.jp/public/gl/invs6.html

107. "Opinion of the EEA Scientific Committee on Greenhouse Gas Accounting in Relation to Bioenergy," EEA, Sep. 15, 2011, https://www.eea.europa.eu/about-us/governance/scientific-committee/sc-opinions/opinions-on-scientific-issues/sc-opinion-on-greenhouse-gas/view

108. "Drax Closed to Coal-Free Future with Fourth Biomass Unite Conversion," Drax, Aug. 20, 2018, https://www.drax.com/press_release/drax-closer-coal-free-future-fourth-biomass-unit-conversion/

109. Sarah Miller, "The Millions of Tons of Carbon Emissions that Don't Officially Exist," *The New Yorker*, https://www.newyorker.com/news/annals-of-a-warming-planet/the-millions-of-tons-of-carbon-emissions-that-dont-officially-exist#:~:text=a%20Warming%20Planet-,The%20Millions%20of%20Tons%20of%20Carbon%20Emissions%20That%20Don't,helped%20create%20the%20biomass%20industry.&text=In%20the%20North%20of%20England,power%20plant%2C%20also%20called%20Drax.

110. Saul Elbein, "Europe's Renewable Energy Policy is Built on Burning American Trees," *Vox*, Mar. 4, 2019, https://www.vox.com/science-and-health/2019/3/4/18216045/renewable-energy-wood-pellets-biomass; Image of Christopher Lloyd by Alex Archambault under Creative Commons License 2.0; Wood burning image by Cristian Janke under Creative Commons License 2.0

111. Phil MacDonald, "Drax Received More than £800m in Biomass Subsidies Last Year," *Ember*, Feb. 25, 2021, https://ember-climate.org/commentary/2021/02/25/drax-biomass-subsidies/

112. Sarah Miller, (See no. 109)

113. "Monthly Densified Biomass Fuel Report," US EIA, Nov. 17, 2021, https://www.eia.gov/biofuels/biomass/#table_data

114. "Nightclub to Convert Dancers' Body Heat Into Renewable Energy," *Cool Hunting*, Nov. 11, 2021, https://coolhunting.com/culture/nightclub-to-convert-dancers-body-heat-into-renewable-energy/; Laughing boy cartoon by hotta

115. Duncan Brack et al., "Greenhouse Gas Emissions from Burning US-sourced Woody Biomass in the EU and UK," Woodwell Climate Research Center, Oct. 2021, https://www.chathamhouse.org/sites/default/files/2021-10/2021-10-14-woody-biomass-us-eu-uk-summary.pdf

116. Sarah Miller, (See no. 109)

117. "Crippling Cost of Ontario's Obsession with Wind Power: 71% Increase in Power Bills," *StopTheseThings*, Oct. 2, 2021, https://stopthesethings.com/2021/10/02/crippling-cost-of-ontarios-obsession-with-wind-power-71-increase-in-power-bills/; Weeping Parisian public domain

Chapter 6: But I'd Like to Keep My Gas Stove

1. Quote by Phyllis Diller, https://www.prizedquotes.com/stove-quotes/

2. "Renewables 2021 Global Stat. Rpt.," REN 21, Jun. 2021, https://www.ren21.net/wp-content/uploads/2019/05/GSR2021_Full_Report.pdf

3. "Stat. Rev. of World Energy," BP, 2021, https://www.bp.com/en/global/corporate/energy-economics/statistical-review-of-world-energy.html;

4. Ibid.; Liquid propane gas flame image by Arivumathi under Creative Commons License 3.0

5. "Energy Consumption in Households," Eurostat, Jun. 29, 2021, https://ec.europa.eu/eurostat/statistics-explained/index.php?title=Energy_consumption_in_households

6. "Energy Use in Homes," US Energy Information Agency, Jun. 23, 2021, https://www.eia.gov/energyexplained/use-of-energy/homes.php

7. "Residential Wood Burning," *Clean Heat*, Mar., 2016, https://www.clean-heat.eu/en/actions/info-material/download/background-paper-residential-wood-burning-3.html

8. "Petroleum & Other Liquids," US Energy Information Agency, 2021, https://www.eia.gov/petroleum/

9. Maulshree Seth, "PM Modi Launches Ujjwala 2nd Phase, Says Migrants Won't Need Address Proof," *The Indian EXPRESS*, Aug. 11, 2021, https://indianexpress.com/article/india/pm-modi-launches-ujjwala-2-0-for-providing-free-lpg-connections-7447111/

10. David Roberts, "The Key to Tackling Climate Change: Electrify Everything," *Vox*, Oct. 27, 2017, https://www.vox.com/2016/9/19/12938086/electrify-everything; Owl and books image by Yamachem

11. Yifan Zhu et al., "Effects of Residential Gas Appliances on Indoor and Outdoor Air Quality and Public Health in California," UCLA Fielding School of Public Health, Apr. 2020, https://coeh.ph.ucla.edu/effects-of-residential-gas-appliances-on-indoor-and-outdoor-air-quality-and-public-health-in-california/

12. Matt Gough, "California's Cities Lead the Way to a Gas-Free Future," Sierra Club, Dec. 13, 2021, https://www.sierraclub.org/articles/2021/07/californias-cities-lead-way-gas-free-future

13. "California Price of Natural Gas Delivered to Residential Customers," US Energy Information Agency, 2021, https://www.eia.gov/naturalgas/data.php#prices; "Electric Power Monthly, US EIA, Feb. 2021, https://www.eia.gov/electricity/monthly/

14. Matt Gough, (See no. 12); Girl surfer image by Daniel Torbekov

15. "Renewable Heating and Cooling Policy Framework," NYSERDA, Feb. 7, 2017, https://www.nyserda.ny.gov/-/media/files/publications/ppser/nyserda/rhc-framework.pdf

16. Emma Newburger, "New York City is Banning Natural Gas Hookups for New Buildings to Fight Climate Change," CNBC, Dec. 15, 2021, https://www.cnbc.com/2021/12/15/new-york-city-is-banning-natural-gas-hookups-for-new-buildings.html

17. Alexander Stevens and Paige Lambermont, "An Overview of Natural Gas Bans in the U.S.," Institute for Energy Research, Aug. 2021, https://www.instituteforenergyresearch.org/wp-content/uploads/2021/08/Natural-Gas-Ban-Report_Updated.pdf

18. Tom DiChristopher, "Gas Ban Monitor: Building Electrification Evolves as 19 States Prohibit Bans," S&P Global, Jul. 20, 2021, https://www.spglobal.com/marketintelligence/en/news-insights/latest-news-headlines/gas-ban-monitor-building-electrification-evolves-as-19-states-prohibit-bans-65518738

19. "Vancouver to Ban Fossil Fuel Appliances for Low-Rise Buildings," Plumbing+HVAC, Jun. 17, 2020, https://plumbingandhvac.ca/vancouver-to-ban-fossil-fuel-appliances-for-low-rise-buildings/

20. "Natural Gas Will Be Outlawed in New Vancouver Homes," Home Builder, Dec. 14, 2020, https://www.homebuildercanada.com/news/news201214-Natural-gas-outlawed.htm

21. "Seven Cities Want to Phase Out Fossil Fuels from Urban Heating & Cooling," Decarb City Pipes 2050, Feb. 3, 2021, https://decarbcitypipes2050.eu/2021/02/03/news-1/

22. "UK Gas Boiler Ban - Everything You Need to Know," EDF, 2021, https://www.edfenergy.com/heating/advice/uk-boiler-ban

23. "Ban Gas Boilers in New Homes by 2025, Says Committee on Climate Change," The Guardian, Feb. 20, 2019, https://www.theguardian.com/environment/2019/feb/20/ban-new-gas-boilers-by-2025-says-committee-on-climate-change; Guillotine image by Mball93 under Creative Commons License 4.0

24. "UK Housing: Fit for the Future?" UK Committee on Climate Change, Feb. 2019, https://www.theccc.org.uk/publication/uk-housing-fit-for-the-future/

25. Ibid

26. Michael, Kelly, "Decarbonizing Housing: The Net Zero Fantasy," The Global Warming Policy Foundation," 2020, https://www.thegwpf.org/content/uploads/2020/02/KellyNetZero-2.pdf

27. Benny Peiser," Press Release: Three in Five Brits Reject Higher Taxes to Reach Net Zero," Net Zero Watch, Dec. 23, 2021, https://www.netzerowatch.com/three-in-five-brits-reject-higher-taxes-to-reach-net-zero/

28. "Gas-Free New Construction from 1 July 2018," Omgevingsweb, Jul. 18, 2018, https://www.omgevingsweb.nl/nieuws/gasvrije-nieuwbouw-vanaf-1-juli-2018-wat-is-de-wetswijziging-en-wat-zijn-de-implicaties-voor-lopende-nieuwbouwprojecten/

29. Gavin Rice, "No One is Being Honest about the Effect of Zero on Britain's Poorest Families," The Telegraph, Nov. 4, 2021, https://www.telegraph.co.uk/news/2021/11/04/no-one-honest-effect-net-zero-britains-poorest-families/; Weeping Parisian public domain

30. Laura Cole, "How the Netherlands is Turning Its Back on Natural Gas," BBC, Oct. 26, 2021, https://www.bbc.com/future/article/20211025-netherlands-the-end-of-europes-largest-gas-field

31. Ibid

32. Image of Gelsenkirchen district heating pipelines by GFDL under Creative Commons License 3.0

33. Yifang Zhu, (See no. 11)

34. Steve Goreham," A Critique of Residential Gas and California Air Pollution Paper: POOR POLICY FOR CALIFORNIA," Climate Science Coalition of America," June, 2020, http://www.stevegoreham.com/wp-content/uploads/2020/07/A-Critique-of-Residential-Gas-and-California-Air-Pollution-Paper-Poor-Policy-for-California.pdf

35. Sabrina Imbler, "Kill Your Gas Stove," The Atlantic, Oct. 15, 2020, https://www.theatlantic.com/science/archive/2020/10/gas-stoves-are-bad-you-and-environment/616700/; Fearful face by Wellcome Images under Creative Commons License 4.0

36. Yifang Zhu, (See no. 11)

37. Goreham, (See no. 34)

38. "Air Quality Guide for Nitrogen Dioxide," US EPA, 2018, https://www.airnow.gov/sites/default/files/2018-06/no2.pdf

39. Goreham, (See no. 34)

40. Lisa Jackson, "Hearing on Regulatory Reform Series #7 - The EPA's Regulatory Planning, Analysis, and Major Actions," US House of Representatives, Subcommittee on Oversight and Investigations, Sep. 22, 2011; https://www.govinfo.gov/content/pkg/CHRG-112hhrg75209/pdf/CHRG-112hhrg75209.pdf

41. "Particulate Matter (PM) Basics," US EPA, 2022, https://www.epa.gov/pm-pollution/particulate-matter-pm-basics#PM

42. "Most Polluted Countries 2021," WorldPopulationReview.com, 2021, https://worldpopulationreview.com/country-rankings/most-polluted-countries

43. "Household Air Pollution and Health," World Health Organization, Sep. 22, 2021, https://www.who.int/news-room/fact-sheets/detail/household-air-pollution-and-health

44. Christopher Olopade, "Indoor Air Pollution from Biomass: A Global Health Disparities Challenge," YouTube.com, Jun. 19, 2014, https://www.youtube.com/watch?v=ShlboeA2Dc8

45. "NAAQS Table," US Environmental Protection Agency, 2022, https://www.epa.gov/criteria-air-pollutants/naaqs-table

46. Clara Chaisson, "Fossil Fuel Air Pollution Kills One in Five People," National Resources Defense Council, Feb. 19, 2021, https://www.nrdc.org/stories/fossil-fuel-air-pollution-kills-one-five-people; Oil pump image by j4p4n and OpenClipart

47. "Our Nation's Air," US Environmental Protection Agency, 2022, https://gispub.epa.gov/air/trendsreport/2021/#home

48. James E. Enstrom, "Fine Particulate Matter and Total Mortality in Cancer Prevention Study Cohort Renalysis," Dose-Response, Jan.-Mar. 2017, https://journals.sagepub.com/doi/full/10.1177/1559325817693345

49. "National Air Quality: Status and Trends of Key Air Pollutants," US Environmental Protection Agency, 2022, https://www.epa.gov/air-trends; Image of North Platte River power plant in 1973 by Boyd Norton, US National Archives

50. Richard Doll and A. Bradford Hill, "Lung Cancer and Other Causes of Death in Relation to Smoking," British Medical Journal, Nov. 10, 1956, https://www.ncbi.nlm.nih.gov/pmc/articles/PMC2035864/

51. Enstrom, (See no. 48); Teaspoon with baking powder image by Rainer Z under GNU Free Documentation License 1.2

52. Douglas W. Dockery et al., "An Association between Air Pollution and Mortality in Six US Cities," New England Journal of Medicine, Dec. 9, 1993, https://pubmed.ncbi.nlm.nih.gov/8179653/

53. C.A. Pope et al., "Particulate Air Pollution as a Predictor of Mortality in a Prospective Study of U.S. Adults," American Journal of Critical Care Medicine, Mar, 1995, file:///C:/Users/goreh/Downloads/EPA-HQ-OAR-2015-0072-0984_attachment_1.pdf

54. Doll and Hill, (See no. 50)

55. Louis Anthony Cox Jr., "Do Causal Concentration-Response Functions Exist? A Critical Review of Associational and Causal Relations Between

Fine Particulate Matter and Mortality," *Critical Reviews in Toxicology*, Aug. 2017, https://pubmed.ncbi.nlm.nih.gov/28657395/

56. "Cutting Carbon Pollution from Power Plants, US EPA, May 9, 2017, https://archive.epa.gov/epa/cleanpowerplan/fact-sheet-overview-clean-power-plan.html
57. Smoking a weed joint by elsaolofsson under Creative Commons License 2.0
58. Steven L. Alderman and Bradley J. Ingebrethsen, "Characterization of Mainstream DMS500 Fast Particulate Spectrometer and Smoking Cycle Simulator," Aerosol Science and Technology, Jun. 2011, https://www.tandfonline.com/doi/full/10.1080/02786826.2011.596862
59. Leslie Eastman, "Wine Country Wildfires Incinerate California's Lofty Air Pollution Goals," *Legal Insurrection*, Oct. 13, 2017, https://legalinsurrection.com/2017/10/wine-country-wildfires-incinerate-californias-lofty-air-pollution-goals/

Chapter 7: Trade My Gasoline Pickup Truck for an Electric Car?

1. Daniel Strohl, "How Henry Ford and Thomas Edison Killed the Electric Car," *Jalopnik*, June. 16, 2010, https://jalopnik.com/how-henry-ford-and-thomas-edison-killed-the-electric-ca-5564999
2. C. C. Chan, "The Rise and Fall of Electric Vehicles in 1828–1930: Lessons Learned," *IEEE.Explore*, Jan., 2013, https://ieeexplore.ieee.org/stamp/stamp.jsp?arnumber=6384804
3. Bonnie Alter, "Electric Milk Trucks Still Working in Jolly Old England," *Treehugger*, Oct. 11, 2018, https://www.treehugger.com/electric-milk-trucks-still-working-jolly-old-england-4857965
4. Kevin A. Wilson, "Worth the Watt: A Brief History of the Electric Car, 1830 to Present," *Car and Driver*, Mar. 15, 2018, https://www.caranddriver.com/features/g15378765/worth-the-watt-a-brief-history-of-the-electric-car-1830-to-present/
5. Loir Steinberg, "It's Time to Admit It: We Are Addicted to Cars," *Humankind*, Jun. 9, 2018, https://www.humankind.city/post/it-s-time-to-admit-it-we-are-addicted-to-cars; Cigarette image by Challiyil Eswaramangalath Vipin under Creative Commons 2.0 License
6. Rebecca Matulka, "The History of the Electric Car," Dept. of Energy, Sep. 15, 2014, https://www.energy.gov/articles/history-electric-car
7. Wilson, (See no. 4)
8. Jamie Gibbs, "Motorway Speed Limits Cut to 60 mph in Bid to Reduce Carbon Emissions," *Confused.com*, Oct. 29, 2020, https://notalotofpeopleknowthat.wordpress.com/2020/11/26/motorway-speed-limits-cut-to-60-mph-in-bid-to-reduce-carbon-emissions/; Tortoise image by Moise Nicu under Creative Commons Attribution 3.0
9. Wilson, (See no. 4)
10. "John B. Goodenough Facts," The Nobel Prize, 2019, https://www.nobelprize.org/prizes/chemistry/2019/goodenough/facts/
11. Virginia McConnell et al., "California's Evolving Zero Emission Vehicle Program: Pulling New Technology into the Market," Resources for the Future, Nov. 2019, https://media.rff.org/documents/RFF_WP_Californias_Evolving_Zero_Emission_Vehicle_Program.pdf
12. Ibid.
13. Wilson, (See no. 4)
14. Joe Clifford, "History of the Toyota Prius," *Toyota UK Magazine*, Feb. 10, 2015, https://mag.toyota.co.uk/history-toyota-prius/
15. Wilson, (See no. 4)
16. Andrew Lambrecht, "The Simplified History of the Electric Car," *InsideEVs*, Nov. 22, 2021, https://insideevs.com/features/549726/electric-car-history/
17. Ibid.
18. Maximilian Holland, "Tesla Passes 1 Million EV Milestone & Model 3 Becomes All Time Best Seller," Mar. 10, 2020, *CleanTechnica*, https://cleantechnica.com/2020/03/10/tesla-passes-1-million-ev-milestone-and-model-3-becomes-all-time-best-seller/
19. Lambrecht, (See no. 16)
20. Image of 2010 Tesla Roadster in San Diego by Tesla Motors, Inc.
21. McConnell, (See no. 11)
22. "The Role of Critical Metals in Clean Energy Transitions," International Energy Agency, Mar. 2022, https://www.iea.org/reports/the-role-of-critical-minerals-in-clean-energy-transitions
23. "Global EV Outlook 2021," International Energy Agency, 2021, https://iea.blob.core.windows.net/assets/ed5f4484-f556-4110-8c5c-4ede8bc-ba637/GlobalEVOutlook2021.pdf
24. Ibid.
25. Roland Irie, "Global EV Sales for 2021," *EVVolumes.com*, 2022, https://www.ev-volumes.com/
26. Michel Rose, "Macron Wants France to be Europe's Top Clean Car Producer," *Reuters*, May 26, 2020, https://www.reuters.com/article/us-health-coronavirus-france-autos/macron-wants-france-to-be-europes-top-clean-car-producer-idUSKBN2322D6
27. Gavin Newsom, Executive Order N-79-20, Sep. 23, 2020, https://www.gov.ca.gov/wp-content/uploads/2020/09/9.23.20-EO-N-79-20-Climate.pdf
28. UK Prime Minister Boris Johnson, presentation at CBI 2021 Annual Conference, Nov. 22, 2021, https://www.youtube.com/watch?v=YtY8yOEOYPw
29. Julie Cooper, "Mary Barra Shares Her Winning Solution to Battling Climate Change," *CEO Magazine*, Jul. 20, 2021, https://www.theceomagazine.com/business/coverstory/mary-barra-general-motors/
30. Irie, (See number 25) and other sources; Image of Tesla Model S in 2013 by Jusdafax under Creative Commons License 3.0
31. Irie, (See number 25)
32. Author's estimate based on several sources
33. Irie, (See number 25) and other sources
34. Global EV Outlook, (See no. 23)
35. Schalk Cloete, "Norway and EV Role Model? Their Pathway is Expensive and Paid for with Oil & Gas Exports," *EnergyPost.eu*, Jun. 4, 2021, https://energypost.eu/norway-an-ev-role-model-their-pathway-is-expensive-and-paid-for-with-oil-gas-exports/
36. Irie, (See number 25)
37. Global EV Outlook, (See no. 23)
38. Irie, (See number 25)
39. "Plug-in Electric Drive Vehicle Credit (IRC 30D)," Internal Revenue Service, Jun. 27, 2021, https://www.irs.gov/businesses/plug-in-electric-vehicle-credit-irc-30-and-irc-30d
40. Leonardi Paoli and Timur Gul, "Electric Cars Fend Off Supply Challenges to More than Double Global Sales," International Energy Agency, Jan. 30, 2022, https://www.iea.org/commentaries/electric-cars-fend-off-supply-challenges-to-more-than-double-global-sales?utm_source=SendGrid&utm_medium=Email&utm_campaign=IEA+newsletters
41. "How Many Cars Are There in the World in 2022?" Hedges & Company, 2022, https://hedgescompany.com/blog/2021/06/how-many-cars-are-there-in-the-world/
42. Sanjay Rishi et al., "Auto. 2020: Clarity Beyond the Chaos," IBM, 2008, https://gerpisa.org/system/files/gbe03079-usen-auto2020.pdf; Tarot card image by Countakeshi under Creative Commons License 4.0
43. Davide Mastracci, "It's Time to Ban the Sale of Pickup Trucks," *Passage*, Jul. 13, 2021, https://readpassage.com/its-time-to-ban-the-sale-of-

pickup-trucks/; Guillotine image by Mball93 under Creative Commons License 4.0

44. Jim Motavalli, "Every Automaker's EV Plans through 2035 and Beyond," *Forbes*, Oct. 4, 2021, https://www.forbes.com/wheels/news/automaker-ev-plans/

45. "Greenhouse Gas Emissions from a Typical Passenger Vehicle," US Environmental Protection Agency, 2022, https://www.epa.gov/greenvehicles/greenhouse-gas-emissions-typical-passenger-vehicle#:~:text=typical%20passenger%20vehicle%3F-,A%20typical%20passenger%20vehicle%20emits%20about%204.6%20metric%20tons%20of,8%2C887%20grams%20of%20CO2.

46. Global EV Outlook, (See no. 23)

47. Candi Tutterrow, "Which Famous Celebrities Drive an Electric Car?" *Plug-in Motorwerks*, Jan. 22, 2015, https://pluginmotorwerks.com/celebrity-electric-cars/

48. "Largest Automakers by Market Capitalization," CompaniesMarketCap.com, Feb., 2022, https://companiesmarketcap.com/automakers/largest-automakers-by-market-cap/

49. Ibid.; Nissan Leaf charging image by Bouchecl under GNU Free Documentation License 1.2

50. Ibid.

51. Ibid.

52. "Tesla Model 3 Performance," Electric Vehicle Database, 2022, https://ev-database.org/car/1620/Tesla-Model-3-Performance

53. Dave Venderwerp,"How EVs Compare to Gas-Powered Vehicles in Seven Performance Metrics," *Car and Driver*, May 5, 2021, https://www.caranddriver.com/features/g36420161/evs-compared-gas-powered-vehicles-performance/

54. David Shepardson, "U.S. Finalizes Long-Delayed "Quiet Cars" Rule, Extending Deadline," *Reuters*, Feb. 26, 2018, https://www.reuters.com/article/us-autos-regulations-sounds/u-s-finalizes-long-delayed-quiet-cars-rule-extending-deadline-idUSKCN1GA2GV

55. "Compare Cars Side-by-Side," Edmonds, 2022, https://www.edmunds.com/car-comparisons/

56. Jennifer A. Kingson, "Cities are Starting to Ban New Gas Stations," *Axios*, Mar. 1, 2021, https://www.axios.com/cities-ban-gas-pollution-fb61cf2f-9893-466f-9559-9c4d27bbc3b6.html; "Out of Gas" sign image from 1973 by David Falconer, U.S. National Archives

57. Patrick L. Anderson and Alston D'Souza, "Comparison: Real World Cost of Fueling EVs and ICE Vehicles," Anderson Economic Group, Oct. 21, 2021, https://www.andersoneconomicgroup.com/wp-content/uploads/2021/10/EVtransition_FuelingCostStudy_10-21-21.pdf

58. Ibid.

59. Ibid.

60. "Lithium-Ion Battery," University of Washington, 2022, https://www.cei.washington.edu/education/science-of-solar/battery-technology/

61. Samantha Gross, "Why are Fossil Fuels so Hard to Quit?" Brookings, Jun. 2020, https://www.brookings.edu/essay/why-are-fossil-fuels-so-hard-to-quit/

62. "Truck Axle Weight Limits by State 2022," World Population Review, 2022, https://worldpopulationreview.com/state-rankings/truck-axle-weight-limits-by-state

63. Pierre L. Gosselin, " 650 km Wintertime Trip with VW E-Car Took 13 Hours, 3 Recharges and Lots of Warm Clothes," *NoTricksZone*, Jan. 18, 2022, https://notrickszone.com/2022/01/18/650-km-wintertime-trip-with-vw-e-car-took-13-hours-3-recharges-and-lots-of-warm-clothes/; Kissy lips image by j4p4n

64. Gustavo Henrique Ruffo, "Biggest Winter Range Test Ever Reveals Best EVs for Cold Weather," *InsideEVs*, Mare. 17, 2020, https://insideevs.com/news/404632/winter-range-test-best-evs-cold-weather/

65. Samantha Gross, (See no. 61); Eco green car icon by dominiquechappard; Weight icon by neorg

66. "Maintenance and Safety of Hybrid and Plug-in Electric Vehicles," US Department of Energy, 2022, https://afdc.energy.gov/vehicles/electric_maintenance.html

67. Sarah LaMonaca and Lisa Ryan, "The State of Play in Electric Vehicle Charging Services—A Review of Infrastructure Provision, Players, and Policies," *Elsevier Renewable and Sustainable Energy Reviews*, Sep. 28, 2021, https://www.sciencedirect.com/science/article/pii/S1364032121010066

68. Global EV Outlook, (See no. 23)

69. LaMonaca and Ryan, (See no. 67)

70. Colin McKerracher, "EV Charging Data Shows a Widely Divergent Global Path," *BloombergNEF*, Mar. 23, 2021, https://www.bloomberg.com/news/articles/2021-03-23/ev-charging-data-shows-a-widely-divergent-global-path

71. Global EV Outlook, (See no. 23)

72. "Making the Transition to Zero-Emission Mobility," ACEA, Jul. 2021, https://www.acea.auto/publication/2021-progress-report-making-the-transition-to-zero-emission-mobility/

73. Abby Brown et al., "Electric Vehicle Charging Infrastructure Trends from the Alternative Fueling Station Locator: Fourth Quarter 2020," NREL, Jun. 2021, https://afdc.energy.gov/files/u/publication/electric_vehicle_charging_infrastructure_trends_fourth_quarter_2020.pdf

74. "Tesla Supercharger Overview," *Electrek*, Oct. 6, 2021, https://electrek.co/guides/tesla-supercharger/

75. Colin McKerracher, (See no. 70)

76. Fred Lambert,"Tesla Gets All Its Supercharger Cables Stolen at Brand New Station," *Electrek*, Feb. 7, 2022, https://electrek.co/2022/02/07/tesla-supercharger-cables-stolen/

77. Australia EV charging station using waste fryer oil image by Jon Edwards

78. Christoph Hammerschmidt, "Fragmented Electric Vehicle Charging Networks Hit Users," *Smart2Zero.com*, June 18, 2020, https://www.smart2zero.com/en/fragmented-electric-vehicle-charging-networks-hit-users/

79. Andrew J. Hawkins, "EV Charging in the US is Broken - Can Joe Biden Fix It?" *The Verge*, May 11, 2021, https://www.theverge.com/22419150/ev-charging-us-joe-biden-infrastructure-plan

80. Jim Motavalli, "Biden Makes a $174 Billion Commitment to Electric Cars," *Autoweek*, Apr. 1, 2021, https://www.autoweek.com/news/a36004838/biden-commitment-to-electric-cars/; Monopoly image by Mike Mozart under Creative Commons License 2.0

81. Abby Brown et al., (See no. 73)

82. Simon Torkington, "This is the Most Popular Type of Home in Europe Right Now," World Economic Forum, Jul. 22, 2021, https://www.weforum.org/agenda/2021/07/flats-houses-types-housing-europe/#:~:text=The%20data%20for%202019%20(the,the%20population%20lived%20in%20flats.

83. Chris Nelder and Emily Rogers, "Reducing EV Charging Infrastructure Costs," Rocky Mountain Institute, 2019, https://rmi.org/insight/reducing-ev-charging-infrastructure-costs/

84. LaMonaca and Ryan, (See no. 67)

85. Katie Lobosco and Tami Luhby," Here's What's in the Bipartisan Infrastructure Package," *CNN*, Nov. 15, 2021, https://www.cnn.com/2021/07/28/politics/infrastructure-bill-explained/index.html

86. Global EV Outlook, (See no. 23)

87. "Research Shows People Are Driving EVs Less than Projected," University of Chicago, Feb. 8, 2021, https://epic.uchicago.edu/news/research-shows-people-are-driving-evs-less-than-projected/?mc_cid=639c3aa187&mc_eid=c70268762a

88. Christian Spencer, "New Study Explains Why Nearly 20 Percent of Electric Car Owners Return to Gas," *The Hill*, Apr. 30, 2021, https://thehill.com/changing-america/sustainability/energy/551207-new-study-explains-why-nearly-20-percent-of-electric

89. Ben Foldy, "Auto Makers Grapple with Battery-Fire Risks in Electric Vehicles," *The Wall Street Journal*, Oct. 19, 2020, https://www.wsj.com/articles/auto-makers-grapple-with-battery-fire-risks-in-electric-vehicles-11603099800

90. Sarah Davidson, "Government Mulls Emergency Measures that Would Enable Networks to SWITCH OFF Your Electricity without Warning or Compensation," *ThisIsMoney.co.uk*, Sep. 17, 2020, https://www.thisismoney.co.uk/money/bills/article-8706033/Smart-meters-used-switch-electricity-without-warning-compensation.html; Image of Bellingham, WA power outage by Robert Ashworth under Creative Commons 2.0

91. John Voelcker, "Chevy Bolt Battery Recall: How Could This Have Happened?" *Car and Driver*, Sep. 13, 2021, https://www.caranddriver.com/news/a37552121/chevy-bolt-battery-recall-deep-dive-details/

92. Steven Loveday, "Recalled 2017 Chevrolet Bolt EV Catches Fire in Parking Lot," *Inside EVs*, Sep. 3, 2021, https://insideevs.com/news/530826/chevy-bolt-fire-unplugged/

93. Voelcker, (See no. 91)

94. Mark Kane, "No Parking Allowed for Chevy Bolt EVs at a Parking Lot in SF," *InsideEVs*, Sep. 8, 2021, https://insideevs.com/news/531854/no-parking-chevrolet-bolt-evs/; Burning Tesla image by Baltimore County Fire Department, public domain

95. Michael Kelly, "Boris's Green Industrial Revolution is Doomed to Fail," *The Spectator*, Nov. 21, 2020, https://www.netzerowatch.com/the-road-to-hell-is-paved-with-green-intentions/

96. "Eight Straight: New-Vehicle Prices Mark Another Record High in November 2021, According to Kelley Blue Book," *Kelley Blue Book*, Dec. 10, 2021, https://www.prnewswire.com/news-releases/eight-straight-new-vehicle-prices-mark-another-record-high-in-november-2021-according-to-kelley-blue-book-301442015.html

97. Mark P. Mills, "Mines, Minerals, and 'Green Energy' a Reality Check," Manhattan Institute, July, 2020, https://www.manhattan-institute.org/mines-minerals-and-green-energy-reality-check

98. Matt Posky, "More Western Leaders Call for the End of Private Vehicle Ownership," *TheTruthAboutCars*, Dec. 29, 2021, https://www.thetruthaboutcars.com/2021/12/western-leaders-call-for-the-end-of-private-vehicle-ownership/; Image of ox head sacrifice by Deeporaj under Creative Commons 3.0 License

99. Global EV Outlook, (See no. 23)

Chapter 8: Green, Leafy Ships, Planes, and Trains

1. *Global Viewpoint*, https://www.myglobalviewpoint.com/inspirational-travel-quotes/

2. Ram S. Singh and Amandeep Walla, "Biofuels Historical Perspectives and Public Opinions," *ResearchGate*, Jan., 2017, https://www.research-gate.net/publication/311575858_Biofuels_Historical_Perspectives_and_Public_opinions

3. Ibid.

4. Guy Adams, "Surgeon Uses Human Fat to Run His Cars," *Independent*, Dec. 26, 2008, https://www.independent.co.uk/life-style/health-and-families/health-news/surgeon-uses-human-fat-to-run-his-cars-1211431.html; Hamster on wheel image by Aaron Denunzio

5. Singh, (See no. 2)

6. "Bush Delivers Speech on Renewable Fuel Sources," *CQ Transcriptions*, Apr. 25, 2006, https://www.washingtonpost.com/wp-dyn/content/article/2006/04/25/AR2006042500762.html

7. "Gordon Brown Speech," Getty Images, Oct. 30, 2006, https://www.gettyimages.com/detail/video/tony-blair-speech-gordon-brown-speech-if-we-take-biofuels-news-footage/697708924

8. "The Way Forward: Strengthening the Transatlantic Partnership," and address by Angela Merkel, Apr. 30, 2007, https://politische--reden.eu.translate.goog/BR/t/1110.html?_x_tr_sl=de&_x_tr_tl=en&_x_tr_hl=en&_x_tr_pto=sc

9. Ivetta Gerasimchuk et al., "State of Play on Biofuel Subsidies: Are Policies Ready to Shift?" International Institute for Sustainable Development, June 2012, https://www.iisd.org/gsi/sites/default/files/bf_stateplay_2012.pdf

10. "Global Bioenergy Statistics 2021," World Bioenergy Association, 2021, https://www.worldbioenergy.org/global-bioenergy-statistics/

11. Ibid.

12. *Power Density: A Key to Understanding Energy Sources and Uses* by Vaclav Smil, (The MIT Press, 2015), pages 89 and 115

13. Hugo Valin et al., "The Land Use Change Impact of Biofuels Consumed in the EU," International Institute for Applied Systems Analysis, Aug. 27, 2015, https://ec.europa.eu/energy/sites/ener/files/documents/Final%20Report_GLOBIOM_publication.pdf

14. "10 Years of EU Fuels Policy Increased EU's Reliance on Unsustainable Biofuels," *Transport & Environment*, Jul. 2021, https://www.transport-environment.org/discover/10-years-of-eu-fuels-policy-increased-eus-reliance-on-unsustainable-biofuels/

15. Winnie Gerbens-Leenes et al., "The Water Footprint of Bioenergy," *PNAS*, Apr. 20, 2009, https://www.pnas.org/doi/pdf/10.1073/pnas.0812619106

16. Meghan Sapp, "Poo-Powered Bus Hits the Road in the UK," *The Digest*, Nov. 20, 2014, https://www.biofuelsdigest.com/bdigest/2014/11/20/poo-powered-bus-hits-the-road-in-the-uk/; Earth in hand image by elconomeno, OpenClipart

17. Valin, (See no. 13)

18. Transport & Environment, (See no. 14)

19. Tiffany A. Groode and John B. Heywood, "Biomass to Ethanol: Potential Production and Environmental Impacts," Massachusetts Institute of Technology, Feb. 2008, http://web.mit.edu/sloan-auto-lab/research/beforeh2/files/TGroode%20PhD%20LFEE%20Report.pdf

20. "Feedgrains Sector at a Glance," US Department of Agriculture, Jun. 28, 2021, https://www.ers.usda.gov/topics/crops/corn-and-other-feedgrains/feedgrains-sector-at-a-glance/#:~:text=Much%20of%20this%20growth%20in,percent%20of%20total%20corn%20use.

21. Lester Brown, "Starving the People to Feed the Cars," *CalCars*, Sep, 14, 2006, http://www.calcars.org/calcars-news/515.html

22. Girl with books image by Timothy Takemoto under Creative Commons License 2.0

23. "Summary for Policymakers and Industry: Charting a Course for Decarbonizing Maritime Transport," The World Bank, 2021, https://openknowledge.worldbank.org/handle/10986/35436

24. *Review of Maritime Transport 2021*, UN Publications, 2021, https://unctad.org/system/files/official-document/rmt2021_en_0.pdf

25. "Fourth IMO Greenhouse Gas Study," International Maritime Organization, 2021, https://wwwcdn.imo.org/localresources/en/OurWork/Environment/Documents/Fourth%20IMO%20GHG%20Study%202020%20-%20Full%20report%20and%20annexes.pdf

26. Maritime Transport, (See no. 24)

27. Maritime Transport, (See no. 24)

28. Matt McGrath, "Climate Change: Speed Limits for Ships Can Have 'Massive' Benefits," *BBC*, Nov. 11, 2019, https://www.bbc.com/news/science-environment-50348321; Tortoise image by Moise Nicu under Creative Commons Attribution 3.0

29. Derek Hammack, "The U.S. National Security Risks of Imposing Idealistic Green Initiatives," *Columbia Political Review*, Aug. 20, 2021, http://www.cpreview.org/blog/2021/8/the-us-national-security-risks-of-imposing-international-green-initiatives

30. "A Conversation with Raymond E. Mabus, Secretary of the Navy," Council on Foreign Relations, Mar. 28, 2011, https://www.cfr.org/event/conversation-raymond-e-mabus-secretary-navy

31. David Alexander, "'Great Green Fleet' Using Biofuels Deployed by U.S. Navy," *Reuters*, Jan. 20, 2016, https://www.reuters.com/article/us-usa-defense-greenfleet/great-green-fleet-using-biofuels-deployed-by-u-s-navy-idUSKCN0UY2U4

32. "Latest US Navy Biofuel Bunkers Are Bad for the Environment, Expensive, Barely Biofuel at All, Says Critic," *Ship & Bunker*, Jul. 6, 2016,

https://www.reuters.com/article/us-usa-defense-greenfleet/great-green-fleet-using-biofuels-deployed-by-u-s-navy-idUSKCN0UY2U4

33. Bonner R. Cohen, "Navy Sink Obama-Era Green Destroyer Program," The Heartland Institute, May 4, 2018, https://www.heartland.org/news-opinion/news/navy-sinks-obama-era-green-destroyer-program

34. Admiral Thomas Hayward presentation at the America First Energy Conference in Houston, Dec. 1, 2017, https://www.youtube.com/watch?v=VuPa8_qIbMU&t=777s

35. "Fiscal Year 2020 Operational Energy Annual Report," US Department of Defense, May, 2021, https://www.acq.osd.mil/eie/Downloads/OE/FY20%20OE%20Annual%20Report.pdf

36. Maritime Transport, (See no. 24)

37. Jasper Faber et al., "Regulating Speed: A Short-Term Measure to Reduce Maritime GHG Emissions," CE Delft, Oct. 18, 2017, https://cedelft.eu/publications/regulating-speed-a-short-term-measure-to-reduce-maritime-ghg-emissions/

38. Maritime Transport, (See no. 24)

39. Christopher Meyer, "Apple's Most Obvious Secret: Reducing Time-to-Value," Working Wider, Oct., 11, 2010, http://www.workingwider.com/strategic_innovation/apples-obvious-secret-reducing-time-to-value/

40. Edwin Lopez and Jennifer McKevitt, "Inside Nike's Plan to cut Lead Times From 60 Days to 10," SupplyChainDive, Nov. 1, 2017, https://www.supplychaindive.com/news/nike-lead-times-innovation-automation-consumer/508606/

41. Ira Breskin, "Breakbulk Europe: Uncertainty Surrounding Future Fuels," gCaptain, May 20, 2022, https://gcaptain.com/breakbulk-europe-uncertainty-surrounding-future-fuels/

42. "Sustainable Aviation Fuel: Review of Technical Pathways," US Dept. of Energy, Sep. 2020, https://www.energy.gov/eere/bioenergy/downloads/sustainable-aviation-fuel-review-technical-pathways-report#:~:text=The%20Sustainable%20Aviation%20Fuel%3A%20Review,proposition%20of%20sustainable%20aviation%20fuel.

43. "France Moves to Ban Short-Haul Domestic Flights," BBC News, Apr. 12, 2021, https://www.bbc.com/news/world-europe-56716708#:~:text=French%20lawmakers%20have%20moved%20to,and%2Da%2Dhalf%20hours.; "Out of Gas" sign image from 1973 by David Falconer, U.S. National Archives

44. Sustainable Aviation Fuel, (See no. 42)

45. Antonia Wilson, "Dutch Airline KLM Calls for People to Fly Less," The Guardian, Jul., 11, 2019; Profit chart image by simpletutorials.net

46. "Sustainable Aviation Fuels (SAF)," Intl. Civil Aviation Organization, 2022, https://www.icao.int/environmental-protection/pages/SAF.aspx

47. "Halving Emissions by 2050 - Aviation Brings its Targets to Copenhagen," International Aviation Transportation Association, Dec. 8, 2009, https://www.iata.org/en/pressroom/2009-releases/2009-12-08-01/

48. "Net Zero 2050: Sustainable Aviation Fuels," IATA, 2021, https://www.icao.int/environmental-protection/pages/SAF.aspx

49. "ICAO Carbon Emissions Calculator Methodology,: International Civil Aviation Organization, Jun. 2018, https://www.icao.int/environmental-protection/CarbonOffset/Documents/Methodology%20ICAO%20Carbon%20Calculator_v11-2018.pdf

50. "Sustainable Aviation Fuels Fact Sheet 5," International Aviation Transportation Association, Dec. 2018, https://www.iata.org/contentassets/d13875e9ed784f75bac90f000760e998/saf-and-sustainability.pdf

51. Sustainable Aviation Fuel, (See no. 42)

52. Tim Gallagher, "These Hybrid Airships Are the Low-Carbon Future of Travel," Euronews.green, Sep. 15, 2021, https://www.euronews.com/green/2021/09/15/these-hybrid-airships-are-the-low-carbon-future-of-travel; Christopher Lloyd image by Creative Commons License 2.0

53. Adele Berti, "Renewable Jet Fuels: How to Handle the Heavy Costs," Airport Technology, Aug. 21, 2018, https://www.airport-technology.com/features/renewable-jet-fuels-how-to-handle-the-heavy-costs/

54. "2019 Environmental Report," International Civil Aviation Organization, 2019, https://www.icao.int/environmental-protection/Documents/ICAO-ENV-Report2019-F1-WEB%20(1).pdf

55. "Rail — Analysis," International Energy Agency, Nov. 2021, https://www.iea.org/reports/rail

56. "The Future of Rail," IEA, 2019, https://iea.blob.core.windows.net/assets/fb7dc9e4-d5ff-4a22-ac07-ef3ca73ac680/The_Future_of_Rail.pdf

57. Rail — Analysis, (See no. 55)

58. Rail — Analysis, (See no. 55)

59. The Future of Rail, (See no. 56)

60. The Future of Rail, (See no. 56)

61. The Future of Rail, (See no. 56)

62. Richard Nunno, "High Speed Rail Development Worldwide," Environmental and Energy Study Institute, Jun., 2018, https://www.eesi.org/files/FactSheet_High_Speed_Rail_Worldwide.pdf

63. Subastian Obando, "California's High-Speed Rail Cost Rises to $105B, More than Double Original Price," Construction Dive, Feb. 15, 2022; https://www.constructiondive.com/news/california-high-speed-rail-costs-rise-to-105-billion/618877/#:~:text=State%20transportation%20officials%20tacked%20on,train%20from%20the%20Cesar%20E.; Monopoly image by Mike Mozart under Creative Commons License 2.0

64. Richard Nunno, (See no. 62)

65. Chris Nickerson, "Urban Density May Be One of Our Best Strategies to Fight Climate Change," Real Estate News Exchange, Feb. 24, 2022, https://renx.ca/urban-density-may-be-one-of-our-best-strategies-to-fight-climate-change/; Kissy lips image by j4p4n

66. The Future of Rail, (See no. 56)

67. "Rail Environment Policy Statement, On Track for a Cleaner, Greener Railway," UK Department for Transport, Jul. 2021, https://assets.publishing.service.gov.uk/government/uploads/system/uploads/attachment_data/file/1002166/rail-environment-policy-statement.pdf

68. The Future of Rail, (See no. 56)

69. "The Future of Hydrogen," International Energy Agency, Jun., 2019, https://www.iea.org/reports/the-future-of-hydrogen

70. John Constable, "Hydrogen, The Once and Future Fuel?" Global Warming Policy Foundation, Oct. 29, 2019, https://www.thegwpf.org/content/uploads/2020/06/Hydrogen-Fuel.pdf

71. The Future of Hydrogen, (See no. 69)

72. The Future of Hydrogen, (See no. 69)

73. "BC Transit's $90M Hydrogen Bus Fleet to Be Sold Off, Converted to Diesel," CBC News, Dec. 4, 2014, https://www.cbc.ca/news/canada/british-columbia/bc-transit-s-90m-hydrogen-bus-fleet-to-be-sold-off-converted-to-diesel-1.2861060; Image of Clint Eastwood by Clint Eastwood under Creative Commons License 2.0

74. "Handbook for Hydrogen-Fuelled Vessels," DNV, Jun., 2021, https://www.dnv.com/maritime/publications/handbook-for-hydrogen-fuelled-vessels-download.html

75. "United to Become First in Aviation History to Fly Aircraft Full of Passengers Using 100% Sustainable Fuel," PR Newswire, Dec. 1, 2021, https://www.prnewswire.com/news-releases/united-to-become-first-in-aviation-history-to-fly-aircraft-full-of-passengers-using-100-sustainable-fuel-301435009.html; Angus cattle image by Scott Bauer, US Department of Agriculture

Chapter 9: Can Renewables Power Heavy Industry?

1. Vaclav Smil, "Why Net-Zero 2050 Really Won't Work," Financial Post, Jul. 21, 2022, https://financialpost.com/opinion/vaclav-smil-why-net-

zero-2050-really-wont-work

2.   Vaclav Smil, "What We Need to Know about the Pace of Decarbonization," *Substantia*, 2019, http://vaclavsmil.com/wp-content/up-loads/2020/01/Substantia.pdf

3.   Dominic Rassool, "Unlocking Private Finance to Support CCS Investments," Global CCS Inst., 2021, https://www.globalccsinstitute.com/

4.   Mathilde Fajardy, "CCUS in Industry and Transformation," IEA, Nov. 2021, https://www.iea.org/reports/ccus-in-industry-and-transformation

5.   Dominic Rassool, (See no. 3)

6.   Elizabeth Segram, "This $110 T-Shirt Sucks Carbon Dioxide fro the Atmosphere," *Fast Company*, Aug. 3, 2021, https://www.fastcompany.com/90661266/this-110-t-shirt-sucks-carbon-dioxide-from-the-atmosphere#:~:text=It's%20partnered%20with%20a%20U.S.,through%20photo-synthesis%20while%20producing%20oxygen.; Planet image by oksmith, public domain

7.   Petya Trendafilova, "What is the 45Q Tax Credit?" *Carbon Herald*, Mar. 17, 2021, https://carbonherald.com/what-is-45q-tax-credit/

8.   "EU Carbon Permits," *Trading Economics*, 2022, https://tradingeconomics.com/commodity/carbon#:~:text=EU%20Carbon%20Permits%20European%20carbon%20prices%20fell%20toward,due%20to%20weaker%20industrial%20output%20across%20the%20region.

9.   Nicola Jones, "Solution or Band-Aid? Carbon Capture Projects Are Moving Ahead," *Yale Environment 360*, Jun. 7, 2022, https://e360.yale.edu/features/solution-or-band-aid-carbon-capture-projects-are-moving-ahead

10.   Mathilde Fajardy, (See no. 4)

11.   Nicholas Kusnetz, "In a Bid to Save Its Coal Industry, Wyoming Has Become a Test Case for Carbon Capture, but Utilities are Balking at the Pricetag," *Inside Climate News*, May 29, 2022, https://insideclimatenews.org/news/29052022/coal-carbon-capture-wyoming/

12.   Ibid.

13.   Emily L. Wegener, "In the Matter of the Appl. of Rocky Mountain Power to Establish Intermediate Low-Carbon Energy Portfolio Standards," Rocky Mt. Power, March, 2022, https://www.documentcloud.org/documents/22035889-rocky-mountain-power#document/p29/a2110522

14.   Dominic Rassool, (See no. 3)

15.   Image of a coal train in Eastern Wyoming in 2006 by Greg Goebel under Creative Commons 2 License

16.   Emily L. Wegener (See no. 13)

17.   "Ammonia Technology Roadmap," International Energy Agency, Oct. 2021, https://www.iea.org/reports/ammonia-technology-roadmap

18.   Ibid.

19.   Ibid.

20.   "Energy Units," American Physical Society, 2020, https://www.aps.org/policy/reports/popa-reports/energy/units.cfm

21.   Ammonia Technology Roadmap, (See no. 17)

22.   Rachael D'Amore, "How Fertilizer in Farming is Pushing Climate Change Past 'Worst-Case Scenarios," *Global News*, Oct. 7, 2020, https://globalnews.ca/news/7378381/nitrous-oxide-climate-change-fertilizer/; Wolfman image by Horror Monsters

23.   Ammonia Technology Roadmap, (See no. 17)

24.   "Concrete Future," Global Cement and Concrete Association," Oct. 12, 2021, https://gccassociation.org/concretefuture/

25.   Tiffany Vass et al., "Cement—Analysis," International Energy Agency, Nov. 2021, https://www.iea.org/reports/cement

26.   "Technology Roadmap: Low-Carbon Transition in the Cement Industry," International Energy Agency, 2018, https://www.iea.org/reports/technology-roadmap-low-carbon-transition-in-the-cement-industry

27.   Stephen Johnson, "Engineers Create World's First Carbon-Neutral Cement Out of Algae," *Freethink*, Jul. 3, 2022, https://www.freethink.com/environment/carbon-neutral-cement

28.   Technology Roadmap (See no. 26)

29.   Technology Roadmap (See no. 26)

30.   Technology Roadmap (See no. 26)

31.   "Cement Science Based Target Setting Guidance," *Sciencebasedtargets.org*, Mar. 2022, sciencebasedtargets.org/resources/files/Cement-guidance-public-consultation.pdf

32.   Cuihong Chen et al., "A Striking Growth of CO_2 Emissions from the Global Cement Industry Driven by New Facilities in Emerging Countries," *Environmental Research Letters*, Mar. 9, 2022, https://iopscience.iop.org/article/10.1088/1748-9326/ac48b5/pdf

33.   "A History of Concrete & Cement," Cemex, 2022, https://www.cemexusa.com/products-and-services/concrete/history-of-concrete-cement#:~:text=Quick%20Historic%20Concrete%20%26%20Cement%20Facts%201%20Cement,75%2C400%20pounds%20of%20sand%2C%20gravel%20and%20bricks.%20

34.   "Three Reasons Why We Should Stop Using Concrete," *Climate Conscious*, May 15, 2020, https://medium.com/climate-conscious/3-reasons-why-we-should-stop-using-concrete-a189d1d9cded#:~:text=%203%20Reasons%20Why%20We%20Should%20Stop%20Using,aggregate%2C%20and...%204%20Final%20Thoughts.%20%20More%20; "Save Our Planet, Kill Yourself" sign by Jorghex

35.   "The Future of Petrochemicals," International Energy Agency, 2018, https://www.iea.org/reports/the-future-of-petrochemicals

36.   Ibid.

37.   Ryan Kh, "The Terrifying Effects of Polyester on the Environment and Our Health," *Blue & Green Tomorrow*, Nov. 1, 2020, https://blueand-greentomorrow.com/environment/terrifying-effects-of-polyester-on-environment-health/; Image of Greta Thunberg by European Parliament under Creative Commons Attribution License 2.0

38.   The Future of Petrochemicals, (See no. 35)

39.   The Future of Petrochemicals, (See no. 35)

40.   Jenna R. Jambeck, et al., "Production, Use, and Fate of All Plastics Ever Made," *Science Advances*, Jul. 19, 2017, https://www.ncbi.nlm.nih.gov/pmc/articles/PMC5517107/

41.   "Iron and Steel Technology Roadmap," IEA Oct. 2020, https://www.iea.org/reports/iron-and-steel-technology-roadmap

42.   Abram Stevens Hewitt et al., "Iron Processing," *Britannica*, Jan. 27, 2017, https://www.britannica.com/technology/iron-processing

43.   Leigh Collins, "World's First Large-Scale Zero-Carbon Steel Plant will Require £500m of Public Money," *Recharge News*, Jul. 20, 2021, https://www.rechargenews.com/energy-transition/world-s-first-large-scale-zero-carbon-steel-plant-will-require-500m-of-public-money/2-1-1042649; Monopoly image by Mike Mozart under Creative Commons License 2.0

44.   Iron and Steel Technology Roadmap, (See no. 41)

45.   Iron and Steel Technology Roadmap, (See no. 41)

46.   Emma Newburger, "Steel Industry to Suffer Major Losses from Rising Carbon Prices and Climate Regs.," *CNBC*, Jul. 30, 2019, https://www.cnbc.com/2019/07/30/steel-sector-to-suffer-losses-rising-carbon-prices-climate-regulation.html; Profit chart image by *simpletutorials.net*

47.   "2022 World Steel in Figures," World Steel Assoc., Apr. 30, 2022, https://worldsteel.org/steel-topics/statistics/world-steel-in-figures-2022/

48.   Iron and Steel Technology Roadmap, (See no. 41)

49.   Iron and Steel Technology Roadmap, (See no. 41)

50.   "Net Zero Steel in Construction: The Way Forward," McKinsey & Company, Apr. 2022, https://www.mckinsey.com/business-functions/sustainability/our-insights/net-zero-steel-in-building-and-construction-the-way-forward

51.   2022 World Steel in Figures, (See no. 47)

52.   Howard Mustoe, "Tata Threatens to Shut Port Talbot Steel Works," *The Telegraph*, Jul. 21, 2022, https://www.msn.com/en-gb/money/other/tata-threatens-to-shut-port-talbot-steel-works/ar-AAZPLPq

53. "The Future of Hydrogen," International Energy Agency, Jun., 2019, https://www.iea.org/reports/the-future-of-hydrogen
54. Ibid.
55. Donn Dears, "Hydrogen and Climate Change," June 15, 2021, https://ddears.com/2021/06/01/special-report-on-hydrogen/
56. "Japan – Its Hydrogen Economy Runs the Risk of Being Powered by Coal," *Hydrogen Central*, Apr. 18, 2022, https://hydrogen-central.com/japan-hydrogen-economy-powered-coal/; Pinwheel image by Kgredi76 under Creative Commons License 4
57. "Stat. Rev. of World Energy 2022," BP, https://www.bp.com/en/global/corporate/energy-economics/statistical-review-of-world-energy.html
58. "Opening Speech by President von der Leyen at the 'H2Poland' Central European Hydrogen Technology Forum," European Commission, May 17, 2022, https://ec.europa.eu/commission/presscorner/detail/en/SPEECH_22_3123
59. Avik Roy, "India to Meet Climate Goals, Be Green Hydrogen Hub: Modi on Indep. Day," *Hindustan Times*, Aug. 15, 2021, https://www.hindustantimes.com/india-news/independence-day-2021-hydrogen-energy-hub-solar-energy-india-climate-goals-modi-101629012924744.html
60. "Ministerial Council on Renewable Energy, Hydrogen and Related Issues," Japan Prime Minister's Office, Dec. 26, 2017, https://japan.kantei.go.jp/98_abe/actions/201712/26article5.html
61. BP Statistical Review, (See no. 57)
62. M. W. Melaina et al., "Blending Hydrogen into Natural Gas Pipeline Networks: A Review of Key Issues," National Renewable Energy Laboratory, Mar. 2013, https://www.nrel.gov/docs/fy13osti/51995.pdf
63. Larry Pearl, "Hydrogen Blends Higher then 5% Raise Leak, Embrittlement Risks for Natural Gas Pipelines: California PUC," *Utility Dive*, Jul. 22, 2022, https://www.utilitydive.com/news/hydrogen-blends-higher-than-5-percent-raise-leak-embrittlement-risks/627895/
64. The Future of Hydrogen, (See no.53)
65. The Future of Hydrogen, (See no.53)
66. The Future of Hydrogen, (See no.53)
67. The Future of Hydrogen, (See no.53)
68. BP Statistical Review, (See no. 57); "United to Become First in Aviation History to Fly Aircraft Full of Passengers Using 100% Sustainable Fuel," *PR Newswire*, Dec. 1, 2021, https://www.prnewswire.com/news-releases/united-to-become-first-in-aviation-history-to-fly-aircraft-full-of-passengers-using-100-sustainable-fuel-301435009.html; Angus cattle image by Scott Bauer, US Department of Agriculture

Chapter 10: The Seeds of Renewable Energy Failure

1. David Schellenberger, "Yes, Solar and Wind Really Do Increase Electricity Prices," *Forbes*, Apr. 25, 2018, https://www.forbes.com/sites/michaelshellenberger/2018/04/25/yes-solar-and-wind-really-do-increase-electricity-prices-and-for-inherently-physical-reasons/?sh=75e0090717e8
2. Sarah Moore, "History of COVID-19," *Medical Lifesciences News*, Sep. 28, 2021, https://www.news-medical.net/health/History-of-COVID-19.aspx
3. "Coronavirus (COVID-19) Statistics," *Microsoft Bing*, 2022, https://www.bing.com/search?q=coronavirus+%28covid-19%29+statistics+microsoft+bing&form=ANNTH1&refig=bd09853b083f4e3a93260ee0184996fd
4. "Global Economic Effects of COVID-19," Congressional Research Service, Nov. 10, 2021, https://sgp.fas.org/crs/row/R46270.pdf
5. "Vehicle Miles Traveled," Federal Reserve Bank of St. Louis, Jun. 2022, https://fred.stlouisfed.org/series/TRFVOLUSM227SFWA
6. Ben Gilbert, "Bill Gates Issued a Stark Warning for the World: 'As Awful as This Pandemic Is, Climate Change Could be Worse,'" *Business Insider*, Aug. 5, 2020, https://www.businessinsider.com/bill-gates-coronavirus-warning-climate-change-worse-than-covid-2020-8; Fearful face by Wellcome Images under Creative Commons License 4.0
7. Robert Rapier, "U.S. Drilling Activity Has Risen 60% in One Year," *OilPrice.com*, Apr. 4, 2022, https://oilprice.com/Energy/Crude-Oil/US-Drilling-Activity-Has-Risen-60-In-One-Year.html
8. "Global Investments in Oil and Gas Upstream," International Energy Agency, 2021, https://www.iea.org/search?q=global%20investments%20in%20oil%20and%20gas%20upstream
9. Antonio Guterres," The Race to a Zero-Emission World Starts Now," *TED Talks*, Oct. 2020, https://www.ted.com/talks/antonio_guterres_the_race_to_a_zero_emission_world_starts_now
10. Global Economic Effects, (See no. 4)
11. "World Economic Outlook Update," International Monetary Fund, Jul. 2022, https://www.imf.org/en/Publications/WEO/Issues/2022/07/26/world-economic-outlook-update-july-2022
12. "Crude Oil," Trading Economics, 2022, https://tradingeconomics.com/commodity/crude-oil
13. Ed Hoskins, "The 2021 European Wind Drought and Weather-Dependent Power Generation," 2022, https://edmhdotme.wordpress.com/2021-european-wind-drought-analysed/; Image of wind turbines at Thornton Bank off the coast of Belgium by Hans Hillewaert under Creative Commons License 4.0
14. "Dutch TTF Gas Futures," Intercontinental Exchange, 2022, https://www.theice.com/products/27996665/Dutch-TTF-Gas-Futures/data?marketId=5419234&span=3; Image of LNG tanker Rivers by Pline under Creative Commons 3.0 License
15. Hoskins, (See no. 13)
16. TTF Gas Futures, (See no. 14)
17. Candiece Cyrus, "Failed UK Energy Suppliers Update," *Forbes*, Feb. 18, 2022, https://www.forbes.com/uk/advisor/energy/failed-uk-energy-suppliers-update/
18. Joe Wallace, "Energy Prices in Europe Hit Records After Wind Stops Blowing," *The Wall Street Journal*, Sep. 13, 2021, https://www.wsj.com/articles/energy-prices-in-europe-hit-records-after-wind-stops-blowing-11631528258; Image of Clint Eastwood by Clint Eastwood under Creative Commons License 2.0
19. "Stat. Rev. of World Energy," BP, 2022, https://www.bp.com/en/global/corporate/energy-economics/statistical-review-of-world-energy.html
20. Ibid; "A 10-Point Plan to Reduce the European Union's Reliance on Russian Natural Gas," International Energy Agency, Mar. 3, 2022, https://iea.blob.core.windows.net/assets/1af70a5f-9059-47b4-a2dd-1b479918f3cb/A10-PointPlantoReducetheEuropeanUnionsRelianceonRussianNaturalGas.pdf; Hilary Hooper et al., "Europe is a Key Destination for Russia's Energy Exports," US Energy Information Administration, Mar. 14, 2022, https://www.eia.gov/todayinenergy/detail.php?id=51618
21. "Europe's Coal Exit," Climate Action Network, Jul. 14, 2022, https://beyond-coal.eu/europes-coal-exit/
22. "Number of Permanent Nuclear Reactor Shutdowns Worldwide as of May 2022, by Country," Statista, Aug. 1, 2022, https://www.statista.com/statistics/513639/number-of-permanent-nuclear-reactor-shutdowns-worldwide/#:~:text=As%20of%20May%202022%2C%20there%20were%20200%20nuclear,units.%20The%20United%20Kingdom%20followed%2C%20with%2034%20reactors.
23. "Average Monthly Electricity Wholesale Prices in Selected Countries in the European Union (EU) from January 2020 to July 2022," Statista, 2022, https://www.statista.com/statistics/1267500/eu-monthly-wholesale-electricity-price-country/;"Electricity Prices: Day Ahead Baseload Contracts - Monthly Average (GB)," Ofgem, 2022, https://www.ofgem.gov.uk/energy-data-and-research/data-portal/all-available-charts?keyword=wholesale%20price%20monthly&sort=relevance
24. Faith Birol, "Coordinated Actions Across Europe Are Essential to Prevent a Major Gas Crunch: Here Are 5 Immediate Measures," International Energy Agency, Jul. 18, 2022, https://www.iea.org/commentaries/coordinated-actions-across-europe-are-essential-to-prevent-a-major-gas-

crunch-here-are-5-immediate-measures

25. Statista, Ofgem, (See no. 23); Powerlines near Laytham, England by JThomas under Creative Commons License 2.0

26. Julia Horowitz, "European Power Prices Shatter Records as Energy Crisis Intensifies," *CNN Business*, Aug. 29, 2022, https://www.msn.com/en-us/news/world/european-power-prices-shatter-records-as-energy-crisis-intensifies/ar-AA11eM9u

27. Victoria Zaretskaya, "U.S. Liquefied Natural Gas Exports to Europe Increased During the First 4 Months of 2022," US Energy Information Administration, Jun. 7, 2022, https://www.eia.gov/todayinenergy/detail.php?id=52659

28. Gerson Freitas Jr. et al., "Natural Gas Soars 700%, Becoming Driving Force in the New Cold War," *Business Std.*, Jul. 4, 2022, https://www.business-standard.com/article/international/natural-gas-soars-700-becoming-driving-force-in-the-new-cold-war-122070500518_1.html

29. Charles Kennedy, "Britons Advised to Stop Showering to Conserve Energy," Aug. 8, 2022, *OilPrice.com*, https://oilprice.com/Latest-Energy-News/World-News/Britons-Advised-To-Stop-Showering-To-Conserve-Energy.html; "Out of Gas" sign image from 1973 by David Falconer, U.S. National Archives

30. Freitas, (See no. 28)

31. Andreas Exarheas, "Europe Rushing to Install New LNG Import Facilities," *Rigzone*, Aug. 29, 2022, https://www.rigzone.com/news/europe_rushing_to_install_new_lng_import_facilities-29-aug-2022-170138-article/

32. Vanessa Dezem and Anna Shiryaevskaya, "Germany's Uniper Suffers 12 Billion Euro Hit in Energy Shock," *Bloomberg*, Aug. 17, 2022, https://www.bloomberg.com/news/articles/2022-08-17/uniper-posts-12-billion-euro-loss-as-a-glimpse-into-crisis#xj4y7vzkg

33. Inke Kappeler et al., "Germany Nationalizes Its Biggest Natural Gas Importer," *CNN Business*, Sep. 22, 2022, https://www.cnn.com/2022/09/21/energy/uniper-germany-energy-crisis/index.html

34. Susanna Twidale and Nora Buli, "EU Races to Shield Industry as Russia Gas Stoppage Shakes Markets," *Reuters*, Sep. 5, 2022, https://finance.yahoo.com/news/eu-races-help-industry-russian-094400766.html

35. Sam Jones et al., "European Energy Groups Secure Government Support Amid Cash Crunch," *Financial Times*, Sep. 6, 2022 , https://www.ft.com/content/cd387e9d-8230-46ec-9e84-042db1057f33

36. Agnieszka de Sousa et al., "Europe's Widening Fertilizer Crisis Threatens Food Supplies," *Bloomberg*, Aug. 25, 2022, https://financialpost.com/pmn/business-pmn/yara-to-further-cut-european-ammonia-production-due-to-gas-spike#:~:text=Europe's%20fertilizer%20crunch%20tightened%20after,%2Dof%2Dliving%20crisis%20intensifies.

37. Joe Wallace, "European Manufacturers Reel from Russian Gas Shutoff," *The Wall Street Journal*, Sep. 11, 2022, https://www.wsj.com/articles/europe-manufacturers-factories-russia-gas-11662938614

38. Harry Dempsey, "More Smelters Face Closure as Europe Enters Power-Starved Winter," *Financial Times*, Aug. 19, 2022, https://www.ft.com/content/0906df5d-1b92-4de1-95d6-3ae7b1055897

39. Wallace, (See no. 37)

40. William Wilkes, "Germany Cranks Up Chemical Imports as Energy Crisis Hikes Costs," *Bloomberg*, Sep. 10, 2022, https://www.bloomberg.com/news/articles/2022-09-11/germany-cranks-up-chemical-imports-as-energy-crisis-hikes-costs

41. "Drought in Europe," EC, Aug. 2022, https://edo.jrc.ec.europa.eu/documents/news/GDO-EDODroughtNews202208_Europe.pdf

42. Ibid.

43. "Measures in Europe to Reduce Energy Consumption," *TheJournal.mt*, Aug. 29, 2022, https://thejournal.mt/measures-in-europe-to-reduce-energy-consumption/

44. Catherine Clifford, "Europe Will Count Natural Gas and Nuclear as Green Energy in Some Circumstances," *CNBC*, Jul. 6, 2022, https://www.cnbc.com/2022/07/06/europe-natural-gas-nuclear-are-green-energy-in-some-circumstances-.html

45. Anna Cooban, "A Third of Brits Face Poverty with Energy Bills Set to Hit $5,000," *CNN Business*, Aug. 9, 2022, https://www.cnn.com/2022/08/09/economy/uk-energy-bills-poverty/index.html; Weeping Parisian public domain

46. Lydia Powell et al., "When the Going Gets Tough, the Tough Burn Coal," Observer Research Foundation, Jul. 25, 2022, https://www.orfonline.org/expert-speak/when-the-going-gets-tough-the-tough-burns-coal/

47. Zahra Tayeb, "Coal is Making a Comeback in Energy-Hungry Europe, Sending Prices Soaring," *Markets Insider*, Sep. 11, 2022, https://www.businessinsider.in/stock-market/news/coal-is-making-a-comeback-in-energy-hungry-europe-sending-prices-soaring-2-analysts-lay-out-whats-going-on-/articleshow/94132719.cms

48. Zahra Tayeb, "Germany is Now Generating Nearly a Third of Its Electricity from Coal as It Scrambles to Replace Russian Gas before Winter," *Business Insider*, Sep. 8, 2022, https://www.businessinsider.in/stock-market/news/germany-is-now-generating-nearly-a-third-of-its-electricity-from-coal-as-it-scrambles-to-replace-russian-gas-before-winter/articleshow/94080029.cms#:~:text=gas%20before%20winter-,Germany%20is%20now%20generating%20nearly%20a%20third%20of%20its%20electricity,replace%20Russian%20gas%20before%20winter&text=Germany%20is%20relying%20more%20on,first%20half%2C%20per%20Destatis%20data.

49. "China Boosts Coal Output to Offset Lower Gas Imports, High Prices," S&P Global, May 18, 2022, https://www.spglobal.com/commodityinsights/en/market-insights/latest-news/lng/051822-china-boosts-coal-output-to-offset-lower-gas-imports-high-prices

50. "India May Need Up to 28 GW of Additional Coal-Based Power Generation Capacity by 2032: CEA," *The Hindu*, Sep. 13, 2022, https://www.thehindu.com/business/Economy/india-may-need-up-to-28gw-of-additional-coal-based-power-generation-capacity-by-2032-cea/article65882403.ece

51. "Coal," *Trading Economics*, Sep. 13, 2022, https://tradingeconomics.com/commodity/coal

52. Elizabeth Piper et al., "Britain to Borrow Big Again to Ease Energy Shock," *Reuters*, Sep. 8, 2022, https://www.reuters.com/world/uk/uk-pm-liz-truss-set-out-bold-plan-tackle-energy-crisis-2022-09-07/

53. Germany Nationalizes, (See no. 33)

54. Bozorgmehr Sharafedin, "Analysis: Forget Showering, It's Eat or Heat for Shocked Europeans Hit by Energy Crisis," *Reuters*, Aug. 29, https://www.reuters.com/markets/europe/forget-showering-its-eat-or-heat-shocked-europeans-hit-by-energy-crisis-2022-08-26/

55. "'Back to the Cave Age': Brussels Diners Eat in the Dark Amid Energy Crisis," *Euronews*, Oct. 3. 2022, https://www.euronews.com/culture/2022/10/03/back-to-the-cave-age-brussels-diners-eat-in-the-dark-amid-energy-crisis; Candlelight master image public domain

56. Statistical Review, (See no. 19)

57. Jorge Liboreiro, " Europe's Gas Prices Have Broken a New World Record. How High Can They Go?" *Euronews*, Aug., 26, 2022, https://www.euronews.com/my-europe/2022/08/25/europes-gas-prices-have-broken-a-new-record-how-high-can-they-go

58. "2021 Economic Study: Future Grid Reliability Study Phase 1," New England ISO, Jul. 29. 2022, https://www.iso-ne.com/static-assets/documents/2022/07/2021_economic_study_future_grid_reliability_study_phase_1_report.pdf

59. "Boston Seeks to Ban Fossil Fuels in New Buildings," *APNews*, Aug. 16, 2022, https://apnews.com/article/boston-charlie-baker-massachusetts-climate-and-environment-government-politics-9930ea6487476c0abfa8369d13a1e0ac?utm_campaign=Hot%20News&utm_medium=email&_hsmi=223075315&_hsenc=p2ANqtz-85DxKS213R_9dqu5ZjUye1w45JqTckArg8POF7h6I2BF0b3uDr5WCdr4Hx3jahkxC9-IfsCfPtI7m0yjHR6Cffk9CNWA&utm_content=223075315&utm_source=hs_email

60. 2021 Economic Study, (See no. 58)

61. 2021 Economic Study, (See no. 58)

62. Will Lockett, "The Solar Panel that Generates Power at Night," *Predict*, Jun. 12, 2022, https://medium.com/predict/the-solar-panel-that-generates-power-at-night-e05b0f5168d4

63. 2021 Economic Study, (See no. 58)
64. 2021 Economic Study, (See no. 58)
65. "How Much Do Wind Turbines Cost?" *Windustry*, 2022, https://www.windustry.org/how_much_do_wind_turbines_cost
66. "Electric Power Monthly," US Energy Information Administration, Feb. 2022, https://www.eia.gov/electricity/monthly/
67. John Clark, "California Asks Residents Not to Charge Electric Vehicles, Days After Announcing Gas Car Ban," *MyStateLine.com*, Aug. 31, 2022, https://www.mystateline.com/news/national/california-asks-residents-not-to-charge-electric-vehicles-days-after-announcing-gas-car-ban; Question mark symbols by Wikipedia under Creative Commons License 4.0
68. Fereidoon P. Sioshansi, "CAISO: The More Renewables, The More Transmission," *Energy Central*, Mar. 8, 2022, https://energycentral.com/c/tr/caiso-more-renewables-more-transmission?utm_medium=eNL&utm_campaign=grid_net&utm_content=431337&utm_source=2022_03_10
69. Ryan Wiser, et al., "Halfway to Zero," Lawrence Berkeley National Laboratory, Apr. 2021, https://eta-publications.lbl.gov/sites/default/files/halfway_to_zero_report.pdf
70. "Annual Electric Power Industry Report," US Energy Information Administration, Nov. 2022, https://www.eia.gov/electricity/annual/
71. Ibid., Hurricane Sandy New York Blackout 2012 image by David Shankbone under Creative Commons 3.0 License
72. Molly Taft, " Making Batteries Out of Crab Shells May Be a Great Idea," *Gizmodo*, Sep. 2, 2022, https://gizmodo.com/batteries-made-from-crabs-chitosan-1849490333; Hamster on wheel image by Aaron Denunzio, public domain
73. Maria Gallucci, Maria Virginai Olano, "How 11 States Are Building the US Offshore Wind Industry from Scratch," *Canary Media*, Feb. 4, 2022, https://www.canarymedia.com/articles/wind/chart-how-11-states-are-building-the-us-offshore-wind-industry-from-scratch
74. "Offshore Wind in Europe - Key Trends and Statistics 2020," Wind Europe, Feb. 8, 2021, https://windeurope.org/intelligence-platform/product/offshore-wind-in-europe-key-trends-and-statistics-2020/
75. "Hurricanes in History," National Hurricane Center, 2022, https://www.nhc.noaa.gov/outreach/history/
76. Mark P. Mills, "Mines, Minerals, and 'Green' Energy: A Reality Check," Manhattan Institute, Jul. 2020, https://www.manhattan-institute.org/mines-minerals-and-green-energy-reality-check
77. Ibid.
78. "The Role of Critical Metals in Clean Energy Transitions," International Energy Agency, Mar. 2022, https://www.iea.org/reports/the-role-of-critical-minerals-in-clean-energy-transitions
79. Stephen Moore, "Beware: 100% Green Energy Could Destroy Planet," *Washington Examiner*, Jun. 2, 2022, https://www.washingtonexaminer.com/opinion/beware-100-green-energy-could-destroy-the-planet; Pinwheel image by Kgredi76 under Creative Commons License 4
80. Critical Metals, (See no. 78)
81. Critical Metals, (See no. 78); Image of copper by Images of Chemical Elements under Creative Commons License 3.0
82. "Electric Power Monthly, February, 2021," Energy Information Administration, Feb. 2021, https://www.eia.gov/electricity/monthly/
83. Rico Luman, "Electric Vehicles to Drive Metals Demand Higher," ING, Oct. 13, 2021, https://think.ing.com/articles/electric-vehicles-to-drive-metals-demand-higher/
84. Critical Metals, (See no. 78)
85. Image of lithium mine at Salinas Grandes salt desert, Jujuy province, Argentina by Earthworks
86. Critical Metals, (See no. 78)
87. "The Massive Environmental Cost of Batteries," *ONiO*, Aug. 19, 2021, https://www.onio.com/article/environmental-cost-of-batteries.html
88. Critical Metals, (See no. 78)
89. Critical Metals, (See no. 78)
90. "Metal Spot Prices by Date," *Daily Metal Prices*, Oct. 2022, https://www.dailymetalprice.com/metaltables.php
91. Michael Wayland, "Raw Material Costs for Electric Vehicles Have Doubled During the Pandemic," *CNBC*, Jun. 22, 2022, https://www.cnbc.com/2022/06/22/electric-vehicle-raw-material-costs-doubled-during-pandemic.html
92. Metal Spot Prices, (See no. 90); Image of lithium hydroxide by Mondalor under Creative Commons License 3.0
93. Mark Z. Jacobson et al., "100% Clean and Renewable Wind, Water, and Sunlight (WWS), Energy & Environmental Science, May 27, 2015, https://web.stanford.edu/group/efmh/jacobson/Articles/I/USStatesWWS.pdf
94. "Useful Life," National Renewable Energy Laboratory, 2022, https://www.nrel.gov/analysis/tech-footprint.html
95. Kandler Smith et al., "Life Prediction Model for Grid-Connected Li-ion Battery Energy Storage System," National Renewable Energy Laboratory, Aug. 2017, https://ieeexplore.ieee.org/document/7963578
96. Image of wind turbine blade waste near Bath, New York in Dec., 2021 by Andy Goodell
97. Aubryn Cooperman et al., "Wind Turbine Blade Material in the United States: Quantities, Costs, and End-of-Life Options," National Renewable Energy Laboratory," May 2021, https://www.sciencedirect.com/science/article/abs/pii/S092134492100046X
98. Jasleen Bhatti, "Europe Bans Disposal of Decommissioned Wind Turbine Blades in Landfills: A Step towards Life Cycle Sustainability," *Downto Earth*, Jul. 7, 2021, https://www.downtoearth.org.in/blog/energy/europe-bans-disposal-of-decommissioned-wind-turbine-blades-in-landfills-a-step-towards-life-cycle-sustainability-77835
99. Atakat Atasu et al., "The Dark Side of Solar Power," *Harvard Business Review*, Jun. 18, 2021, https://hbr.org/2021/06/the-dark-side-of-solar-power
100. Rachel Kisela, "California Went Big on Rooftop Solar. Now That's a Problem for Landfills," *Los Angeles Times*, Jul. 15, 2022,
101. Ibid.
102. "Global EV Outlook 2021," International Energy Agency, 2021, https://iea.blob.core.windows.net/assets/ed5f4484-f556-4110-8c5c-4ede8bcba637/GlobalEVOutlook2021.pdf
103. "US Governmental Entities that Moved to Reject or Restrict Wind Projects," American Experiment, 2022, https://www.americanexperiment.org/windrejectiondatabase/
104. European Platform Against Windfarms, 2022, https://www.epaw.org/about_us.php?lang=en
105. "Public Health Impacts of Wind Turbines," Minnesota Department of Public Health, May 22, 2009, https://apps.commerce.state.mn.us/eera/web/project-file?legacyPath=/opt/documents/Public%20Health%20Impacts%20of%20Wind%20Turbines,%205.22.09%20Revised.pdf
106. Carl V. Phillips, "Epidemiologic Evidence for Health Effects from Wind turbines," Populi Health Institute, Jul. 19, 2011, file:///C:/Users/goreh/OneDrive/Desktop/For%20One%20Drive/Health%20Wind%20Turbines%20Phillips%202012.pdf
107. Stephen Gibbons, "Gone with the Wind: Valuing the Visual Impacts of Wind Turbines through House Prices," London School of Economics, Mar. 2015, file:///C:/Users/goreh/OneDrive/Desktop/For%20One%20Drive/Wind%20Property%20Values%20Gibbons%202015.pdf
108. Yasin Sunak and Reinhard Madlener,"The Impact of Wind Farm Visibility on Property Values: A Spatial Difference-in-Difference Analysis," *Energy Economics*, 2016, https://econpapers.repec.org/article/eeeeneeco/v_3a55_3ay_3a2016_3ai_3ac_3ap_3a79-91.htm
109. Nell Frizzell, "Is Having a Baby in 2021 Pure Environmental Vandalism?" *Vogue*, Apr. 25, 2021, https://www.vogue.co.uk/mini-vogue/article/having-a-child-sustainable
110. "Windfarms Kill 10–20 Times More than Previously Thought," St. Francis Arboreal and Wildlife Association, 2022, https://windmillskill.com/blog/windfarms-kill-10-20-times-more-previously-thought; Image of ox head sacrifice by Deeporaj under Creative Commons 3.0 License

111. K. Shawn Smallwood, "Comparing Bird and Bat Fatality-Rate Estimates Among North American Wind-Energy Projects," *Wildlife Society Bulletin*, 2013, file:///C:/Users/goreh/OneDrive/Desktop/For%20One%20Drive/Wind%20Wildlife%20Deaths%20Smallwood%202013.pdf

112. Paul Denholm et al., "Examining Supply-Side Options to Achieve 100% Clean Electricity by 2035," National Renewable Electricity Laboratory, 2022, https://www.nrel.gov/docs/fy22osti/81644.pdf

113. Image of Ivanpah solar facility by Penny Electric

114. Grzegorz Pawelec and Joana Fonseca, "Steel from Solar Energy," Hydrogen Europe, 2022, https://hydrogeneurope.eu/wp-content/uploads/2022/06/Steel_from_Solar_Energy_Report_05-2022_DIGITAL.pdf

115. "Fuel Prices," *IBISWorld*, Aug. 3, 2022, https://www.ibisworld.com/uk/bed/fuel-prices/44247/

116. Jack Loughran, "Electric Vehicle Owners Face Soaring Charging Costs as Energy Price Cap Rises," *Engineering and Tech.*, Aug. 26, 2022, https://eandt.theiet.org/content/articles/2022/08/electric-vehicle-owners-face-soaring-charging-costs-as-energy-price-cap-rises-again/

117. Hannah Grossman, "Utah School Gives Kids 'Disgusting' Insects to Eat in Class for Climate Assignment on Cows Killing the Earth," FoxNews, Mar. 16, 2023, https://www.foxnews.com/media/utah-school-gives-kids-insects-eat-class-climate-change-assignment-says-will-save-planet?mc_cid=e77f11f62f&mc_eid=5c20d5e304

Chapter 11: Green Breakdown and the Future

1.   Yogi Berra quore from *Goodreads*, https://www.goodreads.com/quotes/261863-it-s-tough-to-make-predictions-especially-about-the-future

2.   Joe Barry, "Struggling to Heat Your Home as Gas and Oil Prices Soar? Why Not Switch to Wood?" *Farming Independent*, Oct. 21, 2022, https://www.independent.ie/business/farming/comment/struggling-to-heat-your-home-as-gas-and-oil-prices-soar-why-not-switch-to-wood-42084137.html; Candlelight master image public domain

3.   BP Statistical Review of World Energy, June, 2022, https://www.bp.com/en/global/corporate/energy-economics/statistical-review-of-world-energy.html

4.   "$1 Trillion: India Submits Its Demand for Raising Emissions Target," *The Quint*, Nov. 11, 2021, https://www.thequint.com/climate-change/1-trillion-india-submits-demands-raising-emissions-targets

5.   *False Alarm: How Climate Change Panic Costs Us Trillions, Hurts the Poor, and Fails to Fix the Planet* by Bjorn Lomborg, (Basic Books, 2021), p. 145

6.   Nick Ferris, "Exclusive: African Civil Society Speaks Out Against Continent's $400 Billion Gas Trap," *Energy Monitor*, Sep. 14, 2022, https://www.energymonitor.ai/sectors/power/exclusive-civil-society-speaks-out-against-africa-400bn-gas-trap

7.   Carolyn Davis,"Some Oil, Gas Execs Cite 'Hypocrisy' as Energy Crisis Upends Security, Climate Goals," *NGI*, Oct. 14, 2022, https://www.naturalgasintel.com/some-oil-gas-execs-cite-hypocrisy-as-energy-crisis-upends-security-climate-goals/

8.   "Captive Coal Plants," *Glob. Energy Monitor*, July, 2022, https://globalenergymonitor.org/projects/global-coal-plant-tracker/summary-data/

9.   Mihir Vora, "Southeast Asia's Steel Surge: How Will the Region Manage Overcapacity?" Wood Mackenzie, May 11, 2021, https://www.woodmac.com/news/opinion/southeast-asias-steel-surge-how-will-the-region-manage-overcapacity/

10. Michael Kern, "Germany is Dismantling a Wind Farm to Make Way for a Coal Mine," *Oil Price*, Oct. 26, 2022, https://oilprice.com/Latest-Energy-News/World-News/Germany-Is-Dismantling-A-Wind-Farm-To-Make-Way-For-A-Coal-Mine.html; Wolfman image by Horror Monsters

11. *Energy Transitions: History, Requirements, Prospects* by Vaclav Smil, (Praeger, 2010), appendix; BP Statistical Review of World Energy, June, 2022, https://www.bp.com/en/global/corporate/energy-economics/statistical-review-of-world-energy.html; "Global Carbon Budget Data," Global Carbon Project, 2022, https://www.globalcarbonproject.org/carbonbudget/20/data.htm; Image of the coal-fired Gladstone Power Station by LBM1948 under Creative Commons License 4

12. Ibid.

13. Alexander Stahel, "The Crisis of the European Energy System," Global Warming Policy Foundation, 2022, https://www.thegwpf.org/content/uploads/2022/09/Stahel-Eurogrid.pdf

14. Johanna Store, "'Fit for 55': EU Strengthens Emission Reduction Targets for Member States," Council of the EU, Nov. 8, 2022, https://www.consilium.europa.eu/en/press/press-releases/2022/11/08/fit-for-55-eu-strengthens-emission-reduction-targets-for-member-states/

15. "Speech by Commissioner Simson for the Opening of the EU Energy Day at COP27," European Commission, Nov. 14, 2022, https://ec.europa.eu/commission/presscorner/detail/en/SPEECH_22_6886

16. BP Statistical Review of World Energy, (See no. 3)

17. Sophie Wallis, "Energy Statistics Australia," *Finder*, Jun. 17, 2022, https://www.finder.com.au/energy-statistics-australia

18. Rhiannon Lewin, "Entire Sydney Suburbs Plunged into Darkness as More Power Outages Loom, *7NEWS*, Jun. 6, 2022, https://7news.com.au/technology/power-outage/entire-sydney-suburbs-plunged-into-darkness-as-more-power-outages-loom-c-7154237, WA power outage by Robert Ashworth under Creative Commons License 2.0

19. BP Statistical Review of World Energy, (See no. 3)

20. "Northeast Regional Assessment of Electrification," NEEP, Jul. 2017, https://neep.org/sites/default/files/Strategic%20Electrification%20Regional%20Assessment.pdf

21. Derek Brower and Myles McCormick, "New England 'Importing European Prices' in Looming Gas Supply Crunch," *Financial Times*, Nov. 17, 2022, https://www.ft.com/content/f9374ff4-3bfd-4b5e-8542-58c3db81514b

22. "Spanish Shops and Restaurants Banned from Setting Air-Conditioners Below 27C Amid Energy Crisis," *ABC News*, Aug. 2, 2022, https://www.abc.net.au/news/2022-08-02/spain-energy-crisis-government-restrictions/101293886, "Out of Gas" sign image from 1973 by David Falconer, U.S. National Archives

23. Climate: Past, Present, and Future vol. 2 by H. H. Lamb, (Metheun, 1977)

24. Jennifer Luden, "Should We Be Having Kids in the Age of Climate Change?" NPR, Aug. 18, 2016, https://www.npr.org/2016/08/18/479349760/should-we-be-having-kids-in-the-age-of-climate-change; "Save Our Planet, Kill Yourself" sign by Jorghex

25. Image of Melbourne Climate Strike, March 15, 2019 by Takver under Creative Commons License 2.0

26. Girl with books image by Timothy Takemoto under Creative Commons License 2.0

27. Paul Berger, "California Looks to Ban Diesel Trucks at Ports by 2035," *The Wall Street Journal*, Nov. 20, 2022, https://www.wsj.com/articles/california-looks-to-ban-diesel-trucks-at-ports-by-2035-11668801812#:~:text=From%202025%2C%20the%20state%20would,to%20clean%20energy%20by%202035.; Girl surfer image by Daniel Torbekov

28. Lindsey Komick, "New York Times Essay Says You Should Mate with Short People to Save the Planet," *New York Post*, Jan. 3, 2023, https://nypost.com/2023/01/03/short-people-better-for-the-environment-mara-altman/?mc_cid=10d657f48f&mc_eid=5c20d5e304; Question guy image by Scout, Open Clip Art

29. "China Has Quickly and Sharply Reduced Pollution Since Enacting Strict Policies," EPIC, Univ. of Chicago, Aug. 15, 2022, https://epic.uchicago.edu/insights/china-has-quickly-and-sharply-reduced-pollution-since-enacting-strict-policies/?mc_cid=8f4efc11a3&mc_eid=c70268762a

30. "The Sustainable Development Goals Report," United Nations, 2022, https://unstats.un.org/sdgs/report/2022/The-Sustainable-Development-Goals-Report-2022.pdf; Chef image by GDJ under Creative Commons Public Domain Dedication

INDEX

ABOUT THE AUTHOR

Steve Goreham is a speaker, author, and researcher on energy and environmental issues and a former engineer and business executive. He is an independent columnist and a frequently invited guest on radio and television programs, including Fox Business Channel and The 700 Club, along with programs hosted by Jim Bohannon, Bill Cunningham, Joe Donlon, Sean Hannity, Dennis Miller, Lars Larson, George Noory, Joe Pags, Janet Parshall, and many others. He's the Executive Director of the Climate Science Coalition of America and a policy advisor to The Heartland Institute.

Green Breakdown is Steve's fourth book. Over 100,000 copies of his previous three books, *Outside the Green Box: Rethinking Sustainable Development*, *The Mad, Mad, Mad World of Climatism: Mankind and Climate Change Mania*, and *Climatism! Science, Common Sense, and the 21st Century's Hottest Topic*, are now in print. Steve devotes full-time efforts to speaking to agriculture groups, businesses, industrial associations, and other organizations to correct misconceptions about energy, resources, climate change, and the environment. He wrote *Green Breakdown* to warn about the coming failure of forced efforts to pursue a green-energy transition.

Steve holds an MS in Electrical Engineering from the University of Illinois and an MBA from the University of Chicago. He has more than 30 years of experience at Fortune 100 and private companies in engineering and executive roles. He is husband and father of three and resides in Illinois in the United States of America.

Steve
Goreham

Speaker/Author/Researcher

Energy, Environment, and Public Policy

Informative and engaging speaker, delivering compelling and provocative programs to business, industry, universities, and other organizations. Effective communicator in the boardroom, conference hall, and on the debate panel regarding:

- Energy, Industry, Agriculture
- Sustainable Development
- Economic Trends
- The Environment
- Climate Change
- Corporate Environmental Policy

www.stevegoreham.com

Enjoy Steve's Other Books

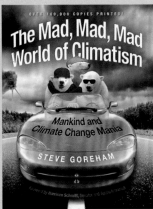

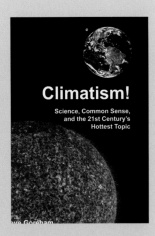

"The antidote for green ideology." — Stephen Moore, Economist, The Heritage Foundation	"An amusing and colorful, yet science-based, look at mankind's obsession with global warming." — *Publishers Weekly*	The complete discussion of the science, politics, and policy implications of the global warming debate.
256-Page Color Soft Cover 122 Sidebars, 69 Figures New Lenox Books (2017)	300-Page Color Soft Cover 150 Sidebars, 113 Figures New Lenox Books (2012)	480-Page Black & White Hard Cover, 135 Figures New Lenox Books (2010)